APPLICATIONS IN
# Recreation
# & Leisure
FOR TODAY AND
THE FUTURE

# APPLICATIONS IN
# Recreation
# & Leisure
## FOR TODAY AND
## THE FUTURE

### THIRD EDITION

**KATHLEEN A. CORDES**

Professor Emeritus
Miramar College

**HILMI M. IBRAHIM**

Professor
Whittier College

Boston   Burr Ridge, IL   Dubuque, IA   Madison, WI   New York   San Francisco   St. Louis
Bangkok   Bogotá   Caracas   Kuala Lumpur   Lisbon   London   Madrid   Mexico City
Milan   Montreal   New Delhi   Santiago   Seoul   Singapore   Sydney   Taipei   Toronto

# McGraw-Hill Higher Education

*A Division of The McGraw-Hill Companies*

APPLICATIONS IN RECREATION AND LEISURE: FOR TODAY AND THE FUTURE, THIRD EDITION

Published by McGraw-Hill, a business unit of The McGraw-Hill Companies, Inc., 1221 Avenue of the Americas, New York, NY 10020. Copyright © 2003, 1999, 1996 by The McGraw-Hill Companies, Inc. All rights reserved. No part of this publication may be reproduced or distributed in any form or by any means, or stored in a database or retrieval system, without the prior written consent of The McGraw-Hill Companies, Inc., including, but not limited to, in any network or other electronic storage or transmission, or broadcast for distance learning.

Some ancillaries, including electronic and print components, may not be available to customers outside the United States.

This book is printed on acid-free paper.

2 3 4 5 6 7 8 9 0 DOC/DOC 0 9 8 7 6 5 4 3

ISBN 0-07-235357-0

Vice president and editor-in-chief: *Thalia Dorwick*
Publisher: *Jane E. Karpacz*
Executive editor: *Vicki Malinee*
Developmental editor: *Carlotta Seely*
Senior marketing manager: *Pamela S. Cooper*
Senior project manager: *Marilyn Rothenberger*
New book production supervisor: *Enboge Chong*
Senior media technology producer: *Lance Gerhart*
Lead designer: *Matthew Baldwin*
Cover Designer: *Joanne Schopler*
Cover Image: *© Getty Images*
Associate supplement producer: *Kate Boylan*
Compositor: *GAC—Indianapolis*
Typeface: *10/12 Palatino*
Printer: *Von Hoffmann Press, Inc.*

The credits section for this book begins on page 330 and is considered an extension of the copyright page.

## Library of Congress Cataloging-in-Publication Data

Cordes, Kathleen A.
    Applications in recreation and leisure : for today and the future / Kathleen Cordes, Hilmi Ibrahim.— 3rd ed.
        p. cm.
    Rev. ed. of: Applications in recreation & leisure. 2nd ed. c1999.
    Includes bibliographical references and index.
    ISBN 0-07-235357-0
    1. Recreation—Sociological aspects. 2. Leisure—Sociological aspects. I. Ibrahim, Hilmi. II. Cordes, Kathleen A. Applications in recreation & leisure. III. Title.

GV14.45 .C65 2003
306.4'8—dc21

2002070273

The Internet addresses listed in the text were accurate at the time of publication. The inclusion of a website does not indicate an endorsement by the authors or McGraw-Hill, and McGraw-Hill does not guarantee the accuracy of the information presented at these sites.

www.mhhe.com

To my colleagues Randy Swedburg and Dale Adkins
for your dedication to our profession and AALR.
It was a pleasure working with you,

KAC


To my wife, Cynthia,
with love

HMI

# Brief Contents

APPENDICES

# Detailed Contents

# Preface

Leisure pursuits and recreational activities play a major role in the lifestyles of most individuals in most societies. Their phenomenal growth has attracted the attention of scholars from all walks of life who have devoted many hours to understanding the factors underlying such growth. These scholars agree that at the core of these desirable human experiences is play. Although the simplest of playforms may appear to be undifferentiated from one society to another, social, economic, and geographic factors have resulted in differences along the evolutionary scale.

## OUR APPROACH

In this new century, leisure pursuits are no longer the sole domain of wealthy individuals or of industrialized nations. Moreover, leisure careers are not limited to the public sector or to specific national boundaries. The approach used in this book is universal and multicultural for today's culturally diverse audience.

With enrollments in introductory recreation and leisure courses rising, the third edition of *Applications in Recreation & Leisure* provides a contemporary examination of leisure issues from philosophical, psychological, and sociological perspectives. The text views the history of leisure; leisure throughout the life course; leisure issues pertaining to aging, and to the physically and developmentally disabled; multicultural and international issues; planning and management issues; and career opportunities. It looks at the past while pointing to the future. In examining leisure and recreation as human rights for all individuals, this text serves as a catalyst for critical thinking by students while providing a broad understanding of the different philosophies of the various providers of leisure services.

With its exciting full-color format, the third edition of *Applications in Recreation & Leisure* provides a very practical look at recreation and leisure with numerous pedagogical elements to help reinforce learning.

## AUDIENCE

This introductory text is written with the student in mind, a student who has chosen to study leisure and recreation as part of his or her college education. The student will gain a meaningful understanding of these activities and how they impact many lives, including his or her own. The student will come to appreciate (1) the important roles that leisure and recreation play in different parts of the world and (2) the complex organization needed to provide leisure services at all levels.

A second audience comprises students who are exploring leisure and recreation for a possible career. Understanding individual tendencies affected by age, gender, or educational background is important for a well-designed recreation program. The planning, organizing, and administering of leisure pursuits and recreational activities help facilitate the services provided for large numbers of people at all levels, whether local, regional, state, or national. *Applications in Recreation & Leisure* looks to the future while considering the rapid changes that have taken place and are still taking place in the field.

## FEATURES

- ◆ A comprehensive and practical look at recreation and leisure from philosophical, psychological, and sociological perspectives is presented. This multidisciplinary approach provides a unifying perspective. It examines current issues and challenges affected by demographic trends, education, finances, public sentiment, laws, and legislation.
- ◆ Leisure and recreation are presented before play to strengthen the theoretical explanation of these important foundational concepts. Scholarly interpretations of the meaning of leisure, recreation, and play are examined. Additional theories, such as Nash's paradigm of free time, have been included.
- ◆ Cultural diversity is examined, such as the evolution of ritual and tradition in enhancing leisure experiences today. A global

approach is used to study a variety of leisure and recreation activities, such as the popularity of Oktoberfest in Germany, bullfighting and soccer in Mexico, and the development of yoga in India.

- ◆ Violence in adolescence is explored, and including the value of well-structured recreation programs, such as outreach programs in urban environments and the Outward Bound program, in modifying inappropriate behavior among "youth at risk."
- ◆ Leisure issues pertaining to the elderly and the physically and developmentally disabled are addressed. With appropriately structured programs of leisure and recreational pursuits, the elderly can be helped to focus on exercise and social interaction, the physically challenged can improve their motor skills and coordination, and the mentally challenged can improve their skills and self-confidence.
- ◆ Leisure throughout the life course, from childhood through adolescence and adulthood, is examined. Play at these different stages is explored, as are the physical, psychological, and social benefits of leisure.
- ◆ Career opportunities are discussed in the areas of leadership, management, and ethics.
- ◆ Trends and future projections are highlighted. Examples include the restructuring of job responsibilities; the need for leisure education and leisure counselors; the benefits of technological and medical advancements; increased environmental concerns; improved services and accommodations for the elderly and the disabled; more single parents and working mothers; community outreach programs to assist the homeless; and counseling programs.

# NEW OR EXPANDED TOPICS

## Chapter 1: The Nature of Leisure, Recreation, and Play
- Leisure as residual time
- Theories of play

## Chapter 2: The Evolution of Leisure, Recreation, and Play
- Historical events and the development of leisure and recreation
- Birth of city parks and national parks in the United States

## Chapter 3: Leisure, Recreation, and the Individual
- Ten most popular recreational pursuits
- Link between leisure pursuits and life satisfaction

## Chapter 4: Play, Recreation, and the Life Course: Children
- Updated population statistics
- Shape of the Nation Report showing obesity as serious health problem
- Low physical activity level as important factor in childhood obesity

## Chapter 5: Recreation, Leisure, and the Life Course: Adolescents
- Current statistics on teenage drug use
- Updates on teen suicide statistics
- Role of leisure provider in influencing identity formation

## Chapter 6: Recreation, Leisure, and the Life Course: Adults and Seniors
- Life expectancy figures updated to 2020
- Population expectations updated to 2025
- Growth of edu-tourism

## Chapter 7: Recreation, Leisure, and Society
- Updated expenditures on leisure
- Current data on work hours in the United States
- Changes in family structure

## Chapter 8: The International Scene
- Status of leisure and recreation in various countries
- Developing nations and leisure

## Chapter 9: Diversity and Inclusiveness
- Importance of family life to individuals
- Challenge of creating family time
- Need for attractive natural resources in and near cities
- Sport/recreation participation and ranking

## Chapter 10: Providers and Resources
- National Scenic Byways Program
- National Wild and Scenic Rivers System and preservation of wildlife and the environment
- Travel and tourism

## Chapter 11: The Profession
- Role of ethics for the leisure professional
- American Therapeutic Recreation Association
- National Therapeutic Recreation Society

## Chapter 12: Planning and Management in Recreation and Leisure
- National, regional, and local approaches to planning and management
- Financial aspects of recreation management

## Chapter 13: Issues and Challenges in Recreation and Leisure
- Updated statistics on TV viewing
- Crowding and carrying capacity

## Chapter 14: The Changing Scene
- Updated crime statistics
- Current work statistics
- Potential for public/private partnership

# PEDAGOGY

- *Full-color design:* The full-color design format is a special feature of this introductory textbook, and it offers a very practical means of enhancing the learning process for students.

◆ *Chapter opening quotes:* Related quotes begin each chapter to further enhance student interest in the chapter topic.

◆ *Chapter at a Glance:* Each chapter begins with a brief overview that sets the theme for the chapter.

◆ *Chapter Objectives:* The chapters open with identification of those concepts to be mastered in each chapter.

◆ *A World of Difference:* Case studies in every chapter provide practical applications of the content. These correspond with *Your Turn* questions at the end of the chapter and allow students to determine solutions for each case discussed.

◆ *Action Guide:* These self-evaluations enable students to apply chapter content to themselves.

◆ *Concept Checks:* These questions are integrated within the text to provide immediate review of chapter content to reinforce learning.

◆ *A Closer Look:* These boxes provide additional coverage of related topics to complement each chapter's content.

◆ *Definition boxes:* New terms that the student will learn in each chapter are identified here.

◆ *Summing Up:* The main concepts of the chapter are summarized for a quick review of chapter content and to help in test preparation.

◆ *Using What You've Learned:* These activities at the conclusion of each chapter provide related activities for student completion.

◆ *Your Turn:* Located at the end of each chapter, these questions correspond with *A World of Difference* case studies and allow students to apply chapter content to determine solutions.

◆ *References:* Concluding each chapter, the references provide thorough documentation of material and are a resource for students to obtain additional information.

## ANCILLARIES

**Downloadable Ancillaries:** The online ancillaries that accompany this text include an Instructor's Manual and Test Bank and a PowerPoint presentation created especially for this book. To access these ancillaries, visit this text's website at www.mhhe.com/hhp.

**Computerized Test Bank:** The Test Bank for this text is available on CD-ROM, which allows the instructor to edit, delete, or add questions as well as construct and print tests and answer keys.

**PowerWeb:** The PowerWeb card packaged with each new copy of this text allows access to a reservoir of course-specific articles and current events. Students can use PowerWeb to take a self-scoring quiz, complete an interactive exercise, click through an interactive glossary, or check the daily news. An expert in each discipline analyzes the day's news to show students how it relates to their field of study.

It has been our pleasure to work with the accomplished individuals from McGraw-Hill, who have contributed to the third edition of *Applications in Recreation & Leisure: For Today and the Future.* We are especially grateful to our Developmental Editor, Carolotta Seely, for guidance and attention to detail. Her sound advice and focus on this project was always appreciated. A special thanks is expressed to Project Manager Marilyn Rothenberger and the production team for their special talents. As always, we are indebted to Pamela Cooper for her help and advice. Her marketing skills are gratefully acknowledged. A very special thank you is extended to Executive Editor Vicky Malinee for assembling this professional and dedicated staff and for demonstrating continued commitment and faith in our project. Thank you!

We credit and thank Jane Lammers for her expressive photographs and graphic contributions. Our gratitude is also offered to the

Whittier College administration for their support and to David Sanderlin and Robert Bacon at Miramar College, for their friendship and unending encouragement.

We graciously thank and acknowledge these reviewers for their helpful comments and suggestions:

For the third edition:
**Denise Anderson**
University of North Carolina–Greensboro

**Chip Cannon**
Humboldt State University

**Amy Goff**
Scottsdale Community College

**Denver Hospodarsky**
Northern Arizona University

For the second edition:
**Barb J. Brock**
Eastern Washington University

**Ernest Coons**
State University College–Plattsburgh

**Patti Freeman**
Murray State University

**Janice Elich Monroe**
Ithaca College

**Ralph W. Weber**
California State University–Fresno

**Edwin K. Lindsay**
North Carolina State University–Ralaigh

For the first edition:
**Don A. Albrecht**
Texas A&M University

**James D. Bigley**
Georgia Southern University

**Jeanne Boyd**
University of Florida

**Barb J. Brock**
Eastern Washington University

**Ronald W. Hodgson**
California State University at Chico

**Joy Joyner**
Mankato State University

**Barbara Klingman**
Western State College of Colorado

**Richard MacNeil**
University of Iowa

**Joseph L. Regna**
University of Florida

**Elaine Rogers**
East Stroudsburg University

**S. Harold Smith**
Brigham Young University

**Daniel E. Wegner**
Southwest Texas State University

**Theodore J. Welch**
SUNY: College at Brockport

**Doris D. Yates**
California State University: Hayward

KATHLEEN A. CORDES
HILMI M. IBRAHIM

There is less leisure now than
in the Middle Ages, when one
third of the year consisted of
festivals and holidays.

J.B. PRIESTLEY

# The Nature of Leisure, Recreation, and Play

CHAPTER 1

## THE CHAPTER AT A GLANCE

In this chapter we define three terms that will be used throughout the text: leisure, recreation, and play. We present various theories of why people play and offer some comments on each. Finally, we present some ideas on the motivation for, and benefits from, engaging in leisure, recreation, and play.

### Chapter Objectives

*After completing this chapter, you should be able to*

- Define leisure, recreation, and play.
- Explain the three essential elements of a leisure experience.
- Discuss leisure in terms of (1) free or residual time, (2) activities, and (3) a state of mind.
- Explain the difference between leisure and recreation.
- Briefly explain the different interpretations of play.
- Describe factors that may motivate individuals to engage in leisure, recreation, and play.

## THE NATURE OF LEISURE

*L*eisure is difficult to define because it means something different to each person, yet scholars have always been interested in the study of leisure. The first attempt to understand leisure probably took place about 300 B.C. The ancient Greeks were intrigued by leisure, and the philosopher Aristotle suggested a paradigm, or model, by which leisure could be categorized. In this paradigm, depicted in Figure 1.1, Aristotle proposed that leisure

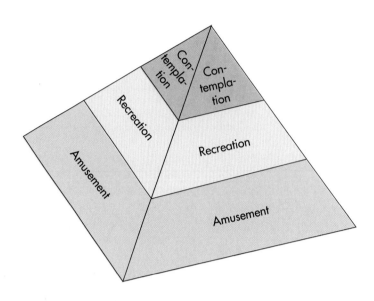

**FIGURE 1.1**  Aristotle's three levels of leisure.

occurs at three levels: amusement, recreation, and contemplation. More on that later.

Almost six hundred years ago, a scholar in another part of the world suggested that the desire for leisure is one of five basic human desires. This scholar, Ibn Khaldun, was a historian who is also considered to be the father of sociology. Khaldun ranked these five desires in ascending order, with leisure at the pinnacle of the pyramid.[1] More recently, American psychologist Abraham Maslow emphasized the importance of certain activities in human life. Figure 1.2 shows his paradigm, which is similar to Khaldun's. Maslow's hierarchy of human needs begins with basic physiological needs, which appear at the bottom of the figure, and culminates with self-actualization, which comprises its highest level. In his early work, Maslow suggested that the human need for aesthetics (appreciation of beauty and order) and cognition (knowledge and understanding) precedes the need for self-actualization.[2]

## DEFINING LEISURE

The term *leisure* came into use only rather recently in the United States. In contrast, the term *recreation* has been used by professionals since the early 20th century. For example, in a pioneering book on recreation in America, published in 1940, the term *leisure* appeared only five times.[3] The author suggested that recreation is a leisure-time activity and that, for most people, recreational opportunities are largely confined to their leisure hours. He noted that an increase in leisure took place in the early 1900s, when working hours became shorter. When people worked 12 to 14 hours a day, six days a week, he pointed out, the problem of recreational use of leisure was nonexistent. In a sense, then, the author equated leisure with free time.

However, having free time does not necessarily mean that one is at leisure. For example, a prisoner or a sick person who is confined to bed has plenty of free time but is not at leisure.

**FIGURE 1.2** A comparison of Maslow's hierarchy of human needs with Khaldun's hierarchy of desires.

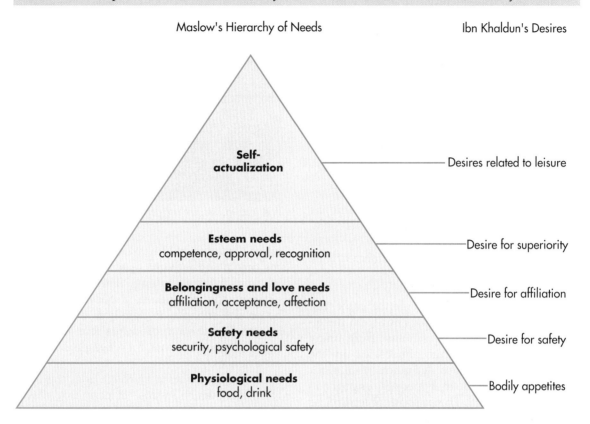

Nevertheless, scholars continued to define *leisure* as free time. In the late 1940s and in the 1950s, several books about leisure were published.[4,5,6,7] Then, in 1960, a scholar of recreation asked the question "What is leisure?" He concluded that the meaning of leisure varies among cultures and that there is little agreement about its meaning and implications. For example, some see leisure as freedom from work, while others view it as an important tool of social control or a symbol of one's status. Still others believe that leisure is simply a state of calm and a form of contemplative dignity.[8]

The debate about the meaning of leisure continues even today. For example, in 1991, a group of scholars met to discuss a book they were writing about leisure. The author of the first chapter had stated his intention of using the words *leisure* and *recreation* interchangeably. The other authors of the book were concerned about the lack of clear definition of the two words. Some of the scholars contended that leisure denotes a desirable state, rather than pleasurable experiences, even though both of these views center on the use of free time.[9]

Developments in Europe and other parts of the world have also highlighted the universality and importance of leisure, recreation, and play in people's lives. For example, a book written in Dutch and translated into English in the 1950s showed the role of leisure activities in different cultures.[10] In another book translated into English, the author asserts, "Culture depends for its very existence on leisure, and leisure, in its turn, is not possible unless it has a durable and consequently living link with the culture, with divine worship."[11]

The following decade, a book on leisure in America began with a chapter in which the author contended that America had entered an age of leisure:[12]

> Every facet of American life is included in the phrase that we are in an age of leisure. Our week is shorter. Our family life has changed its character. Our familiar sources of control, such as church or elders of the community, are no longer in dominance.

Freedom from work and obligation became the definition of *leisure*. According to this view, leisure occurs when people are most free to be themselves. The author suggested that culture can be understood through leisure.

Other clues also indicated that leisure is an element of culture. The evidence came not only from industrial societies but from developing ones as well, and scholars from many countries were becoming interested in the phenomenon of leisure. A French scholar, for example, believed that people engage in leisure by free will. The purpose of leisure, he maintained, is to rest, to amuse oneself, to learn, or to improve personal skills.[13] An East Indian scholar said that the unoccupied space that makes a room habitable is like leisure, which makes life endurable.[14] In the Arab world, one author claimed that free time had increased so much among Egyptian youth that recreational activities should be provided.[15] In Great Britain, books appeared in which the impact of leisure on British society was debated.[16,17,18]

In the United States, one scholar suggested that the term *leisure* is so abstract that it cannot be given a workable definition.[8] Others thought that the abstract nature of the term made it nearly impossible for the average person to grasp its meaning.[19]

Despite these difficulties, scholars continue to try to define *leisure*. These attempts have

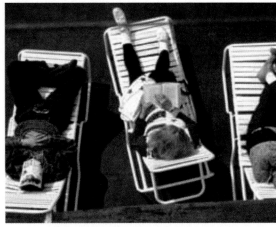

*When at leisure, we are permitted to do as we please.*

taken three general forms. The first is to study the origin of the word as a way of revealing its underlying meaning. The second is to examine the experiences a person has when he or she engages in activities described as leisure. The third approach is to evaluate the motives people have for engaging in such experiences.

The word *leisure* is derived from the Latin word *licer*, which means "to permit or allow." *Licer* is also the Latin root of the word *permission*. This is an important clue, and in this text we will define **leisure** as permission to do as one pleases at one's own pace, to participate in an activity of one's choice, and to abandon the activity at will. The leisure experience has three essential elements:

1. *Perceived freedom*: One embarks on the experience at will and is also able to leave it at will. For example, we have the freedom to drive to the beach on a Sunday, stay as long as we like, and leave when we're tired. If we're employed, realistically we don't have the freedom to make these choices during the workweek.

2. *Autotelic activity*: **Autotelic** means having a purpose in and not apart from itself. An autotelic activity, therefore, is one that is

done through self-motivation and not because of some external factor. For example, a dedicated amateur plays soccer out of love of the game, not for monetary gain.

3. *Beneficial outcome*: One undertakes the activity on the assumption that doing so will yield some benefit. For example, we may work out at the gym to lose weight, increase strength, or improve endurance.

Three distinct approaches to defining the leisure experience are outlined in the next sections.

## Leisure as Residual Time

British sociologist Stanley Parker defined *leisure* as residual time, to be calculated in the following way. Beginning with a 24-hour day, subtract the hours that are *not* devoted to leisure: working, sleeping, eating, attending to physical needs, and so forth.[20] Residual time means, quite simply, time left over—in the case of leisure, time left over after one has performed the tasks necessary to *exist* (continue to be) and to *subsist* (have or acquire the necessities of life, such as food and clothing). Fig. 1.3 shows the overlapping relationship among these times. Time is easily understood in terms of hours, days, and weeks. For this reason, *leisure* is usually defined in terms of these elements.

Yet an overlap among these three sets exists since it is rather hard to separate them. For instance, is a leisurely meal a form of free time activity, or is it an activity for existence?

In 1953, Jay B. Nash, one of the pioneers of recreation and leisure studies in America, supplied us with a paradigm explaining the levels of participation in experiences in which one takes part during free time.[21] In his paradigm (Fig. 1.4), Nash indicated that the abuse of free time is possible. Free time should be differentiated from existence time-the time to fulfill one's physical and psychological needs-and from subsistence time-the time to do work and conduct work-related activities (Fig. 1.3).

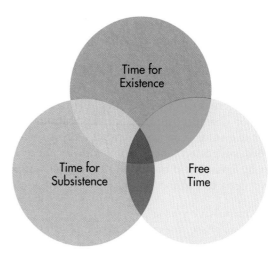

**FIGURE 1.3**  Three sets of time.

**FIGURE 1.4**  Nash's paradigm of free time.

*leisure* permission to do as one pleases at one's own pace, to participate in an activity of one's own choice, and to abandon the activity at will

*autotelic (activity)* having a purpose in and not apart from itself

## Leisure as Activities

**Activity** is commonly defined as the performance of a specific deed or act. Although there is an almost endless variety of human acts, they all have certain characteristics in common. For example, many human acts begin with a condition of disequilibrium. Tamotsu Shibutani, a Japanese-American social psychologist in the 1960s, suggested that one can analyze a human act by breaking it down into functional units, or phases, as outlined below.[22]

### The impulsive phase

In this phase, the condition of disequilibrium sets an organism into motion. The act normally continues until equilibrium is restored. The simplest impulses are physiological: hunger, fatigue, adverse environmental conditions, assault by a predator or an enemy. Disequilibrium also can be of a social or psychological nature, such as the feeling that you are not dressed appropriately. Boredom may also ignite a feeling of disequilibrium.

### The perception phase

Once set in motion by a condition of disequilibrium, the organism seeks to perceive in its environment some means of achieving equilibrium. In the case of boredom, you may perceive reaching equilibrium by engaging in drawing.

### The manipulation phase

After perceiving a means of achieving equilibrium, you next must manipulate yourself, others, or objects in the environment. For example, in the case of boredom, you think of what, where, and when to draw.

### The consummation phase

In this final stage of the act, equilibrium is restored—in the case of hunger, by eating. Except in cases of physiological disequilibrium (hunger, fatigue, adverse environmental conditions, assault), it is not always easy to determine when consummation of an act has occurred. The key is that striving has ceased and the organism is once more in balance.

### Expressive and instrumental acts

For purposes of this discussion, we can identify two types of acts: expressive and instrumental. An expressive act begins with an impulsive phase and emphasizes the processes of perception and manipulation rather than consummation. An instrumental act also begins with an impulsive phase but focuses on consummation rather than perception and manipulation. In the drawing example, is the emphasis on drawing itself (expressive act) or on producing a portrait to be sold (instrumental act)?

Although there clearly is some overlap between these two types of acts, the tendency is to associate instrumental acts with tasks we should or must complete, such as attending class, working, or doing chores, and to associate expressive acts with more enjoyable pursuits such as hobbies, sports, and travel. In this context, leisure activities clearly are more likely to be expressive acts rather than instrumental acts.

## Leisure as a State of Mind

Many scholars have speculated about the importance of one's state of mind in a given leisure experience. One such scholar contended that the opposite of leisure is obligation. To be at leisure, then, one must be free from external forces that prevent one from engaging in a chosen experience.[23] Another scholar maintained the importance of one's perception of freedom in the motivations for, the conditions of, and the attitudes about leisure.[24]

It is also important to understand that the opposite of leisure is not work, it is obligation. Many experiences that are not work or related to work, and which may be thought of as leisurely, are not true leisure experiences. For example, a professional ball player is not at leisure when he or she participates in the sport for its monetary reward. A person who is obligated to mow the lawn is not working but is certainly not at leisure. The term *leisure* is not applicable in these two cases because leisure is not merely an activity engaged in during free

## ACTION GUIDE

### TIME OUT!

Whatever your age, sex, or background, as a college student you definitely have a full plate. You're trying to balance study, work, family, social life, sports, and hobbies and still squeeze in time for meals and sleep. Whether you plan to major in recreation or just check out the field in this one course, you can do yourself a favor by taking time out to conduct your own personal "leisure profile." Just take this quick quiz, and you'll gain some valuable insight into your "leisure personality."

1. In order of preference, rank your five favorite leisure activities. In the spaces that follow, write down first the amount of time you would *like* to devote to each activity and then the time you actually devote to each.

   a. _____  ____  ____

   b. _____  ____  ____

   c. _____  ____  ____

   d. _____  ____  ____

   e. _____  ____  ____

2. How closely does your real-life leisure activity pattern follow your list of favorites?

3. If there's a significant disparity, how might you rearrange your schedule to make your leisure time more rewarding?

time but, rather, is a way of being, a philosophy about living, and, above all, a particular state of mind.[25]

### Concept Check

- What are three approaches to defining *leisure*?
- What is the difference between an expressive act and an instrumental act?

## RECREATION

As with leisure, *recreation* is a term for which there is no universally agreed-on definition. For purposes of this text, we will define **recreation** as voluntary participation in leisure activities that are meaningful and enjoyable to the person involved. The term embraces both indoor and outdoor activities and refers to sports and exercise as well as to less physically active pursuits. As this definition makes clear, recreation is one aspect of the broader term *leisure,* which encompasses not only vigorous activities such as softball and hiking but also sedentary hobbies such as coin and stamp collecting as well as more passive pastimes such as dozing in a hammock or sunbathing.

The link between leisure and recreation was probed by Aristotle. He suggested that leisure can be classified into three overlapping categories: contemplation, recreation, and amusement (Fig. 1.1). Contemplation is the act of considering something with attention. Recreation is the active, participatory aspect of leisure. Amusement is passive reception on the part of an audience or spectators. Contemplation is the core of philosophical thinking, so Aristotle, as a philosopher, understandably viewed contemplation as the highest form of leisure and encouraged its practice. He accepted the recreational use of leisure time but derided amusement.

*activity* performance of a specific deed or act

*recreation* voluntary participation in leisure activities that are meaningful and enjoyable to the person involved

*Kayaking is a popular recreational activity.*

Today the term *recreation* is used to describe activities in a variety of structured settings.

1. *Public recreation* consists of programs offered by nonprofit public agencies that are designed to meet the needs of people of varied ages, backgrounds, and interests. Programs may be conducted indoors or outdoors and may involve sports and fitness activities as well as nature study and crafts. Some activities are free; others are available at a modest cost.
2. *Commercial recreation* describes programs and activities that are offered for profit on a fee basis. Examples are fitness centers, health clubs, indoor tennis and racquetball facilities, yoga and aerobics studios, and driving ranges for golfers.
3. *Corporate recreation* refers to activities sponsored by companies and organizations for the benefit of their employees. Examples are company softball and bowling teams and fitness centers.
4. *Therapeutic recreation* consists of programs offered by both public and private agencies for the benefit of specific populations. Examples are exercise, sports, and craft programs for people with disabilities.
5. *Other recreational settings* are provided on an individual basis as in golfing at a private club or in groups as seen in military recreation.

**Concept Check**

- Briefly explain the relationship between leisure and recreation.
- Identify the key difference between public and commercial recreation programs.

## PLAY: THE NUCLEUS OF LEISURE AND RECREATION

When Thomas Edison was asked how many hours a day he worked, he replied: "I play sixteen hours a day." For Edison, with his curiosity, imagination, energy, and ingenuity, what looked to others like tedious work was actually stimulating and enjoyable—qualities we tend to associate with play rather than with work.

Let's look at some other assumptions about the nature of play. Have you ever wished you could be a professional athlete, a rock star, or a Hollywood producer? On the surface, their lives look glamorous, luxurious, and carefree—the perfect examples of "no work and all play." If you take a closer look at how these celebrities live, however, you'll find they pay a big price for their wealth and fame: long hours of practice and rehearsal; the instability and inconvenience of life on the road; the seemingly endless obligations to fans, investors, and sponsors.

As you can see from these examples, our definitions of *play* tend to be subjective, and they are often based on superficial impressions. For the purposes of this text, we need a collective understanding about the basic elements and characteristics of play; that is, we need an *operational*, or working, definition of *play*.

We will define *play* because it is at the core of the two concepts that we have already introduced: leisure and recreation. **Play** can be defined as activities in which individuals engage freely and from which they derive personal satisfaction.

At this point, we can make three general observations about play:

## A World of Difference

### ONE BOY'S WORK IS ANOTHER BOY'S PLAY

*Strong, healthy, intelligent, successful*— those are all words used by friends and family to describe Chris Makos and John Shu. Best friends since grade school, they're now 17, classmates in their high school's honors program and participants in a wide variety of school activities. They study together, attend the same parties, and travel everywhere in Chris's beat-up VW Rabbit. They both love Cajun music, hate anchovies on pizza, and think America needs a third political party.

As close as Chris and John are in countless ways, when it comes to play they're worlds apart. Stocky, aggressive Chris, the youngest of six sons in a vigorous Greek-American family, has been on a soccer field since he was a toddler. Now captain of the high school team, he's a feisty forward who's spearheaded three undefeated seasons and two state titles. Like his father, uncles, cousins, and five older brothers, Chris thrives on the dirt, sweat, and glory of his rough-and-tumble game. Although he plans to pursue a doctorate in nuclear physics, he's also determined to play

college soccer and is looking at scholarship offers from several top schools.

Where is John while Chris is embroiled in the grit and grind of top-gun soccer? Either huddled intently over a chessboard—often at a regional or state competition—or at the indoor tennis courts, usually before dawn, perfecting an already deadly game of astonishing technical expertise. For both John and his two younger sisters, play and leisure mean taking every opportunity to hone their intellectual skills by mastering the intricacies of chess and the complex strategies of high-intensity tennis. It wouldn't even occur to the Shu kids, second-generation Chinese-Americans, to engage in the down and dirty of soccer, lacrosse, or other physical-contact sports. Like their parents and members of their extended family, they're happiest and most fulfilled when they're tackling strategic, not physical, challenges.

As you study this chapter, think about Chris's and John's extremely different uses of play and leisure time and prepare to answer the questions in Your Turn at the end of the chapter.

1. Play is witnessed among the young of most higher animals, particularly primates. Young chimpanzees, for example, spend most of their time playing.[26]
2. Play seems to be a universal activity among the young of humankind, regardless of race, ethnicity, or culture. The sequence of children's playforms is remarkably stable across populations. Children first learn to manipulate their bodies, then to manipulate objects outside themselves. Their play subsequently becomes repetitive, then expands to include others, and finally becomes rule governed.[27]

3. Research indicates there is some biological basis for play. Some scientists believe the urge to play may be a by-product of some chemical process: that a hormonal code or genetic programming may initiate and propel play.[28] When certain parts of the brains of small animals are destroyed, the animals revert to behaviors that are devoid of play.[29]

> **play** activities in which one engages freely and from which one derives personal satisfaction

## Interpretations of Play

Play is a phenomenon that has intrigued scholars for centuries. Specialists in a variety of disciplines have studied play intensively, seeking to interpret it in terms of their particular scientific orientation. In this section we introduce five interpretations of play: biological, psychological, sociological, cultural, and recent ones.

### Biological Interpretations

In the 18th and 19th centuries, several scholars formulated theories based on the idea that humans and higher animal species, particularly the young, are impelled to play by certain unchangeable biological traits. In essence these theorists believed it is impossible to modify this inborn impulse to play. Although many contemporary scholars believe the tendency to play may have some biological basis, they also recognize other factors that movitate play. We will examine some of those factors in later sections.

Friedrich von Schiller, an 18th-century German poet and philosopher, offered what is considered a classic definition when he described play as "an aimless expenditure of exuberant energy."[30] Herbert Spencer, a 19th-century English philosopher, suggested that lower forms of animals expend all their energies in maintaining life: searching for food, caring for their young, avoiding predators, and seeking shelter. Higher animals, on the other hand, are left with some organs and muscles in a dormant stage. It is this unexpended, dormant, and excess energy, Spencer postulated, that motivates higher animals to engage in play. Rats gnaw at anything; cats fight dogs; dogs chase cats; and human beings "blow off steam" in play.[31]

Karl Groos, a Swiss philosopher of the early 20th century, emphasized the teleological, or purposeful, significance of play. He based his theory on the observation that lower animals are endowed with instincts that appear to be fully developed and ready for use. (An **instinct** is the largely inherited and unalterable tendency of an organism to respond to environmental stimuli without the use of reason.) In contrast, higher animals develop their instincts through play. Long before a kitten actually captures a mouse, it practices the act by playing with a ball or a wad of paper. The more sophisticated the animal, the longer the play-dominated stage. Simple play, Groos theorized, is nature's way of preparing the young of higher animals for the demands of life.[32]

Other scholars believe that some innate tendency not only motivates young humans to play but also systematizes play. For instance, British psychologist G. Stanley Hall in 1916 suggested that a child's play passes through a series of stages that mirrors the cultural epochs of the human race. That is, the child progressively re-enacts in play the animal, savage, nomadic, agricultural, and tribal stages of human development.[33]

### Psychological Interpretations

Attempts to explain human behavior, including play, in psychological terms began in the late 19th century with interpretations based on a belief in inborn instincts as the force that drives behavior. In the early 1920s, William McDougall, a British psychologist, was the chief exponent of the view that instincts are related to certain of an organism's fundamental appetites, desires, and inner energies.[34] Although McDougall would have placed play in this category, he viewed the tendency to play as secondary to such basic instincts as fear, anger, and hunger.

Another advocate of the play-as-instinct theory was American physician-turned-psychologist William James, who wrote:

A boy can no more help running after another boy who runs provokingly near him, than a kitten can help running after a rolling ball . . . . All simple games are attempts to gain excitement yielded by certain primitive instincts . . . . Their special rules are habits, discovered by accident, selected by intelligence, and propagated by tradition.[35]

Other psychologists of the 1920s rejected this notion and instead suggested a reflex or mechanistic theory of play.[36] A **reflex** is a simple segment of behavior in which a direct and immediate response occurs to a particular stimulus. In contrast, an instinct is more complex and does not function as quickly or as automatically as a reflex. Furthermore, an instinct is seen to have an element of continuity because it covers a longer period than a reflex does. The instinct theorists assumed that play is a powerful innate tendency, whereas the reflex theorists assumed that play is triggered by a series of reflexes that are modified and become more complex through experience. Both the instinct and reflex theories of play have long since been abandoned.

Sigmund Freud, the father of psychoanalysis, posited that the behavior of the human infant is governed by the pleasure principle, a concept based on tension reduction (i.e., energy must be instantly discharged to prevent the buildup of tension). The discharge normally occurs through reflex actions that are inherent and automatic. When discharge of energy by this means is impossible, an alternative process—such as play—permits the discharge.[37]

By the middle of the 20th century, the term *instinct* had become unpopular with psychologists, and the term *drive* was used in its place to describe the supply of energy that puts an organism into motion. **Drive** primarily describes behavior directed toward eliminating physiological deprivation or moving away from noxious conditions. Subsequently, psychologists began to use the broader term **motive**, which has many meanings but which encompasses both conscious and unconscious reasons for behavior.

Among the factors that are considered to motivate play is the desire to belong, to undergo new experiences, to achieve recognition, and to express oneself.

American psychiatrist William Menninger in 1960 noted the role of play, specifically competitive sports, in facilitating the release of aggression:

> Competitive games provide an unusually satisfactory social outlet for the instinctive aggressive drive. Psychiatrists postulate the existence in the personality of an aggressive energy drive, which constantly seeks expression.[38]

### Sociological Interpretations

In the mid-1800s, interest began to grow in examining the roles that human groups and institutions play in the lives of individuals. Out of this interest was born the field of sociology. **Sociology** is the study of the development, structure, interaction, and collective behavior of organized groups of human beings.

At the same time, the industrial revolution—the shift from a chiefly agrarian to a chiefly industrial economy—took hold and began to sweep through western Europe and North America. By the early 20th century, this massive transformation not only had brought about fundamental changes in the economy of these regions but also had caused significant social restructuring, not always for the good of everyone. As cities developed around the great manufacturing sites, the tenements built to house workers rapidly degenerated into filthy slums that were breeding grounds for poverty, crime, and disease.

---

*instinct* a largely inherited and unalterable tendency of an organism to respond to environmental stimuli without the use of reason

*reflex* a simple segment of behavior in which a direct and immediate response occurs to a particular stimulus

*drive* behavior motivated toward eliminating physiological deprivation or moving away from noxious conditions

*motive* a conscious or unconscious reason for behavior

*sociology* the study of the development, structure, interaction, and collective behavior of organized groups of human beings

Several social reformers sought public and private support for their efforts to alleviate these problems. In North America, one result of this endeavor was the birth of the recreation movement; we will examine it later in more detail. At the same time, an earnest effort was begun to ascertain the role of play in the socialization of both young people and adults.

In the 1920s, Joseph Lee, an American philosopher and a leader in the American recreation movement, identified the need to belong as the factor that motivates play. He believed that play satisfies this need because, when people play together with a common cause, they fully and meaningfully experience the satisfactions of membership in a group.[39]

A decade later, George Herbert Mead posited that the social conditions under which one's sense of self emerges are illustrated in play and in the game. Play begins as unsystematized movements in the very young child and is described in the myths of primitive peoples. The game, in contrast, is much more complex and requires not only an understanding of the rules but also adherence to them. To play the game correctly, the child (or the uninitiated adult) must incorporate into the self the values, attitudes, and expectations of all others who are involved in the game.[40]

Mead used his theory to develop his well-known concept of the **generalized other**. This concept is defined as the totality of attitudes and values of one's group or social circle whose judgment is used as a standard for one's own behavior. Play and games are the vehicles through which the individual internalizes the values and norms of the group, the community, and ultimately the society.

### Cultural Interpretations

Cultural interpretations of play consider the relationship of play to the customs and symbols of a given society. Some culturally oriented scholars believe that play aids the child not only in understanding his or her culture but also in sustaining it.[41]

Johann Huizinga, a Dutch historian of the 1950s, believed that forms of play have permeated almost all human activities since the dawn of civilization and that play has helped humankind create society:

For many years the conviction has grown upon me that civilization arises and unfolds in and as play.[10]

Huizinga emphasized the relationship between ritual and play. He believed that the spirit of play exists in many rituals, a concept we will explore in Chapter 2.

A recent analysis of play behavior in children from different cultural backgrounds shows that cultural norms mediate role playing, games with rules, and creative play.[42]

### Recent Theories

Recently some scholars focused on the developmental approach to play, which emphasizes the child's attempt to master reality. According to Erik Erikson,

Child's play is an infantile form of the human ability to deal with experience by creating model situations and to master reality by experimenting and planning.[42a]

In this view, a child's play centers first around him/herself. In the second year of life, the scope of play broadens as the child begins to examine objects outside the self. In preschool years, the child learns to physically manipulate both his/her body and outside objects to master social interaction.

Swiss psychologist Jean Piaget viewed play as part of cognitive development, as essentially an attempt at assimilation over accommodation. Whereas assimilation is the repetition of familiar activities and the distortion of reality to match existing forms of thought, accommodation is the process by which thoughts and behaviors are altered to meet the demands of reality. Play is imitative; thus, it facilitates assimilation. Piaget identified three stages of play in a child's cognitive development: sensorimotor (relating to sensory and motor nerve pathways), symbolic/fantasy, and cooperative.[43]

A contemporary scholar believes the human brain contains a "play center."[44] Another had suggested half a century ago that there is a connection between play and ritual, an idea that supports both biological and cultural interpretations of play, as follows:

> Room for play . . . abounds in many kinds of tribal rituals, even in funerary ritual. There is play of symbol vehicles leading to the construction of bizarre masks and costumes . . . there is a play of meanings . . . there is play with words.[44a]

Play activities are dominant in the early stages of life, after which they give way to pursuits such as study and work. Once an adult's basic needs have been satisfied through work-related endeavors, he or she seeks activities that in and of themselves provide pleasure and enjoyment.

The best-known illustration of this concept is Abraham Maslow's hierarchy of human needs (Fig. 1.2), which shows the levels of needs, starting with basic physiological requirements and culminating in self-actualization.[2] At the upper levels of this figure are needs whose satisfaction goes beyond work and even beyond play.

**Concept Check**

- Define *play.*
- Give one example each of a biological and a psychological interpretation of play.

## IN SEARCH OF A THEORY

In 1980 some researchers seeking to identify the factors that motivate leisure, recreation,

***generalized other*** the totality of attitudes and values of one's group or social circle whose judgment is used as the standard of one's behavior

and play listed the clusters shown in Fig. 1.5.[45] In 1991 another group of scholars presented the following findings in a volume titled *Benefits of Leisure:*[46]

1. Studies document strong interest in engaging in regular physical activity.
2. Research findings, although limited, suggest that people recuperate from stress more rapidly in an outdoor setting than in an urban environment.
3. Spirituality appears to be expressed during leisure time in a variety of ways.
4. Leisure activities appear to be associated with positive outcomes in family interaction, satisfaction, and stability.
5. There is conceptual and empirical support for leisure opportunities as contributors to satisfactory community life.

Having established working definitions of three key terms—*leisure, recreation, and play*—in Chapter 2 we will consider the evolution of recreation and leisure from prehistoric times to the present.

**FIGURE 1.5** Factors that motivate leisure, recreation, and play.

- Enjoying nature; escaping civilization
- Escaping from routine and responsibility
- Physical exercise
- Creativity
- Relaxation
- Self-improvement
- Social contact
- Meeting new people
- Contact with prospective mates
- Contact with family members
- Recognition; status
- Social power
- Altruism
- Stimulus seeking
- Self-actualization
- Challenge; achievement; competition
- Aesthetics; intellectual stimulation
- Killing time; boredom

## Summing Up

- In contrast to play, leisure is a phenomenon that is peculiar to humans and that can be viewed as residual time, as particular activities, or as a state of mind.
- Recreation is an active/participative way to experience leisure.
- Recreational opportunities are available in several structured settings: public, commercial, corporate, and therapeutic.
- In its simplest form, play appears to be a

universal phenomenon that is witnessed among the young of higher animals and humans.
- Theories of play are of five main types: biological, psychological, sociological, cultural, and recent ones.
- It may be impractical to apply rigorous scientific analysis to the study of leisure, recreation, and play, but it is possible to create clusters of factors that motivate people to engage in these pursuits.

## Using What You've Learned

1. Select four young people: a toddler, a 5-year-old, a 9-year-old, and a teenager. Observe each of them at play. Which of the play theories you learned in this chapter apply to each young person's play? Report your observations in class.

2. Select eight adults of both sexes but of different ages and backgrounds. In what ways do their ways of playing differ from each other's and from the play you observed in the younger group? Prepare a brief report for class.

## YOUR  Turn

1. What factors that you have learned about in this chapter do you think motivate Chris Makos to play soccer with such dedication and intensity? What factors might explain John Shu's passion for developing technical skills in chess and tennis?

2. What John sees as enjoyable and stimulating Chris experiences as painstaking and tedious; what John sees as grueling and dangerous is Chris's passion. What interpretation of leisure explains why these two best friends have such radically different ideas of what constitutes the ideal leisure-time pursuit?

3. What similarities and/or differences can you identify in your favorite leisure pursuits and those of your closest friend?

### REFERENCES

1. Ibrahim, Hilmi (1988). Leisure, Idleness and Ibn Khaldun. *Leisure Studies* 7:51–58.
2. Maslow, Abraham (1968). *Toward a Psychology of Being.* New York: Von Nostrand Reinhold Co.
3. Butler, George (1940). *Introduction to Community Recreation.* New York: McGraw Hill, p. 2.
4. Nash, J.B. (1953). *The Philosophy of Recreation and Leisure.* Dubuque, IA: Wm. C. Brown.
5. Neumeyer, M. and Neumeyer, E. (1949) *Leisure and Recreation.* New York: Roland Press.
6. Rowntree, B., & Lavers, G. (1951) *English Life and Leisure.* New York: Longmans.
7. Larrabee, E., & Meyersohn (1958). *Mass Leisure.* Glencoe, IL : Free Press.
8. Brightbill, Charles (1960). *The Challenge of Leisure.* Englewood Cliffs, NJ: Prentice-Hall, p. 3.
9. Driver, B. L., et al. (Eds.) (1991). *Benefits of Leisure.* State College, PA: Venture Publishing, p. 7.

10. Huizinga, Johann (1950). *Homo Ludens: A Study of Play Elements in Culture.* Boston: Beacon Press, p. viii.

11. Pieper, Joseph (1964). *Leisure: The Basis of Culture.* New York: Pantheon Press, p. xix.

12. Kaplan, Max (1960). *Leisure in America: A Social Inquiry.* New York: Wiley, p. 3.

13. Dumazedier, Joffre (1967). *Toward a Society of Leisure.* New York: Free Press.

14. Nakhoodu, Z. (1961). *Leisure and Recreation in Society.* Allahabad: Katab Mahal, p. 7.

15. Hafez, M., et al. (1957). *Leisure and Recreation.* Cairo: Modern Press (in Arabic).

16. Roberts, K. (1970). *Leisure.* London: Longmans.

17. Entwistle, H. (1970). *Education, Work and Leisure.* London: Routledge.

18. Smith, M., et al. (Eds.) (1963). *Leisure and Society in Great Britain.* London: Allen Lane.

19. McLean, J., et al. (1985). *Recreation and Leisure: The Changing Scene.* New York: Macmillan.

20. Parker, S. (1976). *Sociology of Leisure.* New York: International Publication Service, pp. 12–20.

21. Nash, Jay B. (1953). *Philosophy of Recreation and Leisure.* Dubuque, IA: Wm C. Brown.

22. Shibutani, T. (1961). *Society and Personality.* Englewood Cliffs, NJ: Prentice-Hall p. 64–70.

23. Godbey, Geoffrey (1994). *Leisure in Your Life: An Exploration.* Philadelphia, PA: Saunders, p. 10.

24. Kraus, Richard (1990). *Recreation and Leisure in Modern Society.* New York: Harper/Collins, p. 12.

25. Russel, Ruth (1996). *Pastimes: The Context of Contemporary Leisure.* Madison, WI: Brown & Benchmark, p. 93.

26. Lancaster, J. B. (1975). *Primate Behavior and the Emergence of Human Culture.* New York: Holt, Rinehart & Winston, p. 49.

27. Wolf, D. P. (1984). Repertoire, Style and Format: Notions Worth Borrowing from Children's Play. In P. Smith (Ed.), *Play in Animals and Humans.* London: Basil Blackwell, p. 178.

28. Eisen, George (1991). A Theory of Play. In G. Gerson, et al. (Eds.), *Understanding Leisure: An Interdisciplinary Approach.* Dubuque, IA: Kendall-Hunt, p. 45.

29. Hooper, J., & Teresi, D. (1986). *The Three Pound Universe.* New York: Macmillan, p. 48.

30. Von Schiller, Friedrich (1781). Cited in Martin H. Neumeyer & Ester S. Neumeyer (1936), *Leisure and Recreation.* New York: A. S. Barnes, p. 134.

31. Spencer, Herbert (1896). *Principles of Psychology.* New York: Appleton-Century-Crofts.

32. Groos, Karl (1911). *The Play of Animals.* New York: Appleton-Century-Crofts.

33. Hall, G. Stanley (1916). *Adolescence: Its Psychology and Its Relations to Physiology, Anthropology, Sociology, Sex, Crime, Religion and Education.* New York: Appleton-Century-Crofts.

34. McDougall, William (1923). *Outline of Psychology.* New York: Scribner's & Sons.

35. James, William (1890). *Principles of Psychology.* New York: Holt, Rinehart & Winston (republished by Dover in 1950), p. 27.

36. Bernard, L. L. (1926). *Introduction to Social Psychology.* New York: Holt, Rinehart & Winston.

37. Freud, Sigmund (1955). Beyond the Pleasure Principle. In J. Stachey (Ed. and Trans.), *The Complete Psychological Work of S. Freud, 1920–1922.* London: Hogarth.

38. Menninger, W. C. (1960). Recreation and Mental Health. In B. Hill (Ed.), *Recreation and Psychiatry.* New York: National Recreation Association.

39. Lee, Joseph (1929). *Play in Education.* New York: Macmillan.

40. Mead, George Herbert (1934). *Mind, Self and Society: From the Standpoint of Social Behaviorist.* Chicago: University of Chicago Press.

41. Roberts, J., & Sutton-Smith, B. (1962). Game Training and Game Inducement. *Ethnology* 1:116–185.

42. Edwards, P.E. (2000). Children Play. *Cross-Cultural Research* 34(4): 318.

42a. Erikson, Erik (1963). *Childhood and Society.* New York: Norton & Sons, p. 222.

43. Piaget, J. (1962). *Play, Dreams and Imitation in Childhood.* New York: Norton & Sons, p. 162.

44. Marano, H.S. (1999). The Power of Play. *Psychology Today* 32(4): 36.

44a. Turner, Victor (1982). *From Ritual to Theatre: The Human Seriousness of Play.* Washington, DC: Smithsonian Institute Press, p. 22.

45. Crandall, R. (1980). Motivations for Leisure. *Journal of Leisure Research* 12:45–54.

46. Driver, B. L., Brown, P., & Peterson, G. (Eds.) (1991). *Benefits of Leisure.* State College, PA: Venture Publishing, p. 7.

Leisure and the cultivation of
human capacities are inextricably interdependent.

MARGARET MEAD
*Redbook, December 1963*

# The Evolution of Leisure, Recreation, and Play

## CHAPTER 2

## THE CHAPTER AT A GLANCE

In this chapter we explore play, leisure, and recreation as they have evolved from prehistoric society to contemporary society. We examine their roles in these societies and discover the contributions of selected societies to some popular forms of modern leisure and recreation.

## Chapter Objectives

*After completing this chapter, you should be able to*

- ◆ Define *evolution*.
- ◆ Identify three forms of leisure.
- ◆ Describe social structures in the following eras: early, middle, Renaissance, and modern.
- ◆ Identify some leisure and recreational activities that were popular in each of the above eras.
- ◆ Explain how the emergence of a middle class changed the nature of leisure and recreation.
- ◆ Describe unique characteristics of leisure and recreation in American society.

## THE NATURE OF EVOLUTION

Most people think of evolution as a biological phenomenon, as made famous by Charles Darwin's groundbreaking book *The Origin of Species*. Evolution also occurs, however, in both social and cultural structures—the context in which forms of play, leisure, and recreation develop. In the broadest sense, evolution means a process of change in a certain direction. In this text we will use the following operational definition of **evolution**: a process of continuous change from a

> **evolution** a process of continuous change from a lower, simpler, or worse to a higher, more complex, or better state

## A World  of Difference

### DANCING: RECREATION OR RITUAL?

"We are going to a dance tonight?" asked Moy Commoro. "Who died?"

"Died?" Jimmy Waters, Moy's host and roommate, was puzzled by his friend's question. "No one died."

Moy Commoro was born a Latuka, a member of a small tribe on the east side of the White Nile, in southern Sudan, a country in northeast Africa. Jimmy's church, which sends missionaries to that part of the world, sponsored Moy's visit to the United States. Moy, a tall, agile boy, is about Jimmy's age, and the two have quickly become good friends.

"Our church holds dances for young people two or three times a year," Jimmy explained, "Do you have dances like that in your country?"

"Yes, we have dances," Moy answered, "but only for special occasions—mainly to honor the dead."

Jimmy was curious about this custom, and Moy told him that the funerary dances take place in his village for many weeks after a person's death. Most members of the tribe, men and women, young and old, participate in the dance. They wear helmets, adorned with beautiful plumes of ostrich feathers. Many dancers wear antelope horns suspended around their necks. The men usually form an inner circle during the dance, with women on the outside.

Jimmy was fascinated and wondered whether the villagers take pleasure in these dances. "Maybe if I explain our dances to him," he thought, "Moy will enjoy himself tonight."

However, when he told Moy that they would be attending a square dance, Moy was confused. "You dance in a square? We dance in a circle."

"No, it's not that we dance in a square—it's just called a square dance. The boys and girls dance as a couple to certain steps, then change partners when the caller tells them to." Moy looked baffled by Jimmy's description of this common American leisure experience. He wasn't sure what to expect at this odd dance, but he was looking forward to seeing what it was all about. As you read this chapter, think about Moy's and Jimmy's very different views of dancing.

lower, simpler, or worse to a higher, more complex, or better state.

In terms of the evolution of play, an easily understood example is the American sport of football. In the early years of the sport, which was first played in the late 1800s at Ivy League colleges, a team consisted of 11 players who played both offense and defense. Today, 100 years later, the game has evolved to the point where a team now consists of more than 40 players: separate units for offense and defense, "special teams" for specific plays, and individuals such as place kickers who perform one narrowly defined task. Understandably, the rules and terminology of football have undergone a similar evolution.

If changes of this number and substance have taken place in just one sport in one country over the span of one century, imagine the magnitude of the evolution in play, leisure, and recreation over the millions of years of human existence! As we examine that process, we will use the following evolutionary continuum:

- Early societies
- Old World societies
- New World societies
- Middle-era societies
- Modern societies

## EARLY SOCIETIES

Evidence exists that several human species lived before the time of *Homo sapiens*, which literally means "intelligent human." A watershed for these early humans was the discovery of fire, because it changed both their physique and their lifestyle and was therefore a quantum leap in the evolution of humankind. Cooking food over fire, which softened it, led to a reduction in the musculature of the jaw, allowing for cranial expansion and a resulting increase in brain capacity. Early humans lived in caves and gathered around the fire not only to prepare food but also for warmth, safety, and companionship. The firelight provided illumination for evening activities, both ritualistic and playful. The Cro-Magnon species left evidence of such activities on the walls of their caves more than 20,000 years ago.[1]

### Tribes and Chiefdoms

The first human social structure was a **dyad**—a unit composed of a male and a female. These units expanded into a family as offspring were born who needed to be nurtured, defended, and fed. A group of families then formed

into a band, consisting of perhaps 16 to 25 persons. Some bands chose to stay together and form tribes. With the expansion of the tribe, a new hierarchical structure evolved. The family that controlled an important resource, such as water, dominated the tribe, creating what is known as a chiefdom. Some contemporary societies, including Native Americans and Africans, continue to live under these structures.

Human bands, tribes, and chiefdoms in general can be characterized as conservative, initiating and accepting little change. The social structure is based on cooperation, and the group is emphasized over the individual. Valuable resources are publicly owned and are often controlled by the elders. Parents and elders raise young people and indoctrinate them into the society's customs and rituals. These societies often are ruled by **taboos**, or prohibitions of certain behaviors, that they believe to be imposed by some supernatural power. Religious practices tend to be closely associated with a belief in magic.

In Chapter 1 we learned that some contemporary researchers believe the human brain contains a "play center."[2] It is close enough to the brain's center for ritualization to suggest that there is a connection between ritual and play. Support for this thesis is found in the reports of several field observers. For example, nearly 125 years ago one observer wrote that the Australian Aborigines did a "canoe dance" in which participants pretended that sticks were paddles. When a signal was given, the participants brought their sticks forward and held them as one holds a paddle, swaying their bodies in unison in a paddling motion.[2a]

In 1932 another observer reported that the Navajo tribe of Native Americans organized wrestling matches whenever there was a

*dyad* a human social unit composed of a male and a female

*taboo* social prohibition of a certain behavior

gathering or a feast.[3] Yet another example of the connection between ritual and play can be seen in the Native American Choctaw chiefdom. They played their traditional game, *toli*, as part of a ritual. *Toli* was described as a fast-moving, dangerous game that later evolved into lacrosse, a popular sport in Canada and the United States.[4]

In tribal societies and chiefdoms, most of these playful rituals involved all members of the society. It was not until the evolution of what is known as the primitive state that social stratification began to occur.

## Primitive States

In these societies, certain members gained greater access to goods, services, and positions of power than was possible in tribes or chiefdoms. Population increased, and a leisure class emerged. An excellent example of a primitive state is the Zulus of Africa, whose kings formed a leisure class. In this structure, public hunts were open to everyone, but royal hunts were organized exclusively for the pleasure of the king.[5]

It was at this stage of societal evolution that the concept of amusive leisure most likely arose. **Amusive leisure** describes a situation in which the most powerful members of a society, the leisure class, are entertained by select performers who have developed a high level of skill in their particular specialty, such as dancing or singing. Here we can identify three distinct social classes: the leisure class, the performer class, and the working class that must provide time for the performers' labor and must support them with food, shelter, and other necessities.[6]

### Concept Check

- Briefly explain the connection between play and ritual in early societies.
- At what point in human development did a leisure class emerge?

# OLD WORLD SOCIETIES

The Old World refers to the world as it was known before the discovery of the Western Hemisphere (the New World). When the advent of agriculture provided a stable food supply, early Old World societies of hunter-gatherers were able to abandon their nomadic lifestyle and establish settled communities. Another major factor in the shift from a nomadic to a settled existence was discovery of a reliable source of water. The security afforded by ready access to food and water spurred the development of complex social systems such as those that originated in the Middle East.

## Mesopotamia

Several civilizations developed in Mesopotamia (the location of modern Iraq), which occupies the land between the Tigris and Euphrates rivers. The first civilization to develop was Sumer, around 3500 B.C.E. (Before the Common Era, or Before the Christian Era—i.e., Before Christ, or B.C.). The united city-states of Ur, Eridu, Uruk, Lagash, and Nippur were among the most powerful, and kings began to rule by what they claimed was divine right. Another union took place to the north, and the Akkadian civilization that emerged from that union subdued the Sumerians around 2300 B.C.E. Babylon gained ascendancy around 1700 B.C.E. under the leadership of Hammurabi. At about that same time, another group, the Assyrians, became powerful. After a period of Persian rule from 539 to 331 B.C.E., Mesopotamia was ruled by the Greeks until the Romans took over in 36 B.C.E.

Their turbulent history notwithstanding, Mesopotamian civilizations made major contributions to the overall evolution of civilization. They created the first system of written communication, the wheel, the 60-minute hour, the 360-degree circle, and the first code of law.[7] A Mesopotamian civilization also created the first park—the Hanging Gardens of Babylon—a key development in the evolution of leisure and recreation.

## Ancient Egypt

The consolidation of settlements around the Nile River resulted in the development of two states, Upper Egypt and Lower Egypt, which were united in 3200 B.C.E. by King Menes. For the next 27 centuries, the social, economic, and political structures of ancient Egypt remained virtually unchanged. Egypt was ruled by a pharaoh who claimed divinity and was supported by the nobility. Beneath the nobility was a large cadre of craftsmen, soldiers, and petty officials, who in turn outranked the lowest level of society, the peasant masses.

Religious ceremonies played a significant role in the life of ancient Egyptians, which was highly ritualized. A major ritual was the reenactment of the myth of Osiris. During the time of Ptolemy, this re-enactment became a puppet play. On certain religious occasions, parades were held in the city of Thebes. During festivals, members of the affluent class were entertained by dancing girls, while commoners celebrated and feasted in garlanded pavilions.

Among the activities of the affluent class was *it sum* (literally, "to occupy oneself with"), or sport.[8] A stock scene from an Egyptian tomb shows a man with his wife and daughter throwing a stick at a flock of geese (Fig. 2.1). A frieze in a temple shows wrestlers in various holds.

> **amusive leisure** a situation in which members of the leisure class are entertained by members of a performer class

**FIGURE 2.1** The recreation of a pharaoh and his family.

## Ancient Israel

The Hebrews originated in Ur in Mesopotamia. Under the patriarch Abraham, they emigrated to Canaan, the land they believed was promised to them by their deity, Jahweh (God). Although initially successful under the leadership of Joshua, the Hebrews subsequently suffered losses and did not begin to reverse the trend until the rule of three consecutive kings—Saul, David, and Solomon. Most of the Hebrews were forced into slavery by the Assyrians in 721 B.C.E.., and the remainder were taken by Babylon in 604 B.C.E. In 539 B.C.E. the Hebrews returned with the intention of practicing the monotheism proclaimed by Abraham. At that time they developed the concept of the six rights of a person:

1. The right to life
2. The right to possession
3. The right to work
4. The right to clothing
5. The right to shelter
6. The right to worship, including a sabbath

To the Hebrews, the sabbath was not intended for rest and recreation but, rather, for cessation of daily work in favor of study and worship. (As we will see later, after the advent of Christianity, the sabbath was also set aside for rest and recreation.) As a people who were subjected to oppression and slavery, the Hebrews tended to have little desire for play. Their religious and seasonal rituals, however, frequently involved singing and dancing.

## Ancient Greece

Whereas the ancient Egyptians and the peoples of Mesopotamia lived in unbroken land masses, the ancient Greeks occupied a series of valleys separated by limestone hills. Rather than dwelling in one large community, the Greeks lived in smaller units in each of these valleys. Despite being separated, the Greeks forged a culture that has had a profound impact on Western thought and behavior. The somewhat harsh environment helped mold a spirit of individualism, coupled with a commitment to local action. In each valley and on the islands surrounding the Greek peninsula emerged city-states called *polis*. Despite strong localism, the city-states, which shared a language and worshipped the same deities, united in the face of common enemies, such as the Persians.

As early as 3000 B.C.E., the great mini-civilization of Minos flourished on the Greek island of Crete. The relics left by the Minoans indicate they were a peaceful people who loved life. In contrast, the Mycenaeans, who lived on the mainland, appear to have been pirates. For 10 years they surrounded the city of Troy, and thereafter Greece fell into a dark age that lasted from 1200 to 750 B.C.E. At that time two significant mini-civilizations emerged. The Dorians of the north settled in Sparta and developed a highly centralized city-state. To the south was Athens, settled by the Mycenaeans, which became a leading center for culture and recreation in the ancient world. A spirit of rebirth was emerging in Greece, and the spark came from distant Ionia, a settlement in Asia Minor. It was in Ionia that Homer produced his two great epic poems, the *Iliad* and the *Odyssey*.

The Greeks also originated the concept of *schole*: schools where the children of the affluent learned the art of gracious living and were taught to engage in a desirable activity for its own sake. In essence the Greeks took leisure seriously. Their religion encouraged inquiry into the nature of things and thus led to contemplation, which (as we learned in Chapter 1) philosopher Aristotle suggested is the highest form of leisure. Recreation, a lower form of leisure, he deemed acceptable, but he derided increasing interest in the lowest form of leisure: amusement (see Fig. 1.1).

Between the fifth and third centuries B.C.E., Greek art, literature, music, poetry, and philosophy flourished, as did sport, which inspired the creation of the Olympic Games. A number of sports competitions took place in ancient Greece, each organized in honor of a different deity. The Olympic Games were considered to be the most important competition because they were held in honor of Zeus, the king of gods. During the games, the city-states were encouraged to set aside their differences and join in a unified celebration. In some ways the spirit of the games in those ancient times survives in the Olympic Games of today; in many other ways the focus of this international competition seems to have shifted in directions never envisioned by the ancient Greeks (see A Closer Look below).

The Greeks at this time also were famous for their Dionysian revels. Dionysus (also known as Bacchus) was the god of wine, and seasonal festivals were held in his honor that featured dramatic presentations as well as orgiastic behavior. (From *Bacchus* comes the word *bacchanal*, which means "orgy.")

A popular private pastime was the symposium held by members of the affluent class. A banquet was followed by a series of entertainments and diversions. A master of ceremonies introduced female dancers and magicians, posed riddles, and organized games among the participants.

## A CLOSER LOOK

### THE OLYMPIC SPIRIT THEN AND NOW

The Olympic Games of ancient Greece were held every four years in a spirit of peace and fellowship, with political differences temporarily forgotten so all could come together in a celebration of skill and achievement. In addition to athletic contests, the games featured both religious and patriotic rituals. The winners of competitions were honored as national heroes and were considered models for youth to emulate.

Begun in 776 B.C.E., the Olympic Games were held until the fourth century C.E., when they were discontinued after having deteriorated under the Roman rule of Greece. The games were revived in the late 19th century in the spirit of unity and harmony that had characterized the ancient contests.

Today the Olympic Games are alive and well—although undoubtedly not in the sense intended by their founders. The exhortation "Go for the gold," made popular in the games of the early 1980s, now refers less to the pursuit of excellence than to the pursuit of material rewards—lucrative product endorsements, movie contracts, and professional tours. It's not just the competitors who seek to cash in on Olympic glory: TV stations vie hotly for the right to broadcast the games, sponsors pay huge sums for 30-second advertising spots, and cities around the world stage multimillion-dollar campaigns to attract the games to their location. Socialist and communist regimes sponsor state programs to groom Olympic athletes, while the United States and other countries send millionaire professional sports stars to compete in what were intended to be amateur contests. Charges of racial and ethnic discrimination, cheating, and illegal drug use abound. Rivalries between members of the same team explode into sensationalistic headlines, as in the Tonya Harding–Nancy Kerrigan affair that dominated the news in the 1994 Winter Olympics. Not only have the Olympic Games become a cash cow, they're also unquestionably a political arena, as evidenced by the following examples of political tensions and conflicts that have marred the spirit of the original Olympic Games. In the 1972 games in Munich, Germany, several Israeli athletes died in a terrorist attack on the Olympic Village. Under President Jimmy Carter, the 1980 U.S. Olympic Team was forbidden to participate in the Moscow summer games because of a dispute with the Soviet Union.

Peace, harmony, unity, fellowship—these lofty ideals now seem to be no more than empty phrases. The acceptance of bribes by members of the International Olympic Committee has further tarnished the organization's reputation.

## Ancient Rome

When it was established in 753 B.C.E., Rome was a small hamlet in the Latium region of Italy. By the fifth century B.C.E., however, it had become a dominant power in the region. Rome's successful wars with Greece made it the undisputed power of the Mediterranean. The captives seized by the Romans in these conflicts became a huge labor force, which gave the upper classes more leisure time, and they began to organize games similar to the Greek Olympics. The Ludi Romani were public games to which even peasants were invited.

Rule in Rome was shared among three groups: the optimares, or old guard; the populares, or common people; and the knights, who were courted by the first two groups. Because government officials served without pay, affluent Romans dominated public life. The public games, which arose out of ritual and religion, began to be used by the wealthy to acquire government favors. Although dramatic performances were enjoyed in ancient Rome over the years, they were eclipsed by the popularity of the games. The Roman theatre attempted to emulate the games, but it soon deteriorated.[9]

By the time of the Common Era, which began with the birth of Christ, Rome was committed to a policy of "bread and circuses" to mitigate civic abuses. The number of recognized holidays in early Rome increased from 50 a year in the first century of the Common Era to 175 in the fourth century. Of these holidays, 101 were dedicated to theatrical entertainment, 64 to chariot racing, and 10 to gladiatorial combats.[10]

### Concept Check

- What civilization created the Hanging Gardens of Babylon, and what was their significance?
- What significant contributions did the ancient Greeks make to leisure and recreation?

## NEW WORLD SOCIETIES

The New World refers to the Western Hemisphere, specifically to the land mass of North and South America. At least two New World societies made significant contributions to contemporary play and recreation: the Mayans and the Aztecs.

### The Mayans

The Mayans built their civilization at the beginning of the Common Era on the Yucatan Peninsula in what is now southern Mexico and northern Central America. Their 18-month year, composed of 20-day months, ended in a 5-day "unlucky period." Each month featured a special festival, and drumming was an important part of these festivals. Conch shells were made into trumpets, and bells of gold and silver were tied to dancers' legs, wrists, and waists. Eventually, dramatic performances became part of these festivals. The Mayans' great passion was a game called pok-a-pok.

### The Aztecs

The Aztecs, the native people of Mexico, evolved to a primitive state over four centuries, from the beginning of the 12th century to the end of the 15th century. Aztec society was highly stratified, and life at the top level was quite

*The Chichen Itza Ball Court on the Yucatan Peninsula of Mexico.*

luxurious.[11] Hunting was a favorite recreational activity of the leisure class, as was a ball game called tlachtli, which was very similar to the Mayan game pok-a-pok. It was played on an elongated, rectangular court with one vertical stone ring placed in the center on either side. The object of the game was to pass a rubber ball through the ring using one's elbow or hip. These games were halted about 1540 C.E. with the advent of the Spanish Conquest.

## MIDDLE-ERA SOCIETIES

In this section we will examine selected Asian and European societies in the period between 500 and 1500 C.E., which is known in European history as the medieval period or the Middle Ages. A common feature of the societies to be discussed is the relative stability of their economic, political, and social systems during this time.

### China

For many centuries, China was composed of several feudal states, each ruled by a prince. When the Chin dynasty unified these states around 200 B.C.E., administrative districts were established that were operated primarily by members of the affluent class. China did not have slaves or serfs, but its huge peasant class, although legally free, was very poor. In the 11th century, China's small number of wealthy landlords were joined by an expanding merchant class. These two groups, along with the top government officials, formed the leisure class of China during this period. Their large households consisted of a master, his chief wife, other wives or concubines, the master's sons and their wives, unmarried daughters, and many servants.

The estates of wealthy Chinese of this period had many buildings, each designed for a specific leisure-time activity, such as admiring the moon, making music, or holding a banquet. Affluent households also retained painters, writers, storytellers, dancers, and musicians to entertain the family and guests. On special occasions the performers were paraded in the neighborhood and announced by fireworks, a Chinese invention.[12]

When Chinese government officials lost their positions after the Mongolian invasion in the 13th century, many began to write novels describing events of the past. Some of the novels became the basis for storytelling and plays. These performances, along with celebratory dances that originated in earlier eras, became the chief form of amusive leisure for the masses in China.

The concept of pleasure grounds emerged during this middle period of Chinese history. These were vast market areas where theatrical presentations, singing, dancing, shadow plays, and puppet and marionette shows took place.[13]

### Japan

By the sixth century of the Common Era, Japan was a united country. Before that time, the Japanese people were organized into several clans whose chiefs held all the wealth and power. At this time, Japan was a feudalistic society in which a small aristocracy was supported by a large class of farmers. The privileged class was composed of nobles, priests, and monks. The nobles' mansions traditionally contained a garden on the southern grounds that featured waterfalls, ponds, and tiny rolling hills.

During this period, public baths in Japan's ancient urban centers grew in popularity.[14] Women attended to the needs of patrons and danced and sang for them. Affluent Japanese gathered in private homes to listen to music and hear poetry recitations. It is out of these gatherings that kabuki, a form of Japanese drama, is believed to have emerged. Women were barred from both attending and performing in dramatic presentations, so puppetry gained popularity during this era because it was permissible for the female form to be represented in a puppet.

Japan's warriors, the samurai, carried swords, whereas common people were forbidden to do so. Commoners defended themselves against marauding samurai by means of jujitsu, a method of self-defense that concentrates on putting an opponent off balance. Jujitsu was the forerunner of judo, now a popular self-defense technique in many parts of the world.

## India

Hinduism, the dominant religion of India, originated the **caste system**. This system is a division of society into several rigid groups based on heredity. In this system, members of a given caste are restricted to certain occupations and are forbidden to associate with members of other castes. Then as now, Hindus sought to be liberated from the material world through purification of desires and eradication of personal identity. Hindus believe in reincarnation of the soul in various forms according to the nature of one's actions in a lifetime; therefore, the faithful devote considerable time to mystic contemplation and ascetic practices.

Like their counterparts in other lands, affluent Indians of the middle era lived a life of luxury. Their ornate palaces had vast gardens and lakes. Young men of the privileged class spent most of their time in graceful idleness, refining leisure to an exquisite art form. Popular pastimes included engaging in amorous adventures, attending literary parties, and writing poetry.[15]

## Islam

The religion of Islam was founded by the prophet Mohammed in 610 C.E. The Islamic society was created when Islam swept across the ancient world and spread into Asia. Although complete political unification was impossible, the adherents of Islam (called Muslims) shared a common culture based on their religious beliefs. Islam was the basis for a civilization in which there was no separation between church and state. Mohammed and his successors, called caliphs, were both the secular leaders and the heads of state. The Islamic civilization flourished and gained impetus from the works of the Greeks, Romans, Persians, and Eastern Indians.

In contrast to the traditional Judeo-Christian view of the sabbath as a day for prayer and reflection, Muslims were permitted to use their sabbath for recreation and leisure. Throughout the history of Islam, holy days such as the Prophet's birthday have been celebrated with large public festivals. One observer gave an account of a religious festival in Cairo, Egypt, that lasted 12 days. The celebrants were amused by poets, rope dancers, sleight-of-hand tricksters, magicians, and acrobats.[16] Similar activities occur today in many Muslim cities and communities.

During Ramadan, the Muslim month of fasting, the faithful refrain from eating, drinking, and smoking from sunrise to sunset. After breaking the fast at sunset, Muslims begin an evening of socializing. Women get together to chat, play cards or table games, or engage in similar recreational pastimes. Men spend their evening in the coffee house (the equivalent of bars and taverns in the West), where they play chess and backgammon, games the Muslims imported from Persia and India. The children of Cairo carried candle lanterns as they paraded and caroled through the city. Today the children use battery-powered lanterns.

A 3-day feast celebrates the end of the month of fasting. The area around the mosque (house of worship) is crowded with families dressed in new clothes. Children enjoy the hand-powered rides in simple amusement parks set up by the many entrepreneurs who occupy spaces around the mosque. A 4-day festival is held 2 months later to celebrate the return of the hajjis (pilgrims) from the holy city of Mecca.

Wealthy Muslims try to create heaven on earth in their verdant courtyards, adorned with fountains and singing birds. In these courtyards members of the privileged class occupy their time playing chess, talking to friends, or relaxing. Traditionally, Muslim women do not socialize with Muslim men. Therefore, the women remain in their quarters and are entertained by female dancers who perform what is known in the West as belly dancing.

## Europe

Rome had been the central authority in the Western world for more than four centuries. However, its fall in the fifth century led to the rise of a feudalistic system that dominated Europe for the next several centuries. Under this system, life was miserable for the common people, many of whom lived in hovels surrounding the manor houses of feudal lords. Life was drudgery for commoners except for fairs in some cities and the celebrations of saints' days. On these purportedly religious occasions, ironically, the commoners temporarily forgot their misery by singing bawdy songs and engaging in other forms of raucous behavior.

### European revival

By the 10th century, a revival had started in Europe that originated in Venice, a port city in northeastern Italy. Trade with both the East and the West was increasing, which caused Venice to prosper and fostered the emergence of a strong merchant class. Soon other cities began to enjoy the rebirth Venice was experiencing. As affluence spread and urban populations increased, so did the desires of city dwellers for enjoyable leisure-time activities. Guilds of merchants and craftsmen became social and recreational centers for their members, and the middle class flourished.

Freed from the onerous existence of commoners and peasants, merchants and craftsmen were able to devote more time to the pursuit of leisure. They enjoyed longer, more relaxed meals and enjoyed celebrating numerous saints' days. Trade fairs, ostensibly intended for commerce, also offered opportunities for amusive leisure: attendees could see wrestling matches, stage shows, and acrobatic performances. People of the Middle Ages also enjoyed the entertainment provided by wandering minstrels and troubadours.

With cooperation from the clergy, the aristocracy gained control of virtually all aspects of life in medieval Europe. As wars subsided, an era of peace, stability, and prosperity prevailed.

*Jousting tournaments are often re-enacted today.*

Small churches were rebuilt as cathedrals, while modest manor houses were enlarged into castles. Life in a castle offered many opportunities for leisure. On certain days the lord and his entourage would hunt, ride horseback, or engage in falconry. Evening entertainment featured singing, dancing, and games. Knights organized tournaments in which participants jousted and engaged in other contests of skill.

By the 15th century the city-states of Europe were giving way to a new political structure: the nation-state. Leaders in this direction were

**caste system** a division of society into rigid groups based on heredity, in which members of a given caste are restricted to certain occupations and are forbidden to associate with members of other castes; originated with the Hindu sect of India

France and England; entities in other areas of Europe were slower to follow. Celebrations expanded to include national occasions as well as religious holidays, and elaborate festivities were organized at royal palaces. Europe's nobility attended masquerades, balls, and tournaments and began to enjoy new games such as tennis and lawn bowling.

Although the "new leisure" was opposed by Protestant reformers as idle and even immoral, Europe in the late Middle Ages clearly was on the verge of a rebirth: a renaissance.

### The European Renaissance

By the 14th century, intellectual curiosity had largely been liberated from the iron fist of the church in Rome, and this new freedom paved the way for a European revival. Affluent Italians, who were the first to open their estates to leisure activities for common people, also opened their purses to finance scientific endeavors and the exploration of uncharted territories. Contemplation, which according to Aristotle was the highest form of leisure pur-

*Kings College Chapel in Cambridge.*

suit, was encouraged by the new secular authority. The other two forms of leisure, recreation and amusement, also flourished.

During this period, each European city had a patron saint whose day was celebrated by both nobles and commoners. Religious processions played a major role in these celebrations. A feast usually followed the procession, and the remainder of the day was spent playing and watching games. Some of the games were crude; others were more refined.

An excellent illustration of the evolution of games and sport can be seen in the British experience, which we will examine in the next section. Later we will explore the modern societies of France, Germany, and the United States.

**Concept Check**

- What were some hallmarks of Chinese and Japanese leisure and recreation in the Middle Ages?
- What is the caste system?
- How does the Islamic view of the sabbath differ from the traditional Judeo-Christian view?

## MODERN SOCIETIES

The term *modern* has many meanings and, therefore, is difficult to define in only one way. To help us define *modern* in the context of society, we can examine a given society's legal and behavioral code. If the society uses a two-code system in which the rights of one group (for example, the aristocracy) are broader and more generous than the rights of the rest of the society, that society is governed by a feudal structure. A **modern society**, in contrast, either has adopted or is moving toward adopting a unified code of behavior. A society well known for having followed this path is Great Britain, whose democratic institutions have their roots in the Magna Carta. Issued in 1215 during the reign of King John, the Magna Carta established a series of legal principles, such as the right to due process and a requirement that the legislature approve any taxes requested by the king.

## The British Experience

What today is known as the United Kingdom (UK) of Great Britain is composed of England, Scotland, Wales, and Northern Ireland. Ruled by monarchs, Great Britain for many centuries had a social structure that consisted of royalty, aristocrats, and commoners. This last class included the large number of peasants who composed the primarily agricultural labor force. Unlike their counterparts on the European continent, these laborers were not slaves but free agents, a factor that greatly enhanced their social mobility.

*Hampton Court Gardens in England.*

As Great Britain began to shift from an agricultural to an industrial economy in the middle of the 18th century, much of the labor force moved from rural areas into the cities that housed the country's expanding manufacturing base. Factory supervisors and managers, together with skilled craftsmen, merchants, and bankers, formed the nucleus of a British middle class that grew rapidly in number and influence. Understandably, the middle class tried to emulate the upper class in manners and behavior, including the cultivation of the leisure pursuits enjoyed by the upper class.

As noted earlier in this chapter, these pursuits included hunting, horseback riding, falconry, tennis, and lawn bowling. The upper class, and eventually the upper middle and middle classes, also enjoyed sports that first became popular at Great Britain's public schools. (Called "public" because their purpose was to prepare privileged young men for positions in public service, these schools were, and are, privately owned.) Among these public school sports were rowing, rugby, cricket, and badminton—traditional British sports that now are played in many other parts of the world that were part of the once-vast British Empire.

Among modern Great Britain's other significant contributions to the world of leisure is the establishment of a second home for rest and relaxation. Although this form of indulgence traditionally was possible only for the upper class, many members of the upper middle class began to acquire small second homes in the country. Middle-class people who could not afford a second home traveled to the seashore and rented a "holiday flat," a small apartment designed for vacationers of modest means. As the middle class expanded, seaside resorts

> **modern society** a society that has adopted or is moving toward a unified code of behavior; e.g., Great Britain

expanded and flourished by providing housing and entertainment on an affordable scale.[17]

By far the most popular sport of the masses in Great Britain was, and is, soccer (a shortening of the term association football). This game is played throughout the UK, in many other European countries, and in North and South America. Soccer—or football, as it is called in the UK—is played professionally in the UK and has fanatically loyal followers who sometimes have caused riots while attending games between intense rivals.

## The French Experience

Before the French Revolution in 1789 in which the monarchy was overthrown and a republic established, French kings built elaborate palaces to replace the modest hunting cottages of their predecessors. The most ornate and famous palace is at Versailles, which is a major attraction for tourists from around the world. As in Great Britain, hunting was the chief recreational occupation of the French aristocracy.

Before the revolution, ordinary citizens of France enjoyed a generous holiday schedule: 52 sabbaths per year, 90 so-called rest days, and 38 holidays from work.[18] After the revolution, under the new republican government, the French lost much of the free time they had enjoyed under the monarchy. In partial compensation, the new government enacted legislation that granted commoners access to and use of the great estates of the aristocracy. Under this law the public was permitted to visit the palace at Versailles, which during the reign of Louis XIII had undergone impressive enhancements: a grand canal, a full mile long and 200 feet wide, with gondolas for the king's pleasure; waterfalls and an artificial lake stocked with waterfowl; and a now world-famous botanical garden.

## The German Experience

The kingdoms and city-states of Germany were not united until the French conquest of Germany under Napoleon in 1806. The humiliating defeat gave rise to a wave of intense German nationalism, of which one facet was the movement known as the Turnen (gymnastics). The immediate aim of this program was to strengthen German youth for the purpose of liberating the country from its conquerors. In 1811 the first Turnplatz (playground) was opened on the outskirts of Berlin.[19] Although the Turnen were abolished after Germany was freed from the French, commitment to the discipline of gymnastics remained strong, and the sport is the hallmark of contemporary united Germany.

Modern-day Germans continue to celebrate several holidays that originated in early Christian times and in the earlier pagan era. A major pagan festival was held at the time of the winter solstice. The Germans combined this event with the celebration of Christmas, which throughout the contemporary Western world features remnants of old pagan customs, such as the use of evergreens for decoration, lavish feasting, and the burning of the Yule log.

Another traditional German celebration that has gained fame worldwide is the Oktoberfest, an annual event of several days' duration that centers on sampling the brews for which the country is famous. The streets are filled with merrymakers, and taverns and restaurants are taken over by revelers who hoist their steins and lustily sing traditional German drinking songs. In the United States, many communities with a strong German-American component host their own versions of this centuries-old ritual as a means of attracting tourists.

## The American Experience

Life for the first American settlers was harsh and demanding, and there was little time for leisure. Furthermore, frivolous pursuits of any sort were frowned on by the Puritans, a group of Protestants from England who preached asceticism and self-denial. Described by many as religious fanatics, the Puritans wielded considerable influence over life in the colonies and imposed severe punishments on those who dared to violate their rigid rules of personal conduct. A somewhat more moderate view was expressed by the spiritual leader of New England, Cotton Mather:

> Laudable recreations may be used now and then, but I beseech you, let those recreations be used for the sauce but not for the meat.[20]

As the Puritan influence waned, more 18th-century Americans chose to pass their Sunday leisurely, enjoying such previously forbidden activities as hunting, fishing, horse racing, card playing, and dancing.

Hunting, which was essential to keep families supplied with food, became an end in itself when settlers found the time to hunt raccoon and opossum for sport. In the 17th century, Americans enjoyed such spectator sports as horse racing, cock fighting, and bull baiting—all imported from England. Horse racing, as in the mother country, was primarily the sport of the privileged. In the Chesapeake Bay area in the early 18th century, a tailor was fined 100 pounds of tobacco for racing his horse in a contest reserved for gentlemen.[20]

After the War of Independence in 1776, in which the American colonies gained their freedom from British rule, Americans began to develop their own distinctive rituals. In rural areas barn raisings, cornhusking, apple paring,

and quilting bees combined work with socializing and usually culminated in dances. Similar gatherings were held to clear timber, remove rocks from fields, and spread manure. Drinking became part of the ritual as men smoked, gossiped, told tall tales, and sometimes fought and wrestled.[21]

Taverns for many years were the major social centers for American males. There, hard drinking, heavy smoking, and betting took place. Men shot billiards, threw dice, and played cards. In many cities and rural areas, taverns continue to be a male bastion.

In the 19th and early 20th centuries, Americans were entertained by theatrical productions ranging from opera and serious drama to melodrama, burlesque, vaudeville, and minstrel shows. Affluent people often invited friends to their homes for an evening of music: a string quartet, a chamber ensemble, or a vocal soloist. Traveling shows became popular at this time, especially among rural Americans, whose opportunities to see professional entertainment were few. There was always great excitement when a circus or carnival came to town, an event usually marked by a parade down Main Street. Throughout small-town America, people enjoyed such simple

*Rose Parade in Pasadena, California.*

*The Rose Bowl football game.*

gatherings as ice cream socials, church suppers, and town and county fairs.

By the mid-19th century, more and more Americans were joining the sports craze that today continues to dominate the U.S. leisure scene. Both men and women enjoyed playing tennis, badminton, and croquet, as well as ice skating, cycling, and archery. The less affluent availed themselves of the athletic facilities provided by the Young Men's and Young Women's Christian Associations (YM/YWCA) and the Young Men's and Young Women's Hebrew Associations (YM/YWHA). Americans of many different ethnic backgrounds played games and sports from their native lands and formed social clubs that organized sports competitions (see the Action Guide on p. 33). As Americans' interest in sports and fitness grew, national magazines on these topics began to appear.

A number of sports began to draw audiences. Prizefighting and wrestling gained popularity throughout the 19th century.[22] Football games at colleges and universities drew not only students and alumni but also others who loved the rough and tumble of what rapidly became America's autumn sports ritual. During this time, however, baseball became America's national pastime. In addition, the concept of a city park was born,[22a] followed by a uniquely American concept: national park.[22b]

Over time, the U.S. calendar began to fill up with uniquely American holidays: Washington's and Lincoln's birthdays, Memorial Day (in honor of soldiers who died in World War I), Labor Day, Columbus Day, Veterans Day, Thanksgiving, and Independence Day or the Fourth of July. Each of these special days has become the occasion for a host of celebratory rituals and leisure-time activities. As an ethnic "melting pot," America also boasts a variety of regional and national celebrations with their roots in other cultures: St. Patrick's Day, Valentine's Day, Cinco de Mayo, Oktoberfest, Halloween. In later chapters we will learn more about the contemporary experience in American leisure and recreation.

Despite the increase in both free time and holidays, the pace of the American leisure experience is demanding. One scholar of leisure notes that Americans believe that useful activities are the most valuable and meaningful; thus, they stay busy taking extension courses, running church groups, redecorating their homes, and jogging in the streets and parks of America.[23]

Nevertheless, certain popular forms of leisure, such as watching television, are sedentary activities. According to Nielsen surveys, in the evening hours across the United States, one-third of Americans, or about 90 million people, are watching television.[24] United Nations data show that the United States has the highest ratio in the world of television sets to people, with one set to each 1.68 people, compared with 1 to 98 in Britain and 1 to 375.5 in India.[25]

Volunteering one's free time to help others has been an American tradition since colonial times. Today, new forms of volunteerism are seen in America. According to the U.S. Census Bureau, almost 40 million Americans volunteer at jobs such as assisting in hospitals, cooking for the needy, and building houses for low-income families.[26]

Mobility has always been a characteristic of the American people. Whether for work or pleasure, Americans are always on the move. Travel for pleasure began with the desire to see America's magnificent natural resources and continues with an increase in travel abroad.[27]

In this chapter we have provided an overview of the evolution of leisure experiences in the United States. Details about the contemporary leisure scene are given in Chapters 9, 10, 12, and 13.

**Concept Check**

- Compare the British experience with the French experience.
- What are the German contributions to leisure?
- What is a typical American leisure pursuit?

# ᴀCTION GUIDE

## WHAT'S YOUR GAME?

Whether your ancestors came to America on the *Mayflower*, entered at Ellis Island in the great immigration wave of the late 19th and early 20th centuries, or are relative newcomers to the country, along with their luggage they brought a host of customs and rituals, including the games of their native land. If you don't know yourself, find out from your parents or other older relatives what favorite game they brought to America from their country of origin.

1. What is the game called? What is the origin of the name?

   _____

   _____

2. When and how did the game originate?

   _____

   _____

3. Who played the game (people of all ages and both sexes; males only; females only; children only)?

   _____

   _____

4. How, if at all, did the game change when it was brought to the United States?

   _____

   _____

5. Do you and/or other members of your family play the game today? If so, what changes, if any, have you made in the game?

   _____

   _____

## Summing Up

- Throughout human history, there appears to have been a strong connection between play and ritual.
- In early human societies such as bands, tribes, and chiefdoms, leisure and recreational activities were open to all members of the society.
- Social stratification began to appear in primitive societies, with the result that members of the privileged group began to exclude the less fortunate from certain leisure activities.
- The ancient societies of Mesopotamia, Egypt, Israel, Greece, and Rome created many forms of leisure that are still popular today: the sabbath, or day of rest; public games; dramatic performances; and public gardens. The Greek philosopher Aristotle identified three forms of leisure: amusement, recreation, and contemplation.
- The years between 500 and 1500 C.E. saw the emergence of a middle class from the ranks of serfs and peasants, which created strong demand for access to leisure pursuits previously enjoyed only by royalty and members of the affluent class.
- In the modern era, sports, dramatic performances, and other leisure-time opportunities gradually became available to a wider spectrum of society.
- The American experience of leisure is unique, in part because of the impact of the harsh existence of the early settlers and in part because of the many ethnic and cultural influences that have contributed to recreation and leisure in America.

## Using What You've Learned

1. Select a sport or game that was played in a New World society and do research to find out when and how the activity originated; how it was played; and, if applicable, in what form the activity exists today.
2. Select a contemporary sport and prepare a one-page report on the origin of the sport and its evolution to the present day.
3. Interview a fellow student from another country or culture. Ask him/her to describe that country's or culture's favorite traditional pastime and to explain its origin and evolution. Prepare a report for the class.
4. Determine what is the most important holiday in your ethnic or cultural background. Find out what the holiday commemorates, how it was celebrated, and how it has changed over the years.

## YOUR  Turn

1 What factors might help explain why Moy and Jimmy have such radically different views of dancing as a form of recreation?
2 What factors might have contributed to people's enjoyment of hunting as a sport instead of a necessity for survival?

3 Is there any recreational activity you enjoy that someone you know finds strange or offensive? Conversely, is there anything a friend or acquaintance does for recreation that you either don't understand or object to? In each case, why?

# REFERENCES

1. Shivers, J. (1979). The Origin of Man, Leisure and Culture. In H. Ibrahim & J. Shivers (Eds.), *Leisure: Emergency and Expansion.* Los Alamitos, CA: Hwong Publishing.

2. Marano, H.E. (1999). The Power of Play. *Psychology Today* 32:36.

2a. Wood, J. (1872). *The Uncivilized Races of Men.* Hartford, CT: J. B. Burr, p. 751.

3. Reagan, A. (1932). Navajo Sports. *Primitive Man,* 5:68–71.

4. Cushman, H. B. (1899). *History of the Choctaw, Chickasaw and the Natchez Indians.* Stillwater, OK: The Redlands Press (1962 Edition).

5. Blanchard, K., & Cheska, A. (1985). *The Anthropology of Sports: An Introduction.* South Hadley, MA: Bergin & Garvey, p. 7.

6. Royce, A. P. (1977). *The Anthropology of Dance.* Bloomington, IN: Indiana University Press.

7. Whitrow, G. J. (1989). *Time in History: Views of Time from Prehistory to the Present Day.* New York: Oxford University Press, pp. 92–96.

8. Routney, A. D., & Wening, S. (1969). *Sport in Ancient Egypt.* Leipzig.

9. Butler, J. (1972). *The Theatre and Drama of Greece and Rome.* San Francisco: Chandler, p. 143.

10. Roberts, V. M. (1962). *On Stage: A History of Theatre.* New York: Harper & Row, p. 57.

11. Farb, P. (1968). *Man's Rise to Civilization.* New York: Avon Books, p. 221.

12. Gernet, J. (1962). *Daily Life in China.* Stanford: Stanford University Press, pp. 118, 256.

13. Fitzgerald, C. P. (1933). *China: A Short Cultural History.* New York: Praeger.

14. Sansom, G. B. (1936). *Japan: A Short Cultural History.* New York: Appleton-Century-Crofts, p. 41.

15. Basham, A. (1963). *The Wonder That Was India.* New York: Hathorn.

16. Lane, E. W. (1973). *An Account of the Manners and Customs of the Modern Egyptians.* New York: Dover.

17. Lawerson, J., & Myerscough, J. C. (1977). *Time to Spare in Victorian England.* Hassocks, Sussex: Harvester Press, p. 32.

18. de Grazia, S. (1962). *Of Time, Work and Leisure.* New York: Anchor Books.

19. Mechinkoff, Robert, & Estes, Steven (1993). *A History and Philosophy of Sport and Physical Education.* Madison, WI: Brown & Benchmark, p. 145.

20. Hawke, D. F. (1988). *Everyday Life in Early America.* New York: Harper & Row, pp. 96, 99.

21. Larkin, J. (1988). *The Reshaping of Everyday Life.* New York: Harper & Row, p. 266.

22. Sutherland, E. D. (1989). *The Expansion of Everyday Life.* New York: Harper & Row, p. 244

22a. Taylor, D.E.(1999). Central Park as a Model for Social Control. *Journal of Leisure Research* 31(4): 320.

22b. Knudson, D. (1984). *Outdoor Recreation.* New York: MacMillan.

23. Russell, R. (1996). *Pastimes: The Context of Contemporary Leisure.* Madison, WI: Brown & Benchmark.

24. Nielsen, A.C. *Nielsen Estimates: National Audience Demographic Reports.* Northbrook, IL: Nielsen.

25. Ibrahim, H. (1991). *Leisure and Society: A Comparative Approach.* Dubuque, IA: Wm. C. Brown.

26. United States Bureau of Labor Statistics (1996). *News.*

27. United States Bureau of Labor Statistics (1996). *Statistical Abstracts of the United States, 1993.* Washington, DC: U.S. Government Printing Office.

There is only one success—to be able to spend your life in your own way.

CHRISTOPHER MORLEY
*Where the Blue Begins, 1922*

# Leisure, Recreation, and the Individual

CHAPTER 3

THE CHAPTER AT A GLANCE

In this chapter we explore the relationship between participation in leisure pursuits and the impact of such participation on the individual physically, emotionally, psychologically, and socially. We examine the ways in which demographic factors affect people's choice of leisure pursuits, and we learn about the benefits of participating in outdoor leisure activities. Finally, we discuss the importance of providing recreational services to members of special populations.

## Chapter Objectives

After studying this chapter, you should be able to

- Discuss four aspects of leisure: physical, emotional, psychological, and social.
- Name the skill-related and health-related components of physical fitness.
- Identify general and activity-specific psychological benefits of leisure.
- Explain Csikszentmihalyi's concept of flow experience.
- Explain how an individual's choice of leisure pursuits is affected by these demographic factors: age, gender, occupation, residence, and lifestyle.
- Describe some of the social benefits of leisure.
- Identify four special populations who need leisure and recreation programs designed for their specific situations.

## A World  of Difference

### ALL IN THE FAMILY: MEETING VARIED NEEDS FOR RECREATION

Meet the Timmons family: Bob, 36, Kathy, 35, and their three kids—Dan, 13, Kelly, 10, and Jake, 8. Like the majority of American parents today, Bob and Kathy both work outside the home. Bob, an accountant in the municipal water department, also runs his own small financial services business to earn money for the kids' college educations. Kathy is a high school history teacher who also does alterations and dressmaking for a small clientele. Their long hours of work leave little time for recreation. Bob's preferred mode of relaxation is sleeping late on Sundays and napping in front of the TV later in the day. Kathy loves gardening and bird-watching, but this year she's been too busy to plant flowerbeds, let alone join her birding club on its weekly walks.

Dan is the family bookworm; a straight-*A* student, he's the star of his school's chess team and already has won a regional science project competition. Big for his age, he dislikes physical exercise and relaxes by reading books on astronomy and botany while eating snack foods. Kelly, in contrast, is a human dynamo whose only mode is full speed ahead. Bubbly and outgoing, she's a dedicated athlete who powers her school's girls' softball team and keeps opponents scoreless as an ace soccer goalie. She loves the outdoors, and her idea of heaven is a long bike ride on a wooded trail with plenty of hills. Little brother Jake is a friendly, sweet-tempered child who attends special school because he has Down syndrome. Because of the physical problems inherent in his condition, he can't engage in many activities enjoyed by other 8-year-olds, and he sometimes becomes frustrated when he has difficulty keeping up with them.

As you study this chapter, think about the individual situation and preferences of each member of the Timmons family and prepare to answer the questions in Your Turn at the end of the chapter.

## PHYSICAL ASPECTS OF LEISURE

Leisure activities cover a wide spectrum, from intensely physical to sedentary. In this section we will focus on the beneficial aspects of physical exercise as a leisure pursuit.

Described as the "incredible machine," the human body performs so efficiently that few if any man-made machines can rival it. Interestingly, this highly complex and elegant machine has a very simple beginning.

After a gestation period of approximately 280 days, a very dependent human being is born. The growth and development of a human occur over 16 to 18 years. *Growth* refers to changes in the structure and shape of body organs and systems; *development* refers to

increases in their complexity. Growth in height and weight proceeds rapidly during infancy and early childhood, slows down briefly during middle childhood, and accelerates again during early adolescence. Of course, there are wide variations among individuals in rates of growth and development.

Growth and development are influenced by two main factors: genetics and environment. Heredity determines skeletal structure and body shape. Muscles increase in size and strength from birth to young adulthood as the result not only of hormonal secretions but also of environmental factors, such as diet and exercise.

Appropriate physical activity is essential to a healthy course of growth and development, not only of bones and muscles but also of the heart and lungs. An active lifestyle also improves a growing child's locomotor development, which requires coordination between the muscular and nervous systems. The growing child experiences the benefits of exercise and establishes habits that can form the blueprint for a lifetime of healthful activity. Physiologic changes will occur over the years, nonetheless regular physical activity can reduce the risk of obesity, diabetes, high blood pressure, heart disease, and stroke in later life.

In the section that follows, we will learn the components of physical fitness and will examine some trends in the American sports and fitness scene.

## Physical Fitness

There is no single, universal standard of physical fitness. Optimum levels of fitness vary, depending on age, sex, physical ability, and overall health. Despite these variations, there is general agreement among experts that the components of physical fitness should be grouped into two broad categories that correspond to two levels of performance: athletes and nonathletes.[1]

### Skill-related components

The following six components of physical fitness should be pursued by an athlete:
1. *Agility*: The ability to change body position quickly
2. *Balance*: The ability to regain upright posture, or equilibrium, while moving or standing still
3. *Coordination*: The ability to use vision, touch, and muscle sense (the degree of responsiveness to stimuli) to achieve precise body movements
4. *Power*: Strength
5. *Reaction time*: The amount of time it takes to start moving after a decision to move is made
6. *Speed*: The rate at which one covers a distance or completes a movement or sequence of movements

### Health-related components

The five components of physical fitness outlined below are recommended for the development and maintenance of a healthy body, but at a lower level of fitness than is required for athletes:
1. *Cardiovascular fitness*: The ability to exercise at an elevated heart rate for a designated time while supplying adequate oxygen to the body
2. *Flexibility*: The ability to move joints and muscles to their fullest extent
3. *Endurance*: The ability to exercise without tiring for a designated time
4. *Strength*: The ability to exert force against resistance
5. *Body composition*: Ideally, a state in which body fat does not exceed 20% to 25% of total body composition

### General principles of exercise

Both athletes and nonathletes should follow three general principles of exercise:
1. *The overload principle*: To achieve benefit from exercise, the body must work above and beyond its normal activity level.

*Water aerobics enhance all of the components of fitness.*

2. *The progression principle*: As physical abilities improve, the exercise regimen should increase in intensity and duration. One should start slowly and apply overload gradually.

3. *The specificity principle*: Specific exercises should be used to achieve specific results.

## The American Fitness Scene

Since the early 1970s, there has been a strong and growing interest in physical fitness among North Americans. Research shows that in 1990, 40% of Americans engaged in some form of physical activity every day and that, 70% did so once a week. The same participation levels were reported for Canadians. In 1992 joggers in America participated in more than 15,000 marathons. In the same year, more than 3 million Americans belonged to fitness clubs.[2]

In 1993, 217 million Americans reported their participation in these physical/recreational activities:[3]

- ◆ Swimming      32.8 million
- ◆ Fishing      24.3 million
- ◆ Basketball      10.7 million
- ◆ Running/jogging    10.6 million
- ◆ Baseball/softball    6.2 million

Fig. 3.1 shows the 10 most popular physical pursuits identified by the U.S. Bureau of the Census for 2000.

**FIGURE 3.1**   The 10 most popular physical/recreational pursuits.

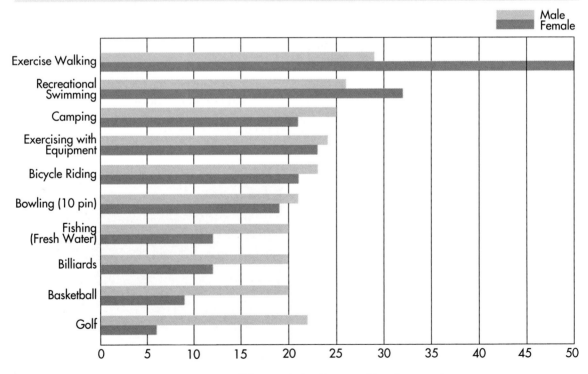

Percent of the population 7 years old and over

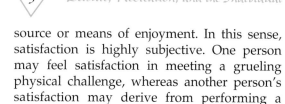

## EMOTIONAL ASPECTS OF LEISURE

As we have seen, the benefits of physically active forms of leisure are fairly easy to identify and quantify. Equally important are the emotional aspects and benefits of all forms of leisure, including sports and exercise. In this section we will explore the emotional aspects of leisure.

In Chapter 1 we learned several theories about the factors that motivate humans to engage in play, leisure, and recreation. As we discovered, humans most likely are motivated to engage in these pursuits by a combination of biological, psychological, sociological, and cultural factors. In the discussion that follows, we will focus on three emotional aspects of participating in leisure activities: satisfaction, attitude, and values.

### Satisfaction with Leisure Experiences

**Satisfaction** can be defined as the fulfillment of a need or want, as contentment, or as a

*Recreation in nature may influence attitudes toward the environment.*

source or means of enjoyment. In this sense, satisfaction is highly subjective. One person may feel satisfaction in meeting a grueling physical challenge, whereas another person's satisfaction may derive from performing a complex technical task. Still others may experience satisfaction while gardening, washing a car, or basking on a sunny beach.

Some authors advocate that participation in leisure pursuits provide a sense of worth and allows for sharing which in turn leads to satisfaction in life.[4]

### Attitudes Toward Leisure

An **attitude** is reflected in the tendency to feel toward or react to a given object or subject in a certain way. In terms of leisure, this means each of us can develop a certain attitude toward leisure in general or toward a specific leisure activity. You may love to travel but shy away from sports; your classmate may be a champion swimmer but be uninterested in nature hikes. Attitudes also may develop as the result of engaging in certain activities. For example, does participating in "appreciative" activities such as cross-country skiing and hiking foster a more pro-environment attitude than participating in "consumptive" activities such as snowmobiling and dirt biking? Conversely, one may choose hiking over snowmobiling precisely because one already has a pro-environment attitude.

### Leisure and Values

When something holds **value** for us, we find it important, worthwhile, and desirable. Some values are individual; in many cases values are held in common by a group such as a family, a

---

**satisfaction** the fulfillment of a want or need; contentment; a source or means of enjoyment

**attitude** the tendency to feel toward or react to a given object or subject in a certain way

**value** the quality of being worthwhile, important, and desirable

community, a religious sect, or a political party. In the example above, people whose attitude is pro-environment will agree that there is value in protecting the environment from the damage caused by snowmobiling and dirt biking.

There are two types of values that affect our view of leisure: instrumental values and terminal values.[5] **Instrumental values** are both observable and testable. Examples of instrumental values are responsibility, courage, and good health. These values may affect one's choice of leisure activities; for example, a person who values good health may participate in aerobic exercise or yoga, and a person for whom courage is a value may engage in a challenging activity such as rock climbing or hang gliding.

**Terminal values** are conceptual and have meaning within themselves. Examples of terminal values are concepts such as peace, freedom, and harmony. Like instrumental values, terminal values may affect one's choice of leisure pursuits. A solitary wilderness hike, involvement in a group committed to world peace, or a quiet gathering for the purpose of meditating are some activities that might be appealing to one who values peace, freedom, and harmony.

**Concept Check**

- What are three emotional aspects of participation in leisure activities?
- Give your own examples of an instrumental value and a terminal value.

## PSYCHOLOGICAL BENEFITS OF LEISURE AND RECREATION

Quantifying the psychological benefits of leisure experiences is a challenging task. However, one scale, the Recreation Experience Preference (REP) scale, has been developed to measure the psychological benefits derived from participating in outdoor recreation experiences.[6] (The REP scale was later used in a wider study of leisure experiences overall.) In outdoor recreation, according to the scale, one may enjoy psychological benefits from any or all of the elements listed in Fig. 3.2. In A Closer Look on p. 43 you can learn more about the benefits and effects of engaging in outdoor leisure pursuits.

In another study, responses from more than 4,000 participants led researchers to identify two kinds of psychological benefits that can be derived from engaging in leisure activities of all sorts: general benefits and activity-specific benefits.[7] General benefits are gained to approximately the same degree from any leisure activity, whereas activity-specific benefits are gained in greater or lesser degree, depending on the specific leisure activity undertaken. Fig. 3.3 lists the general and activ-

**FIGURE 3.2** Psychological benefits of outdoor recreation.

- Challenge/achievement
- Reflection on personal values
- Leadership
- Creativity
- Autonomy/independence/freedom
- Nostalgia
- Risk taking/action/excitement
- Exercise/physical fitness
- Use and care of equipment
- Physical rest
- Family togetherness
- Escape from personal pressure
- Social contact
- Escape from physical pressure
- Meeting/observing new people
- Escape from family
- Learning/discovery
- Security
- Relationship with nature
- Enjoyment of climate

# A CLOSER LOOK

## THE OUTDOOR EXPERIENCE

Earlier we learned about some of the psychological benefits that have been associated with participation in outdoor leisure activities. Now we will explore additional aspects of leisure in this special setting that some scientists believe to be psychologically beneficial. For instance, one study showed that an outdoor setting has what humans find to be an appropriate density. Density can be understood by comparing two paintings, one of which has two colors and the other four colors. The second picture has greater density than the first. In addition, a slower change of pace is found in an outdoor setting.[8] This means that in an outdoor setting our brain operates at a low **information rate** (the rate at which the brain processes information during a given time). Too much visual information can lead to confusion; too little visual input can also cause psychological discomfort. Many experts believe an outdoor setting provides the most comfortable information rate in comparison with other settings and that this helps us perceive ourselves as functioning competently.[8]

Interacting with nature may have profound effects on some people, although not everyone is comfortable or happy in an outdoor environment. Some experts have suggested that we are sensitive to the spatial characteristics of outdoor environments and that we tend to categorize these characteristics based on individual preferences. One study identifies three such categories: (1) dense woods and wide-open vistas, (2) manicured settings such as lawns, and (3) transparent woods in which the sun filters through the trees. The authors of this study found that humans tend to prefer the second and third categories to the first.[9]

As we learned in Chapter 1, American psychologist Abraham Maslow developed the hierarchy of needs (Fig. 3.4) to show the order in which humans seek to meet their needs. Maslow believed that, after fulfilling their basic physiological needs, humans will move upward on the hierarchy and ultimately seek the "full use and exploration of talents, capacities, and potentialities,"[10] that is, self-actualization. Clearly, leisure can be a means by which one achieves self-actualization. (See the Action Guide on p. 46)

## Leisure and Flow Experience

Another concept that has some bearing on leisure is Mihalyi Csikszentmihalyi's idea of "flow experience."[11] Central to this concept is the idea that our perception of the experience we are undergoing is of utmost importance. If we perceive an experience as too difficult to handle, we will feel anxiety. If, in contrast, the experience is perceived as too easy, we will feel boredom. Between anxiety and boredom, Csikszentmihalyi believes, lies an optimum condition in which one may experience "flow."

What is flow? Csikszentmihalyi interviewed hundreds of people who engaged in various forms of leisure activities to discover what features of those activities the subjects found rewarding and how they felt while engaging in the activities. Whether rock climbing, dancing, playing basketball, composing music, reading, or writing a poem, the participants who became intensely involved in an activity said they felt as if they were being carried along on a current—like being in a flow. The dimensions of these experiences are the same regardless of

ity-specific psychological benefits identified by the researchers.

## Leisure and Self-Actualization

One school of thought in the field of psychology suggests that human behavior is motivated by the attempt to satisfy certain needs.

***instrumental value*** a value that is both observable and testable

***terminal value*** a value that is conceptual and has meaning within itself

***information rate*** the rate at which the brain processes information during a given time

**FIGURE 3.3**   General and activity-specific psychological benefits of leisure.

| GENERAL BENEFITS | | |
| --- | --- | --- |
| Abasement | Justice | Relaxation |
| Autonomy | Moral values | Self-control |
| Counteraction | Order | Succorance |
| Deference | Recognition | Task generalization |
| Harm avoidance | Rejection | Tolerance |

| ACTIVITY-SPECIFIC BENEFITS | | |
| --- | --- | --- |
| Ability utilization | Cooperation | Reward |
| Achievement | Creativity | Security |
| Activity | Dominance | Self-esteem |
| Advancement | Exhibition | Sentience |
| Affiliation | Independence | Sex |
| Aggression | Nurturance | Social service |
| Authority | Play | Social status |
| Catharsis | Responsibility | Supervision |
| Compensation | | Understanding variety |

age, gender, or nationality.[12] It is in this state of consciousness that what Csikszentmihalyi describes as a *flow experience* occurs. A flow experience, he says, requires intense involvement that is possible only when one believes the opportunities for action in the given situation "are more or less in balance with his or her ability to respond to the opportunities that match his or her skills." A **skill** is the learned ability to perform a task competently. We will now explore the dimensions of the relationship between leisure and learning.

## Leisure and Learning

In Chapter 1 we defined a leisure pastime in part as being autotelic, or having meaning in itself, as opposed to being undertaken for financial gain or some other purpose external to the participant. It is possible, however, to enjoy an activity for its own sake and at the same time gain some knowledge from the pursuit. Although there is no general agreement on

the relationship between leisure and learning, experts suggest several kinds of knowledge one might acquire while engaging in leisure activities:[13]

1. *New behavior and skill learning*: Outdoor experiences provide opportunities to learn new skills such as building shelters and preparing food.
2. *Memory learning*: Participation in some leisure activities has been shown to improve recall and recognition memory. Memory learning of directions, rules, techniques, and strategies is important for later participation in and enjoyment of many activities.
3. *Factual learning*: One can gain useful knowledge while engaging in leisure pursuits such as traveling, visiting art galleries and museums, exploring the wilderness, gardening, tinkering with machinery, and a host of other activities.

**FIGURE 3.4** A schematic representation of Maslow's hierarchy of human needs.

| ORDER LEVEL | | NEED | BEHAVIOR SET |
|---|---|---|---|
| HIGHEST | GROWTH-MOTIVATED | SELF-ACTU-ALIZATION | Self-fulfillment through sports, music, art, religion, philosophy, etc. To become everything one is capable of becoming. Harmony between self, others, and environment. |
| | | SELF-ESTEEM | Very dominant need in the "Achievement" and "Performance" oriented society—need for strength, achievement, mastery, competence, independence, etc. Includes deference and esteem from others—need for prestige, reputation, power, status, recognition, appreciation, etc. |
| CONFLICT AND ANXIETY | DEFICIENCY-MOTIVATED | LOVE and BELONGINGNESS | Need to love, be loved, and be included—need to associate, interact, mingle, communicate, belong, join, etc. |
| | | SAFETY | Orderliness, justice, consistency, routine, predictability, control, safety—parental security, police, army, referees, rules, boundaries, maps, insurance policies, savings account, unions, job security, etc. |
| LOWEST | | PHYSIOLOGICAL NEEDS | Hunger, thirst, sex, bodily secretions, rest, activity, etc. |

4. *Attitude and value learning*: Often the acquisition of new knowledge leads to the development of new, positive attitudes and values. For example, after visiting a sanctuary for an endangered animal species, one might gain a new appreciation for the value of the species and participate in efforts to protect it.

## Spiritual Benefits of Leisure

There are many different ways to define and describe a "spiritual experience." In general, it is an experience in which one gains greater insight into his or her place in the universe.

*skill* the learned ability to perform a task competently

## ACTION GUIDE

### WHAT DO YOU WANT FROM YOUR LEISURE?

Although we usually just assume we want to use leisure time to relax, there are, in fact, a variety of motivations that influence how we spend our free time. The same activity might even be chosen for different reasons. One woman may garden to express her creativity, another to unwind from work, and still another for the feeling of accomplishment. A 1992 Leisure Trends/Gallup poll identified a variety of motivations for choosing leisure activities, from "recuperative" to "intellectual" to "competitive." Our leisure motivations change dramatically with age, as recuperating from work takes on more importance. The data below rate how important each motivation is to different age groups as compared with the average for the total population.

For 16- to 24-year-olds, socializing is the biggest motivator, followed by competition, such as sports, and escape. This is reflected in the most popular activities among this age group: spending time with friends and watching TV. But, after 24 years of age, we reserve much of our free time for recuperation and the desire to escape. Reading, the top leisure choice for 25- to 34-year-olds, satisfies both these needs.

The average amount of leisure time is 38 hours per week; surprisingly, 24- to 35-year-olds have slightly more free time than 16- to 24-year-olds. But "no one feels like he or she has enough leisure time to do all the things they want to do," observed Bill Danner of Leisure Trends, so it becomes essential to evaluate which activities best meet your leisure "goals."

*Fishing is serene on Lake Powell.*

1. Enhanced personal development—for example, building self-confidence by mastering the skills needed for rock climbing
2. Greater appreciation for the wonders of nature, such as one might gain while observing the intricacies of a tidepool
3. An expanded social consciousness, perhaps as a result of participating in a project to help clean up the environment
4. A sense of well-being one may feel because of being part of the great web of life
5. The pleasure of creativity one may enjoy while writing a poem, designing an item of clothing, planting a new garden bed, or painting a watercolor

Some experts have suggested ways in which it is possible to have a spiritual experience while engaging in certain forms of leisure.[14]

## Concept Check

- What is the concept of "flow experience"?
- Identify four kinds of learning one can acquire by engaging in leisure pursuits.

## SOCIAL ASPECTS OF LEISURE

By nature and necessity, humans are social beings. By interacting and cooperating with others, we are able to meet not only our basic physiological needs (food, shelter, rest) but also our needs for affiliation, participation, and acceptance. New members first must learn what is expected of them in the society. The process through which a novice gains understanding of the society's customs, values, and expectations is called **socialization**. Socialization is also the means by which new members, whether they were born into the society or moved into it, learn its attitudes toward and practices of leisure behavior.

### Socialization into Leisure

Socialization is a lifelong process, and the same is true of socialization into leisure. It is during childhood and early adolescence, however, that participation in particular leisure activities seems to take a "permanent" shape and become established as lifelong preferences.[15–18]

Among the agents for socialization into leisure, by far the most influential is the family. Schools socialize children into certain leisure pursuits on the playground and in the gymnasium, and children also are socialized into both indoor and outdoor recreational activities by a host of agencies that serve youth: the YM/YWCA, YM/YWHA, Boy Scouts and Girl Scouts, Little League, and American Youth Hostel, to name a few.

Leisure itself may serve as an agent for socialization, especially in later life after a person retires. Senior citizens who have ample leisure time often learn new skills and develop new interests as part of a group, and many

*World Explorer Cruises—with its motto "Mind, body, and soul"—offer excitement ranging from rafting in an eagle sanctuary in Haines, Alaska, to onboard lectures about geology, history, anthropology, and art.*

seniors volunteer time to serve their community or religious organization.

### Demographic Correlates of Leisure Behavior

To a great extent, our choice of leisure pursuits depends on the demographic variables of age, gender, occupation, residence, and lifestyle. In the sections that follow, we will explore these variables and how they affect our use of leisure time.

#### Age

Over the course of a lifetime, people may lose interest in some leisure activities and become more interested in others. For example, children abandon simple pastimes such as playing tag and fingerpainting when they become old enough to master more complex activities such as baseball and computer games. When people marry and become parents, they tend to move away from spending leisure hours with friends and devote more free

> ***socialization*** the process through which a novice gains understanding of the society's customs, values, and expectations

time to family outings. As people age, they may reduce their proportion of vigorous activity and increase the amount of time they spend on less strenuous pastimes. An older person also may forgo active leisure pursuits in favor of increased attendance at spectator sports.

### Gender

Not only do the play patterns of boys differ from those of girls, but men's leisure pursuits tend to be different from women's.[19,20] Furthermore, there is a significant disparity between men and women in the amount of time allotted for leisure. Despite the many improvements in women's status over the past generation, women overall devote less time to recreation than men do. This is primarily because, even when they work outside the home, women still assume more domestic responsibilities than men do and, thus, have significantly less time to spend on leisure pursuits. This has been found to be true not only in the United States but also in other countries.[21–26]

### Occupation

A clear correlation has been identified between one's occupation and both the amount of time one devotes to leisure and the kinds of leisure pursuits one undertakes. A study reported in 1969 showed that members of the higher professional occupations engage in a greater variety of leisure pursuits than do people with less prestigious occupations.[27] A later study supported this conclusion.[28] Professionals have more money to spend on leisure, and in the course of their education they develop more interests that lead them to hobbies and avocations. Furthermore, people who do manual labor tend to participate in fewer leisure activities because of lower income, longer working hours, and physical exhaustion.

### Residence

To a considerable extent, people's opportunities for and choices of leisure pursuits depend on their geographic location (north-east, southwest, seacoast, inland, desert, woods); whether they live in a large city, a suburb, or a small rural town; and their proximity to parks, playgrounds, active and spectator sports, cultural centers, movie theatres, shopping malls, and natural attractions. One study found that people who live in urban areas participate more in recreational activities than rural residents do.[29]

### Lifestyle

The term **lifestyle** is used to describe the way people live based on the demographic factors outlined above: age, gender, occupation, and residence. In the United States, *lifestyle* is now commonly used in place of the more traditional term *social class*. One author has identified nine lifestyles in contemporary America:[30]

1. *Survivors*: Very poor people who may lack the energy to play sports and who spend their leisure time watching television
2. *Sustainers*: People who work in manual and service occupations and who may like to go fishing and watch X-rated movies; these people may tend to be angry and combative
3. *Belongers*: Middle-class Americans who tend to like soap operas and romance novels and to prefer home and family activities
4. *Emulators*: People under 30 years of age who are improving their financial position and who may enjoy bowling and night clubs
5. *Achievers*: Professionals such as teachers, lawyers, physicians, and engineers who are likely to attend cocktail parties and enjoy traveling
6. *I am me*: People who tend to own exercise equipment, bicycles, and other recreational gear and to enjoy vigorous activity; those who seem to have an inner direction that causes them to develop new interests
7. *Experiential*: People who practice yoga, eat health food, and attend foreign films

8. *Socially conscious*: People who have little need for self-display and who are likely to engage in healthful outdoor pursuits

9. *Integrated*: People who experience both inner and outer direction as being equally beneficial and powerful; socially mature people who tend to have a sense of what is appropriate in a given situation, who tend to blend work and play, and who develop close relationships with others

## Social Benefits of Leisure

Although many people prefer to engage in solitary leisure activities or choose pursuits such as watching television that tend not to involve dialogue with others, it is through group activities that we learn to interact productively with others and to gain the benefits of socialization. Families and groups of friends are important vehicles in this process. In addition to offering social benefits, group activities also help participants satisfy their need to belong.

Recreation and leisure services and opportunities have been found to contribute to people's satisfaction with community life.[31] Likewise, experts in family bonding say that leisure activities are associated with positive outcomes on a relatively consistent basis.[32]

Another significant social benefit that may accrue from participating in group leisure activities is the opportunity to build one's sense of self-identity. In this connection, a question to consider is, do we seek leisure situations that serve to validate our preconceived notions of who we are, or do we seek situations that move us toward our desired view of ourselves?[33] Although research provides no answers to this question, it is reasonable to believe that group leisure activities offer us the opportunity to validate our desired self-identity.

The relationship between identity and leisure has not been clearly established; nonetheless, it appears that engagement in leisure pursuits may provide at least a secondary identity for many of us.

> Thousands wear insignia of their football teams . . . and bowling team league shirts . . . [and] caps identify those who own a particular brand of motorized leisure vehicle.[34]

Another important social benefit that can result from participating in group leisure activities is bonding among members of the group. For instance, a group that engages in a challenging activity such as whitewater rafting, mountain climbing, or rappelling may forge a strong bond because each member of the group is both dependent on and responsible for the others. Participating in group leisure activities also provides opportunities to develop long-lasting friendships and love relationships.

To many people, participating in some form of group leisure activities has the benefit of enhancing their status. For example, some people play golf, tennis, or polo or join country clubs in the belief that doing so will enhance their social status or help them make important business connections.

One's lifestyle is dramatically enhanced when it includes many pleasurable leisure experiences. Despite individual differences that result from these variables, a lifestyle that includes leisure experiences is possible for everyone when the following variables are considered.

The person, regardless of individual circumstances, must try to engage in autotelic activities (those that are meaningful in themselves). The repertoire of activities should include active and passive activites, solitary

> **lifestyle** the way one lives based on one's age, gender, occupation, and residence

and social ones, and those that take place both at home and away from home. The most important guiding principle is the wise selection of activities that improve one's physical conditioning and reduce emotional stress.[35]

**Concept Check**

- What is the relationship between leisure and socialization?
- Briefly explain the relevance of demographic factors to leisure experience.

## LEISURE AND SPECIAL POPULATIONS

The term **special population** describes a group of people who have particular needs that require special attention. Examples of such groups are physically and mentally challenged persons, socially deviant persons, and elderly persons. In contemporary society, considerable effort is devoted to meeting the needs of these special populations, including structuring appropriate programs of leisure and recreational pursuits. The following sections discuss the characteristics and needs of these special populations.

### Physically Challenged Persons

This group includes people who have orthopedic impairments, cerebral palsy, muscular dystrophy, multiple sclerosis, and cardiac malfunction, as well as persons whose sight and/or hearing are impaired. Appropriately designed programs of recreation and leisure not only can help many people with physical challenges improve their motor skills and coordination but also can offer opportunities for social interaction and emotional satisfaction.

### Mentally Challenged Persons

People with mental retardation often are affected by multiple impairments, not only in intellectual development and in motor and speech skills but also in the ability to conform socially and culturally, to form meaningful personal relationships, and to deal with the problems of attention deficit disorder. Members of this special population can benefit significantly from leisure and recreation programs that consider their challenges and help them build skills and self-confidence.

### Socially Deviant Persons

This special population includes juvenile offenders and prison inmates. In many cases these people have responded favorably to programs that allow them to experience self-discovery and enhance their self-concept. Of particular benefit are programs such as Outward Bound, which is based on participation in challenging outdoor activities. This program also offers opportunities to build self-reliance by solving problems related to outdoor survival. Although there is no empirical evidence, these programs can play a significant role in rehabilitating members of this special population and in helping them adjust to the demands of life outside the penal institution.

### Elderly Persons

The "the graying of America" describes the continuing increase in the number of Americans over 65 years of age. As the post–World War II baby boom generation moves toward retirement, the population of elderly persons will swell to even greater proportions. Thanks to advances in medical science and to increased interest in physical fitness and good nutrition, senior citizens are enjoying a notable increase in life expectancy over previous generations. Today's seniors are far more likely than their predecessors to remain physically active in later life. Leisure and recreation programs are designed to meet the needs of this rapidly expanding special population, focusing on moderate physical exercise and providing varied opportunities for social interaction.

With Chapters 1, 2, and 3 providing the background and framework for our exploration of recreation and leisure, in Chapter 4 we examine the roles of play and recreation in the lives of children.

**Concept Check**

- What is meant by *special populations*?
- Identify four types of special populations.

> ***special population*** a group of people who share characteristics and needs that distinguish them from the general population

---

## Summing Up

- Physical fitness is essential to healthy growth and development. The components of physical fitness can be grouped into two broad categories: skill-related and health-related.
- The three general principles of exercise are the overload principle, the progression principle, and the specificity principle.
- The three emotional aspects of participating in leisure activities are satisfaction, attitude, and values.
- Two kinds of psychological benefits can be derived from participating in leisure activities: general benefits and activity-specific benefits.
- As described by Csikszentmihalyi, a flow experience is one in which we become so intensely involved in an activity that we feel as if we are being carried away on a current—as if we are in a flow.
- Leisure activities offer opportunities for four kinds of learning: behavior change and skill learning, memory learning, factual learning, and attitude and value learning.
- Our choice of leisure pursuits is strongly influenced by the demographic variables of age, gender, occupation, residence, and lifestyle.
- Leisure and recreation programs are designed for the specific needs of special populations: physically and mentally challenged persons, socially deviant persons, and elderly persons.

---

## Using What You've Learned

1. Ask six people of both sexes and different ages whether they participate in regular physical exercise. Ask them why they exercise or why they do not. Find out what is an important participatory leisure experience for each person.
2. Write a two-page essay on how you benefitted from participating in a particular leisure or recreational experience in the past few weeks. Compare your experience with what you have learned in this chapter.
3. Visit your local community recreation center and find out what kinds of activities the center offers. From your city hall, obtain demographic information about your community. Do the activities offered by the recreation center appear to meet the needs of the local population as indicated by the demographic data?
4. In researching the demographics of your community, obtain data on the special populations in your area. Find out what kinds of services, including recreational programs, the local government offers each of these special populations.
5. Climb to the top of a hill, hike through the woods, or sit by a body of water. Take note of your feelings. Record them later and share them with your classmates.

## YOUR  Turn

1   Given the differences in their preferences and needs, what are some leisure activities the Timmons family might enjoy participating in together? How would the activities you suggest be beneficial to family members physically, emotionally, psychologically, and socially?

2   How could 13-year-old Dan combine his love of astronomy and botany with some leisure-time activities that would involve physical exercise?

3   What would be some advantages to 8-year-old Jake of participating in a leisure and recreation program especially designed for children with Down syndrome?

## REFERENCES

1. Corbin, C., & Lindsey, R. (1984). *The Ultimate Fitness Book*. New York: Leisure Press, p. 10.
2. Eitzen, D. S., & Sage G. (1991). *Sociology of North American Sport*. Dubuque, IA: Wm. C. Brown, p. 390.
3. Phillips, J. (1993). *Sociology of Sport*. Boston: Allyn & Bacon, p. 5.
4. Edington, C.R., et al. (1998). *Leisure and Life Satisfaction*. St. Louis: McGraw-Hill, p.11.
5. Feather, N. (1975). *Values in Education and Society*. New York: Free Press.
6. Driver, B. L., Tinsley, H., et al. (1976). Quantification of Outdoor Recreationists' Preferences. In B. Vander Smissen (Ed.), *Research, Camping and Environment Education*. University Park, PA: Pennsylvania State University, HPER Series No. 11.
7. Tinsley, H., Barrett, T. C., & Kass, R. A. (1977). Leisure Activities and Need Satisfaction. *Journal of Leisure Research* 9:110–120.
8. Mehrebian, J., & Russell, J. (1974). *An Approach to Environmental Psychology*. Cambridge, MA: MIT Press, p. 84.
9. Kaplan, R., & Kaplan, S. (1989). *The Experience of Nature: A Psychological Perspective*. Cambridge: Cambridge University Press.
10. Maslow, A. (1970). *Motivation and Personality*. New York: Harper & Row.
11. Csikszentmihalyi, M. (1975). *Beyond Boredom and Anxiety: The Experience of Play in Work and Games*. San Francisco: Jossey-Bass.
12. Mannell, R.C., & Kleiber, D.A. (1997). *A Social Psychology of Leisure*. State College, PA: Venture Publishing, p. 290.
13. Roggenbuck, J., Loomis, R., & Dasgostino, J. (1991). The Learning Benefits of Leisure. In B. L. Driver, et al. (Eds.), *Benefits of Leisure*. State College, PA: Venture Publishing, p. 195.
14. McDonald, B. & Schreyer, R. (1991). Spiritual Benefits of Leisure Participation and Leisure Settings. In B. L. Driver, et al. (Eds.), *Benefits of Leisure*. State College, PA: Venture Publishing, p. 179.
15. Orthner, D.K. (1998). Strengthening Today's Families: A Challenge to Parks and Recreation. *Parks and Recreation* March: 87.
16. Hemingway, J.L. (1999). Leisure, Social Capitol and Democratic Citizenship. *Journal of Leisure Research* 31(2): 150.
17. Parr, M.G., & Oslin, J. (1998). Promoting Lifelong Involvement Through Physical Activity. *JPERD* 69(2): 72.
18. Bradshaw, R., & Jackson, J. (1979). Socialization for Leisure. In H. Ibrahim & R. Crandall (Eds.), *Leisure: A Psychological Approach*. Los Alamitos, CA: Hwong Publishing.
19. DiPetro, J. (1981). Rough and Tumble Play: A Function of Gender. *Developmental Psychology* 17:50–58.
20. Kelly, J. R. (1983). Leisure Styles: A Hidden Core. *Leisure Studies* 5(4):321–337.
21. Bialeschki, M., & Henderson, K. (1986). Leisure in the Common World of Women. *Leisure Studies* 5(3):299–308.
22. Fasting, K., & Sisjord, M. K. (1985). Gender Roles and Barriers to Participation in Sport. *Sociology of Sport Journal* 2(4):345–351.

## REFERENCES (cont'd)

23. Ibrahim, H., et al. (1981). Leisure Behavior Among Contemporary Egyptians. *Journal of Leisure Research* 13:89–104.
24. Philipp, S.F. (1998). Race and Gender Differences in Adolescent Peer Group Approval of Leisure Activities. *Journal of Leisure Research* 30(2): 214.
25. Thrane, C. (2000). Men, Woman and Leisure Time. *Leisure Sciences* 22: 109.
26. Shaw, S. (1985). Gender and Leisure: Inequality in the Distribution of Leisure Time. *Journal of Leisure Research* 17(4):266–282.
27. Burdge, R. J. (1969). Levels of Occupational Prestige and Leisure Activity. *Journal of Leisure Research* 13:262–274.
28. Bultena, G., & Field, D. (1978). Visitors to National Parks: Test of Elitism Argument. *Leisure Sciences* 1(4):228–239.
29. Foret, C. M. (1985). *Life Satisfaction and Leisure Satisfaction Among Young-Old and Old-Old Adults with Rural-Urban Residence.* Unpublished Ph.D. Dissertation. Denton, TX, 1985.
30. Mitchell, Arnold (1983). *The Nine American Lifestyles: Who We Are and Where We're Going.* New York: Macmillan.
31. Allen, L. (1991). Benefits of Leisure Services to Community Satisfaction. In B. L. Driver, et al. (Eds.), *Benefits of Leisure.* State College, PA: Venture Publishing.
32. Orthner, D., & Mancini, J. (1991). Benefits of Leisure for Family Bonding. In B. L. Driver, et al. (Eds.), *Benefits of Leisure.* State College, PA: Venture Publishing.
33. Haggard, L., & Williams, D. (1991). In B.L. Driver, et al. (Eds.), *Self-identity Benefits of Leisure Activities.* State College, PA: Venture Publishing.
34. Kelly, John R. (1987). *Freedom to Be.* New York: Macmillan, p. 115.
35. Gerson, G., & Ibrahim, H. (1991). *Understanding Leisure: An Interdisciplinary Approach.* Dubuque, IA: Kendall-Hunt

There are only two lasting bequests we can hope to give our children. One of these is roots; the other is wings.

HODDING CARTER

# Play, Recreation, and the Life Course

## CHILDREN

## CHAPTER 4

### THE CHAPTER AT A GLANCE

In this chapter we explore the developmental stages of childhood and the forms of play activity children engage in at each stage. We learn about children's play objects and toys; examine the history, characteristics, and benefits of various kinds of playgrounds; discuss the role of games and sports in children's development; and consider ways of preventing and minimizing play-related injuries to children.

### Chapter Objectives

*After completing this chapter, you should be able to*

- Identify and briefly describe each of the developmental stages of childhood.
- Describe appropriate play objects and activities for children at each stage of development.
- Outline the history of playgrounds and describe the four kinds of playgrounds commonly found in the United States.
- Discuss guidelines and procedures that can prevent or minimize play-related injuries to children.
- Explain the differences between child-sponsored and adult-sponsored games.
- State the risks and drawbacks of children's participation in organized competitive sports.

## CHILDHOOD: TRENDS AND CHALLENGES

Developing children need constructive, age-appropriate activities that challenge but do not overtax them. Such activities help children acquire knowledge, skills, and attitudes that can serve as the foundation for a lifetime of healthy, wholesome recreation and leisure.

## A World  of Difference

### ALL WORK + NO PLAY = PROBLEM FOR KIDS

"Ric, I don't know where you left your math book. I asked you to help Anita get into her coat. Hurry up, you're late for school, and I'm late for work!" Dan Hernandez scoops dry food into the kitten's dish, grabs his mug of lukewarm coffee, and hurries to the living room, casting a despairing backward glance at the dirty dishes in the sink, the piles of laundry on the dryer, and the stack of unopened mail on the kitchen counter. In the living room, Dan helps his daughter into her parka while Ric retrieves his math book from under a pile of newspapers on the coffee table.

Outside, Dan gets the kids into the car, fastens their seatbelts, and grits his teeth as he turns the key in the ignition, praying that the aging starter in his old Ford pickup will catch just one more time. After a couple of dispiriting whines the starter kicks in, and Dan sighs with relief as he pulls out into rush-hour traffic. First stop, 9-year-old Ric's elementary school a mile away. Next, Dan's sister's house, where 3-year-old Anita spends the day with

Aunt Gloria and her three kids. Then onto the jammed freeway for the usual nerve-jangling commute to the industrial park where Dan works as a welder in a machine shop.

As traffic slows to a halt because of construction ahead, Dan drinks the last sip of his now-cold coffee and asks himself what's happened to his life. Not so long ago he and his wife, Maria, were a happy, hard-working couple, saving for a house and enjoying simple family outings with their kids. While Dan worked his usual 40- to 50-hour week at the machine shop, Maria ran a small dressmaking business and sold cosmetics out of their home so she could be a full-time mother to the kids. Weekends were family time—at the zoo, the playground, the science museum or in Grandma and Grandpa's big back yard with its playhouse, swings, slides, and assortment of colorful toys, plus plenty of cousins to play with. Dan was teaching Ric to enjoy his recreational passion, fly-fishing, and he also coached his son's church baseball team.

Recreation and leisure for the family as a whole, and for children in particular, are strongly influenced by social trends that shape behavior, tastes, values, and motivation. For example, most middle-class children born in the post–World War II baby boom between 1946 and 1964 had mothers who did not work outside the home. During this time, after-school activities centered on spontaneous play with other neighborhood children. Today, with more than 19 million American working mothers, along with a significant increase in single-parent households, there is a strong and growing demand for organized play programs for children.

According to the U.S. Bureau of the Census, there will be over 35.5 million children between

ages 5 and 13 and over 20 million children under age 5 by 2010 (Fig. 4.1). Population growth is expected to increase by over 7 million in these age categories by 2025. These children need our earnest efforts, especially if there is validity to this statement of one expert:

> It is not uncommon for youth to play games, surf the internet, or do homework on computers for hours every day. They are building the skills they'll need in a computer-oriented world, but they are becoming high-tech couch potatoes.[1]

### Obstacles to Healthy Development

Overall, today's American children are far less physically active than those of the post–World War II baby boom years. Among the factors often

# A World 🌐 of Difference

## ALL WORK + NO PLAY = PROBLEM FOR KIDS (CONT'D)

That all ended four months ago when Maria was called to Puerto Rico to help take care of her ailing father after Maria's mother died of heart failure. Torn between loyalty to her husband and children and devotion to her family of origin, Maria wavered back and forth between going to Puerto Rico and staying home. Dan finally urged her to go, knowing she'd always regret not helping her father when he was in need.

Since then, Dan has tried his best to be both mother and father to Ric and Anita. As he increased his hours at work to make up for lost income, however, Dan found himself spending less and less time with the kids. Ric, seeing his dad's weariness at the end of the day, has stopped asking Dan to help him practice batting or take him fishing and has started hanging out with some kids in the convenience store parking lot. Too tired to read to Anita and play dolls with her, Dan tends to let her sit for hours watching cartoons while he tries to keep up with the ever-

increasing burden of housework and laundry. He knows Ric is hanging out with a questionable crowd and wishes he had time to play ball and go fishing with his son. He also knows that, at his sister Gloria's house, Anita and her three cousins spend most of the day eating junk food and watching tabloid TV. Divorced and living on alimony, Gloria loves her kids but finds it easier to let them do what they want than to direct them into useful activities.

Dan and the kids talk on the phone with Maria every Sunday, and last week she said she'd almost certainly be home by Christmas. In the meantime, however, Dan feels he's becoming less and less effective as a parent and more and more caught up in the daily struggle just to get by—with no time out for his kids or himself.

As you study this chapter, think about the Hernandez family's situation and prepare to answer the questions in Your Turn at the end of the chapter.

---

blamed for the decrease in children's activity levels are television and video games. Statistics show that 13 percent of American children are overweight, compared to seven percent in the 1970s, and that even more are headed toward becoming overweight.[2] This indicates a need for physical activity in community recreation programs more than ever before. While researchers agree that diet contributes to this serious health problem, a Mayo Clinic study indicates that physical activity may play an even greater role.[3] One study of 8- to 12-year-old girls showed, for example, that they burned fewer calories while watching one 30-minute television episode than they did while lying in bed for 25 minutes.[4]

Also challenging the healthy development of today's children are the previously men-

tioned increases in the numbers of working mothers and single-parent households. Whereas some working parents leave their children to their own devices during after-school hours, others may feel guilty about spending little time with the kids and compensate by making too many formal arrangements for them. Children need a routine, direction, and guidance; they also need time to themselves and opportunities to play with other children in unstructured settings.

Another obstacle today's children face is parental pressure. According to Elkind, the child

> has become the unwilling, unintended victim of overwhelming stress—the stress born of rapid, bewildering social change and constantly rising expectations.[5]

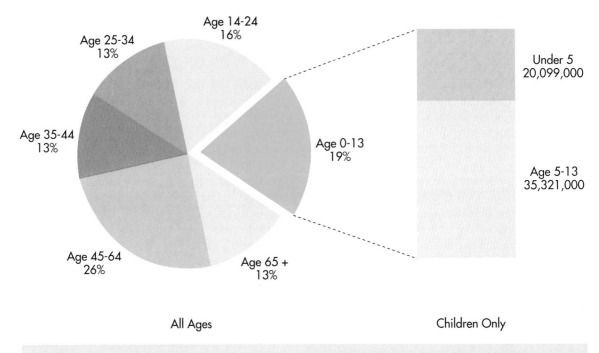

Age 14-24 16%

Age 25-34 13%

Age 35-44 13%

Age 45-64 26%

Age 65 + 13%

Age 0-13 19%

Under 5 20,099,000

Age 5-13 35,321,000

All Ages                                Children Only

**FIGURE 4.1**    Children as part of the United States population projected for the year 2010.

Elkind cautions that children should not be hurried through childhood or pressured to grow up too fast. Too commonly, he believes, children are asked to learn too much at too young an age, and their normal play is displaced as they compete for prestigious positions in sports, music, drama, and other activities. Children need balance to foster creativity. Professionals and parents should respond by allowing children time to be themselves and to explore their own interests.[5a]

Play and recreational activities provide pivotal experiences for children as they develop the skills needed to move from one stage to the next. Children should be encouraged to be creative and inventive in their play. With guidance and age-appropriate activities, children can discover a world of opportunities. In the sections that follow we describe the normal course of children's maturation and discuss the activities best suited for children at each stage of development.

Concept Check

- In what ways do play environments and opportunities differ between children of the baby boom era and children of today?
- What are some obstacles to healthy development for today's children?

## CHILDHOOD AND PLAY

All children play, and playing is a large component of their activities. Play gives children an important opportunity to learn about their abilities and limitations. It allows them to explore a wide range of possibilities without rigid rules or required outcomes. Children can engage in play for its own sake, not to achieve specific goals, and through make-believe games can transform reality.

Without being forced, children can learn naturally while playing as they interact with materials and objects in their immediate environment. Through play experiences such as imitation, experimentation, construction, representation, and dramatization, children begin to shape an understanding of their culture and language. As action is translated into meaningful concepts, play becomes a basis for reasoning, communicating, socializing, and achieving. Both recreational and educational institutions offer play experiences to encourage learning and behavioral development. A rich play setting provides a wide variety of active and passive play opportunities suited to children at each developmental level.

A child's play process and stage of game playing are determined by the child's level of physical, emotional, cognitive, and social development. Table 4.1 presents a simplified analysis of the stages of play.

The stages of a child's development are infancy, early childhood (includes toddler and preschooler), and middle childhood. In the following sections we explore each of these stages and learn what constitutes appropriate play for each stage.

## Infancy

**Infancy** encompasses the period between birth and 18 months of age. During this time most children progress through a definite order of motor (movement) activities (Table 4.2). Motor activities contribute significantly to development of the infant's brain and are essential for organization of the nervous system. With ample and appropriate motor stimulation, the infant's brain actually develops more neurons (nerve cells) and nerve pathways, which can enhance intelligence and learning capabilities. Without motor stimulation, however, unused neurons atrophy and disappear.[6]

Because infants move in response to natural instincts, adults need not force the development of motor skills. Gentle stimulation may be helpful if it is provided in a relaxed, pressure-free setting. Infants begin to learn through trial-and-error motor activity; through play they experiment with and master skills such as grasping and eye-hand coordination. At this stage what infants need most is freedom and

> *infancy* the period of childhood between birth and 18 months

## TABLE 4.1 Stages of Game Playing

| AGE (YEARS) | STAGE | LEVEL | PROCESS OF PLAY | TEACHING APPROACH |
| --- | --- | --- | --- | --- |
| 1 to 5 | Egocentric | Self-play<br>Parallel play | Exploration<br>Imitation | Exploration<br>Problem solving |
| 4 to 8 | Cooperative | Partner<br>Small group | Imitation<br>Prediction<br>Analysis<br>Synthesis | Problem solving<br>Guided discovery |
| 7 to 12 | Competitive | Small group<br>Team | Testing<br>Contesting<br>Analysis<br>Synthesis<br>Evaluation | Problem solving<br>Guided discovery<br>Command |

**TABLE 4.2**  Milestones of Motor Development

| SKILL | 25 PERCENT* | 50 PERCENT | 90 PERCENT |
| --- | --- | --- | --- |
| Rolling over | 2.1 months | 3.2 months | 5.4 months |
| Grasping rattle | 2.6 months | 3.3 months | 4.0 months |
| Sitting without support | 5.4 months | 5.9 months | 6.8 months |
| Standing while holding on | 6.5 months | 7.2 months | 8.5 months |
| Grasping with thumb and finger | 7.2 months | 8.2 months | 10.2 months |
| Standing alone well | 10.4 months | 11.5 months | 13.7 months |
| Walking well | 11.1 months | 12.3 months | 14.9 months |
| Building tower of two cubes | 13.5 months | 14.8 months | 20.6 months |
| Walking up steps | 14.1 months | 16.6 months | 21.6 months |
| Jumping in place | 21.4 months | 23.8 months | 2.4 years |
| Copying circle | 3.1 years | 3.4 years | 4.0 years |

*Approximate ages when 25%, 50%, and 90% of children can perform each skill.

space to move. Simple games such as peekaboo and pat-a-cake help teach infants about their physical world, their abilities, and their relationships with objects. These games also aid in coordination of motor activity. Infants can develop their muscles by playing and rolling on slightly deflated beach balls. They can experience new sensations of touch by crawling on different kinds of surfaces.

Experts differ in their opinions as to whether and how much adults should intervene to promote an infant's motor development. Some experts advocate as little intervention as possible, whereas others encourage adults to stimulate purposeful movement by changing the infant's position. Some pediatricians criticize walkers that are designed to help infants walk earlier than they normally would; they fear negative consequences from turning infants into toddlers before they are developmentally ready. Furthermore, walkers have been the source of serious injuries from falls and burns.[7]

In recent years exercise classes for the diaper set have become big business. In addition to

*Through play, children discover a world of opportunities.*

commercial enterprises such as Gymboree, nonprofit entities such as community recreation centers, YM/YWCAs, and YM/YWHAs offer programs for infants as young as 3 months. Most programs teach balance, strengthen muscles, and develop eye-hand coordination. Parents are shown how to help infants use their motor abilities to the degree consistent with the infant's stage of development. Motor activity also is encouraged through swim classes.

Many pediatricians believe infant exercise classes can be beneficial provided the activities are medically sound and are not performed to excess. One study shows that, the more vigorous the newborn, the more active he or she will be in later childhood.[8] In addition, pleasurable play and physical activities should begin early to promote continued movement experiences and interests throughout life.[9]

## Early Childhood

**Early childhood** begins at 18 months of age and extends to 5 years of age. This period of childhood represents a major transformation that includes the process of learning a language. By 5 years of age, most children are able to form and use complex sentences, although their thinking is still unsophisticated. Adults need patience to answer the young child's abundance of questions. During this period children develop a unique personality. However, they typically are still **egocentric**— concerned or preoccupied with the self—and see things only from their own point of view. The more young children are helped to become independent, the less likely they are to become negative and rebellious.

Children at this stage take play quite seriously as they tackle new activities and develop new skills. Play not only serves as a means of self-expression but also is an indicator of emotional and social adjustment. This is a crucial time for children to build self-confidence and self-esteem, so professionals should emphasize success and minimize failure.

Indoor play areas should be colorful, orderly, and conveniently arranged so that children feel comfortable and secure. Children should be encouraged to help organize displays. Space is needed for individual, quiet, and creative pursuits. Outdoor play areas are discussed later in the chapter.

## Toddlers

**Toddlerhood** encompasses the period between 18 months and 3 years of age. Moving unsteadily but independently in the upright posture, children grow faster during this stage than at any other time in their life. The body shape of toddlers becomes less round and more linear. They become more mobile, verbal, and independent. Active explorers, they are absorbed in discovering the world around them. They are eager to try new things and use materials in different ways. Toddlers like to have their own way and are not likely to share or take turns. Because their attention span is short, planned activities are easily disrupted as they wander around and interrupt.

From birth to 2 years of age, children are at what Swiss psychologist Jean Piaget called the **sensorimotor stage of development**, during which they learn to deal with objects, time, and space on a concrete basis. Children cannot form abstract concepts at this stage. They tend to learn more through movement and sensation than through listening and reasoning.

One expert outlines some play settings that are appropriate for toddlers:[10]

**early childhood**  the period of childhood between 18 months and 5 years of age

**egocentric**  concerned or preoccupied with the self

**toddlerhood**  the period of childhood between 18 months and 3 years of age

**sensorimotor stage of development**  the stage from birth to 2 years of age during which children learn to deal with objects, time, and space on a concrete basis

1. Play environments that provide space and equipment for **gross motor activity**, that is, activity that uses the large muscle groups that coordinate body movements required for normal living, such as walking, running, jumping, throwing, and balance
2. Toys that are touchable and mouthable and can be used in many ways, such as blocks
3. New activities and play items that can be rotated or changed for fresh appeal
4. Plenty of alternatives
5. Only a few group activities; at this age, children easily lose interest
6. Avoidance of arbitrary decisions so toddlers can learn to reach constructive solutions
7. Expectation of difficult behavior, which is normal at this stage
8. Self-care activities that encourage children to learn to cope with separation; free play

Settings away from home can give toddlers an opportunity for interactive play. Side-by-side activity with another child, known as **parallel play**, helps children learn to relate to others. A relationship often begins when one toddler notices something about another, such as a red ribbon, and begins to investigate; the next step is mutual exploration. Adults can encourage interaction among toddlers by playing with them.

During this period children also engage in pretend play and imaginative role playing. These forms of activity are important ways for toddlers to experiment with expressing emotions and with communicating ideas through language and gestures. Children often imitate adult behavior in their play, and pretend play gradually becomes more reality oriented. By becoming play partners, adults can help toddlers understand cause-and-effect relationships through play sequences. For example, when a doll or stuffed animal falls, the child can help

take it to the "doctor" or "hospital" and can be shown how to treat the toy with loving care.

### Preschoolers

As toddlers become **preschoolers** (3 to 5 years of age), they enjoy greater mobility and increasing mental powers. They develop a conscience and an awareness of gender differences and of their relationships with others. They experience an increased ability to reason and some decrease in egocentricity. Preschoolers enjoy exploring and experimenting as they attempt to find out about themselves and the world around them. A success-oriented play environment becomes less important as preschoolers' energy and enthusiasm allow them to forget failure quickly while they move on to other endeavors.

Play continues to occupy most of the preschooler's waking hours, although it still is not highly structured or directive. Children at this stage need an abundance of opportunities for gross motor play in both controlled and uncontrolled settings. Through such movement experiences, children learn more about their physical abilities and can enhance their problem-solving skills. At this stage short rest periods are needed, especially after vigorous play. Preschoolers also enjoy handling objects, eye-hand coordination exercises, creative opportunities, and sensory experiences. Activities such as show-and-tell help alleviate shyness and improve language skills. Carefully chosen toys provide stimulation and offer opportunities for manipulation; we describe toys in more detail later in the chapter.

By 5 years of age, children are actively seeking out others and are beginning to enjoy some competition.

### Concept Check

- In what specific ways can children learn as they play?
- What are the three stages of child development?

## Middle Childhood

**Middle childhood** spans the years between 5 and 12 and is marked by slower, steadier growth that allows children to engage in activities without the energy-draining changes that result from rapid physical growth during early childhood. Increased heart and lung capacity allow children to be active for longer periods without rest. As bones and muscles develop, children become stronger and more flexible, and they react faster. They continue to master more complex motor skills and to improve their **fine motor skills**, that is, the use of precise, coordinated movements in such activities as writing, buttoning, cutting, tracing, or visual tracking.

Because of variation in growth rates during middle childhood, some children are self-conscious about their appearance compared with that of their peers. Physical differences between the sexes are minimal during this stage, so age is a far more significant factor than gender in the levels of skills children acquire. Girls generally are superior in accuracy of movement, whereas boys tend to excel at less complex and more forceful acts. By the end of middle childhood, girls may be taller, heavier, and stronger than boys, and some girls will have experienced their first menstrual period.

Emotions during middle childhood are in the process of transition and refinement, and marked development is apparent in thinking, memory, learning ability, and capacity for knowledge. Children's thought process is more understandable to adults, and children are better able to control their behavior and cooperate with others. With appropriate opportunities, encouragement, and practice, children are able to acquire many new skills. These new skills, along with a more cooperative spirit, give children more opportunities for interaction by participating in games, sports, and social functions. Through these activities children can move toward forming their first close relationships outside the family.

For children in this age group, activities with simple rules work best. Among popular activi-ties are rhythms, tumbling, fitness, and swimming. Children in this age group want to build skill competence. Cooperative play develops into competitive play through small-group activity. Children gradually prepare for full team play, and skills learned during this stage may lay the foundation for a lifetime of sports activity.

*Learning to swim and float is a popular activity for children ages 5 to 12.*

***gross motor activity*** activity that uses the large muscle groups that coordinate body movements required for normal living, such as walking, running, jumping, throwing, and balance

***parallel play*** side-by-side activity with another child

***preschooler*** a child between 3 and 5 years of age

***middle childhood*** the period of childhood between 5 and 12 years of age

***fine motor skills*** precise, coordinated movements in such activities as writing, buttoning, cutting, tracing, and visual tracking

Physical activity is particularly helpful for children who have the extreme variations in activity level associated with attention deficit disorder (ADD). Also called hyperactivity, ADD primarily affects children and adolescents and is characterized by behavior and learning disabilities. Symptoms include impairment in perception, conceptualization, language, memory, and motor skills; increased impulsivity and emotional instability; and hyperactivity. Physical activity helps children with ADD by allowing them to release excess energy.

Between 6 and 10 years of age, sex play begins to occur.[11] When adults respond calmly, they help prevent children from feeling guilty. These are times when children can be invited to talk about their bodies. To children on the verge of adolescence, gender identification begins to take on increased meaning.

Middle childhood is a time of great enthusiasm, imagination, and exuberance. Children enter into informal social groups; as they mature, they are drawn into more formal groups and clubs. By the end of this stage they may have formed a close circle with two or three other friends, usually of the same sex.

### Concept Check

- Identify three specific ways in which abilities and behavior in middle childhood differ from those in early childhood.
- What are some ways in which girls and boys differ in middle childhood?

## PLAY OPPORTUNITIES

The UN Declaration of the Rights of the Child suggested that children should have the full opportunity for play and recreation. Play opportunities and playthings stimulate children's development—physical, mental, emotional, and social. Children can improve their gross and fine motor skills, learn cooperation and teamwork, satisfy their curiosity, and add to their knowledge of the world.

### Toys and Playthings

Toys inspire the imagination and help children learn new skills. As children express their thoughts and feelings through play, toys assist in the process. Children who have access to a wide variety of playthings designed for both sexes appear to have the advantage over those whose choices are restricted. Although boys tend to play more aggressively with dolls than girls do, dolls provide better outlets for working through problems than do trucks or cars.

Experts recommend that children have access to toys that enhance the development of a wide variety of skills—imagination, cooperation, turn taking, organizing, physical coordination, and spatial relationships. Well-designed playthings provoke exploration, investigation, manipulation, and contemplation. If an object is sufficiently complex and responsive, the child will investigate its physical properties and seek answers to questions that arise during the investigation, thus developing problem-solving skills. One expert offers these guidelines for selecting play objects:[12]

1. Children play for stimulation.
2. Stimulation must contain elements of uncertainty, novelty, or complexity.

*Children learn about Old Glory McHenry National Monument and Historic Shrine in Baltimore.*

3. Objects must be complex or become more complex with the accumulation of knowledge about or experience with the object.

With due consideration for issues of safety, children should be allowed to use toys as they wish, not necessarily as a parent, teacher, or manufacturer thinks they should be used. Adults can use toys to encourage learning, such as by asking children to name colors or count objects. One psychologist used toys to help reduce differences in verbal and other skills between middle-income and low-income children. A "toy demonstrator" went to the homes of low-income preschool children and taught their mothers how to play with their children in ways that would stimulate their children's ability to think and learn. When the children were in the third grade, they were given follow-up tests that showed they outperformed a control group by about 10 percentage points in both reading and arithmetic, which brought the children up to the national average.[13]

Children can enjoy playing with new toys every other week by visiting a toy library. Safe utensils and tools can stimulate a child's imagination and enhance creativity, cognition, and flexibility. For children with disabilities, an organization called Lekotek offers a well-stocked library of adapted toys that can be borrowed on a monthly basis.[14]

**Concept Check**

- What are some attributes of effective playthings?
- What kinds of skills can children develop by playing with toys?

## Playgrounds

Playgrounds offer a combination of large playthings in one location, usually outdoors. To arouse children's interest, a playground must provide stimulation, variety, challenge, and change. Such a playground will engender enthusiasm and curiosity that will promote observation, problem solving, and creative expression.

### Playground History

The first American playground, the Boston Sand Garden, was established in 1885 (see A Closer Look on p. 66), and in 1900 Joseph Lee, the father of the American playground, proposed that a model playground be developed. The experimental model, which attracted 300 children per week, provided an early foundation for other playgrounds in Boston and various towns and cities throughout the country. During the Great Depression of the 1930s, the federal government built some 13,000 playgrounds. These playgrounds offered city children a substitute for a natural setting, and climbing apparatus took the place of trees.

### Playground Styles

Over time, four general playground styles have developed in the United States:

- *Traditional*: This style of playground consists of steel slides, seesaws, swings, merry-go-rounds, and climbing apparatus placed on dirt, asphalt, or grass. The advantages of this style are that it provides opportunities for gross motor exercise and requires little maintenance. Disadvantages are that children tend to get bored easily because there are few choices of apparatus; the nature of

*Nature's playground inspires respect for the environment.*

## A CLOSER LOOK

### THE BOSTON SAND GARDEN: AMERICA'S FIRST PLAYGROUND

The famous Boston Sand Garden is regarded as a landmark in the development of recreation in the United States because it was the first American playground designed specifically for children. Sponsored by a women's reform organization called the Massachusetts Emergency & Hygiene Association, the playground literally was a pile of sand placed in a working-class district in Boston's North End. Initially the children who came to play there with pails and shovels were supervised by volunteers. Within 2 years of the facility's founding in 1885, however, 10 more such playgrounds were opened, with women employed to supervise. Subsequently, the city of Boston began to subsidize the maintenance of the sand gardens, thus allowing underprivileged children the opportunity to play in a safe environment.[15,16]

the equipment tends not to encourage social interaction; and injury rates are higher than is the case with other kinds of playgrounds.

◆ *Contemporary*: Sometimes called creative playgrounds, these facilities offer more stimulation than traditional playgrounds because children can modify equipment to create new challenges. Items such as tires, railroad ties, and cable spools are used to make wooden climbing platforms, ladders, tire nets, suspension bridges, pulley cables, tire swings, balance beams, tunnels, and slides. The pieces are connected, so creative play and social interaction are facilitated. The advantages of contemporary playgrounds are the wider variety of opportunities for creative play and social interaction, and the apparatus can be altered to offer children new experiences. Disadvantages are the liabilities associated with this kind of playground and the difficulty of obtaining insurance.

◆ *Adventure*: This playground style began in post–World War II Europe when children designed their own imaginative playgrounds on the sites of bombed-out buildings. In today's version, children use hand tools, wood, and ropes to build and rebuild their own structures. The playground environment can be altered by building, digging, or adding water to expand opportunities for maneuverability, creativity, and skill development. The advantages of adventure playgrounds are low initial cost, a stimulating environment, and proven popularity. Disadvantages are the often unattractive appearance and difficulty in obtaining liability insurance.

◆ *Modern*: Today, designers are combining some elements of each of the playground styles described above to create safer and more varied play environments that offer a developmental progression of challenges and skill-building opportunities. Modern playgrounds provide places for quiet play and social interaction and large areas for gross motor play. Equipment is safe, reliable, easy to install, and manufactured in an array of colors and shapes. Some equipment will harmonize with the environment. Soft contained play equipment (SCPE) playgrounds offer soft, pliable tunnels; climbers; slides; and other moving components.

### Playground Planning and Supervision

Playground planning is an important part of public recreation planning, and recreation professionals must develop a philosophy and set goals that can be translated into a stimulating, effective playground design. Such a design will offer choices, safety, and challenges; facilities for solo play and group interaction, muscle-building and energy-releasing exercises for creativity, and younger and older children; opportunities for creativity fun, and confidence; variation in topography, surfaces, and textures; and the capacity for change, relocation, and additions.[17a]

To appeal to children and hold their interest, playground design must emphasize exploration, investigation, and manipulation; offer opportunities for play and exercise that go beyond gross motor activity; and provide both sun and shade. One study showed that the average visit to playgrounds that lacked these features lasted only 15 minutes; during peak usage, equipment that could not be manipulated was deserted as much as 89% to 98% of the time.

**Playground Safety**

Playground safety is an issue of great concern to children, parents, recreation professionals, and government bodies at all levels (see A Closer Look). Far too many playgrounds are antiquated, hazardous, and inappropriate for the developmental needs of children. Problems with salvaged and aging equipment have motivated many local governments and private groups to upgrade to newer and safer apparatus. A growing number of playgrounds are structured to enhance children's development while protecting them from injury, and many modern, imaginative playscapes are designed to harmonize with nature. Guidelines and standards for playground design are available from the U.S. Consumer Product Safety Commission (CPSC) and the American Society for Testing and Materials (ASTM) (see Appendix A).

The National Program for Playground Safety, established through a grant from the Centers for Disease Control and Prevention, stresses that all children should be supervised. To improve playground safety, many local parks and recreation departments hire supervisors or play leaders, particularly during the summer months. These employees must be appropriately prepared for the responsibilities they are assuming. They need to know

1. The basic physical and cognitive skills of children at various stages of development
2. Potential playground dangers
3. A set of rules that can help prevent accidents
4. An established crisis management procedure

Regardless of their training, playground leaders cannot compensate for hazardous surfaces or unsafe design, installation, or maintenance.

Over the past several years, increases in both lawsuits and insurance rates have caused many

## A CLOSER LOOK

### PREVENTING PLAYGROUND INJURIES

Studies rank playgrounds among the five greatest hazards to our nation's children.[18] More than 200,000 people a year are treated in hospital emergency rooms for playground injuries, and about 17 children die each year.[19] These fatal injuries involve falls, entanglement of clothing or other items in equipment, entanglement of ropes tied to or caught on equipment, head entrapment, impact from equipment tipovers or failures, and collisions with moving swings.[20]

About 70%[21] of all playground injuries and 90% of all serious injuries are caused by falls.[22] Head injuries are involved in about 75% of falls (Fig. 4.2). A fall onto a hard surface can be life threatening. Alternative surfaces, such as hard wood fiber or mulch, pea gravel, sand, and rubber tiles, mats, or poured surfaces, are acceptable when measured to the appropriate depth. For equipment up to eight feet in height, the depth should fall to 12 inches.[23]

New, safer playgrounds are evolving. One trend is equipment that is lower to the ground—20-foot-tall corkscrew slides have seen their last days. There will be no more merry-go-rounds that can trap children underneath. Traditional seesaws are giving way to spring-loaded ones so that, if one child jumps off, the other child is not injured. High swings, which call for extra expense to pad the area, may be removed.[18] Donna Thompson, director of the National Program for Playground Safety, suggests removing animal swings, replacing metal and wooden seats with soft seats, and not attaching swings to other equipment.[23]

The National Playground Safety Institute, a program of the National Recreation and Park Association (NRPA), trains communities in playground safety and certifies playground safety inspectors. Unfortunately, many playgrounds are used by children before they receive a third-party safety audit.[24]

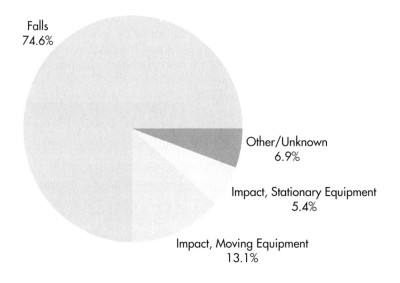

Falls
74.6%

Other/Unknown
6.9%

Impact, Stationary Equipment
5.4%

Impact, Moving Equipment
13.1%

**FIGURE 4.2**   Hazard patterns of incidents involving public playground equipment.

municipalities to shut down playgrounds altogether or to be extremely cautious in playground design. These trends do help keep playgrounds safe, but they also are used as an excuse for not designing more creative and challenging playgrounds. Children need to play in an environment that is safe without being overprotected. As one expert observes,

> We need as much play value as we can possibly get, whereas we only need as much safety as necessary. Any other approach would seem to be defeating the purpose of children's play.[25]

**Current Trends**

A current trend in playground design is creating facilities for a broad range of users. Many playground injuries result when small children with less developed cognitive and motor skills play on equipment designed for older children. Postings at playground entrances should advise caregivers of the age range for which a particular play area is designed. An important extension of the CPSC guidelines addresses playground design for children under 6 years

of age. The commission recommends that children start using playgrounds when they are toddlers, provided the play environment and equipment are appropriate.

Playground equipment helps toddlers and preschoolers enhance their orientation ability, and moving in space helps build a foundation for symbolic learning in later years. Play areas for this age group should accommodate no more than six children at a time to prevent social interaction from becoming too complex. Equipment should be accessible to adults. After the first grade, children need more challenge and complexity. If playground apparatus is not challenging, children are likely to create their own challenges by misusing equipment, causing risk to themselves and others.

Ongoing research shows that children particularly value play structures that have the following characteristics:[19]

- ◆ Complexity and variety
- ◆ Mystery and suspense
- ◆ Perceived risk and challenge

*Soft contained play equipment even offers toddlers a safe play environment and an opportunity for social interaction.*

◆ Linkage and creative opportunities
◆ Lookouts and private hideaways
◆ Refuges for social and dramatic play
◆ Potential for adult interaction

Since passage of the 1990 Americans with Disabilities Act (see Chapter 14), there has been a revolution in playground design to make facilities accessible to children with disabilities. Handholds and footholds give a sense of security to children who are without sight or hearing or who are mentally challenged. Play areas and pathways are designed so that all children can play together. Along the pathways are exercise stations and easy-access apparatus. Challenging playground equipment consists of several slides—one with a wheelchair ramp—an accessible swing set, climbing apparatus, concrete tunnels, and a wheelchair sports course. The ASTM provides information on play areas and equipment accessibility for children with disabilities.

### Concept Check

- What are the four kinds of playgrounds commonly found in the United States?
- What are some common playground injuries? How can they be prevented?
- Name five specific characteristics of good playground design.

## Games

Although the words *play* and *game* may seem synonymous, games represent a more mature stage of development than play does. Playing a game is the voluntary attempt to overcome unnecessary obstacles.[27] In games children test their competence within the limits of a pre-established structure; they use equipment in specified ways and conform to a set of rules. Games are played not just for the sake of enjoyment but in pursuit of a goal, such as winning. Play is fun, but involvement in games may cause children considerable stress. Thus, as children grow and mature, the rules, skills, and social structure of games increase in complexity.

According to Piaget, learning the rules of a game is an important part of the socialization process. By participating in games, children learn to control selfish and aggressive behavior, and they eventually discover that bending the rules causes the game to break down.

When left to their own devices, children spend a great deal of time creating rules for backyard games or sandlot sports. In this process children develop their ability to reason and work with others. To keep the game going as long as possible, children tend to give more highly skilled participants handicaps and offer others special concessions. Rules serve the needs of the group by equalizing opportunities, promoting fun, and allowing children to build positive relationships and work out problems.[28] Supervised by the participants, these games can be played without the expectations, standards, and values of adult-sponsored sports. Table 4.3 contrasts the characteristics and outcomes of the child-directed and adult-directed approaches to games. The Action Guide on p. 71 gives you the chance to recall and analyze your own experiences.

The preceding discussion should not be taken to mean that child-sponsored games are superior to organized sports. As we will see later, however, the intense pressure and competition that characterize many organized sports can have negative effects on children. An alternative is the cooperative games approach, in which winning is secondary to fun. Exemplified by the so-called New Games movement, this approach encourages participation by everyone, requires little equipment or expense, and is not oriented to spectators. Emphasizing cooperation over competition, the approach focuses on fun, fitness, striving, and social growth and minimizes stress and anxiety. Noncompetitive versions of both new and traditional games are used in many school and public recreation programs.

**TABLE 4.3** Comparison of Two Groups*

| THE SPONTANEOUS PLAY GROUP | THE SPONSORED COMPETITIVE TEAM |
|---|---|
| No formal organizaton | Very formal organization |
| Action is an outgrowth of the participants' interpersonal relationships and decision-making processes | Action is an outgrowth of a predesignated system of role relationships and of the participants' role-learning abilities |
| Rewards are primarily intrinsic and are a function of the participants' experience and the extent of their interpersonal skills | Rewards are primarily extrinsic and are a function of the participants' combined technical skills |
| Meanings attached to actions and situations are emergent and are subject to change | Meanings are predominantly predefined and are relatively static from one situation to the next |
| Group integration is based on exchanges among participants | Group integration is based on an awareness of and conformance with a formalized set of norms |
| Norms governing action are emergent and interpretation is variable | Norms are highly formalized and specific, with variability resulting from official judgments |
| Social control is internally generated among members and depends on commitment | Social control is administered by an external agent and depends on obedience |
| Sanctions are informal and are directly related to the maintenance of action in the situation | Sanctions are formal and are related to the preservation of values as well as order |
| Individual freedom is high, with variability a function of the group's status structure | Individual freedom is limited to the flexibility tolerated within role expectations |
| The group is generally characterized by structured instability | The group is generally characterized by structured stability |

*A study of the game-playing behavior of elementary school children conducted by Sylvia Polgar (1976) provides empirical support for the comparisons made in this table.

# ACTION GUIDE

## CHILD'S PLAY OR ADULT AGENDA?

If you were like most kids, you created your own games or were part of a group that did the same thing. By answering the questions that follow, you'll gain—or regain—insight into the kinds of activities you engaged in as a child and how you felt about participating in them.

1. As a child, did you create a game—alone, with brothers or sisters, or with a neighborhood group? _____

2. Briefly describe the game: its name if any; the rules; the sex(es), ages, and number of participants; the equipment involved, if any; and the play site (yard, woods, field, etc.).

   _____

   _____

   _____

   _____

3. As time went on, did you change any of the rules of the game? If so, why?

   _____

   _____

   _____

4. What did you like about the game, and why?

   _____

   _____

5. What, if anything, did you dislike about the game, and why?

   _____

   _____

6. If you also participated in an adult-sponsored sport or activity as a child, compare and contrast your feelings about the organized activity with your feelings about the game you created yourself. If you had the choice today, which activity would you engage in, and why?

   _____

   _____

   _____

   _____

   _____

**Concept Check**

- In what ways does participating in games differ from simply playing?
- In what ways do games organized and directed by children differ from those sponsored by adults?

## Sports

Youth sports programs have existed in the United States since the beginning of the 20th century. Initially, such programs were supervised primarily by recreation professionals, athletic coaches, and physical educators. As competition and training intensified in the 1930s, many recreation professionals and physical educators began to withdraw from sports programs because they opposed what they considered excessive training and overemphasis on competition. The gaps were filled by volunteer organizations.

In the past 20 years, the age at which American children begin their involvement in competitive sports has steadily lowered. Some children start as early as 3 years of age. Organized in 1939, Little League Baseball, with its televised world series, has attained international prominence. It is the only youth sports organization with a charter granted by the U.S. Congress. It was incorporated under a bill signed by President Lyndon B. Johnson in 1964. The law was amended in 1974 to admit girls. Nearly 3 million players participated in 1997, up 16,000 from 1996. To qualify for the Little League World Series, a team comprising the best 11- and 12-year-olds in a Little League program enter the world's largest elimination tournament. More than 7,000 teams on six continents begin the tournament, playing in district, sectional, state, and regional tournaments before the eight World Series entrants are determined.[29]

Levels of participation and intensity of competition in youth sports programs have risen to all-time highs. Reportedly, some 6-year-olds are completing marathons and running 80 miles per week in training; 8-year-olds are swimming up to 20,000 meters per day; 10-year-old hockey players are participating in 90-game seasons; and 12-year-olds are competing in intensive national championships in gymnastics, tennis, swimming, and other sports.[30,31] Some children are abusing steroids, becoming dehydrated, and suffering from nutritional deficiencies.

### Injury Prevention

To minimize the risk of injury, younger children must learn basic skills and should not be placed into competitive situations before they are ready. Many experts recommend that athletes be grouped according to weight, stage of maturation, and skill level, rather than simply by age.

Children's overall maturational status and readiness can be assessed in physical examinations. This information is important because early injuries can disrupt the development of bones and muscles, and continued overuse can cause serious injury. The risk of injury to young athletes can be minimized by helping them achieve the appropriate level of fitness before beginning a sports program; by placing reasonable limits on the duration and intensity of practice sessions; and by structuring sessions to allow adequate time for warming up, stretching, and cooling down. Two-thirds of youth sports injuries occur during practice, and specialty sports camps have been shown to have high overuse-injury rates from long practice and playing times. The American College of Sports Medicine recommends only 20 to 30 minutes of intensive daily activity.

Youth sports injuries also can be minimized by the use of appropriate protective gear. The CPSC reports that since 1973 more than 50 children have been fatally injured while playing baseball, usually when the ball strikes the youngster in the chest and damages the heart.[32] Baseball-related injuries can be prevented or minimized by the use of protective gear such as a face mask and chest protector for the catcher and a helmet for the batter, as well as chest and eye protection. Playing areas must also be carefully maintained and routinely checked for hazards.

### Children with Special Needs

Children who are physically, mentally, or emotionally challenged can benefit greatly from participating in carefully structured organized sports programs. Some special-needs children may be able to take part in certain regular programs; others require programs that are designed to meet their specific needs. The oustanding example of a sports program for children with disabilities is the Special Olympics, in which everyone who participates is cheered as a winner just for taking part and trying. Programs such as the Special Olympics contribute significantly to the enhancement of special-needs children's pride, self-confidence, and self-esteem. Appendix B lists several sports programs for children with disabilities.

### The Sports Dilemma

In addition to promoting physical fitness and helping children acquire skills, appropriately coached organized sports can teach discipline, respect for authority, dedication, teamwork, and healthy competition. Competitive team sports can provide opportunities for social development and for building character, self-confidence, and self-esteem. On the down side, if mishandled, such programs can have serious adverse effects on children's development.[33]

Adults hold the key to the success or failure of children's sports programs. When adults are good sports, children are likely to be good sports. Too often, however, adults' expectations extend beyond children's ability and maturity level. Team organizers and leaders must educate adult volunteers to be empathetic and supportive and to be realistic about children's abilities. Events should be organized so that every child will experience some

*Children should be rewarded for their efforts as well as their accomplishments.*

success. Children's feelings of self-worth derive not only from the outcome but also from their efforts and accomplishments. Children should never be punished, verbally or physically, for losing. Instead, they should be encouraged to learn from defeat, praised for trying, and commended for good sportsmanship. The National Youth Sports Coaches Association (NYSCA) offers volunteer coach certification.

Why do children quit organized sports? One expert has identified the following reasons:[34]

- ◆ Not getting to play
- ◆ Negative reinforcement
- ◆ Mismatching (for example, body weights in wrestling or ages in gymnastics)
- ◆ Psychological stress
- ◆ Failure
- ◆ Over-organization

Likewise, music and dance recitals and other events present opportunities for children to display their new-found skills unless demands of perfection interfere with an otherwise fulfilling experience. With appropriate sport supervision, studies show that most children will have fun, improve their physical and social skills, and learn about discipline, cooperation, and fair play, building a solid foundation for later success.

**Concept Check**

- In what ways do children's sports become too intense?

- How might the risk of injury be reduced in children's sports?

## Summing Up

- The developmental stages of childhood are infancy (birth to 18 months of age), early childhood (toddlers, 18 months to 3 years of age); preschoolers, (3 to 5 years of age), and middle childhood (5 to 12 years of age).
- Through play, infants explore their bodies, learn to manipulate objects in their environment, and begin to experience themselves as separate beings.
- In early and middle childhood, children use play to develop and improve their physical skills, to acquire and refine social skills, and to gain peer acceptance and approval.
- Playthings for children should be capable of manipulation, responsive, and complex enough to stimulate exploration and investigation.
- Four kinds of playgrounds are commonly found in the United States: traditional, contemporary, adventure, and modern.

- Playground design should promote safety while stimulating creativity and exploration, should accommodate children of all ages and ability levels, and should offer variety and choices.
- By playing games, children can enhance their physical skills while learning how to cooperate and how to play by a set of rules.
- Organized sports programs have both benefits and drawbacks for children. Among the benefits are the opportunity to achieve physical fitness and master complex skills, to learn teamwork and discipline, and to enhance self-esteem and self-confidence. Drawbacks include overtraining, inappropriate emphasis on winning, high risks of injury, and intense pressure from coaches and adult volunteers.

## Using What You've Learned

1. Meet with an adult who has children and discuss his or her needs for supervised recreational activity for the children.
2. Locate a recreation program for preschoolers in your area and ask if you may observe. Take notes on your observations of
   (a) Whether children play alone or in groups
   (b) Which playthings appeal to them and which do not

   (c) How long certain objects or activities hold children's interest
   Report your findings in class.
3. Visit a playground in your neighborhood. If you were a child, would you find it stimulating? Why or why not?
4. Did you ever compete in a sport as a child? Imagine you are a child again and write a one-page paper describing what you like most and least about participating.

## YOUR Turn

1 Ric Hernandez is 9 and his sister Anita is 3. In what developmental stage is each child?
2 What play activities are appropriate for each child? What skills should each be acquiring?
3 What are the disadvantages to Ric and Anita of the play activities currently available to them?

4 How would Ric and Anita benefit from organized, supervised recreational activities?
5 How could their father Dan Hernandez foster healthful, age-appropriate recreation opportunities for them?

## REFERENCES

1. National Association for Sport and Physical Education (October 28, 1997). *Shape of the Nation Report Release.* Reston, VA: NASPE, p. 2.
2. Centers for Disease Control and Prevention (2001) *Physical Activity and Good Nutrition: Essential Elements for Good Health At-A-Glance 1999.* Atlanta, GA: U.S. Department of Health and Human Services, p. 2-5; Hellmich, N. (March 13, 2001). Children Add on the Pounds. *USA Today.* 6D.
3. American Alliance for Health, Physical Education, Recreation, and Dance (August 1999). *Journal of Physical Education, Recreation, and Dance* 70(6): 8.
4. Rubin, R., Hannon, K., & Mannix, M. (1993). News You Can Use. *U.S. News and World Report* 114(7):68.
5. Elkind, D. (1981). *The Hurried Child.* Menlo Park, CA: Addison-Wesley.
5a. The Independent (June 13, 2000) Helping Children to Play May Stunt Creativity. *InteliHealth, Inc.,* p.2.
6. Beck, J. (April 21, 1993). Learning Is Linked to IQ. *The San Diego Union Tribune,* p. B9.
7. Keefer, A. (May 2001) Baby Walkers: Many Parents Still Unaware of All the Dangers. *San Diego Family Magazine* 20(2): 62.
8. Harris, C. (1986). *Child Development.* St. Paul, MN: West., p. 196.
9. Stoll, S., Matthews, A., Trainer, M., McLaughline, C., Beller, J., Matthews, J., Freitas, B., and Mike M. (November/December 2000) I Play, Therefore I Am. *Journal of Physical Education, Recreation, and Dance* 71(9): 54.
10. Gonzalez-Mena, X. (1986). Toddlers: What to Expect. *Young Children* 42(1):49.
11. Perry, S. (Oct 1992). I'll Show You Mine. *Parenting,* p. 187
12. Ellis, M. J. (1973). *Why People Play.* Englewood Cliffs, NJ: Prentice-Hall, pp. 135–136, 138.
13. Fong, B., & Resnick, M. R. (1986). *The Child.* Palo Alto, CA: Mayfield. p. 342.
14. All in a Day's PLAY (1994). *Mosby Publishers Newsletter,* p. 9.
15. Edginton, C., et al. (1995). *Leisure and Life Satisfaction.* Madison, WI: Brown & Benchmark, p. 73.
16. Kraus, R. (1990). *Recreation and Leisure in Modern Society.* Glenview, IL: Scott, Foresman/Little, Brown, pp. 158–159.
17. Ellison, G. (1975). *Play Structures.* Pasadena, CA: Pacific Oaks College and Children's School, p. 1.
17a. Hudson, S. and Thompson, D. (April 2001) Are Playgrounds Still Viable in the 21st Century? *Parks and Recreation* 36(4): 55, 62.

18. Hamilton, K., & King, P. (May 5, 1997). Playgrounds of the Future: They Ain't Got Swing. *Newsweek* CXXIX(19):14.
19. Kutska, K. and Kalousek, T. (April 2000) A Vision for the Future. *Parks and Recreation* 35(4): 93.
20. Tinsworth, D. K., & Kramer, J. T. (Apr 1990). *Playground Equipment—Related Injuries and Deaths.* Washington, DC: U.S. Consumer Product Safety Commission.
21. Mack, M. and Henderson, W. (April 2000) Risk Factor Three: Fall Surfacing on Safe Playground. *Journal of Physical Education, Recreation, and Dance* 71(4): 17.
22. Frost, J. (Apr 1994). Preventing Playground Injuries and Litigation. *Journal of Physical Education, Recreation, and Dance* 29(4):57.
23. American Alliance for Health, Physical Education, Recreation, and Dance (Apr 1996). Director Answers to Common Questions About Playground Safety. *Journal of Physical Education, Recreation, and Dance* 67(4):8.
24. Christiansen, M. (April 1999) An Evaluation of Playground Management. *Parks & Recreation* 34(4): 78-79.
25. Jensen, M. (1990). Playground Safety: Is It Child's Play? *Parks & Recreation* 25(8):38.
26. Bigtoys. (1993). *Catalog 18,* p. 5.
27. Suits, B. (1979) *What is a Game? In Sport and the Body: A Philosophical Symposium In* E. Gerber and W. Morgan (Ed). Philadelphia, P.A.: Lea & Febiger.
28. Coakley, J. (1993). Play Group Versus Organized Competitive Team: A Comparison. In D. S. Eitzen (Ed.), *Sport in Contemporary Society.* New York: St. Martin's Press.
29. _____ (1997). *Little League World Series Media Guide,* pp. 6, 23.
30. Kibler, B., & Chandler, T. J. (1993). Musculoskeletal Adaptations and Injuries Associated with Intense Participation in Youth Sports. In B. Cahill & A. Pearl (Eds.), *Intensive Participation in Children's Sports.* Champaign, IL: Human Kinetics, p. 204.
31. Donnelly, P. (1993). Problems Associated with Youth Involvement in High-Performance Sport. In B. Cahill & A. Pearl (Eds.), *Intensive Participation in Children's Sports.* Champaign, IL: Human Kinetics, p. 97.
32. Ignelzi, R. (May 1, 1993). Play It Safe. *The San Diego Union Tribune,* p. F-1.
33. Butler, L. (February 2000) Fair Play: Respect for All. *Journal of Physical Education, Recreation, and Dance* 71(2): 32.
34. Leonard II, W. (1993). *A Sociological Perspective of Sport.* New York: Macmillan, p. 127.

*An adolescent is both an impulsive child and a self-starting adult.*

MASON COOLEY

# Recreation, Leisure, and the Life Course

## ADOLESCENTS

### THE CHAPTER AT A GLANCE

The adolescent years are a search for both identity and independence. Adolescents are no longer children but have not yet entered the adult world. They need their own activities, challenges, and recognition. In this chapter we explore the recreational needs of adolescents, consider ways in which those needs may be met, and learn about activities that are popular with this age group.

### Chapter Objectives

*After completing this chapter, you should be able to*

- ◆ Describe the key characteristics and challenges of younger and older adolescents.
- ◆ Describe the physiological changes that take place in both girls and boys during puberty.
- ◆ Explain the challenges adolescents face in developing their own identity.
- ◆ Describe the kinds of recreational activities that are enjoyable and beneficial to adolescents and explain how youth programs can be structured to provide those activities.
- ◆ Identify the special needs of youth at risk and outline ways in which recreational opportunities can be a positive influence on such youth.
- ◆ Explain the ways in which adolescents are affected by involvement in adventure, sports, music, and travel.

## A World  of Difference

### HOW DO YOU SPELL "BELONGING"?

Tracy had been thinking continually about the camping trip ever since it was announced, but she acted a little bored as she boarded the bus, bumped past her classmates, and sank into a seat in the back. How could this trip be much different from her daily life? After all, she had noticed the hand signs and gang colors as she made her way onto the bus. Like Tracy, each of the students had been forced to enroll at Vincent, the alternative school. Tracy had been caught dealing drugs, Bill was sent because he not only packed a knife but used it, and Anita had so much misdirected energy that she bounced right off the walls of her middle school and into their class. Home life for each of them was marked by poverty, abuse, and unrealized dreams. Among these three students were two alcoholic parents, two who were abusive, and none who had enjoyed the success everyone on television seemed to achieve. With the city budget cuts, the local teen activity center had closed, so the kids spent their time after school hanging out on the streets. The downward spiral continued for these 11- and 12-year-olds. They were all considered to be "at risk," a distinction that earned all 40 of them their free trip to camp.

On the ride up into the mountains, Tracy doodled and sketched in her notebook. She thought about the fact that she had spent her entire 11 years in the city. She knew from movies that the woods were dark and unsafe. Besides, why did she need to learn how to use a compass, anyway? And who would buy the food that week and cook for her two younger sisters and her baby brother if her dad didn't come home at night again? Suddenly a loud cheer went up from the people at camp who were waiting to greet them. The driver turned and parked the bus in the grassy field. As they left the bus, a news photographer snapped lots of pictures, including one of Tracy, and at that moment the constant camp activity began.

Like the bright flash from the photographer's camera, the civic leaders wanted to brighten the lives of these at-risk students. They wanted them to know the joy of learning to swim, of hiking and seeing a wildflower in bloom, of sitting around a campfire, of riding a horse. They wanted the camp to provide a spark of hope that transforms a life, or at least a week of happiness that would be one good childhood memory to cherish. But overcoming the grim circumstances of these at-risk students would take more than a week at camp.

Along with the camp experience, how would you use recreation to give these students a way out and a better future? As you study this chapter, think about Tracy's situation and prepare to answer the questions in Your Turn at the end of the chapter.

## CHARACTERISTICS OF ADOLESCENTS

Adolescence is a period of major physical and psychological transitions that strongly influence the recreational preferences of this age group. Responding appropriately to the recreational needs of adolescents is important because the patterns and habits formed during this stage are the blueprints for lifelong attitudes and behavior.

Believing that adolescents do not become mature adults without guidance, the task force on youth development of the Carnegie Council on Adolescent Development said[1]

*Snowboarding is a popular sport among adolescents.*

Americans must rebuild a sense of community in their neighborhoods. The nation cannot afford to raise another generation of young adolescents without the supervision, guidance, and preparation for life that caring adults and strong organizations once provided in communities.

**Adolescence** is a developmental transition from childhood to adulthood that begins at the onset of puberty, between 10 and 12 years of age, and ends at 19 or 20 years of age. In addition to the characteristic physiological changes, adoles-

cents also face the challenge of achieving emotional maturity: acquiring an identity, becoming independent, developing a set of values, and forming adult intimate relationships. In later sections we will divide adolescence into early adolescence, the period of physical changes and growth, and late adolescence, when the focus is on emotional development and increasing awareness of adult concerns.

Although the concepts and rituals of adolescence may vary among cultures and social classes, the years between 10 and 20 years of age are almost certainly the most challenging period of the lifecycle. Rapid growth, major hormonal changes, and the emotional struggle for identity, independence, and freedom make adolescence a time of conflict and uncertainty. Stress is exacerbated because adolescents tend to compare themselves with others on the basis of chronological age rather than maturational age.

The number of teenagers from age 15 to 19 is expected to increase 9% over this decade and is expected to reach 21.7 million by 2010.[2] Fig. 5.1 shows the size of this population in relation to the overall U.S. population for the year 2010. Fig. 5.2 shows the expected populations for three age groups of adolescents for the years 1992, 2000, and 2010.

## Positive Traits of Adolescents

Despite the self-centered and rebellious behavior most people associate with adolescents, researchers observe that young people exhibit a variety of positive characteristics:[3]

- ◆ Energetic; full of life
- ◆ Idealistic; genuinely concerned for the future of the country and the world
- ◆ Intellectually curious; question contemporary values, philosophies, ideologies, and institutions

***adolescence*** a developmental transition from childhood to adulthood that begins at the onset of puberty, between 10 and 12 years of age, and ends at 19 or 20 years of age

- Perceptive
- Courageous; willing to "stick their necks out"
- Independent
- Fair; intolerant of injustice or wrongdoing
- Reliable; responsible
- Flexible; responsive to change
- Honest; open; straightforward
- Loyal; supportive
- Good sense of humor
- Optimistic; positive outlook on life
- Take things seriously
- Sensitive to and aware of others' needs

By focusing on these strengths and on the challenges and needs of adolescents, professionals can design positive recreational programming that maximizes their success, happiness, and physical and emotional development.

## Challenges of Adolescents

Surveys have been used to demonstrate trends in youth risk behavior. Although adolescents represent a collection of complex lives, data from the Centers for Disease Control and Prevention (CDC) show that more of today's teenagers are taking various types of safety precautions. Fewer teens ride with drunk drivers, and more wear seatbelts and bicycle helments. In addition, while fewer teens are sexually active, a greater percentage of those who are use condoms. Pregnancy is also on the decline, and episodic heavy drinking has leveled off.[4]

Trends alone do not tell the entire story, however. Teenagers are about twice as likely as any other segment of the population to be in automobile collisions that result in fatalities or injuries.[5] Three out of four say that they speed when they drive, and 40% say that they have ridden with a teen driver who was intoxicated or impaired.[6] Exhaustion also figures in. Since melatonin, the chemical that prompts sleep, does not kick in for teenagers until 10:30 p.m. or later, many teens are sleep impaired. Moreover, they learn from adults that sleep holds a low priority.[7]

Youth also remain at considerable risk for contracting many kinds of sexually transmitted diseases. Because unprotected sex remains common, HIV (human immunodeficiency virus) continues to affect them. Many do not even know that they are infected. Additionally, about 43% of American adolescent girls will have been pregnant at least once by the time they are 20.[8]

**FIGURE 5.1** Adolescents as part of the population in the United States projected for the year 2010.

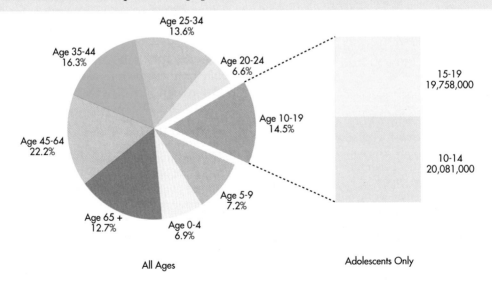

Age 25-34
13.6%

Age 35-44
16.3%

Age 20-24
6.6%

Age 45-64
22.2%

Age 10-19
14.5%

Age 65 +
12.7%

Age 0-4
6.9%

Age 5-9
7.2%

15-19
19,758,000

10-14
20,081,000

All Ages

Adolescents Only

Population 274,815,000; 10-19 Yrs. 39,849,000

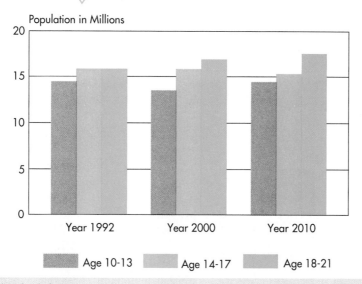

**FIGURE 5.2** Growth of adolescent groups comparing years 1992, 2000, and 2010.

According to a Kaiser Family Foundation report, only about 30% will have discussed birth control with their parents by the time they are teenagers, and more than 75% of them will never have discussed when it is appropriate to begin a sexual relationship.[5,9] Although the National Household Survey on Drug Abuse shows that drug use decreased in 1999 to 9.0% (see Figure 5.3 for other drug use statistics that decade), CDC data indicates that more teenagers are smoking and using marijuana, cocaine, or steroids.[4,10] It is estimated that 250,000 high school students may be using anabolic steroids, at grave risk to their health.[11] Fourteen percent of youth ages 12 to 19 were overweight in 1999, up from 11% in 1988-1994.[12-13] These overweight teens are at risk for developing various conditions including cardiovascular diseases, diabetes, and other serious health problems.

Although CDC data shows that fewer teens seriously consider suicide (one in five high school students), more American adolescents (one in 14) are actually attempting it. Sadly about 2,000 do actually kill themselves each year, making it the third leading cause of death for teenagers after accidents and homicides.[4,13a] Self-esteem, substance abuse, and depression are commonly asso-

ciated with suicide. Other provocations are AIDS, pregnancy, school failure, conflict with a parent, and loss of a loved one. Challenged to help youth make healthy choices, after-school programs and youth services are best built upon a pro-social philosophical concept that focuses on the positive aspects of helping youth build success, as opposed to a problem-focused approach.[13b] This is accomplished by furnishing recreational programs that reflect age-appropriate needs while providing a means of helping them achieve competencies necessary for positive development.[13c]

## YOUNGER ADOLESCENTS

Younger adolescents are between 12 and 16 years of age. With the onset of **puberty**, the period of life at which the ability to reproduce begins, comes a rapid growth spurt and various physical and hormonal changes. The reproductive structures mature, the sex organs enlarge, and secondary sex characteristics emerge. **Secondary sex characteristics** are

*puberty* the period of life at which the ability to reproduce begins

## Drug Use by Teens on the Rise

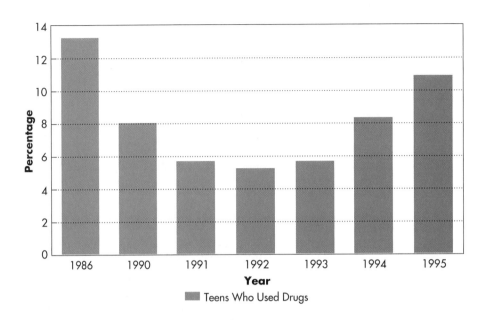

Teens Who Used Drugs

**FIGURE 5.3**  Percentage of teens 12 to 17 who said they used illegal drugs in the past month.

physical characteristics that appear in only one sex and are not directly related to reproduction; examples are breasts in females and thickened vocal cords in males. It can take four to eight years to complete the growth process and reach physiological maturity. Because the process begins a year or two earlier for girls than for boys, girls often find themselves taller than boys at this stage.

Both girls and boys develop axillary (underarm) and pubic hair. Overactive sebaceous glands may produce acne, which causes affected adolescents to become extremely self-conscious. The brain is no longer growing, but the brain's efficiency is increasing.

For girls, gradual changes in body shape include breast development and hip widening. A milestone of sexual maturity in girls is **menarche**, the onset of menstruation. When menstruation is treated as a forbidden subject, as is the case in some cultures and families,

girls tend to view it negatively. In contrast, pride in womanhood seems to be instilled in girls whose cultures celebrate the onset of menstruation.[14]

In boys the first sign of puberty is enlargement of the sex organs, and the principal indicator of sexual maturity is the presence of sperm in the urine. Involuntary ejaculation may occur during sleep. Boys' hips become narrower, their bodies become more heavily muscled, and they develop facial and chest hair. Their voices deepen as vocal cords thicken.

### Self-Image

Given all the physical changes that accompany puberty, it is easy to understand adolescents' combination of vanity, self-consciousness, and discomfort with their bodies. With more adolescents headed toward obesity, after-school programs presenting physical activities are badly needed to help combat the problem. Contributing factors are the high-fat, high-sugar diet and sedentary lifestyle of many teens; body weight also is influenced by inherited metabolic rate and developmental history. At the other end of the spectrum are teens who are obsessive about controlling their body weight. Boys may engage in demanding body-building regimens and abuse steroids; girls—both serious athletes and dancers as well as those responding to social pressures to be thin—are likely to go on rigid diets without medical supervision (see A Closer Look).

## Relationships

Two hallmarks of adolescence are increased sexual awareness and attraction to members of the opposite sex. Boys' interests tend to be erotic, whereas girls' are more likely to be romantic. Many teens are discovering their sexual orientation is homosexual; they require strong social support.

Overall, friendships are extremely important to adolescents in both the early and late stages. Friends provide acceptance, empathy, and emotional support. In the early adolescent years, bonds tend to be formed on the basis of shared interests, values, and backgrounds. Conformity and acceptance by the peer group are dominant factors in social relationships and help maintain self-esteem. As adolescents develop more self-confidence and become less dependent on the group, they begin

---

**secondary sex characteristics** physical characteristics that appear in only one sex and are not directly related to reproduction (e.g., breasts in females, thickened vocal cords in males)

**menarche** onset of menstruation

**anorexia nervosa** a disorder characterized by a prolonged refusal to eat, resulting in emaciation, cessation of menstruation, emotional disturbance concerning body image, and an abnormal fear of becoming obese

**bulimia** an insatiable craving for food, often resulting in episodes of continuous eating and often followed by purging, depression, and self-deprivation

---

## A CLOSER LOOK

### TEENS AND EATING DISORDERS

The two most prevalent eating disorders are anorexia nervosa and bulimia. **Anorexia nervosa** is characterized by a refusal to eat, which results in emaciation, cessation of menstruation, distorted body image, and an abnormal fear of becoming obese. **Bulimia** is an insatiable craving for food, often resulting in episodes of continuous eating and often followed by purging, depression, and self-deprivation. Almost all (90% to 95%) cases of anorexia nervosa and bulimia are found in females, and most of these live in North America and Europe.[15]

Anorexia nervosa is most prevalent among teenage girls and is characterized by starvation. Persons with the disorder see themselves as fat. Although preoccupied with food, they eat very little. Usually well behaved and successful in school, they are obsessive perfectionists who tend to be socially withdrawn and depressed. They may further compromise their health by overexercising. In addition to severe weight loss, they also may experience decreased heart size, loss of hair, and osteoporosis.

Bulimia is more prevalent in the late teens and early to mid-twenties. Bulimics believe they are overweight and follow a binge-purge cycle. Their usually secret eating binges are followed by self-induced vomiting and use of laxatives and diuretics. Not abnormally thin, they experience shame, self-contempt, and depression. They suffer from gastric irritation and tooth decay caused by the repeated vomiting of stomach acid.

Eating disorders are extremely serious. 5% to 10% of all patients die of complications such as cardiac arrest, extreme hypoglycemia (low blood sugar), and suicide.[15] The most successful approaches to treating these disorders involve psychotherapy or behavior therapy. Teens who exhibit any symptoms of an eating disorder should be carefully observed and encouraged to seek appropriate treatment. Many patients learn to structure their time and improve their quality of life through leisure activities. Female athletes, on the other hand, are particularly susceptible to these disorders because many of them believe that losing weight will enhance performance. Body fat percentage and proper nutrition are much more relevant, however.[16] For more information, visit the National Eating Disorders Organization online at www.laureate.com/eating/nedomerg.asp.

experimenting with and expressing their own individuality and may develop friendships with people of different backgrounds and interests.

## Identity and Role Confusion

As adolescents strive to complete the major task of this life stage—establishing their own identity—they require more independence and privacy at home. Changing needs and expectations often cause family conflicts. Girls at this stage tend to stay closer to the family than do boys, but they may be moody and inward looking. Boys may become withdrawn and uncommunicative, or they may become heavily involved in sports, music, or other activities. Some boys express their feelings in aggressive, antisocial behavior, and this tendency may be exacerbated by prolonged exposure to violence either in the home or through the media.

Developing a healthy sense of identity requires strong support from family, friends, and adult leaders such as teachers, guidance counselors, coaches, pastors, and directors of youth activities. Adolescents need to feel free to experiment within structures that are safe and supportive but not constrictive or oppressive. Adults must set reasonable boundaries and rules to help teens learn respect for authority and be sensitive to the needs and rights of others. Behavior becomes more predictable and consistent as adolescents develop their identity in a positive setting.

Adolescents who have not achieved a sense of identity are said to suffer from **role confusion**. These youth exhibit erratic behavior because they have no consistent set of values, beliefs, goals, or standards to guide their behavior. Adolescents who lack a sense of identity may become strict conformists, letting the group dictate their attitudes and behavior. Teens whose emotional and recreational needs are not met by family and the community are more likely than others to form gangs,[17] which provide acceptance and offer security through elaborate rules and rituals. Others may turn to drugs, alcohol, or other self-destructive pursuits. Adolescents who lack appropriate emotional support and outlets

also may fail to foresee the consequences of their actions and take unreasonable risks in an effort to prove their self-worth.

Leisure service providers should consider the extent to which they influence the process of identity formation. One leisure educator explains[18]

> Leisure as a context for identity formation among youth can be examined from three perspectives: (1) leisure contexts provide young people with opportunities to successfully integrate both personal and social identity; (2) leisure contexts serve as a transition from childhood to adulthood; and (3) leisure contexts provide a space for embedding identities.

## OLDER ADOLESCENTS

Older adolescents are between 17 and 20 years of age. In American society, young people make the transition to adulthood in a variety of ways. These steps toward independence, if undertaken with appropriate guidance and forethought, provide positive experiences, enhance self-confidence, and promote the building of a healthy sense of identity. According to Erik Erikson, a leading figure in the field of psychoanalysis and human development, after successfully establishing an identity and a sense of independence, young people tend to return to closer emotional relationships with their families than they experienced in the turbulent adolescent years.

During older adolescence, young people usually develop an enhanced sense of self-esteem and become more emotionally stable. They take on more adult roles and responsibilities and in turn are granted more privileges. They tend to impose on themselves fewer standards of success or failure and become less concerned with what others think. Older adolescents may make a stronger commitment to a romantic relationship, although today marriage is likely to be postponed to later years. Ultimately the successful conclusion of adolescence brings increased stability and insight as well as enhanced abilities to make plans, pursue goals, and reach decisions.

*During older adolescence, young people often develop an enhanced sense of self-esteem.*

**Concept Check**

- Identify three ways in which older adolescents differ from younger adolescents.

# RECREATION FOR ADOLESCENTS

According to one study, adolescents spend about 60% of their time on essential activities such as school, personal care, and employment, with the remaining 40% available for discretionary activities (Fig. 5.4). In this section we will explore leisure-time opportunities for adolescents in two categories: youth development programs that focus on teens' social, emotional, and psychological needs and programs that are oriented toward physical activities such as sports, fitness, and outdoor adventures.

## Youth Development Programs

Adolescents want to engage in constructive activities during their discretionary time. They also want regular contact with caring, responsive adults; opportunities to contribute to worthwhile causes; and protection from hazardous and antisocial activity.

The Carnegie task force report[1] identified five themes of adolescent development that can

be used to structure community-based youth development programs:

- Young people, their parents, and other adults want such programs.
- Young people value and want opportunities to build their personal and social skills.
- Young people and adult alumni value their participation in community-based youth programs.
- Participation in such programs is especially appreciated by minority youth and youth from single-parent families.
- Participation in community-based youth development programs can promote positive behavior and reduce high-risk behavior.

Community recreation professionals have unparallelled opportunities to help adolescents through creative programming. Professionals can encourage young people to make healthful lifestyle choices by presenting videotapes, arranging for guest speakers, and sharing news and ideas from public information campaigns. Youth programs play a vital role in helping participants learn about and appreciate others of different backgrounds. Programs that focus on racism and oppression of minorities help young people develop the ability to communicate in a multicultural context. Most important, a youth center can offer young people an opportunity to express their feelings in a supportive environment under the guidance of trusted leaders.

The best source of information about what young people like and want in a youth program is young people themselves. To ensure that programming is responsive to adolescents' needs, professionals should include them in the planning process. Community programs whose leaders recognize the value of teens' diverse

**role confusion** experienced by adolescents who have not achieved a sense of identity and who tend to exhibit erratic and sometimes self-destructive behavior

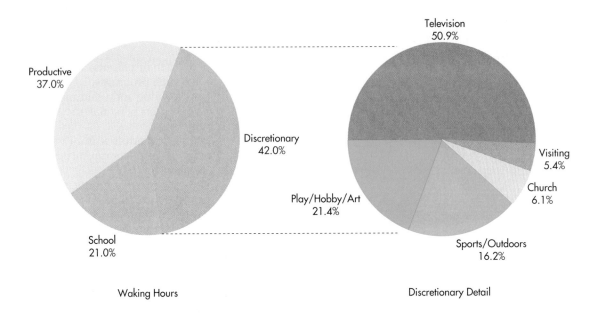

**FIGURE 5.4** Discretionary time of adolescents.

backgrounds and experiences are placing teens on youth boards. These leaders are also evaluating their current programs to make them more responsive to young people's needs and concerns. For example, teens particularly value programs that help them identify and accept who they are in terms of gender, race, and culture. Other topics of concern for today's adolescents are AIDS, sexuality, sexual abuse, and substance abuse. They are attracted to programs that involve peer responses, counseling, and mentors and that help them develop positive relationships with others and resolve conflicts constructively.

Adolescents also seek to acquire work experience and learn about career options. They often appreciate volunteer or paid opportunities to assume a leadership role—for example, by working with younger children. To respond to these needs, youth programs can teach young people vital skills such as goal setting, communication, problem solving, social competence, citizenship, and leadership.

Because families and schools often lack the time and resources to meet the many needs of adolescents, strong community programming is needed to guide adolescents during non-school hours and to give them a sense of place and belonging. Without structured, supervised after-school activities, young people are at significant risk for involvement in dangerous and illegal activities. All adolescents should have the opportunity to maximize their potential with the guidance and support of community-based programming.

Many young people from economically disadvantaged families and neighborhoods are excluded from beneficial recreational activities that are available to teens in more affluent circumstances. Lacking these opportunities, such youth are often easily led into destructive pastimes. Fortunately, more community leaders are beginning to recognize the advantages of targeting programs to youth at risk. **Youth at risk** describes adolescents who are in trouble at home or school, who may be involved in drug or alcohol abuse, and who may or may not have been brought into the juvenile justice system.[19] These young people need constructive outlets for their energy and responsible adult leadership to help them set and achieve positive goals.

Studies indicate that intervention strategies can effectively foster resilience in at-risk youth. Leisure programs and services can give youth a base by providing a caring and supportive environment, positive interaction with adults, opportunities for communication, social relationship skills, positive attention, leader involvement, high expectations, leadership opportunities, participation in planning and decision making, community service, skill development for success, and integration with prosocial peers.[20]

## Youth Recreation Programs

One study ranked the recreation preferences of an ethnically diverse group of adolescents between 10 and 18 years of age who came from both rural and urban areas of Arizona (Table 5.1). Recreation professionals may find these rankings helpful when designing programs that respond to the needs and interests of young people.

Too old for traditional playgrounds yet too young to drive, many young adolescents spend most of their leisure time hanging out in malls. Fortunately, playground designers and equipment manufacturers are beginning to address the needs of 10- to 15-year olds by designing leisure areas intended to move this age group out of the mall and back into the community. Young people can sit on benches to talk or relax; they also can use equipment to strengthen upper body, arms, legs, and hips.

Young people are strongly drawn to informal drop-in centers where they can "hang out," talk, listen to music, or participate in low-key activities in an unstructured setting without obvious adult supervision. Many teens enjoy watching movies, both comic and serious, and discussing what they've seen. Many also like computer games, table tennis, drawing murals,

> **youth at risk** adolescents who are in trouble at home or school, who may be involved in substance abuse, and who may or may not have been brought into the juvenile justice system

**TABLE 5.1** Youth Activities and Participation Rates

| FAVORITE ACTIVITIES OF YOUTH | | PARTICIPATION RATES | | ACTIVITIES YOUTH WOULD MOST LIKE TO TRY | |
|---|---|---|---|---|---|
| Rank | Activity | Rank | Activity | Rank | Activity |
| 1 | Basketball | 1 | Hanging out | 1 | Horseback riding |
| 2 | Public swimming | 2 | Spectator sports | 2 | Water jet skiing |
| 3 | Hanging out | 3 | Basketball | 3 | Downhill skiing |
| 4 | Baseball | 4 | Walking | 4 | Air sports |
| 5 | Tent camping | 5 | Private swimming | 5 | Public swimming |
| 6 | Horseback riding | 6 | Park playground | 6 | Rock climbing |
| 7 | Football/soccer | 7 | Attending a concert | | |
| 8 | Motorcycle riding | 8 | Jogging | | |
| 9 | Roller skating | 9 | Bicycling | | |
| 10 | Fishing in a natural setting | 10 | Baseball/softball | | |

dancing, and taking part in dramatic performances. Also popular with young people are sports, fitness, and outdoor adventures.

## Adventures

Many teens are attracted to adventurous and risky activities, partly because they crave excitement and partly because they believe they are invincible. Risk does not necessarily mean recklessness, and activities with an element of risk offer young people some significant benefits. Adventure programs allow teens to take on challenges; test their courage and skill; develop their leadership and problem-solving abilities; share exhilarating experiences with others; and build self-confidence, self-reliance, and self-esteem. Teens learn how to take responsibility, cooperate with others, and recognize the differences between challenge and real danger.

Community recreation programs offer a variety of constructive opportunities for adolescents to satisfy their desire for risk taking and adventure. For example, they can try wall climbing to practice the skills needed for rock climbing, and introductory scuba diving can be taught in an indoor swimming pool. Some recreation programs teach orienteering, camp-craft, and trust-based exercises, such as the rope course, that

*Teens build self-confidence as they participate in outdoor activities.*

require both individual and group efforts. Designed to develop individuals' self-confidence and build trust within the group, the rope course challenges participants to climb, swing, jump, and balance on rope and log structures while group members call out encouragement.

In addition to recreation centers, adventure classes meet at local parks, farms, or reservoirs. Both at outdoor adventure camps and in organizations such as Boy Scouts and Girl Scouts, young people can acquire outdoor survival skills, learn about nature and ecology, and improve their level of physical fitness. They also may develop expertise in horseback riding, canoeing, rafting, kayaking, sailing, cross-country skiing, and rock climbing.

Adolescents also can participate in outdoor recreation programs that focus on environmental concerns and teach the no-trace ethic. This ethic encourages the use of methods that help protect outdoor recreation areas and the surrounding environment, particularly in the back country at developed campsites, by leaving no trace of occupancy. Furthermore, lessons on air currents, river patterns, gravity, and altitude can help young people achieve an understanding of the laws of nature.

Communities must also make a wide range of adventure opportunities available to young people from economically disadvantaged backgrounds and single-parent homes, as well as to youth at risk. Perhaps to even a greater extent than their more fortunate peers, these young people can benefit from participating in carefully structured adventure programs.

## Sports

Sports opportunities for adolescents are available through many sources: schools, clubs, church/synagogue groups, YM/YWCA and YM/YWHA, youth leagues with national affiliations (for example, Little League, Youth Soccer), adult service clubs such as Rotary and Kiwanis, and community recreation programs. Club programs usually operate on a for-profit basis and charge fees to participants; in some nonprofit programs young people can participate free of charge but may be required to pay all or part of the cost of uniforms and equipment. Table 5.2 provides information about selected national youth sports programs.

Wheelchair and ambulatory sports competitions are available to young people with cerebral palsy and lower-body paralysis and to *les autres*[21] (French for "the others"), a sports term for people who have locomotor disabilities that make

**TABLE 5.2** Characteristics of Selected National Youth Sports Programs

| ORGANIZATION | AGE RANGE | COMPETITION AT NATIONAL LEVEL | EMPHASIZE FUN, SOCIAL AND SKILL DEVELOPMENT | PROVISION FOR LOW INCOME | FEE FOR PLAY |
|---|---|---|---|---|---|
| Amateur Athletic Union | N/A | Yes | Yes | Yes | Yes |
| American Youth Soccer Organization | 5–19 | Yes | Yes | Yes | No |
| Dixie Youth Baseball | 8–17 | No | Yes | Yes | Yes |
| Hershey Track and Field | N/A | Yes | Yes | No | No |
| Little League Baseball | 6–18 | Yes | Yes | No | Yes |
| National Jr. Tennis League | 8–18 | Yes | Yes | Yes | Yes |
| National Youth Sports Program | 10–16 | No | Yes | Yes | No |
| Police Athletic League | N/A | Yes | Yes | Yes | N/A |
| Pony Baseball | 5–18 | Yes | Yes | No | Yes |
| Pop Warner Football | 6–16 | Yes | Yes | No | Yes |
| Soccer Association for Youth | 6–18 | Yes | Yes | No | Yes |
| U.S. Ice Hockey Association | 5–18 | Yes | Yes | No | Yes |
| U.S. Volleyball Association | 6–adult | Yes | Yes | No | Yes |
| U.S. Wrestling Association | 8–adult | Yes | No | No | Yes |
| U.S. Youth Soccer Association | 4–19 | Yes | Yes | Yes | Yes |
| Young American Bowling Alliance | 8–21 | Yes | Yes | No | Yes |

them ineligible to compete as spinal-paralyzed or cerebral-palsied athletes. Included in *les autres* are people with muscular dystrophy and multiple sclerosis and those who have experienced amputation. The Les Autres Sports Association was organized in 1986. The world-renowned Special Olympics offers youngsters with physical and mental disabilities the opportunity to compete in a structured, supportive environment where the emphasis is on trying rather than on winning. Appendix B lists addresses of organizations that offer sports activities to persons with disabilities.

In 2000 at least 6.5 million young people in the United States participated in interscholastic sports programs.[22] Accompanying the many values of high school sports programs are concerns about exploitation of young athletes, high injury potential, emphasis on winning at all costs, long and grueling practice sessions, and the precedence given to sports over studies, social life, and other opportunities to enjoy new experiences and acquire useful skills. Pressure is increasing to restore the original purpose of school sports programs: to instill cooperation, loyalty, perseverance, and leadership skills (see the Action Guide on p. 92).

Asked to rank various aspects of playing a game, junior high students chose fairness above winning or playing well. High school students rated playing well above fairness or winning.[23] These priorities should be considered in the design of school sports programs.

Like children, adolescents benefit from unstructured as well as intramural and structured sports programs. In fact, one study showed that 70% of high school boys drop out of organized sports as early as 15 years old and never return.[24] These young people most likely prefer to play sports in a more relaxed, less competitive atmosphere. Teenagers enjoy an informal pickup game of basketball, where they can relax and socialize while shooting hoops. This also is an excellent activity for youth at risk because it offers camaraderie and peer group acceptance that such youth otherwise might

seek by joining a gang. Non-traditional sports are proving to be less calamitous than some of the traditional sports. The freestyle biking population has been exploding right along with skateboarders.[24a] In-line skating is outgrowing baseball, tennis, soccer, and many other traditional sports, while skateparks offer clinics, camps, competition, and special events.[24b]

## Music

Each generation of teenagers has its favorite music and performers, and listening to music occupies a great part of teens' discretionary time. In embracing "their" music, young people sometimes express resistance to authority and begin to move away from family and toward their peer group. Adolescents' involvement with music is a key part of their search for identity and independence. Rock music, often disparaged by parents who do not understand it, offers teens a means of creating and controlling their own culture. Music also serves as a source of information about sexuality, alternative lifestyles, politics, and racial issues. Music heightens emotions, serves as an outlet for the release of stress, and encourages movement through dancing. Teens can listen to music without doing anything else, while engaging in other activities, or while attending a party or concert.

Because music preferences may provide clues to the adolescent's mental and emotional health, experts advise parents and other involved adults to be aware of the role of music in a teenager's life. Lyrics can be found on the Internet. Music preferences sometimes reflect the problems adolescents are experiencing during their transition into adulthood. Some studies suggest that music preference may be related to school performance.[25] For instance, significant preoccupation with music may be associated with poor academic performance and with rebellion against the structures of society.

Given the rates of homicide, suicide, and pregnancy among teens, parents and other professionals understandably are concerned about popular music whose lyrics contain references to homicide, suicide, drugs, racial hatred, rape, torture, and satanism. Rock concerts have also been scenes of violence, sometimes involving serious injuries and even deaths.

Although more studies need to be undertaken, there is a respectable amount of evidence that young people are influenced by music lyrics. One study found that, of 203 chemically dependent adolescents, 59% were heavy metal fans and 79% of those had problems with violence.[26] Interpretations of music vary widely, however, and its effects may be subtle. In general, says one team of experts, healthy, well-adjusted teenagers are minimally affected by rock music. Music interpretation programs offer teens and adults an opportunity to share thoughts about music. Communication barriers can be lifted and adults may ultimately be able to help teens place life's ups and downs in a clearer perspective.[27]

**Travel**

Travel offers adolescents unparalleled opportunities to broaden their experience, increase their knowledge, and enhance their understanding of different ways of life. A major barrier to travel traditionally has been cost, but some attractive options include camping opportunities on nationnal trails, water trails, and federal lands.

Eager to see the world and to learn about themselves and others, older adolescents can also take advantage of affordable travel housing around the United States through American Youth Hostels (AYH) and around the world through the International Youth Hostel Federation (IYHF). Empty school buildings and college dormitories serve as inexpensive sleeping quarters (hostels) for cyclists, hikers, and travelers by road or rail.

Founded in 1932, the IYHF today has field study centers, cultural centers, and recreational activities for hostelers in and around the hostels. Discovery Tours, the organization's travel program, offers hiking and cycling tours for young people 15 years of age and over. Today there are approximately 5 million active IYHF members, hundreds of millions of alumni, and an operating network of 4,200 hostels recording 35 million overnight stays annually in 60 countries.

The mission of the IYHF is to help all people, especially young people, gain a greater understanding of the world and its diverse cultures. Friendships are made by sharing affordable living quarters with others. Evening programs provide opportunities to meet other travelers from around the world, and some locations offer nature hikes, lectures, and discounted trips. The IYHF program gives young people opportunities to enhance self-discovery and cultural awareness and exposes them to a variety of environments.

For both American teens and young people from other countries who are traveling in the United States and Canada, the AYH offers a wide variety of activities: historic neighborhood walking tours, nature excursions, lectures, and seminars. AYH leaders give hostelers recommendations about and directions to cultural, historic, and recreational attractions in the surrounding area. AYH councils provide local members and visitors a wide range of special programs, events, trips, and activities. Many such activities are designed for physically challenged persons, disadvantaged youth, and senior citizens.[28]

*The Cascadia Marine Trail in Washington has camping sites reserved for kayakers.*

## ACTION GUIDE

### DO HIGH SCHOOL ATHLETES GET A SPORTING CHANCE?

Were you a high school athlete, or did you choose not to be? In either case, taking this quiz can give you some insight into the consequences of your decision. Questions 1 through 5 are for students who participated in athletics; questions 6 through 8 are for those who did not; and questions 9 and 10 are for both. When you've finished the quiz, share your answers with your classmates and compare your experiences with theirs.

1. As an athlete, why did you choose to join a high school sports team?

   _____

   _____

2. How many hours per week did you devote to practice, travel to and from games, play, and pre- and post-game sessions? _____

3. Given your academic program, job (if you worked), family responsibilities, and social life, do you think the hours per week you spent on sports were excessive, just right, or inadequate? _____ Why or why not?

   _____

   _____

4. What specific benefits did you enjoy as a result of participating in school sports?

   _____

   _____

5. What disadvantages, if any, were associated with your participation in school sports?

   _____

   _____

*Continued*

An increasing number of public, nonprofit, and private organizations offer travel opportunities for youth, with the emphasis on variety, safety, and affordability.

As adolescents become young adults, their needs and desires for recreational activities begin to shift as school, work, and relationships occupy an increasing amount of their time. Moving toward middle age brings yet more changes in needs, interests, and preferences, and the post-retirement years present their own set of challenges and opportunities. In Chapter 6 we explore the evolving recreational needs of young, middle-aged, and senior adults.

## $\mathcal{A}$CTION GUIDE (cont'd)

### DO HIGH SCHOOL ATHLETES GET A SPORTING CHANCE? (cont'd)

6. As a nonathlete, why did you decide not to participate in school sports?

   _____

   _____

7. What specific benefits did you enjoy as a result of not participating in school sports?

   _____

   _____

8. What disadvantages, if any, were associated with your decision not to participate in school sports?

   _____

   _____

9. Whether you were or were not a high school athlete, have you ever had reason to regret your decision about school sports? Give reasons for your answer.

   _____

   _____

10. Whether athlete or nonathlete, in what specific ways, if any, do you think high school sports programs should be changed, and why?

   _____

   _____

   _____

   _____

   _____

**Concept Check**

- Identify ways that community recreation programs can help adolescents.

## Summing Up

- Adolescence is the developmental transition from child to adult. It begins at the onset of puberty, between 10 and 12 years of age, and ends at about 19 or 20 years of age.
- The primary challenges of adolescents are developing identity, values, independence, and mature relationships.
- Appropriately designed school and community recreation programs offer teens the opportunity to relax, socialize, and play games and sports in a supportive, positive environment.
- Such programs are particularly important for youth at risk and for economically disadvantaged and minority youth because they provide positive alternatives to illegal and dangerous activities, including drug use and gang membership.
- Recreation for adolescents is available in a variety of forms: adventure programs, sports, music, and travel.

## Using What You've Learned

1. List 10 characteristics of adolescents. For each characteristic, briefly explain how it might influence the choice of leisure-time activities.
2. Interview three adolescents about the kinds of recreation they enjoy. How might their chosen activities benefit themselves, their families, and society in general?
3. Describe a significant event in your adolescent life that occurred during or as the result of participation in a recreational activity.
4. Contact a neighborhood youth agency and determine the three most popular activities it offers. Ask if you can observe one of the activities. Take notes of your observations of the individuals and the group as a whole. How do these behaviors influence your understanding of recreational preferences during this phase of the life course?

## YOUR  Turn

1. What factors that you have learned about in this chapter make Tracy a youth at risk?
2. What factors in Tracy's life can work in her favor to keep her life on a positive track?
3. What special needs does Tracy have that a community recreation program might meet?

# REFERENCES

1. *A Matter of Time: Report of the Task Force on Youth Development* (1992). New York: Carnegie Corp., pp. 13–86.

2. Population Division (Jan. 2, 2001). Population Estimates Program. Washington, DC: U.S. Census Bureau, p. 1.

3. Harris, J. R., & Liebert, R. M. (1991). *The Child.* Englewood Cliffs, NJ: Prentice Hall, pp. 522, 659.

4. Centers for Disease Control and Prevention (Feb. 2001). *Fact Sheet: Youth Risk Behavior Trends.* Atlanta, GA: U.S. Department of Health and Human Services, pp. 1-2.

5. Modler, H. (Sept./Oct. 1997). Privilege. *San Diego Avenues* 2(3):23.

6. _____ (Jan. 2001). How to Keep Teens Safe. *Parade*, p. 21.

7. _____ (Feb. 6, 2000) Overworked Teens Running on Empty. *Washington Post*, p. A1.

8. Associated Press (Dec. 2, 1997). Clinton Asks America's Youth to 'Keep Yourselves Safe' from HIV. *The San Diego Union Tribune*, p. A-5.

9. Leblanc, A. (Dec 2, 1997). Adolescent Health in America. *American Health* 16(10):69-71.

10. U.S. Department of Health and Human Services (1999). National Household Survey on Drug Abuse. Washington, DC: U.S. Department of Health and Human Services, p. 1.

11. O'Shea, M. (Dec. 7, 1997). Better Fitness. *Parade*, p. 13.

12. Hellmich, N. (Mar. 13, 2001). Children Add the Pounds. *USA Today*, p. 13A.

13. Centers for Disease Control and Prevention (2001). *Physical Activity and Good Nutrition: Essential Elements for Good Health At-A-Glance 1999.* Atlanta, GA: U.S. Department of Health and Human Services, p. 2-5.

13a. The Associated Press (June 12, 2000). High School Trauma of Suicide. *InteliHealth Inc.*, p. 1.

13b. Edington, C. (Nov/Dec. 1997). Enabling the Future. *Journal of Physical Education, Recreation, and Dance* 68(9):15.

13c. Hudson, S. (Nov./Dec. 1997). Helping Youth Grow. *Journal of Physical Education, Recreation, and Dance* 68(9):17.

14. Papalia, D., & Olds, S.W. (1990) *A Child's World.* New York: McGraw-Hill, p. 522.

15. Bemben, D. (1993). Female Health and Fitness. In T. Thomas (Ed.), *Fitness and Health Promotion.* Dubuque, IA: Eddie Bowers, pp. 157–158.

16. Beals, K. (Sept. 2000). Subclinical Eating Disorders in Female Athletes. *Journal of Physical Education, Recreation, and Dance* 71(7):28.

17. Miller, D. (1974). *Adolescence.* New York: Jason Aronson, pp. 46–47.

18. Kivel, B. (Jan. 1998). Adolescent Identity Formation and Leisure Contexts: A Selective Review of Literature. *Journal of Physical Education, Recreation, and Dance* 69(1):36.

19. DeMers, G., & Cedillo, M. (1994). Society at Risk. *Journal/Times* 56(7):5.

20. Mundy, J. (Mar. 1996). Tipping the Scales from Risk to Resiliency. *Parks & Recreation* 3(3):78–85.

21. Auxter, D., Pyfer, J., & Huettig, C. (1993). *Principles and Methods of Adapted Physical Education and Recreation,* ed. 7. St. Louis: Mosby.

22. National Federation of State High School Associations (2001). *1999-2000 Athletics Participation Summary.* Indianapolis, IN: National Federation of State High School Associations, p. 1.

23. Phillips, J. C. (1993). *Sociology of Sport.* Boston: Allyn & Bacon, p. 95.

24. Rumpf, E. A. (Sept. 1992). Just for Fun. *Current Health* 19(1):23.

24a. Spohn, J. (Aug.2001). Doing It Right. *Parks & Recreation* 36(8):87.

24b. Winn, K. (July 1998). The Politics of Building a Skate Park. *Parks & Recreation* 33(7):63.

25. Brown, E. F., & Hendee, W. R. (September 22/29, 1989). Adolescents and Their Music. *Journal of the American Medical Association* 262(12):1600.

26. Miedziam, M. (1991). *Boys Will Be Boys.* New York: Doubleday.

27. Corwin, M. (July 2001). Listen Closely and You Will Hear. *Parks & Recreation* 36(7):108.

28. Hosteling International (1995). *The Mission of American Youth Hostels* (press kit). Washington, DC: American Youth Hostels.

How old would you be if you didn't know how old you was?

SATCHEL PAIGE

# Recreation, Leisure, and the Life Course

## ADULTS AND SENIORS

## CHAPTER 6

### THE CHAPTER AT A GLANCE

The adult population in the United States is growing rapidly, and it is an increasingly active group. Although many adults seek active recreational and leisure pursuits, some tend to be more passive about leisure. In this chapter we describe the life course of the adult, examine the mental and physical benefits of an active lifestyle, and discuss some of the most popular and successful recreation and leisure programs for adults and seniors.

### Chapter Objectives

*After completing this chapter, you should be able to*

- Describe key characteristics, goals, and interests of young adults, middle adults, and senior adults.
- Explain what is meant by successful aging.
- Describe the activity theory, the disengagement theory, and the attribution theory.
- Describe the characteristics of four personality types of seniors and explain their implications for leisure.
- Outline the issues and challenges of post-retirement life in the United States.
- State the three major goals of recreation for older adults.
- Describe some recreation opportunities available to older adults.

## A World  of Difference

### TWO FACES OF RETIREMENT

"Good morning, Helen! Isn't it a beautiful day?" Walking briskly down the corridor to the dining room, Jane Stanfield pauses to greet Helen Waters, who lives in the apartment next door at Garden Grove, the independent senior community to which Jane moved after her husband's death 3 years ago.

"Oh, hello," Helen replies without much enthusiasm. Seated on a comfortable upholstered bench in the hallway, she's been staring dispiritedly at a colorful painting on the opposite wall. It's a cottage garden scene that reminds her of the small house she and her late husband, Tom, moved into as newlyweds. How they laughed as they carried their few possessions into what wasn't much bigger than a playhouse . . . how they loved relaxing in their lovingly tended garden after dinner, watching warm summer evenings fade peacefully into darkness . . . how they rejoiced when they brought their first child, Anna, home to the tiny nursery they'd carefully decorated in sunny pastels.

*How can she be so cheerful?* Helen wonders as she looks up into Jane's smiling face. *Just like me, she's lost her husband and her home; her children and grandchildren live far away; her vision isn't good enough to let her drive anymore; . . . and here she is, smiling and acting like life is just a bowl of cherries.* Helen doesn't actually resent Jane's pleasant outlook—she just doesn't understand it. Since her husband's death 6 years ago, Helen has felt herself sinking deeper into depression and despair. It seems as if her whole life collapsed when Tom died, and now she's sitting amid the ruins of what was once a full and happy existence. She declines invitations from Jane and other neighbors to join them for bridge or

lunch; when she receives flyers about activities from the community's recreation director, she throws them into the wastebasket without reading them. Most of the time she stays in her apartment, watching television, sleeping, or just staring into space. Her health is good, but she has no energy for exercise in the community's well-equipped fitness center. For Helen, the golden years are anything but bright and shiny; all she sees is tarnish.

*I wish I could help her*, Jane thinks as she looks into Helen's almost expressionless face. *I know just how she feels. When John died after fighting cancer for 3 years, in some ways I thought I'd died with him. There were so many times I just wanted to give up . . . but I kept forcing myself to go to church every Sunday and to keep up with my volunteer work at the children's home. It was hard . . . but after a few months I stopped dreading waking up in the morning and started actually looking forward to the day. I still miss John so much, and I wish Chris and Jeannie and the grandchildren didn't live so far away, but I'm really enjoying living here because there's so much to do and so many interesting people to talk with. Sometimes I wish I still had my house and garden, but I'm having fun helping plant perennials in the new flowerbeds here, and I love watching the birds at the feeder outside my bedroom window. And now I'm starting to get really excited about the Elderhostel trip to Maine this summer.*

As you study this chapter, think about the ways in which Helen Waters and Jane Stanfield are handling the transitions involved in aging and prepare to answer the questions in Your Turn at the end of the chapter.

## ADULT STAGES

Psychological, intellectual, and social development are most rapid and dramatic during early life; however, such development continues through adult life, with discernible stages at which generally identifiable milestones are reached. Attitudes and behavior at each stage differ among adults, influenced by generational and socioeconomic factors and by individual life experiences and perceptions. For example, some people delight in reaching middle age, whereas others undergo a "midlife crisis" in which fear of advancing age causes anxiety, depression, and futile efforts to stop or turn back the clock.

By acquiring a basic understanding of the behaviors, tasks, and challenges associated with each stage of adult life, adults can become more familiar with their own needs, and recreation professionals can provide programs to meet those needs effectively.

Since the beginning of the 20th century, the average life expectancy of North Americans has risen dramatically, from less than 50 years to 75 years or more today. By the middle of the next century, life expectancy could extend into the nineties. Table 6.1 shows some trends in life expectancy over the past 5,000 years.

The fact that, on average, people are living longer today does not necessarily mean they are living well. Too many Americans are consuming high-fat diets, living sedentary lives, and dealing with a variety of stress factors. Advances in medical and scientific technology and improvements in overall living conditions will not on their own transform an aging population into fit, contented human beings. As we will learn in this chapter, recreation professionals can provide effective leisure programming to enhance the quality of adult life as life expectancy continues to increase.

Among experts in many disciplines, support is growing for a holistic approach to adult living that encompasses the physical, intellectual, emotional, social, and spiritual dimensions of activity.[1] More adults are turning to leisure education, which helps them learn about new pursuits and opportunities and which has helped eliminate barriers and encourage participation. Table 6.2 shows the percentages of American adults who participate in various activities, categorized by age, sex, race, and family income.

Another factor that affects the development of adult leisure and recreation programs is the growth trends in various age groups of American adults (Table 6.3). The U.S. Bureau of the Census predicts that for the period from 2000 to 2010 the 55- to 64-year-old age group will experience the greatest increase, from 24 million in 2000 to 35.3 million in 2010. This growth of 11.3 million persons will represent half of the nation's population increase during this period.

---

**TABLE 6.1** Average Length of Life 3000 B.C.E.–1990 C.E.

| | |
|---|---|
| Early Iron and Bronze Ages, Greece, 3000 B.C.E.–100 C.E. | 18 years |
| Rome, first century B.C.E. | 22 years |
| Middle Ages, England, 400–1400 C.E. | 33 years |
| Breslau, Poland, 1687–1691 | 34 years |
| England and Wales, 1838–1854 | 41 years |
| United States, 1900–1902 | 49 years |
| United States, 1946 | 67 years |
| United States, 1978 | 73 years |
| United States, 1990 | 75 years |
| United States, 2020 | 78 years |

**TABLE 6.2    Participation Rates for Leisure Activities by Demographic Group: 1997**

| | U.S. ADULT POPULATION (MILLIONS) | MOVIES | SPORTS EVENTS | AMUSEMENT PARK | EXERCISE PROGRAM | PLAYING SPORTS | OUTDOOR ACTIVITIES | CHARITY WORK | HOME IMPROVEMENT REPAIR | GARDENING | COMPUTER HOBBIES |
|---|---|---|---|---|---|---|---|---|---|---|---|
| **All Adults** | 195.6 | 65.5% | 41.2% | 57.0% | 75.7% | 44.9% | 44.3% | 43.2% | 65.9% | 65.4% | 40.4% |
| Male | 94.2 | 66.1 | 49.2 | 57.7 | 74.8 | 56.1 | 51.0 | 40.3 | 71.2 | 56.7 | 44.0 |
| Female | 101.4 | 65.0 | 33.8 | 56.5 | 76.5 | 34.6 | 38.3 | 46.0 | 60.9 | 73.3 | 37.2 |
| **Race** | | | | | | | | | | | |
| Hispanic (any race) | 19.1 | 59.4 | 34.8 | 66.0 | 68.9 | 34.9 | 33.5 | 31.3 | 60.6 | 58.7 | 24.9 |
| White | 146.1 | 67.5 | 44.0 | 56.3 | 77.7 | 48.0 | 50.3 | 45.1 | 69.7 | 69.0 | 42.8 |
| African American | 22.1 | 59.8 | 34.8 | 54.7 | 73.6 | 34.0 | 16.6 | 44.4 | 51.2 | 54.3 | 37.4 |
| American Indian | 3.0 | 65.4 | 34.3 | 59.4 | 82.9 | 49.2 | 51.2 | 33.6 | 57.6 | 64.2 | 37.1 |
| Asian | 5.3 | 76.1 | 28.7 | 58.0 | 69.5 | 47.9 | 45.9 | 41.4 | 58.3 | 51.5 | 61.6 |
| **Age** | | | | | | | | | | | |
| 18 to 24 | 23.7 | 88.2 | 51.0 | 76.4 | 84.8 | 66.7 | 54.3 | 35.3 | 57.3 | 46.1 | 67.7 |
| 25 to 34 | 40.1 | 78.9 | 50.5 | 70.1 | 81.6 | 62.7 | 52.5 | 40.6 | 62.7 | 59.6 | 51.2 |
| 35 to 44 | 45.3 | 73.3 | 46.4 | 68.3 | 78.5 | 51.6 | 54.5 | 49.6 | 75.6 | 71.4 | 47.1 |
| 45 to 54 | 33.7 | 65.0 | 42.3 | 53.3 | 76.9 | 40.0 | 44.7 | 46.3 | 74.6 | 70.7 | 39.9 |
| 55 to 64 | 20.9 | 46.0 | 32.9 | 40.2 | 69.4 | 19.1 | 33.0 | 43.5 | 70.6 | 68.8 | 22.7 |
| 65 to 74 | 19.6 | 38.4 | 20.8 | 28.8 | 64.9 | 22.5 | 23.8 | 39.9 | 55.2 | 75.0 | 10.6 |
| 75 and older | 12.3 | 28.2 | 16.3 | 18.4 | 55.7 | 12.9 | 13.8 | 39.8 | 44.3 | 65.2 | 7.3 |
| **Income** | | | | | | | | | | | |
| $10,000 or less | 15.0 | 36.6 | 15.0 | 38.7 | 55.3 | 19.0 | 22.9 | 31.8 | 41.7 | 56.6 | 18.6 |
| $10,001 to $20,000 | 26.5 | 45.5 | 26.0 | 50.6 | 68.9 | 27.3 | 31.1 | 34.1 | 53.4 | 58.7 | 22.3 |
| $20,001 to $30,000 | 29.4 | 56.2 | 27.9 | 54.8 | 72.1 | 40.2 | 38.0 | 36.6 | 60.6 | 63.5 | 30.1 |
| $30,001 to $40,000 | 32.1 | 70.7 | 41.7 | 63.7 | 77.2 | 45.5 | 46.8 | 46.6 | 68.3 | 65.5 | 40.2 |
| $40,001 to $50,000 | 25.9 | 72.7 | 50.7 | 66.5 | 80.3 | 50.8 | 51.6 | 41.9 | 75.3 | 70.4 | 47.1 |
| $50,001 to $75,000 | 35.0 | 82.4 | 53.9 | 65.4 | 85.8 | 59.7 | 58.4 | 50.3 | 79.6 | 69.5 | 54.3 |
| $75,001 to $100,000 | 16.2 | 81.0 | 65.7 | 64.3 | 86.1 | 60.9 | 52.2 | 51.2 | 79.2 | 72.1 | 64.4 |
| Over $100,000 | 15.5 | 86.7 | 65.4 | 56.0 | 90.5 | 66.1 | 58.4 | 59.4 | 81.4 | 69.6 | 68.6 |
| **Education** | | | | | | | | | | | |
| Grade School | 13.7 | 13.9 | 13.0 | 34.2 | 46.3 | 12.5 | 20.8 | 20.0 | 39.9 | 59.7 | 1.4 |
| Some High School | 26.9 | 51.7 | 24.6 | 54.0 | 65.5 | 30.0 | 31.8 | 30.7 | 58.9 | 57.6 | 19.1 |
| High School Graduate | 62.0 | 62.4 | 38.2 | 57.9 | 74.4 | 41.3 | 42.8 | 36.2 | 64.8 | 66.2 | 35.0 |
| Some College | 50.3 | 77.6 | 47.7 | 64.0 | 81.3 | 53.8 | 49.7 | 50.2 | 70.8 | 65.7 | 51.8 |
| College Graduate | 25.2 | 81.9 | 59.4 | 60.7 | 87.2 | 60.8 | 55.3 | 54.8 | 76.4 | 70.4 | 62.7 |
| Graduate School | 17.4 | 80.5 | 55.3 | 52.7 | 88.0 | 57.3 | 56.4 | 66.7 | 73.1 | 70.9 | 59.1 |

**TABLE 6.3** Population Expectations for the Years 2000, 2005, 2010, and 2025 (in millions)

| AGES | 2000 | 2005 | 2010 | 2025 |
|---|---|---|---|---|
| 18–24 | 26.3 | 28.3 | 30.1 | 30.4 |
| 25–34 | 37.2 | 36.3 | 38.3 | 43.1 |
| 35–44 | 44.7 | 42.2 | 38.5 | 42.4 |
| 45–54 | 37.0 | 41.5 | 43.6 | 36.9 |
| 55–64 | 24.0 | 29.6 | 35.3 | 39.5 |
| 65–74 | 18.1 | 18.4 | 21.1 | 35.4 |
| 75–84 | 12.3 | 12.9 | 12.7 | 19.5 |
| 85+ | 4.2 | 4.9 | 5.7 | 7.0 |

### Concept Check

- What is the average life expectancy of an American today?
- What U.S. age group is expected to experience the greatest increase between 2000 and 2010?

## Young Adults: 20 to 40 Years of Age

**Young adulthood** is a crucial period in the life course during which young people's focus changes from growing up to settling down. Status and privilege are no longer conferred according to age but instead derive from knowledge, skill, achievement, and business and social connections. As young adults strive for competence, self-actualization, and power, new tasks and challenges often arise before existing ones are completed or resolved. At the same time as young adults are taking on additional roles and responsibilities, their personal relationships are intensifying. Success in this stage of adulthood requires an understanding of new rules and standards, flexibility to adjust and change, and the ability to develop new personal styles and self-concepts.

The twenties generally can be characterized as a time of confidence and optimism, whereas in their thirties adults tend to become more reflective. Health choices made in these years have a tremendous effect on how well those in their twenties and thirties will age and how long they can maintain a high quality of life. This group tends to be more active than older adults and takes more risks. The National Center for Health Statistics ranks accidents—especially those involving motor vehicles and motorcycles—as the leading cause of death for people ages 20 to 34. After AIDS, accidents are the second leading cause of death for people ages 35 to 39.[2] Minor injuries can often be prevented with proper warm-up before recreational pursuits. Unfortunately, many young adults consider themselves invincible and fail to practice this technique, which becomes particularly important in the mid-thirties. Though each person responds to his or her own internal clock, aging begins at this time with a modest loss of muscle strength and bone mass. Hearing and vision become less acute, the immune system loses some of its resistance, hormone levels drop, and the body gets a little shorter every year.[3] Some weight gain can also be expected, and learning new motor skills becomes more challenging. As a result, people in their thirties start to become more concerned about their health and about signs of aging.

As young people make the transition from adolescence to young adulthood, their search for independence sometimes involves breaking away from the family, which can cause a loss of security and a sense of loneliness or isolation. Career opportunities often demand relocation and result in the loss of some friendships. The selection of a career itself is a major task of young adulthood: social and economic status; personal values, goals, and attitudes; and friendships all are affected by the choice of an occupation or a profession. Young adults who choose careers that require advanced education may find themselves almost as dependent as they were during adolescence. In contrast, the lives of unskilled or semi-skilled workers seem to move along at a faster pace because they start work right after high

*young adulthood* the period of adulthood between 20 and 40 years of age

school and tend to marry and have children at younger ages than people who go to college and graduate school.

Erik Erikson believed that adults emerge from a search for identity ready to establish more intimate relationships that require commitment, compromise, and sacrifice.[4] If a close relationship culminates in marriage, a new social role develops, and with it the challenge of new tasks. Adults who choose to have children undergo the psychological transformations associated with becoming parents. Insecurity about marital relationships and income may begin to develop. Some marriages end, forcing or facilitating the adjustments involved in adopting a new lifestyle. Some people begin second marriages.

Not all young adults marry, of course; some postpone marriage and parenthood until their middle years, whereas others choose different lifestyles. Many people choose to remain single and are perfectly content, although studies show this to be truer for women than for men. Loneliness is the greatest threat to singles who would prefer to be in relationships, and they invest a great deal of energy in looking for companionship.

Americans born between 1965 and 1976 are referred to as the post-boom generation, meaning they were born after the end of the post-World War II baby boom in 1964. Popularly called **Generation X**, they have been described as the most culturally diverse generation of adults in American history. Compared with the 77.6 million American children born in the post-war boom, the 73 million members born in the echo boom, between 1977 and 1993, and 68.3 million members born before 1946, Generation X numbers 44.6 million.[5]

A bright and savvy group, they are better educated than previous generations. Unlike most baby boomers, many Generation Xers were latchkey children who learned independence early. They came from families with high rates of divorce. Because a large number of Xers were raised in single-parent homes or homes where both parents worked, they

learned to respect women in leadership roles. Members of this generation are concerned about the future, the national debt, environmental issues, racial strife, homelessness, AIDS, and fractured families. Because of both a strong aversion to divorce and economic constraints, many Xers postpone marriage.

Generation X has been described as a group who would rather climb the Himalayas than the corporate ladder. They are less conventionally ambitious than recent generations, although they are competitive, determined, and committed. They seek a rich family and spiritual life, rewarding work, and the chance to help others. This generation cherishes the outdoors, supports preservation of natural settings, and engages in activism at the local level. Their favorite recreational activities promote social interaction and can be enjoyed outdoors and close to home. They like a wide range of fitness activities, including roller blading, yoga, tai chi, aerobics, working out with fitness videos that resemble music videos, and participating in sports and adventure programs. Generation Xers grew up with VCRs and video games and spend their discretionary income on these items, radios, electronics, mountain bikes, movies, and food. In response to one survey, 52% said they believed they would have less leisure time available to them than their predecessors,[6] but another survey showed that 96% of Xers feel very sure that they will get to where they want to be in life.[5]

**Concept Check**

- In what important respects does young adulthood differ from adolescence?
- What age group constitutes Generation X, and what are their priorities in leisure and recreation?

## Middle Adults: 40 to 60 Years of Age

The **middle adult years** begin with a transition that, according to social psychologist Daniel Levinson,[7] occurs between 40 and 45 years of age, when people realize their youth has come to a close. Most people enter middle age with feelings of satisfaction and relief at easing up on the drive toward achievement that dominates the young adult years. For some, however, growing older is accompanied by anxiety and by sometimes frantic efforts to stay young. The key task of middle age, Levinson says, is to outgrow some of the illusions of youth to build and lead a fuller, more balanced life. This is a time to develop new insights into and understanding of the self and to make choices that result in a better quality of life. Among the healthy techniques for moving through middle adulthood are taking time out for leisure and relaxation, engaging in exercise and social interaction, enjoying nature, learning new skills, volunteering, and establishing a life philosophy that focuses on values and productivity.[8]

One of the primary developmental tasks of this period is adjusting to change. The physiological changes that accompany aging take place gradually but perceptibly, and middle adults need to slow down from the faster pace of young adulthood. Bone density decreases, tissues become less elastic, wrinkles develop, and reaction time begins to slow. Both men and women experience hormonal changes, and women undergo **menopause**, or termination of menstruation, which marks the end of childbearing capability. Some women may remain fertile into their fifties, but childbirth is likely to be both riskier and more difficult. Men lose some of their physical vitality and begin to experience a decline in sexual potency. All of these changes can be emotionally as well as physically challenging for both men and women.

The physical and psychological changes that mark middle age occur at different times for different people and have varying effects on individuals. Some people want nothing more than to lie in a hammock just as others are seeking new challenges. Many middle adults discover new talents and interests and even make career changes, whereas others are grateful for job stability. While some are advancing to new heights in their careers, others are opting for early retire-

ment, while still others are retiring, retraining, and starting second careers. Some middle adults are watching their children leave home and experiencing the "empty nest" syndrome; others are just starting their families; and still others are becoming grandparents. With more time available, many empty-nest mothers continue their education, enter or re-enter the job market, or accelerate existing careers.

Many middle adults of today face the multiple challenges of caring for their aging parents, sending their children off to college, and preparing for their own retirement. The weight of these responsibilities can cause both emotional and financial strain. To complicate matters, for some people the changes of middle age cause a traumatic response known as a midlife crisis. This is a period of great upheaval during which the affected person may try to cast aside many aspects of his or her life and attempt to start over—possibly with a new job or career and sometimes even a new spouse. Some people become obsessed with their physical appearance and undergo cosmetic surgery in an effort to turn back the clock. Especially for men, there is a tendency to focus on failures rather than on successes and to see one's life as having been empty and pointless. Eventually the crisis comes to an end, and most affected people settle into middle age with a renewed sense of security and fulfillment.

### The Baby Boom Generation and Leisure Interests

**Baby boomers**, the term used for Americans born between 1946 and 1964, are the largest segment of our society, making up nearly one-third

---

*Generation X* Americans born between 1965 and 1976; this generation numbers about 41 million people

*middle adult years* the period of adulthood between 40 and 60 years of age

*menopause* termination of menstruation and the end of childbearing capability

*Rancho la Puerto in Mexico is the original health spa in North America.*

of the nation's population. Boomers are one of America's best nurtured and best educated generations. Exposed to more organized sports and other recreational activities than any previous generation, many have attained a state of fitness and well-being that some believe will forestall the onset of "old age" until they are well into their seventies. In fact, those who reach the age of 65 are now expected to live into their eighties—well beyond their average life expectancy. Millions more will live far beyond this milestone.

In addition to health and fitness, boomers place high value on service, quality, and convenience. They also enjoy a wide range of cultural interests, including theatre, dance, music, and art. They are, according to one study, stronger supporters of the environment than the generation following them.[5] Boomers consider leisure activities to be a necessity and have learned to expect a choice of enjoyable pursuits. They are not afraid to develop new skills or seek new opportunities. They make the active-adult market younger and look forward to active-adult housing rather than larger retirement communities.[9] Their future pensions will help them remain financially secure. These boomers are expected to continue to spend time and money on entertainment, including home entertainment, travel, recreational vehicles, midlife learning, and leisure pursuits.

### Middle Adult Lifestyles and Leisure

The **nuclear family** (mother, father, and children only) that predominated in the 1950s and 1960s is now just one of a variety of family structures that includes single parents, joint custody arrangements between divorced parents, and same-sex parents. New parents are almost as likely to be in their forties as in their twenties, and many more households have two working parents than in the past. As we will learn in Chapter 9, recreational and leisure interests of families depend on background, values, geographical location, socioeconomic status, age, occupation, discretionary time, and income.

Another significant segment of the adult population is single people. By 2010, the U.S. Bureau of the Census expects that more than one in seven adults will reach the age of 44 without having married. Others will be unattached as result of divorce. In addition, a Scripps Howard survey found that only about half of today's singles say that they will marry.[10] Single adults often have more discretionary time and income than do those who are married and/or have children. Many of their social commitments revolve around friends and parents. Singles often seek recreational opportunities available from commercial sources, such as cruises, sports trips, outdoor adventures, and cultural outings. Other singles turn to programs offered by religious organizations, singles clubs, and groups such as Parents Without Partners. Volunteer work and fitness activities also are popular with many singles.

Most American adults spend the majority of their waking hours earning a living. Are we working more and enjoying it less? A Louis Harris poll shows that since 1973 Americans have been working 20% more hours and have 32% less leisure time than in the past.[11] The question is, Are they enjoying it? A survey of 1,200 successful lawyers, artists, blue-collar workers, teachers, and students indicated that 80% do enjoy their work but do not enjoy their personal lives; 15% percent said they did not enjoy their work or their personal lives; and only 4% found both their work and their personal lives satisfying.[11] Living a balanced life involves learning to slow down and to make careful choices about how to use one's time. We examine these issues in greater depth in Chapter 9.

Conflicting demands on their time have caused many adults to re-examine the role their careers play in their lives. Some are backing away from intense work and travel schedules and are less receptive to relocating as a means of advancement. Between 40 and 60 years of age, when spirituality and the inner life take on greater meaning, some adults are choosing literally to reinvent their lives. Many are turning to programs in meditation, relaxation, and stress reduction to help them reduce anxiety, become more focused, and improve general health and well-being. Also useful in alleviating adult stress are such popular activities as exercise and sports, outdoor adventures, hobbies, creative endeavors, short trips, and spectator events.

Clearly, the need is increasing for both public and private recreation programs that address the physical, emotional, social, intellectual, and aesthetic needs of today's young and middle adults.

**Concept Check**

- What is a primary developmental task of middle adulthood?
- What is the age span of the baby boom generation, and what are their recreational priorities and interests?

## Senior Adults: 60 Years of Age and Over

**Senior adulthood** can be divided into two stages: *early seniors*, from 60 years of age to the midseventies, who tend to identify more with middle age than with old age; and *seniors*, from 75 years of age on, an increasing number of whom remain healthy and active for many years. Senior adults generally have more time available for leisure and welcome the opportunity for relaxation and enrichment. They may continue to participate in the same leisure activities they enjoyed in earlier years, and many are eager to try new endeavors. Opportunities for senior recreation and leisure will become increasingly important as this segment of the population continues to grow over the next several decades.

Thanks to improvements in medical care, nutrition, and fitness, as well as the healthful

---

**baby boomers** Americans born in the post–World War II years between 1946 and 1964; this generation numbers about 77 million people

**nuclear family** a family that consists only of mother, father, and children; named for the "nuclear age" that began after World War II

**senior adulthood** the period of adulthood that begins at 60 years of age

environment of many retirement communities and centers, older adults today enjoy a significantly higher quality of life than previous generations of seniors. Staying healthy and active allows many seniors to delay the decline in functioning that may lead to the loss of independence. Some experts believe that in time we actually could spend more years of our lives as older adults than as children. For example, the life expectancy for an American born in 2020 is 78.1 years, which represents 18.1 years of senior adulthood—almost the same number of years that constitute the childhood/adolescent period.[12]

The group of people age 100 and older is among the fastest-growing segments of the United States population. Demographers predict that the 61,000 people already in this age group will increase to an estimated 214,000 by 2020[13] and to half a million by 2030.[14] Many of these people will continue to be in good health well into their second century. Early studies indicate that the aging process appears to decelerate at about age 80, leveling off sharply at age 110.[15] The U.S. Bureau of the Census also expects that the 65- to 74-year-old and 75- to 84-year old segments will increase as a percentage of the population, growing from 11.4% in 2010 to 16.4% by 2025.

### Dispelling Myths of Old Age

In some societies elders are respected for their wisdom and appreciated for their contributions, whereas in others they are viewed as unproductive or even as a burden. As a society, we need to dispel unfavorable misconceptions and stereotypical notions associated with growing older. Instead, we must view and treat older adults as being worthwhile and welcome members of our society. Also to be discouraged is **ageism**, which is discrimination based on age. Older people do not inevitably experience intellectual deterioration, nor should they be tagged with such discriminatory epithets as *feeble, cranky, out of touch,* or *over the hill.* Ageism in America is combated by several organizations, including the Gray Panthers, the American Association for Retired Persons (AARP), and the National Council on Aging, which supports research into the physiological causes of aging and improvement of the quality of life during the aging process. Appendix C is a comprehensive listing of organizations that provide resources for older adults.

### Successful Aging

People age at different rates, and perhaps the most significant factor in successful aging is appropriate care of the body and mind. The old saying "You're only as old as you feel" may actually have some merit. According to some researchers, chronological age is a much less important factor than are biological age and psychological outlook. In fact, the founding director of the National Institute on Aging says, "What was old in the last century is not old anymore."[3] Several theories that have been proposed to explain the process of successful aging are discussed next.

### *The activity theory*

The **activity theory** suggests that, except for physical changes, older adults are no different from middle adults and have the same psychological and social needs. Feelings of social isolation among this age group are reduced when seniors learn to substitute new interests and activities for lost roles such as parent, spouse, or employee. In this view, the person who ages most successfully stays active and socially involved.[16] This theory does not account for people who have found satisfaction in inactivity throughout their lives and continue to do so in old age, nor does it consider the fact that no activities can replace certain roles in life that have been lost.

### *The disengagement theory*

The **disengagement theory** defines successful aging in the context of mutual withdrawal from interaction: the individual from society and society from the individual. For example, many individuals are moved to withdraw from society upon retirement or widowhood, and society traditionally has sanctioned this withdrawal. Seen as normal and mutually satisfying, such withdrawal is accompanied by increased opportunities for reflection, a growing preoccupation with the self, and a declining interest in others and the world. If one disengages before the other is ready, however, disengagement is seen as dysfunctional, resulting in a loss of morale.[17] This theory has been criticized on the grounds that substantial evidence shows that seniors who remain socially connected and active are happier than those who withdraw.

### The attribution theory

The **attribution theory** holds that the individual is constantly searching for the underlying causes of everyday occurrences in his or her life. According to this theory, people perceive causes in two ways. The first is called *dispositional*, in which the cause of an event is attributed to inherent qualities of the individual. The second form of perception is called *environmental*, in which the cause of the event is attributed to external factors or simply to luck. People who primarily use dispositional perception believe they influence events through their unique personal qualities and attitudes. People in this category tend to be confident, vibrant, and generally healthy. In contrast, people who use environmental perception tend to feel they lack control of situations and thus experience feelings of helplessness that can lead to despair.[18]

### Personality and Leisure

Researchers conducting the Baltimore Longitudinal Study of Aging report that personality is a constant after age 30, and people do not become more cantankerous as they age. However, a key to growing older lies in the capacity to make reasonable adjustments.[3] Most experts believe that positive adjustment to aging is directly linked to the ability to maintain a positive view of oneself and the world in spite of experiencing age-related changes. The validity of this notion is borne out when

we look at four distinct personality types[19] and their influence on seniors' approach to leisure.[18]

### Integrated personality

Persons with an integrated personality enjoy a high degree of self-esteem and life satisfaction. Perhaps their outstanding characteristic is their acceptance of the circumstances and experiences of their lives. They adjust well to the aging process and have a wide range of activity levels, from very active to voluntarily passive.

### Armored-defense personality

Persons with an armored-defense personality tend to rely on defense mechanisms to help them cope with the situations that arise in later life. For example, uncomfortable feelings may be repressed or "forgotten," or the individual may use denial and refuse to accept some obvious reality. These persons usually are most comfortable when continuing to engage in activities they enjoyed in middle age. Although their personalities are not fully integrated, they tend to be reasonably well adjusted.

### Passive-dependent personality

Persons with a passive-dependent personality usually rely heavily on others for motivation and emotional support. They tend to have

*ageism* discrimination based on age

*activity theory* suggests that successful aging depends on remaining active and socially involved

*disengagement theory* views aging as a process of mutual (and mutually satisfactory) withdrawal: the individual from society and society from the individual

*attribution theory* holds that whether people perceive the causes of events as being internal or external to themselves determines whether they feel confident or inadequate in dealing with situations

*Participants in Elderhostel meet others in classes, field trips, and recreational activities.*

limited interest in their surroundings and low activity levels. As seniors, their life satisfaction is most often ranked as medium to low.

### Unintegrated personality

Persons with an unintegrated personality generally have low self-concept, personal adjustment, and life satisfaction. This personality type includes the "angry," the "self-haters," and the "disorganized."[16] They generally are depressed and have a pessimistic outlook. They often blame themselves or others for their frustrations in life.

### Meeting needs with recreation programs

Recreation professionals can design programs for seniors that meet the needs of each of these personality types. Programs that offer a wide array of challenging and enjoyable activities give seniors the opportunity to assume roles and levels of responsibility with which they can be comfortable. For example, a class in woodworking would allow some participants to learn new skills. Other programs provide expertise and direction for seniors for whom familiarity and control are important. Seniors who view this time of life as an opportunity to broaden their horizons can enjoy travel, outdoor adventures, and cultural outings. For those who are responding to the aging process by disengaging, other programming challenges exist. These seniors can be encouraged to continue familiar recreational activities and social contacts with drop-in programs that do not require commitment.

### Retirement, Recreation, and Leisure

The idea that older people should stop working and retire while still in good health is of relatively recent origin. Not many generations ago older adults often worked until they died. Technological and social changes subsequently gave rise to laws that mandated retirement at 65 years of age. The Social Security Act was passed in 1935, and soon afterward private pension plans were introduced. Some businesses and labor unions developed retirement options for employees in their midfifties, and the military and some civil service entities offer options for retirement after just 20 years of service. In 1978 Congress increased the mandatory retirement age in private business and industry from 65 to 70 and removed the age limit for federal employees. Given this wide array of options, some people are choosing to retire from one position to work part-time or full-time at another.

Seniors who are financially secure can enjoy retirement by traveling, pursuing hobbies, volunteering, and simply relaxing. Even for these fortunate people, however, retirement represents a significant transition, and many react to their loss of role and status with irritability and depression. Marital disputes may erupt. Retirees literally must reorganize their lives and must make psychological, social, and financial adjustments to their new situation.

Seniors today are becoming more active and adventurous, both physically and intellectually, and recreation is playing an increasing role in fulfilling retirees' physical, educational, social, and spiritual needs.

### Physical fitness for older adults

In one survey, 95% of the respondents age 65 and older said they do exercise.[3] No age group can benefit more from exercise than older adults. Whereas a young person can increase physical function by 10% through exercise, an older person can achieve an increase of 50%.[20] Even if started late in life, exercise enhances both physical and cognitive function and allows older adults to remain independent for as much as 10 years longer than is the case for sedentary seniors. Conversely, a sedentary lifestyle has been estimated to account for 50% of the decline in aerobic capacity, strength, flexibility, balance, and reaction time—declines that trigger mobility problems and lead to the loss of independence.[21]

### Leisure education

Despite the wide variety of recreation and leisure opportunities available to older adults, some seniors complain that they are tired most of the time and have nothing to do. Others may consider recreation frivolous, inappropriate, and childish. Seniors who have this attitude lack knowledge about recreation resources and during their middle years may not have prepared for retirement. They can benefit from learning to redefine leisure and recreation in a broader perspective than simply a list of activities. They

need to understand why leisure is important for them and analyze their attitude toward playfulness and leisure. Seniors may gain appreciation for the benefits of leisure and recreation by attending classes in leisure education.

Older adults can benefit from recreation in at least three major ways, and leisure education classes emphasize these benefits. First, recreation offers seniors an opportunity to develop and maintain friendships. Second, recreation can enhance seniors' self-esteem by fostering independence, encouraging decision making and problem solving, and helping seniors make positive use of disappointments and negative experiences. Third, recreation promotes health and fitness, which enhances seniors' quality of life and may reduce the need for health care services and drugs.[22]

The immediate purpose of leisure education programs is to assist seniors in making the transition to retirement. The overall aim, however, is to help seniors enrich their lives by building self-confidence, maintaining independence, providing each other emotional support, and making commitments to specific plans of action.[23]

In designing programs of leisure education for seniors, recreation professionals must understand the factors that influence the decision to retire.[18] Among these factors are

*The Iditarod National Historic Trail in Alaska challenges adults of all ages.*

- Philosophical attitudes toward work
- Degree of job satisfaction
- Reactions of significant others
- Health
- Financial situation
- Individual interests
- Ability to adapt to change
- Current leisure pursuits

Barriers to successful retirement have been identified as

- Loss of friends through moving or death
- Loss of opportunities to give and receive nurturance
- Lack of preparation for the transition to retirement

How an individual adapts to change has a significant impact on his or her transition into retirement. A team of sociologists constructed a scale of adaptability that classifies individuals according to how well they adapt to life changes.[24] People classified as *reorganizers* are focused and are able to disengage successfully from past responsibilities. They are able to substitute new activities for their former work and, thus, are more likely to have a successful retirement. Less successful are seniors classified as *disorganized*; they have difficulty restructuring their lives after retirement and often become apathetic. On the positive side, several studies show a trend toward increased feelings of stability and satisfaction among both men and women as they enter this stage of life.[25] They are more realistic, insightful, self-sufficient, and skilled at problem solving. They are better able to engage in close relationships and are more likely to pursue interests beyond the purely personal.

### Preretirement planning

People in the middle stage of adulthood can benefit significantly from approaching retirement planning early. In this way middle adults can shape their future by examining their values and exploring their options. Preretirement programs of leisure education focus specifically on adults whose work is at the center of their lives and who may have difficulty leaving the work environment. By participating in leisure education such people can begin early to identify and participate in leisure activities that not only promote relaxation but also offer opportunities to build competence and achieve recognition. Working adults who have varied interests and a positive attitude toward leisure appear to make the transition to retirement more successfully than do those whose lives are dominated by work and who have few leisure interests.[21]

One Pre-Retirement Planning Center has identified four major areas of concern for people who face retirement.[26]

1. Role-defining activities
2. Legal and financial planning
3. Health and welfare
4. Continuing education and leisure time

Offering an opportunity for long-term preretirement planning, leisure education programs help middle and older adults acquire information that enables them to build positive images. Over 67% are planning for more recreation in their retirement years.[26a] Recreation professionals identify personal preferences, interests, and goals by means of questionnaires, wish lists, and other tools.

Some adults resist the idea of preretirement planning because they do not want to admit they are getting older. Others equate retirement with poverty, frailty, and loss of independence. It is exactly these negative notions that prevent many seniors from enjoying satisfactions and accomplishments in their post-retirement years. The reality is that today's retirees are healthier and more active, have more disposable income, and are participating in leisure activities to a greater extent than any previous generation.

Preretirement planning assistance and leisure education opportunities may be available from community recreation agencies, schools, colleges, religious organizations, corporations, and organizations such as the YM/YWCA and the YM/YWHA. Such entities can assist adults in several ways:[27]

1. Offer a wide variety of activities and courses for middle and older adults—for example, eco-tourism, organic gardening, bike repair, gourmet cooking for two, aerobics, walking, art appreciation, creative writing, preretirement planning
2. Cooperate with other agencies that offer opportunities for preretirees and retirees
3. Serve as a resource for information about group tours and other travel opportunities for older adults, as well as special packages offered by banks and retail stores and discounted services available from banks
4. Arrange to give lectures about the importance of preretirement planning
5. Realize that most older adults need to be needed and feel useful; create and coordinate opportunities for older adults to volunteer at hospitals, nursing homes, cultural institutions, literacy programs, and animal shelters, among others; serve as a resource for information about companies and other organizations in the community that are interested in hiring older workers; encourage adults to share their knowledge and experience by serving as instructors, participating in outreach programs, and giving speeches
6. Ease the transition into retirement for older adults and their children and grandchildren by providing regular intergenerational activities
7. Keep current with developments in gerontology (the study of aging) by reading and by talking with professionals in the field

**Concept Check**

- What are three theories that can be used to explain successful aging?
- In what three ways can older adults benefit from recreation?

- What factors affect how an older adult makes the transition into retirement?

## RECREATIONAL AND LEISURE ACTIVITIES

In this section we will learn about several enjoyable and challenging activities that are available to senior adults. In later chapters we will explore opportunities for all adults in outdoor recreation, fitness, hobbies, and cultural events.

### Sports

Men and women 55 years of age and over are being encouraged to enter or re-enter competitive sports by participating in the increasing variety of athletic events organized specifically for older adults. A large number of competitors are found in swimming, distance running, track and field, and bowling. Other popular sports for this age group are tennis, badminton, cycling, golf, archery, flycasting, orienteering, rowing, canoeing, sailing, trapshooting, table tennis, shuffleboard, fencing, horseshoes, and horseback riding.

In organized athletic competitions, seniors often are assigned to age groups that are divided into five-year segments, such as 55 to 59. Tournaments and championships are held at the local, state, national, and international levels. The U.S. National Senior Sports Classic, a biennial event hosted by the U.S. National Senior Sports Organization, is open to adults 55 years of age and over and offers competitions in 18 sports, including the triathlon, track and field, basketball, tennis, swimming, and cycling.

The first World Masters Games were held in Toronto, Canada, in 1985. Most events had a minimum age of 35 for men and 30 for women. Entrants competed in 22 sports and included 1,600 swimmers, 500 rowers, and 64 ice hockey teams. The opening day festival featured a parade in which athletes marched in groups organized by age rather than by country.

The United States Senior Olympics made its debut in St. Louis in 1987 with 2,500 participants. Within eight years, the participation rate rose more than 300% when over 8,000 seniors took part in the U.S. National Senior Sports Classic V.

The first World Veterans Games, the biennial masters track and field championships, were held at the University of Oregon. This program is designed for adults 35 years of age and over. In 1999, the 13th World Association of Veteran Athletes (WAVA) Games, held in Gateshead, Great Britain, attracted 5,804 men and women from 66 countries. Competitors ranged from 35 to 96 years old.[28]

The United States Masters Swimming program, which was started in the early 1970s, is one of the fastest growing participatory/competitive adult sports programs in the country. Open to adults 19 years of age and over, the program emphasizes swimming for health and fitness and offers competitive swimming to age groups in five-year increments, all the way up to 95 years of age and over.

Participation in competitive sports benefits older adults in many ways. Training regimens help seniors improve fitness and health. Competition enhances skills, builds self-confidence, and offers opportunities for social interaction.

## Travel and Adventure

The nation's leisure industry is shifting focus to seniors' travel as this segment of the population continues to grow.[13] Older adults can choose from a wide variety of opportunities for travel and tourism both within the United States and around the world. Many travel packages designed for seniors are discounted, and itineraries are structured with seniors in mind. Guided tours provide a measure of safety and security that many seniors find more comfortable than traveling on their own. Adventure tours, such as windjammer cruises, whale-watching excursions, and music cruises, also are popular with older adults. In addition, more Americans age 60 and over are participating in physically challenging, muscle-powered outdoor activities than ever before.[3]

The trend toward edu-tourism is also growing.[29] For older adults who seek opportunities to acquire knowledge and take on challenges, perhaps the premier program is Elderhostel, which offers short-term, inexpensive academic programs throughout the United States and the world (see A Closer Look on p. 113). Adults and their families are finding educational travel experiences at the Disney Institute in Orlando, at resorts, on cruises, and through universities, museums, and other institutions. A number of travel agencies are also specializing in tours to educational destinations.

## Reminiscence Programs

At one time or another, all of us reminisce. From a philosophical perspective, reminiscing qualifies as contemplation, which Greek philosopher Aristotle believed to be the highest form of leisure. Reminiscing can be a very rewarding use of leisure time. Programs of recreational reminiscence encourage participants to recall positive experiences through guided exercises that result in sharing, focusing, and preserving memories.

Participants write their memories in play or narrative form, record them on audiotape or videotape, or document them in a scrapbook or notebook illustrated with personalized artwork or photographs. Sharing memories with others adds a new dimension to the lives of the participants, the program leader, and relatives who are eager to learn more about their loved ones. Reminiscence programs are also offered to residents of nursing homes to stimulate both long-term and short-term memory while promoting social interaction.

As a process, recreational reminiscing has three elements: sharing, focusing, and preserving. A program leader encourages a participant to share reminiscences in a small group. The leader serves as a receptive audience and helps

# A CLOSER LOOK

## ELDERHOSTEL: ADVENTURES IN LEARNING

Elderhostel, a new movement in American adult education, began in 1975 with a small number of programs offered on New England college campuses. Today nearly 250,000 older adults attend programs conducted by some 2,000 institutions located in every American state and Canadian province and in more than 45 other countries.

Students live modestly on college campuses or at other educational or commercial facilities. Faculty members or other experts teach classes on a not-for-credit basis. Students are of all educational levels and backgrounds, and there are no class preparations, homework, exams, or grades. Participants have the opportunity to socialize and to enjoy a variety of extracurricular offerings that include sightseeing trips and cultural and recreational activities.

Programs vary widely, from intensive classes that focus on a single subject to programs designed to foster interaction among different age groups. For example, young people from local schools or colleges might be invited to join hostelers. Special programs are offered for persons with hearing impairment and for people with mobility challenges. Seasonal catalogs that describe current Elderhostel programs are sent to every public library in the United States. The spirit of Elderhostel encourages older adults to enjoy adventures in learning, to visit new locations, and to have the pleasure of making new friendships.

and prevents the reminiscence session from becoming a life history recital.

A participant who chooses to document memories in a scrapbook or notebook can personalize the material by choosing artwork or photographs to illustrate the narrative. The scrapbook also might contain items such as old letters and other documents as well as samples of the participant's work, such as a piece of a handmade quilt. The completed scrapbook can be photocopied and bound for preservation; additional copies can be made for family members. The process is especially rewarding for families who are geographically separated. At a later time participants may add new chapters to their reminiscences. Using the Action Guide on p. 114, you can learn first-hand how to design a reminiscence exercise.

Another way in which older adults can share reminiscences is by participating in a playwriting class where their own lives serve as material for intriguing or inspiring dramas. With help from program leaders, seniors can use both high and low points of their lives to create scenes, develop characters, write dialogue, and set time periods for various phases of the action. In developing characters, participants can draw on their own memories or exchange reminiscences with other participants. In many cases engaging in this playwriting exercise helps participants work out personal conflicts and tragedies and shows them how to draw on their own creative resources to enjoy new and rewarding experiences.

the participant minimize ambiguity and focus on specific events. In some cases the participant may be asked to complete a questionnaire before the sharing session. This technique ensures confidentiality, helps the participant feel comfortable and in control of the process,

## In-Home Recreation

Many older adults do not participate in leisure and recreational activities outside their homes because of health challenges, poor vision, mobility problems, lack of access to transportation, fear of crime in their neighborhoods, or

## ACTION GUIDE

### MAKING MEMORIES LAST

You've undoubtedly listened to an older relative recall what life was like in the "old days." Over the past 50 years, so many changes have taken place in society and technology that senior adults often feel as if they're living in a different world.

Listening to their stories about the past, you may have trouble believing that there was ever a time when people didn't have television, dishwashers, or computers; didn't shop at malls; and walked to school instead of drove. Here's a way for you to temporarily enter your older relative's "lost world":

1.  Ask an older relative to share his or her reminiscences with you.

2.  If he or she is willing, make an audio or video recording of the session, and invite your relative to prepare a scrapbook to augment the recording.

3.  How did your relative respond to this invitation to reminisce?

    _____

    _____

4.  What feelings did he or she seem to be experiencing while recalling people and events from the past?

    _____

    _____

5.  On the basis of this experience, what do you see as the advantages to seniors of sharing reminiscences?

    _____

    _____

6.  If you see any disadvantages, what are they?

    _____

    _____

7.  In what ways did you benefit from participating in this reminiscence exercise with your older friend or relative?

    _____

    _____

lack of knowledge of available programs.[30] As a result, these seniors often suffer from boredom and social isolation. Recreation and leisure professionals can provide relief and improve the well-being of these seniors by taking services to their homes and encouraging them to participate. In-home recreational activities such as hobbies, crafts, card and table games, and special interests engage the interest of homebound adults and promote social interaction. As such, they are an attractive alternative to watching television, sleeping, or remaining idle.[31]

As the U.S. population continues to age, the need is increasing for older adults to remain independent and to avoid or delay receiving institutional care. In the 1950s, people entered nursing homes at about age 65. Now they are more likely to be in their eighties.[3] In-home recreational activities can help seniors remain mentally alert, socially involved, and psychologically well adjusted. The challenge for

*Recreational activities help seniors remain mentally alert, socially involved, and psychologically well-adjusted.*

recreational providers is to market their services effectively to the participants and their adult children.

## Summing Up

◆ Life expectancy in the United States today averages about 75 years, compared with about 50 years at the beginning of this century. It could extend into the mid-nineties by the middle of the 21st century.

◆ Young adulthood is the period between 20 and 40 years of age; it is a period of settling down as opposed to growing up and is characterized by striving in the areas of career, marriage, and family.

◆ Middle adulthood, the period between 40 and 60 years of age, is a time for recognizing and accepting the end of youth, for easing up in the struggle for achievement, and for learning techniques for healthy aging.

◆ Given the variety of lifestyles in American society today, the need is increasing to develop programs of leisure and recreation that respond to the interests of these different groups.

◆ Older adulthood begins at 60 years of age and is a time for retirement planning, relaxing, reflecting on achievements, and developing new interests and pursuits. In this regard, many seniors benefit from attending programs in leisure education and preretirement planning.

◆ Personality type is a strong influence on seniors' attitudes toward recreation and leisure.

◆ Among the enjoyable activities available to seniors are sports, Elderhostel, reminiscence programs, and in-home recreation programs.

## Using What You've Learned

1. Interview three adults—one young adult, one middle adult, and one senior adult—about their leisure activities, taking special note of their preferences and how their chosen activities affect their lives. Prepare a three-page report for class.

2. Interview three adults of any age group about the priority they assign to leisure and recreation in their lives. Observe and take note of the constraints or lack of constraints in each person's schedule. On the basis of the information you have gathered, what recommendations would you make to the directors of local recreational facilities that would be helpful to these adults?

3. Call your local Chamber of Commerce or other appropriate agency and ask for a list of senior day centers or senior communities for active adults. Visit one and take note of its recreational facilities and programs. Are the facilities and programs responsive to seniors' needs and constraints? In what specific ways? What roles do the seniors themselves play in the programs? Report your observations in class.

## YOUR  Turn

1 Of the theories of aging you learned in this chapter, which seems to apply to Helen Waters? To Jane Stansfield? Give reasons for your answers.

2 Think about some older adults you know—perhaps your grandparents—and try to determine which theory of aging applies to each person.

3 Helen and Jane appear to have similar backgrounds. What factors do you think might account for their different responses to the changes that come with aging?

4 Based on what you have learned in this chapter, what would you suggest as ways to help Helen Waters enjoy her senior years?

# REFERENCES

1. Mahon, M., & Searle, M. (1994). Leisure Education: Its Effect On Older Adults. *JOPERD*.

2. Clark, C. (Oct. 6, 1996). Chart Health Path in 20s and 30s. *The San Diego Union Tribune*, p. H-10.

3. Shute, N. (June 9, 1997). A Study for the Ages. *U.S. News & World Report* 122(22):69, 72, 78.

4. Erikson, E. H. (1963). *Childhood and Society*. New York: W. W. Norton & Co., p. 266.

5. Hornblower, M. (June 9, 1997). Great Xpectations. *Time* 149 (23): 58, 62.

6. Richardson, J. E., & Sago, B. (1993). Baby Busters: The Neglected Generation. *Marketing 93/94*. Guilford, CT: Dushkin Publishing Group, Inc., p. 97.

7. Levinson, D. (1977). The Midlife Transition: A Period in Adult Psychosocial Development. *Psychiatry* 40(99):112.

8. Bruess, C., & Richardson, G. (1992). *Decisions for Health*. Dubuque, IA: Wm. C. Brown Publishers, pp. 510, 511.

9. Heavens, A. (July 23, 2000). Baby Boomers Likely to Reinvent Retirement Living. *The San Diego Union Tribune*, p. H12.

10. Hargrove, H., & Stempel III, G. (Feb 12, 1998). Those Who Said "I Do" Would Take the Same Mate Again. *The San Diego Union Tribune*, p. E-3.

11. Keeler, G. (August 15, 1993). Block That Stress! Limit Your Choices. *The San Diego Union Tribune*, pp. D1 and D8.

12. Gibbs, N. (February 22, 1988). Grays on the Go. *Time* 131(8):70.

13. Cowley, G. ( June 30, 1997). How to Live to 100. *Newsweek* CXXIX(26):58, 63.

14. El Nasser, H. (Dec. 29, 1997). Age-Old Question: Why So Healthy? *USA Today,* p. 2A.

15. Wade, N. (Jan 28, 1998). Fountain of Youth May Not Be Myth. *New York Times News Service*, p. E-1.

16. Havinghurst, R., Neugarten, B., & Tobin, S. (1968). Disengagement and Patterns of Aging. In B. L. Neugarten (Ed.), *Middle Age and Aging*. Chicago, IL: University of Chicago Press, p. 160.

17. Cummings, E., & Henry, W. (1961). *Growing Old*. New York: Basic Books.

18. MacNeil, R. D., & Teague, M. L. (1987). *Aging and Leisure: Vitality in Later Life*. Englewood Cliffs, NJ: Prentice-Hall, pp. 144–145, 330–331.

19. Personality types devised by MacNeil and Teague from personality typologies produced by Richard, Lirson, and Peterson (1962) and by Neugarten, Havinghurst, and Tobin (1968).

20. Toufexis, A. (February 22, 1988). Older but Coming on Strong. *Time* 131(8):79.

21. Jones, C. J., & Rikli, R. E. (1993). The Gerontology Movement—Is It Passing by Us? *JOPERD* 64(1):19-20.

22. Tabourne, C. (1992). Name That Tune. *Parks & Recreation* 27(4):82.

23. Thompson, R., & Cruse, D. (1993). Leisure Awareness and Education: Preparing for Retirement. *JOPERD* 64(4):36–37.

24. Neugarten, B. L. (1968). Adult Personality Toward a Psychology of the Life-Cycle. In B. L. Neugarten (Ed.), *Middle Age and Aging*. Chicago, IL: University of Chicago Press.

25. Van Hoose, W. H., & Worth, M. R. (1982). *Adulthood in the Life Cycle*. Dubuque, IA: Wm. C. Brown Publishers, p. 50.

26. MacNeil, R., & Teague, M. (1987). *Aging and Leisure*. Englewood Cliffs, NJ: Prentice-Hall, p. 331.

26a. Shapiro, J. (June 28, 1999). No Sunset for Sun City. *U.S. News & World Report* 126(25):78.

27. Blanding, C. (1992). Planning for Retirement: Can We Help? *Parks & Recreation* 27(3):38–40.

28. World Association of Veteran Athletes (2000). *Latest News* www.wava.org/latest_news/.

29. Holdnak, A., & Holland, S. (Sept 1996). Edu Tourism: Vacationing to Learn. *Parks & Recreation* 31(9):73.

30. MacNeil, R. D., Teague, M. L., McGuire, F. A., & O'Leary, T. T. (1986). *Aging and Leisure: A Literature Synthesis*. Washington, DC: U.S. Government Printing Office, p. S-107.

31. Wilhite, B. (1992). In-Home Alternatives. *JOPERD* 63(8):45.

*To be able to use leisure intelligently will be the last product of an intelligent civilization.*

BERTRAND RUSSELL

# Recreation, Leisure, and Society

In this chapter we examine recreation and leisure as they are affected by the social system and its substructures: the family, religion, government, economics, and technology. Each of these substructures in turn has individual components—law, science, education, the media—and we consider each of these in the context of its relationship to recreation and leisure.

## Chapter Objectives

*After completing this chapter, you should be able to*

◆ State the four criteria a human group must meet to be called a society.
◆ Explain the structure of a social system.
◆ Explain how a society is influenced by its culture.
◆ Define and explain *customs* and *mores*.
◆ Explain how leisure and recreation are influenced by the social subsystems of family, religion, government, economics, and technology and by the individual components of each subsystem.

## THE NATURE OF SOCIETY

*W*hat impact does society and its structures have on play, recreational activities, and leisure pursuits? To answer this question, we first must determine what constitutes a society. A society may be broadly defined as an enduring and cooperating social group whose members have developed organized patterns of relationships through interactions with one another.

## A World  of Difference

### NATURE AND SOCIETY: A DELICATE BALANCE

"Let's hit the beach!"

Christy Morelli brakes her rusty old pickup to a sand-scattering halt and leaps out the door, followed by three eager friends who are relieved to escape from the hot, tiny cab. It's a perfect beach day: brilliant sun, temperature in the low 80s, and a brisk offshore breeze. Christy and her friends, Andrew, Sean, and Kathy, unload coolers full of soda and food, blankets, towels, a bright beach umbrella, and the ubiquitous boombox. They've chosen a nearly deserted stretch of beach near the federal marine preserve, so they feel free to turn up the volume and kick back.

Delighted by the terrific weather, the idyllic beach scene, and the temporary freedom from work, school, and parents, the friends laugh and talk: college plans, the upcoming Pearl Jam concert, who is—and isn't—dating whom. They apply sunscreen to each other's back, pass around bags of chips and pretzels, and watch small planes crisscross the horizon, trailing their messages: "Frank's Foot-Long Subs," "Tan—Don't Burn," "Salt Water Taffy 4th & Atlantic."

A couple of hours later, noticing that his companions have started to doze off, Sean stands up, pulls on his T-shirt, and starts walking toward the marine preserve. It's posted "No Trespassing: Authorized Personnel Only," but his curiosity prevails and he carefully enters the preserve. At first this quiet area looks no different to him from the rest of the beach, but soon he's hovering over a tidal pool, fascinated by the rich variety of plant and animal life in this tiny universe. He begins to recall lessons from the unit on marine life in his honors biology class and wishes he had a notebook to record his findings.

Walking farther down the beach, Sean is dismayed to see its pristine surface littered with styrofoam cups, aluminum cans, and plastic six-pack holders. He's angry, sad, and frightened to think that this fragile, beautiful place, teeming with life, is being threatened by careless humans who use the beach for their own enjoyment and leave their trash to pollute the environment and endanger wildlife.

Across the water he hears the angry snarl of a big outboard engine and sees a glittering powerboat pulling up at the jetty. The driver jumps off, leaving the huge engine running, and lights a cigar. He's soon joined by friends who load coolers, bait buckets, and fishing rods onto the boat. That task finished, the driver reboards the boat with his friends and tosses his cigar onto the jetty, where it's quickly followed by the crash of a beer bottle. The engine at full throttle, the boat blasts back into open water with its laughing passengers.

*I don't get it*, Sean thinks. *How can they—we—all of us—be so careless with our natural resources? Why can't we have fun without wrecking the environment? I'm no saint where all this is concerned*, Sean thinks, *but I know there has to be a better way.*

As you study this chapter, think about the relationship between leisure behavior and the environment, and prepare to answer the questions in Your Turn at the end of the chapter.

Four criteria are used to classify a human group as a **society:**

- The group is capable of living longer than the life expectancy of any individual member.
- The society acquires new members mainly through sexual reproduction.
- The members are united in allegiance to a general system of action.
- The system of action is self-sufficient, with defining roles, statuses, goals, rewards, and punishments.

At the core of any social system is the system of action mentioned above. The impact of that system on human behavior, including leisure behavior, varies according to the degree of sophistication in the society. For example, the system of action of a small tribal society determines who will play the role of warrior and thus achieve the concomitant status of hero. In a modern industrial society, however, there is no need for a warrior class; its heroes are athletes and entertainers, who achieve high social status by virtue of their wealth and celebrity.

Despite the difference in sophistication between these two kinds of societies, roles and statuses within each are reinforced through the same kind of mechanism: positive sanctions, or rewards, and negative sanctions, or punishments.

The social system in turn exists within two larger systems that have a direct impact on social life: the cultural system and the physical environment (see Fig. 7.1). The cultural system surrounds the social system and to a great extent determines the society's values and norms (see Chapter 3). The physical environment strongly affects the structure of a society. For example, a tribal society whose land is fertile; well endowed with water, game, and vegetation; and protected by natural barriers may have no need for a warrior class to seek out and conquer other territories. The society instead needs classes of farmers, hunters, and possibly guards to defend the desirable territory from

invaders. As these examples make clear, a social system is directly affected by its interaction with its culture and its physical environment.

Sociologists agree that a social system consists of five basic subsystems:

- family
- religion
- government
- economy
- technology

Later we will examine each of these subsystems in terms of its relationship to recreation and leisure. First, however, we will consider the social system in the context of the larger entity within which it exists: its cultural system.

## The Cultural System

As we learned earlier, a culture is a system of norms and values that define what is acceptable behavior in a society. In many societies, for example, a central value is "Work is good" and its corollary, "Idleness is bad." The rewards for adherence to these and other norms and values

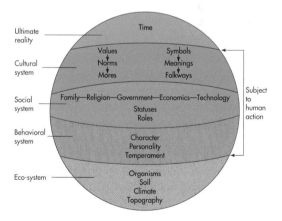

**FIGURE 7.1** *Society and its environment.*

*society* an enduring and cooperating social group whose members have developed organized patterns of relationships through interactions with one another

are acceptance and a sense of belonging and security; the consequences of nonadherence include disapproval, rejection, and ostracism. Each society also adopts norms and values concerning the scheduling and use of leisure time. In contemporary Western societies, for example, evenings and weekends are generally acknowledged to be appropriate times to engage in leisure pursuits, and individuals can choose from a wide variety of acceptable solo and group activities. Generally considered unacceptable are pastimes that offend prevailing public notions of decency, that are illegal, that harm or endanger other persons or animals, or that cause damage to property.

### Customs

Cultural norms evolve over time into **customs**: the whole body of usages, practices, or conventions that regulates social life. Customs are enforced not by law but, rather, by informal social control. Americans customarily celebrate the new year by drinking champagne and cheering when the clock strikes midnight on December 31. It is perfectly legal to perform this social ritual on January 31 or at any other time—but it is not customary to do so.

### Mores

A culture also establishes and expects conformance to a set of **mores**: the fixed, morally binding customs of the group. Some societies, for example, establish moral prohibitions against cheating at games, playing while one should be working, and using one's money for leisure pursuits instead of for the support of one's family. In many cases informal social control is sufficient to enforce conformance to a society's mores; in other cases conformance must be achieved by more formal means.

### Laws

When informal social control is inadequate to ensure conformance to mores and values, a society may adopt the more formal approach of establishing and enforcing laws. Basing laws on accepted cultural values facilitates law enforcement because the typical member of society already has internalized these values and adheres to them as a matter of course. When the desired behavior is not internalized, formal social control becomes important for enforcement. Persons who see no need to stop for a red light are penalized for their behavior. In recreation and leisure, government entities have laws that govern fishing, boating, swimming, cycling, skateboarding, horseback riding, and the use of public recreational facilities from national parks to local playgrounds. Laws also are enacted to create and maintain national, state, and local parks, forests, and beaches.

We next begin to explore the influences on recreation and leisure of the five major social subsystems: the family, religion, government, economics, and technology. We also consider the impact of recreation and leisure on the ecosystem.

**Concept Check**

- What are the five subsystems of a social system?
- What is the difference between customs and mores?

## THE FAMILY

The basic social unit is the **family**, which traditionally consists of two parents rearing their own or adopted children. As we learned earlier, in the post–World War II "nuclear age" this structure was dubbed the nuclear family. A family that also includes relatives such as grandparents or cousins is called an **extended family**. Despite the changes in family structures, such as step families, one-parent families, and so on, the family still plays a very important role in the socialization of the young.

As the primary agent for socializing children, the family plays a key role in introducing children to recreation and leisure pursuits. In this process parents teach their children values as well as skills, and children benefit psychologically from interacting with other family members while engaging in pleasurable pursuits.

Although the notion that the family that plays together stays together is not supported by research,[1] it has been found that leisure in which parents and children participate is satisfying only to the fathers.[2] Nevertheless, studies conducted on the family's role in socializing children into leisure, recreation, and play show that activities in which children take part during childhood through age 13 will be continued into adulthood.[3] The family's role in leisure experiences, recreational activities, and forms of play is discussed further in Chapter 9.

## RITUAL AND RELIGION

Ritual and religion exert a powerful influence over human behavior, including leisure activities. As we learned earlier, some scientists believe the human brain may actually have a center for ritual that causes people to seek and establish rituals in their lives. The ancient Greeks were motivated by their religious beliefs to participate in physical activities. This participation led eventually to the establishment of an elaborate sports competition, the Olympics, which was intended to please and honor the Greek gods. The gladiator contests and chariot races staged by ancient Romans were also rooted in religious myth and ritual. The early Christians, in contrast, frowned on such activities. As the influence of Christianity expanded, the games that once flourished in Athens and Rome sank into oblivion.

With the spread of Roman Catholicism throughout Europe, the church's holy days began to be superimposed on pagan rituals. In the 16th century, distressed by what they saw as corruption and excess in the church, reformers such as Martin Luther and John Wycliffe rejected many of the church's doctrines and practices. Their work gave rise to the Protestant Reformation and the establishment of Protestant churches. Subsequently, King Henry VIII of England broke away from the Roman Catholic Church when it refused to grant him a divorce. In 1635, he formed the Church of England, a key force in the Protestant movement.

When the British began to colonize North America in the early 17th century, a key motivation of the first settlers was freedom from religious strictures imposed by England. The Puritans, a group of Protestant religious dissidents, wielded strong influence over every aspect of life in the colonies, especially in New England. Although the Puritans sought religious freedom for themselves, they sought to impose their own rigid code of behavior on other settlers. They forced adherence to their strict observance of the sabbath as a day of worship. They also established and enforced stringent prohibitions against what they viewed as ungodly amusements such as cards, dice, dancing, dramatic performances, and other leisure activities.

After the colonies achieved independence from England in 1776, the new nation began to expand geographically and to attract immigrants from throughout Europe. The variety of cultural and religious traditions thus introduced served to dilute the influence of the Puritans and to increase tolerance for different lifestyles, including leisure pursuits. Religious organizations were and continue to be centers of social and leisure activities for their members,

---

**customs** the whole body of usages, practices, or conventions that regulates social life

**mores** the fixed, morally binding customs of a group

**family** the basic social unit, traditionally consisting of two parents rearing their own or adopted offspring

**extended family** a family that includes other relatives such as grandparents or cousins in addition to parents and their children

particularly new immigrants who seek support and companionship as they learn to adapt to life in their adopted country.

Today many religious institutions in America sponsor leisure activities to promote camaraderie among their members and to provide wholesome opportunities to achieve balance in their lives. Among their offerings for young people are sports teams, camps, youth groups, and scout troops. Also available are a variety of activities for adults, ranging from sports to social outings to discussion and special-interest groups. Some religious organizations use sports as a means of recruiting new members throughout the world; examples are the Fellowship of Christian Athletes and Missionary Athletes International.

With the rise of secularism in modern times, coupled with the ideologies of socialism and liberalism, it seemed to many observers that religion's role in people's lives would gradually become less important. On the contrary, religion is witnessing a resurgence that is expected to continue for some time.[4]

- What is an extended family?
- Identify three ways in which religious organizations may influence leisure behavior.

# GOVERNMENT

Throughout history, people of all social and economic classes have pursued their own forms of leisure activity, regardless of the prevailing form of government or political structure. As we learned earlier, the leaders of early societies often claimed for themselves the choicest leisure pursuits and sometimes used their power to prevent members of the lower classes from engaging in certain leisure activities. With public pressure and outright revolution spurring the emergence of democratic and republican forms of government, power and authority began to be shared between rulers

and representatives of the people. One consequence of this sharing was the removal or dilution of traditional strictures on leisure activities.

## Local Government

In the United States, local government was a representative structure from the start, with each town being governed by a committee of men chosen by citizens to supervise the town's affairs. Initially these committees' agendas were not concerned with recreation or with the preservation or use of open space. As towns expanded in size and population, however, natural resources were subjected to abuse, and local governments initiated efforts to protect them. Governments also took steps to establish public recreation sites, such as the creation in the 1850s of New York City's Central Park on an 843-acre site in the middle of the city.

A leader in the U.S. public recreation movement was renowned social worker Jane Addams, who established the famed Hull House settlement in Chicago in 1892 for members of the poor and underprivileged classes. In 1892 a model playground was opened at Hull House. In 1908, after a meeting with President Theodore Roosevelt, Addams and others organized the Playground Association of America, predecessor of the National Recreation and Park Association.

Following the example of New York City, other large cities established their own parks, and smaller municipalities followed suit. Today every large city in the United States has at least one major public park and several smaller neighborhood parks. Parks in large cities offer a wide array of facilities for both cultural and physical leisure pursuits.

Local government has become less important in American's lives during the past few years. Its diminished role can be attributed mainly to the general shortage of funding caused by reduced taxes. Local recreational programs have suffered from budget declines, and many local parks and recreation departments have found it necessary to resort to fundraising, a practice often used by semi-public agencies such as the Boy Scouts and the YMCA. This situation is expected to continue, with pressures on inadequate budgets becoming even greater. An increase in the U.S. population, particularly among the elderly and the very young, will increase the demand for leisure services. To meet this demand, local parks and recreation departments may have to become revenue-generating agencies.[5]

## State and Provincial Government

According to one expert, state and provincial governments can support the public recreation efforts of cities and counties through:[6]

- *Legislation*: Laws passed by an elected body allow local governments to impose taxes so they can provide services such as community recreation centers and playgrounds.
- *Resources*: Most states and provinces have open spaces that could be used as public parks, beaches, and forests.
- *Programs*: States and provinces can sponsor recreation programs on their own land or on historic sites.
- *Conservation*: State and provincial governments can pass laws to promote conservation of natural sites used for recreation.
- *Standards*: State and provincial governments should provide staff for recreational activities and should set the standards for behavior in public recreational settings.
- *Promotion*: States and provinces should participate in public relations campaigns that promote local and regional recreational facilities and tourism.

## Federal Government

In both the United States and Canada, the most important role of the federal government in recreation and leisure is to establish and maintain national parks, forests, beaches, and other sites. Another significant role is the allocation of funds to support facilities and programs at the regional, state, and local levels.

The U.S. government is responsible for public recreation and leisure in the following ways:[7]

- Ownership and management of approximately 740 million acres of land that have potential for recreational use. These lands constitute approximately one-third of total U.S. acreage
- Grants to state and local governments for the acquisition of land and facilities and for the organization of recreational programs
- Regulation of such leisure pursuits as boating, camping, fishing, and hunting, as well as setting standards for environmental quality
- Regulation of concessionaires and recreational programs in national parks, forests, and historic sites
- Conducting research and providing technical support to regional and state agencies in planning and constructing new facilities and developing relevant programs
- Coordinating the efforts of federal government agencies that deal with natural resources, such as the National Park Service, U.S. Forest Service, and Bureau of Land Management
- Overseeing international agreements related to outdoor recreation in areas such as water quality, fish and game, and tourism

Further discussion on the roles of the three levels of government is provided in future chapters.

### Concept Check

- Name three ways in which state governments support the efforts of local governments to provide recreation services.
- Name three ways in which the federal government help state governments provide recreation services.

# ECONOMICS

The nature and status of a society's economy are inextricably linked with the society's leisure-related attitudes, opportunities, and practices. One authority has identified three levels of an economy: primary, secondary, and tertiary.[8] In a **primary economy**, the majority of the labor force is engaged in farming and extractive work (for example, mining and drilling for gas and oil). A **secondary economy** is based on manufacturing, and an economy at the **tertiary** level is service based. A society's evolution through these three economic stages is a function of technological advancement.

It has been suggested that technological advancement in America thus far has taken place in three stages:[9] a scientific revolution early in the 17th century, followed by the industrial revolution from 1750 to 1850, which marked the transition from an agricultural to a manufacturing economy; and, beginning around 1850, the discoveries and inventions that transformed the economic landscape in terms of travel, communication, and entertainment. Advances in science and technology continue to proliferate in America and in other highly developed economies, spurring the ongoing transition to a strongly service-based global economy.

According to one expert, these economic developments have strongly influenced the leisure attitudes and practices of contemporary societies in three ways. First, increased productivity creates more discretionary time that can be devoted to leisure pursuits; second, increases in discretionary income expand people's leisure and recreation options; third, technological advances permit the production of more recreational equipment and facilities.[10]

## Expenditures on Leisure and Recreation

The U.S. Bureau of the Census estimates that personal expenditure on recreation and leisure increased from $116.3 billion in 1985 to $282.6 billion in 1990 and $401.7 billion in 1995. Today it is approaching $500 billion. Most of the spending increase was generated by the purchase of sport, photographic, audio, video, and computer equipment and products and admission to spectator amusements, such as theme parks, theatres, and sport events.

During the same time period, recreational travel also increased dramatically. Census Bureau figures indicate that the number of pleasure trips of 100 miles or more rose from 301.2 million in 1985 to 361.1 million in 1990 and reached 413 million in 1995. The average household on these trips comprised 1.9 people, who stayed an average of 3.8 nights and traveled an average of 781 miles by car. In 1995, the household income of 47% of these travelers was less than $40,000 per year. The other 53% of travelers earned a household income greater than $40,000 per year.[11]

## Economic Benefits of Leisure

Participation in leisure pursuits may produce economic benefits in several ways. First, individuals who engage in healthful recreational activities may become more productive and thus increase their earning power. Second, such increased productivity may benefit employers. Other beneficiaries are the entities that provide leisure goods and services: equipment manufacturers, sporting goods stores, health clubs, fitness trainers, resorts, spas, the travel industry, and professional sports teams and entertainers. Promoters, broadcasters, and the owners of event venues also stand to gain financially from the public's interest in spectator sports and other forms of entertainment, as do the product manufacturers who receive endorsements from star athletes and entertainers. Also benefiting from the public's pursuit of leisure are movie, play, and television producers, the owners of movie theatres and live theatres, and the writers and publishers of the vast array of magazines and books devoted to every conceivable aspect of leisure and recreation.

## Future Economic Trends

Many societies are still trying to achieve modern industrial status. The societies that already have attained this status, such as the United States, for many years have been developing models that suggest the shape of the post-industrial society, including the nature of recreation and leisure.

Some scholars suggest that beyond the tertiary economy we discussed earlier is a **quaternary economy** in which a shorter workweek will permit more participation in leisure pursuits of all kinds: amusive, recreational, and contemplative. Another prediction for the future is based on the HE/SHE model of society. The HE model posits a hyperexpansionist society that continues to emphasize economic growth. In this model, values and goods are quantitative; priorities are masculine; and emphasis is placed on organizational values, rationality, contractual relationships, money, technocracy, and specialization. In contrast, the SHE model envisions a sane, humane society in which feminine priorities predominate. Values and goals are qualitative; human development is emphasized over economic growth; relationships are intuitive, experiential, and empathic; and real needs and aspirations take precedence over money. In both the HE and SHE models, the author predicts that pleasure travel, hobbies, and personal development efforts will increase.[12]

**Concept Check**

- Name the three ways in which economic developments influence leisure attitudes and behavior in contemporary society.
- Identify five entities that benefit from contemporary societies' pursuit of recreational and leisure activities.

## TECHNOLOGY

In the preceding section we learned that a society's economy evolves as the result of technological advancement, which in turn creates opportunities for greater numbers of people to participate in leisure activities. Although, as observed earlier, people at even the lowest socioeconomic levels traditionally have been able to enjoy at least some form of leisure, not until the industrial revolution peaked in the mid-1800s did the average person have access to the time and money necessary to engage regularly in leisure pursuits. As you can see in Fig. 7.2, working hours in the United States gradually declined as the result of increased mechanization and the use of time-saving devices. Thanks to technology, the average workweek decreased from 53+ hours in 1890 to about 40 hours today. And the demand for more free time continues.[13]

In the sections that follow we examine two aspects of technology: the material and the social. Material technology encompasses scientific knowledge and skills and their application—that is, industrialization. Social technology embraces education, both formal (as acquired by attending school and college) and informal (as acquired through travel and by visiting cultural institutions); the mass media, both print and electronic; and amusements such as movies and the theatre.

## The Scientific Revolution

The industrial revolution of the 18th and 19th centuries and the electronic revolution in which we are living today are solidly based in a scientific revolution that began in the 16th century. Observations of the natural world led

---

*primary economy* an economy in which the majority of the labor force is engaged in farming or extractive work

*secondary economy* an economy based on manufacturing

*tertiary economy* a service-based economy

*quaternary economy* a predicted post-industrial economy in which more time will be available for recreation and leisure

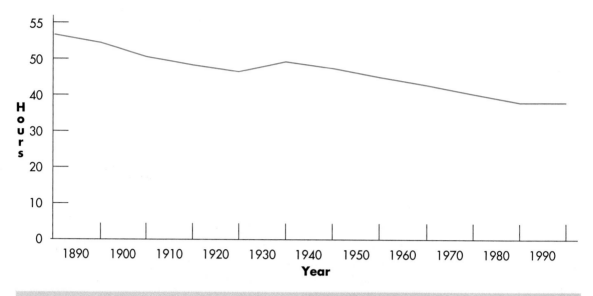

**FIGURE 7.2** Average weekly hours per worker, U.S., 1890-1990.

Italian astronomer and physicist Galileo to declare that the earth revolves around the sun and not the reverse (an idea condemned as heresy by the Roman Catholic Church). In the 17th century, Isaac Newton, a British mathematician and physicist, discovered the principles of gravity that underlie the study of matter and motion. Later scholars attempted to use scientific observation to understand human and animal behavior, thus laying the foundation for the development of two key sciences: biology and psychology.

Medical professionals and others used important discoveries in biology to improve people's health and the quality of their living conditions. The study of biology also persuaded many physicians of the benefits of sports and physical culture. In 1887, 25 physicians attended a meeting of physical education that resulted in the formation of the American Association for the Advancement of Physical Education (AAAPE).[13] Today this organization is called the American Alliance for Health, Physical Education, Recreation, and Dance (AAHPERD). A few years after the formation of AAAPE, the Playground Association of America was formed. Later it was renamed the National Recreation and Parks

Association (NRPA). AAHPERD and NRPA are the two most important professional associations in the field of leisure and recreation.

Influential psychologists such as William James and William McDougall helped explain and enhance understanding of the value of play and leisure in a society that was still dominated by Puritan attitudes.

Through biology and psychology, the foundations were established for Americans of all ages to enjoy a lifestyle that is both playful and healthful. The scientific revolution, which helped change old attitudes and support new values, was to be enhanced by another important revolution, the industrial revolution, which continues to have a great impact on contemporary recreation and leisure.

### Industrialization

In addition to the increase in leisure time made possible by mechanization and automation, industrialization has had a strong impact on the evolution of leisure in modern society. For example, the invention of the steamboat and the train not only allowed people to travel for pleasure but also enabled traveling entertainment troupes to visit towns and cities throughout the country. These inventions, followed later by the airplane, also facilitated the expansion of both intercollegiate and professional sports competitions. Perhaps the single greatest impact on individual leisure pursuits, however, has been exerted by the automobile, which was invented in the late 19th century

(see A Closer Look below).

The harnessing of electrical power permitted significant increases in opportunities for night-time leisure activities such as dances, parties, concerts, and sporting events. The invention of the camera drew many people into the new leisure pastime of photography. The creation of

## A CLOSER LOOK

### THE AUTOMOBILE: LEISURE ON WHEELS

Few if any inventions have altered the American landscape as radically as the automobile. When the first "horseless carriages" started rolling down American roads in the 1890s (using technology pioneered by German automakers Daimler and Benz), skeptics and detractors vastly outnumbered enthusiasts. Many intelligent and thoughtful people believed the automobile was a passing fancy, a rich man's conceit, and towns passed elaborate laws governing the behavior of motorists. Children in rural areas delighted in gathering at the site of a broken-down automobile (a frequent occurrence in those early days) and mocking the hapless driver with the taunt "Get a horse!"

In 1914 Henry Ford was using a moving assembly line to produce his vastly popular Model T, which was largely responsible for putting America on wheels. Simple and economical, the Model T was the first reliable automobile to come within reach of the average American. No longer forced to rely on public transportation, families found their horizons expanding along a growing network of roads and highways.

As auto design and technology became increasingly refined, drivers were offered a dazzling variety of choices in makes, models, horsepower, colors, and levels of luxury. Low-slung speedsters and glamorous 12- and 16-valve luxury cars began to share the road with modest family sedans. Governments started to finance construction of the highways needed to accommodate the increasing tide of vehicular traffic as America took to the road for everything from daily commuting to family outings. The year 1933 marked the birth of an American institution, the drive-in movie theatre, proof of the indelible mark the auto-

mobile was making on the nation's culture. Drive-in restaurants and roadside taverns began to flourish, offering both food and entertainment to their new patrons, and motels and tourist courts started popping up along increasingly well-traveled highways.

Increasingly, Americans were identifying themselves and others by the vehicles they drove: big and glamorous, like the elaborately tailfinned Cadillacs of the 1950s; sleek and racy, like the wildly popular Corvette and two-seater Thunderbird; sedate and reliable, like the utilitarian family station wagon. Convertibles were for carefree, fun-loving types; the old wood-sided station wagon, or "woody," became the emblem of the California surfer crowd and its landlocked admirers; British sports cars were the vehicles of choice for the children of the affluent; and for decades the Volkswagen "Beetle" was prized by college students for its high gas mileage and economical maintenance. Beat-up vans with handpainted motifs often served as homes for hippies on the road, and the 1965 Mustang dashingly introduced the era of muscle cars. In the 1990s reverse chic came to rule the road. Rejecting the gas guzzlers driven by their parents, baby boomers made sport utility vehicles their emblem—glamorized trucks with a rugged look and lots of luxury appointments. The once-humble pickup truck was streamlined and upgraded with extended cabs, air conditioning, power locks and windows, and cruise control.

In the more than 100 years since its birth, the automobile has had a deep and wide-ranging impact on almost every aspect of leisure in America. As such, it truly merits the label "leisure on wheels."

synthetic materials such as nylon, dacron, and fiberglass has enabled manufacturers to produce more durable and longer lasting equipment for boating, hunting, fishing, camping, and mountain climbing. At the same time, the invention of snow- and ice-making devices allows for longer skiing seasons and for ice skating in the summer. The development of sophisticated electronic technology has literally revolutionized contemporary lifestyles with such inventions as the telephone, the phonograph, radio, television, and computers. On the leisure side, such technology permits fishermen to locate fish by sonar depth sounding, allows for automated scorekeeping in sports such as bowling, and has given birth to the rapidly growing video game and slot machine industries.

## Education

The traditional function of education has been to prepare young people of varied socioeconomic backgrounds for the roles and duties they will assume as adults. The primary focus has been on training young people for an occupation or profession, the latter often in combination with education in the humanities. Although competitive sports programs had been offered at private schools for centuries, it was not until the early 20th century that progressive educators began to advocate incorporating play and recreation into the educational experience for all young people.

One such educator was John Dewey, who suggested that

> . . . education has no more serious responsibility than making adequate provision for the enjoyment of recreative leisure, not only for the fact of immediate health but still more for the fact of its lasting effect upon habits of the mind.[14]

Progressive educators such as Dewey spearheaded major transformations in the American educational system and in Americans' attitudes toward and practices of leisure.

A wide variety of programs supplements the academic curriculum in today's schools and

colleges. These programs broaden young people's cultural horizons, help them achieve physical fitness and develop sports skills, and generally prepare them to enjoy productive leisure pursuits. Among these offerings are

- ◆ *Music*: Students can take courses in music appreciation and music theory, receive vocal and instrumental training, and participate in a chorus, glee club, band, jazz combo, or orchestra as well as in recitals and other performances.
- ◆ *Arts and crafts*: Students can learn drawing, painting, photography, ceramics, sculpture, printmaking, silkscreening, jewelry design, glassblowing, woodworking, metalworking, leathercraft, needlework, and a host of other skills.

- *Drama*: In addition to reading and studying plays in academic coursework, students can participate in skits, pantomimes, puppet shows, musicals, and plays. They also can learn related skills such as stage set design, lighting, costume making, direction, and production.
- *Physical education*: In Chapters 4 and 5 we learned in detail how young people can benefit from participating in appropriately structured school-sponsored programs of physical education. Through such participation, young people can develop interests and skills that will lead to enjoyable leisure pursuits throughout their lives.
- *Outdoor education*: Many schools sponsor extracurricular programs for students who are interested in botany, biology, astronomy, geology, ecology, and the environment. Here students can put to work the knowledge they acquire in the classroom and can gain experiences that may lead to lifelong interests, or perhaps even a profession or career.

As we learned in Chapter 6, leisure education itself is gaining prominence as the U.S. population ages and the need increases to provide leisure services to senior adults. If, as many experts anticipate, technological advances continue to allow workers more discretionary time,

*High-tech materials have influenced leisure activities. This synthetic surface makes it possible to play broomball in socks rather than in skates.*

*Outdoor education.*

there will also be an increase in demand for leisure education for younger people as well as for seniors. More and more people will want to learn how to live rewarding lives outside of their employment and how to make productive and enjoyable use of their leisure time.

## The Media

The media, both print and electronic, are a powerful force in shaping attitudes in contemporary society. The key media we will consider here are newspapers, magazines, radio, and television. Both print and electronic media perform two key functions: disseminating information and providing entertainment. Reading, listening, and viewing are themselves forms of leisure activity, and the media also offer countless opportunities to learn about popular leisure activities and lifestyles.

### Newspapers

Perhaps the best evidence of the impact of newspaper journalism on leisure behavior can be seen in the area of sport. Historian Peter Levine suggested that the role played by newspapers (and radio) in reaching millions and shaping a national cultural experience encouraged the development of sport as a commercial venture that set the tone for the 20th century.[15] In the last three decades of the 19th century, owners and editors of newspapers across the country realized the scope of popular interest in sport. Although sport was covered by many newspapers, it was publishing giant William Randolph Hearst who developed the first sports section in his *New York Journal*.[16] Today virtually every daily newspaper has a sports page or section.

Over the past several years many American newspapers have begun to include a section devoted to leisure pursuits. Called "Leisure," "Arts and Leisure," "Lifestyle," and a host of other names, this section contains features on movies, books, and events in the arts: exhibit openings, concerts, plays, musicals, the opera. Also included may be one or more features on cooking, often with a gourmet flair or emphasis on healthful, "light" eating. The section contains listings of television and radio programs and movies and is a popular advertising vehicle for providers of leisure goods and services.

Despite their efforts to cater to people's demand for information, including news of recreation and leisure, newspapers today are in a state of decline because of competition from electronic media. The number of daily papers is declining, and existing papers are experiencing a serious decrease in both advertising revenue and number of subscribers.

## Magazines

In comparison with newspapers, American magazines are enjoying a reasonably good state of health. The American magazine industry celebrated its 250th anniversary in 1991. As it enters the 21st century, it is pursuing a new direction and emphasis with the aim of becoming more responsive to readers' changing needs and tastes. Despite a difficult period in which many well-established magazines disappeared from the market, since 1988 a total of 491 new magazines have entered the scene.[17]

Not surprisingly, the hot market today is at either end of the age scale: young people and older adults—the two groups of Americans who have the most free time.[18] Another important development in magazine publishing is an increase in the number of highly specialized magazines, many of which are designed to appeal to the leisure interests of specific groups. For example, sports and fitness magazines are published for males and for females, for young people and for seniors. Numerous magazines are available for lovers of the outdoors (fishing, hunting, camping) and for hobbyists of all descriptions: gardeners, stamp collectors, photographers. Also popular are travel magazines, some of which are aimed at affluent Americans and others that focus on rustic accommodations. Health, wellness, and fitness magazines cater to people of every age and interest in today's culturally diverse America.

## Radio

With the introduction of radio technology in the early part of the 20th century, the United States and ultimately the entire world were swept into an entirely new area of both information and entertainment. Beginning in the 1920s, the radio gradually became the center of home entertainment as families gathered to listen to comedies, dramas, westerns, soap operas, serials, sporting events, news broadcasts, and, of course, advertisements for every conceivable kind of product. People in even the most remote rural areas suddenly gained access to a whole world of news, information, and entertainment that previously was unavailable to them. Until the advent of television in the late 1930s, radio ruled supreme as the predominant mass media vehicle, influencing the attitudes, tastes, perceptions, and choices of millions of listeners around the world. Despite the influence of television, radio continues to be a powerful force in contemporary society; according to one study, there are 2.3 radios for every person in America.[19]

## Television

By the end of World War II in 1945, astonishing strides in electronic technology were enabling the launch of the vast, powerful, and ongoing television era. Throughout the postwar era, television has played a powerful role in shaping American culture. Watching television continues to be one of the most popular leisure pursuits in the United States: 74% of the respondents to one study said they watched television an average of almost three hours a day.[18] Use the Action Guide on p. 134 to check out your television viewing habits.

As with radio, television initially was a family affair, with everyone gathered around one black-and-white set to watch comedy and variety shows, westerns, and dramas. Today many homes have sophisticated big-screen color TVs as well as several smaller sets so each family member can watch what he or she chooses. Truly dedicated (or obsessed) viewers can even carry tiny portable sets wherever they go. Over the past 50 years, television programming has broadened exponentially beyond the white, middle-class family situation and variety shows of the early days, when blacks and other racial and ethnic groups were largely either ignored or parodied. On the negative side, TV producers are coming under increasing fire for what many viewers believe are excessive sex and violence in programming.

Not only is television viewing itself a widely popular leisure activity, but also the lifestyles portrayed on much current programming have a strong influence on people's perception of "the good life." Many TV characters are attractive, fit, and well dressed; live in glamorous homes; drive expensive cars; and seem to spend little time working and much time playing.

As with radio, although on a much larger scale, television is an extremely powerful vehicle for disseminating advertising messages about countless products and services, many of them related to leisure and "the good life." Advertisements urge viewers to take cruises, install swimming pools, purchase fitness equipment, visit gambling casinos, and travel to huge theme parks. Groups of carefree young people cavort and socialize while drinking beer. Cheerful, wholesome-looking families prepare for adventure by loading up costly sport utility vehicles. Shapely women and well-muscled men boast glowing, "healthful" suntans acquired by using "safe tanning" products with sunscreen. Professional athletes endorse a host of merchandise, subtly creating in many viewers' minds the perception, that if they purchase the athletic shoes, the swimsuit, or the sports beverage, they will be buying themselves a bit of reflected glamour and glory.

With the advent of cable television in the early 1970s, the television menu became increasingly broad and varied. Viewers can now choose from a vast menu of comedy, drama, sports, news, documentaries, music, and special-interest programming, such as art, science, education, women's issues, senior citizens' forums, and a wide variety of offerings for children. While sitting in your living room you can earn college credit, watch a major heavyweight fight, or follow a floor debate in Congress. Television technology marches on, and the next big breakthrough, interactive TV, will allow individual viewers to select programming to suit their particular tastes and schedules.

## The Computer and the Internet

About four of every 10 homes in the United States have at least one personal computer. This relatively new technological tool has changed many aspects of our lives. The computer affects leisure, recreation, and play in two ways. First, the computer speeds the tempo of life itself. The Babylonians introduced the world to the concept of the minute, which comprises 60 seconds; the computer has introduced us to the nanosecond, a unit of time equal to one-billionth of a second. Although such a fleeting span of time cannot be experienced by humans, its effect will be to necessitate more precise measurement of time.[20]

Second, the personal computer erodes free time gained as a result of the industrial revolution. Television has already encroached on that valuable time and has encouraged an unhealthy, sedentary lifestyle. Daily use of the computer, and especailly the Internet, may have the same result.

On the bright side, the computer provides opportunities for contemplation, which Greek philosopher Aristotle considered to be the highest form of leisure.

# ACTION GUIDE

## TV VIEWING—WHAT'S YOUR SCORE?

If you're like most people, you spend some time watching television almost every day. By answering the questions in this quiz, you can identify your particular TV viewing patterns and gain insight into why you watch what you watch as well as how your tastes, attitudes, and behavior are being influenced by your choice of TV fare. For one week, keep a detailed daily log of your television viewing, following the format shown below for each program or event you watch.

1. Date/day of week _____

2. Program/event watched (title and/or description) _____

3. Watched alone or with others? _____

4. Why did you choose to watch this show or event?

   _____

   _____

5. What specifically did you like or dislike about this program or event?

   _____

   _____

6. What did you do when commercial messages came on?
   a. Ignored, changed channel, or left room
   b. Watched, but with little interest or attention
   c. Actively liked or disliked some commercials

7. Why did you behave/react the way you did during commercial breaks? Which commercials did you like? Why? Which did you dislike? Why?

   _____

   _____

8. In what specific ways, if any, were your tastes, attitudes, and desires influenced by watching this program/event and the accompanying commercial messages?

   _____

   _____

At the end of the week, review your responses and ask yourself whether you are satisfied or dissatisfied with your viewing habits and what if any of those habits you might want to change.

- Identify five leisure-related educational opportunities available to today's students.
- State three ways in which your own leisure tastes, attitudes, and behaviors are influenced by your television viewing habits.

## RECREATION, LEISURE, AND THE ENVIRONMENT

Leisure behavior is affected by and has an impact on the physical environment in which members of a society live, work, and play. To a great extent our choices of leisure and recreational activities are shaped by factors such as geographical location, climate, and topography. People who live in the mountains of the Northwest can enjoy skiing and snowshoeing; those who live on either coast or on large lakes can choose from a variety of water sports; and the desert Southwest offers a wide range of land-based activities.

As North Americans take to the outdoors in increasing numbers, many natural resources are becoming crowded with people, especially on weekends and during the summer. Such mass leisure activity represents a serious threat to the delicate balance of the ecosystem and its components: water, vegetation, and wildlife. The number of visitor hours spent in federal recreation areas increased by almost 25%, considerably more than the U.S. population grew in the last two decades.[21]

A major concern over the increasing recreational use of fragile natural resources is the environmental problems created by such use. Examples are air and water pollution, forest fires, and destruction of plant life and wildlife. Destruction of freshwater aquatic systems has led to the extinction of many species of fish. Also affected by human use is the estuarine system, which is the coastal area over which the tide ebbs

and flows and which includes the wide mouth of a river flowing to the sea. The food chain has been severely disrupted by decisions to convert some of these areas into real estate developments. Dredging of estuaries to create canals and marinas is equally as destructive to sea life.

On seacoasts, human activities, including leisure pursuits, have adversely affected marine ecosystems. *Offshore iceberg* is the term used to describe the masses of discarded cups, cans, bottles, and straws that gather at the end of the surf line. Coral reefs that have existed for thousands if not millions of years are being destroyed by humans in pursuit of leisure. Pleasure boats crash into them; swimmers bump, scrape, and stand on them; and undisciplined persons yank pieces of them for souvenirs.

At the same time, forests are disappearing at an alarming rate. Careless campers start forest fires that ravage thousands of acres, destroying vegetation and wildlife. The North American prairie, which at one time supported innumerable species of wild game, is being depleted of its wealth of wildlife. Equally tragic is the wanton destruction of our fragile deserts by the users of vehicles such as motorbikes, dune buggies, and ATVs.

Innumerable laws to protect the environment have been passed at all levels of government, with the objective of allowing appropriate recreational use and enjoyment of nature while preserving its precious resources, yet it is not laws but, rather, human decency and concern that ultimately have the greatest power to save our environment. Leisure experiences, recreational activities, and forms of play will undoubtedly be affected by a growing population, changing demographics, increased urbanization, diminished energy resources, global warming, and water scarcity.

In this chapter we have discussed recreation and leisure largely in terms of their relationship with North American society. In the next chapter we will widen our perspective and explore the international aspects of recreation and leisure.

## Summing Up

♦ A society exists within a cultural system that by various means creates and enforces the society's values, norms, customs, mores, and laws.

♦ A social system can be seen as consisting of five subsystems: the family, religion, government, economics, and technology.

♦ The family is the basic unit of social life; by socializing children, it affects their recreation and leisure-related attitudes and behaviors.

♦ Ritual and religion form the basis for much leisure activity, such as the celebration of holy days and the honoring of deities through pursuits such as the Greek Olympics. Religion also defines what kinds of leisure activities are and are not acceptable for adherents.

♦ Governments at the local, state, and federal levels serve as both guardians and providers of many recreation and leisure opportunities.

♦ A society's level of economic achievement determines both the time and income available for leisure pursuits.

♦ Technology, both material and social, influences a society's recreational and leisure activities in many ways. Science and industry facilitate leisure pursuits with inventions such as the automobile and television; education and the mass media provide information on how to enjoy recreation and leisure.

♦ To a large extent the kinds of recreational opportunities available to people are determined by the physical environment in which they live: geographical location, topography, and climate.

♦ Overuse and abuse of fragile natural resources by recreation and leisure seekers are destructive to the environment and to the delicate balance of the ecosystem.

♦ Concerned citizens and governments seek to protect the environment through prudent management of natural resources and through enactment of laws to regulate their use.

## Using What You've Learned

1. Write a three-page paper on your first leisure pursuit. Who or what influenced you to become involved in it? Discuss the role of whichever of these factors is applicable: family, religion, school, television.

2. Contact your state's department of parks and recreation and request a list of the facilities it provides. Write a short summary of your findings.

3. Visit a nearby elementary school. What formal and informal activities for students might influence their future choice of leisure pursuits?

4. Make an appointment with your local public librarian. Find out what books and magazines the library is purchasing in these areas related to recreation and leisure: sports, fitness, travel, hobbies, relaxation. Approximately what percentage do these materials represent of the library's total collection?

5. Visit a county, state, or national recreation area. Ask various tourists to identify their favorite pursuits and find out from the on-site manager what activities are permitted and prohibited in the area.

## YOUR  Turn

1  When you use a natural area for recreation and leisure, what responsibility, if any, do you feel to preserve the environment?

2  What would you do if you saw someone—friend or stranger—in some way causing harm to a natural recreation area?

3  How do you feel about powerboats, snowmobiles, dune buggies, and ATVs being used in natural recreation facilities designed for public use?

4  Whatever your response to question 3, how, if at all, do you think accommodation might be reached between the users of these mechanized devices and people who believe they should be banned from natural recreation facilities?

## REFERENCES

1. Mannell, R. & Kleiber, D. (1997). *A Social Psychology of Leisure.* State College, PA: Venture Publishing.

2. Russell, R. (1996). *Pastimes: The Contemporary Context of Leisure.* Madison, WI: Brown & Benchmark, p. 133.

3. Bradshaw, R., & Jackson, J. (1979). Socialization for Leisure. In H. Ibrahim & R. Crandal (Eds.), *Leisure: A Psychological Approach.* Los Alamitos, CA: Hwong Publishing.

4. Zeldin, T. (1994). *An Intimate History of Humanity.* London: Harper.

5. Godby, G. (1997). *Leisure and Leisure Services in the 21st Century.* State College, PA: Venture Publishing, pp. 18–55.

6. Kraus, Richard (1984). *Recreation and Leisure in Modern Society.* New York: Appleton-Century-Crofts, pp. 51-55.

7. McLean, J., Peterson, J., & Martin, D. (1985). *Recreation and Leisure: The Changing Scene.* New York: Macmillan, p. 116.

8. Clarke, C. (1942). *The Economics of the 1960s.* London: Macmillan.

9. Johnson, R., & Brown, T. (1991). Beneficial Economic Consequences of Leisure and Recreation. In B. L. Driver, et al. (Eds.), *Benefits of Leisure.* State College, PA: Venture Publishing.

10. Kahn, H., et al. (1976). *The New 200 Years: A Scenario for America and the World.* New York: Wm. Morrow & Co.

11. Statistical Abstracts of the United States (1992). *Characteristics of Business Trips and Pleasure Trips: 1980-1990.* Washington, DC: U.S. Government Printing Office, p. 245.

12. Robertson, J. (1985). *Future Work: Jobs, Self-Employment and Leisure After the Industrial Age.* New York: Universe Books.

13. Boggis, J.J. (2001). The Eradication of Leisure. *New Technology, Work and Employment* 16:2.

14. Dewey, John (1921). *Democracy and Education.* New York: Macmillan, p. 48.

15. Levine, P. (1989). *American Sport: A Documentary History.* Englewood Cliffs, NJ: Prentice-Hall, p. 98.

16. Eitzen, D. S., & Sage, G. (1993). *Sociology of North American Sport.* Madison, WI: Brown & Benchmark, p. 39.

17. Tebbel, J., & Zukerman, M. E. (1991). *The Magazine in America: 1741-1990.* New York: Oxford University Press, p. 371.

18. United Media Enterprises (1983). *Where Does the Time Go.* New York: Newspaper Enterprise Association.

19. Statistical Abstracts of the United States (1994). *Telephone, Newspapers, Television and Radio by Country.* Washington, DC: U.S. Government Printing Office, p. 866.

20. Russell, R. *(1996) Pastimes: The Contemporary Context of Leisure.* Madison, WI: Brown & Benchmark, p. 241.

21. Statistical Abstracts of the United States (1980, 1990, 2000). *Visitation to Federal Recreation Areas, by Administering Federal Agency: 1980 to 1992.* Washington, DC: U.S. Government Printing Office.

If we are to achieve a richer culture, rich in contrasting values, we must recognize the whole gamut of human potentialities, and so weave a less arbitrary human fabric, one in which each diverse human gift will find a fitting place.

MARGARET MEAD
*Sex and Temperament in Three Primitive Societies*
(1935)

# The International Scene

## CHAPTER 8

## THE CHAPTER AT A GLANCE

This chapter attempts to show the universality of leisure behavior. Article 24 of the United Nations Declaration of Human Rights emphasizes that everyone has the right to rest and recreation, including reasonable limitation of working hours and periodic holidays with pay. Samples from the Western bloc, Eastern bloc, and Third World nation are presented here to show that some nations are doing that. For each nation we trace the history of recreation and leisure and then learn about some popular current pursuits and activities.

## Chapter Objectives

*After completing this chapter, you should be able to*

◆ Define the terms *Western bloc, Eastern bloc,* and *Third World.*
◆ Identify popular leisure pastimes in countries of each of the above three areas.
◆ Discuss the impact of politics, religion, and culture on recreation and leisure in the three areas of the world studied in this chapter.

## WESTERN BLOC

Western bloc, Eastern bloc, and Third World are political classifications that came into use after World War II when communism became a powerful ideological force in eastern Europe in competition with the democracies, republics, and constitutional monarchies of western Europe and its allies. The **Western bloc** is a group of noncommunist countries with free-market economies, including the

## A World  of Difference

### BUILDING BRIDGES ACROSS CULTURES

"Your foreign exchange student, Franz Heilig, will arrive in Chicago on Tuesday, August 17. . . ."

"*YES!*" Tossing the letter from the American Field Service high in the air, 17-year-old Jeff Kasten pumps his right arm in the ultimate victory salute. For as long as he can remember he's wanted to have a student from another country live with his family and attend school with him for a year. His parents and younger sister, Kim, have always been fully in favor of the idea, but after their father was seriously injured in an automobile accident 2 years ago there was no money for extras, let alone enough to feed and shelter another person. Jeff's dad was 100% recovered several months ago, and he gave the green light for the family to register with the AFS for a foreign exchange student.

Now Jeff's dream is finally coming true. In just 2 months he and his family will meet Franz at Chicago's O'Hare Airport and welcome him to their comfortable home in suburban Hinsdale. A couple of weeks later, after the usual boisterous family Labor Day barbecue, Franz will join Jeff for his senior year at Hinsdale High.

Picking up the letter from the kitchen floor, Jeff removes a paperclip and finds a photograph of Franz along with a sheet of biographical information. The photo shows an unsmiling young man with high cheekbones, a square jaw, and dark, close-cut curly hair. *Looks pretty serious*, Jeff muses, thinking of the smiling faces in the class photos in his high school yearbook. *I sure hope he has a sense of humor.*

"Franz is 17 years old and speaks fluent English," the narrative on the bio sheet begins. "He attends the *gymnasium* (a secondary school that prepares students for university), where he excels in mathematics and chemistry and has won honors for his work in the classics. Franz plays fullback on his school's football team, is a talented cellist, and is the school chess champion. He plans a career as a chemical engineer."

*Wow,* Jeff thinks, *this is pretty heavy*. Jeff, a second-string basketball player and solid B student, feels somewhat overwhelmed by the string of superlatives that describes his future roommate, companion, and classmate. *What if he thinks I'm a lightweight?* As far as career plans are concerned, Jeff hasn't decided between being a history teacher and following in his father's footsteps as an accountant. Neither has he narrowed down his choice of colleges; so far all he knows is that he wants to go to school on either the east or the west coast. *And here's this guy, with his future already all planned out.*

After eagerly waiting all this time to host a foreign exchange student, Jeff now wonders if he and his family actually have anything to offer Franz. *OK,* he tells himself, *forget the fact that this guy sounds like Superman. How can I make him feel welcome—in the United States, in Chicago, in our home, in my school? I want to introduce him to my friends, but I don't want him to think he always has to do what they want to do. I wonder what he likes to do in his spare time. . . .*

As you study this chapter, think about Jeff's and Franz's situations, and prepare to answer the questions in Your Turn at the end of the chapter.

United States, Canada, Great Britain, western Europe, Australia, and New Zealand. The **Eastern bloc** is made up of eastern European nations that, until the fall of the Berlin Wall in 1989, were under the domain of the Soviet Union. The **Third World** consists of nations, located mainly in Asia and Africa, that were not aligned with either the communist or the noncommunist blocs and that can be considered developing nations.

The Western bloc countries we will discuss are Great Britain, France, Germany, and Australia. These countries were selected for two reasons. First, Great Britain, France, and Germany have had a significant impact on recreation and leisure not only in the United States and Canada but also worldwide. Second, data on these countries are available in English. It is also important to note that these countries share a common historical and cultural background. In Chapter 2, The Evolution of Leisure, Recreation, and Play, we learned about that common background, traces of which are still found in the Western world today.

## Great Britain

The British Empire, and particularly England, could be described as the mother of modern sport. England gave the world its most popular contemporary spectator sport, soccer (or football, as it is called outside the United States). But the story began long before the invention of soccer.

The Saxons, a Germanic people who conquered England in the fifth century with the Angles and the Jutes, were fond of parades that featured their king accompanied by thousands of guards. From that time on, parades became a major tradition in England and were conducted to mark every important occasion. In 1066 the Norman invasion brought new pastimes to the British Isles, including jousting (engaging in combat with lances while on horseback) and other kinds of tournaments. The combination of tournaments and parades resulted in the

extravagant celebrations that took place in the Middle Ages, with kings and nobles displaying their finery and trumpeting their accomplishments.[1]

The Roman Catholic Church acquiesced to the celebration of saints' days and other religious occasions. For example, in the Middle Ages, images of the Virgin Mary and St. Martin were paraded through the streets of Leicester, accompanied by 12 singing men costumed as the 12 apostles. Moreover, the church adopted and popularized ball games by providing times and places for them to be played. Although royal edicts and local statutes prohibited playing soccer on Shrove Tuesday, the final celebration before the onset of Lenten austerity, soccer games were played between two parishes in Derby from the early 15th century into the 19th century. The purpose of the game, for which no written rules existed, was to kick, carry, or throw the ball against the opponent's goal. The two goals in this case were a prominent gate in the parish of St. Peter at one end and a water wheel in All Saints parish, three miles away. Local pride and Shrovetide ale exacerbated the hostility between the two teams and their supporters. These altercations resulted not only in broken

---

*Western bloc* a political classification formerly used to describe noncommunist countries with free-market economies, including the United States, Canada, Great Britain, western Europe, Australia, and New Zealand

*Eastern bloc* countries of eastern Europe that were under Soviet communist domination from the end of World War II until the collapse of communism in 1989

*Third World* a group of developing nations with largely agrarian economies, located mainly in Asia and Africa, that generally is not aligned with the ideologies of either the East or the West

bones and other injuries but also in death.[2] Religious leaders tolerated these and similar events and their consequences but in 1578 obtained an edict from Queen Elizabeth I that prohibited such events from being conducted on the sabbath, which was designated for rest and worship.[1]

Meanwhile, members of England's privileged classes were hunting and hawking on horseback, not for survival but as recreation. Bear, fox, and deer were hunted by the nobility; the hunting of this finer wild game was forbidden to the commoners, who were allowed to hunt small game for food only.

### Puritan Dissidents

All of these activities brought down the wrath of the Puritans, a dissident Protestant sect that demanded adherence to a strictly regulated Christian regimen. The Puritans became critical not only of political machinations but also of many popular social and leisure practices. They strongly opposed the sporting events and festivities championed by the Stuart monarchs of Scotland, who ruled England for most of the 17th century into the early 18th century.

In 1641 Oliver Cromwell led the Puritans in a war against the Stuarts, after which the Puritans gained control of the government. They immediately banned Sunday amusements; abolished church festivals; and prohibited horse racing, cockfighting, bear baiting, dancing, and drama. These prohibitions were short lived, however. They were repealed shortly after Charles II of the House of Stuart returned to power in 1660. Despite this setback, the Puritans succeeded in forcing the people of England and later of the United States to curb their recreational activities, at least as far as the sabbath was concerned. For some 300 years, from the mid-17th to the mid-20th century, both England and the United States set aside the sabbath for rest and worship.

### The Restoration

Upon his return from exile, Charles II reestablished the monarchy and revived the traditional customs of festivities and sport. This period of English history is called the Restoration, meaning the restoration of the monarchy, and it extended from 1660 to the death of Charles II in 1685. Maypoles reappeared on village greens, and kingly sports such as tennis and golf were revived. Horse racing was resumed for the aristocracy, and boxing evolved as "the manly art of self-defense."

The Scottish kings tried repeatedly but unsuccessfully to prohibit commoners from playing their favorite sport, golf, which originated in Scotland. Instead, they wanted their subjects to practice archery, a skill that was useful militarily. Golf today is an extremely popular sport around the world, particularly in the United States, where it is played both in elegant private clubs and on public courses.

### Class Distinctions

Great Britain is sometimes described as "the mother of democracy" because the average person is free to express his or her opinion. Nonetheless, a strict line of demarcation still exists between the upper class and the lower class. Horse racing, fox hunting, and regattas continue to be enjoyed almost exclusively by England's aristocracy; although others are not forbidden by law to participate, they are effectively prevented by centuries-old conventions. In 1541 a royal edict prohibited commoners from bowling; the edict was not rescinded until 1845.

Forbidden by law to participate in the sport of royalty, commoners vented their frustrations by devising for themselves several boisterous, violent, and sometimes cruel pastimes that became known as "blood sport." Cock throwing, for example, consisted of throwing missiles at a tethered cock until the cock died. Other blood sports favored by commoners were cockfighting and bear baiting, the practice of setting dogs on a chained bear.

## Industrial Revolution

With the advent of the industrial revolution in the mid-17th century, many commoners migrated from rural villages to cities in search of better paying work. Between 1801 and 1850 the populations of some British cities doubled or tripled. In these sprawling urban centers, workers found respite from monotonous factory work in the public house, or pub, which offered food, drink, companionship, and recreation. Billiards, quoits (similar to horseshoes), and darts were played inside, bowls (the predecessor of modern bowling) outside.

As the growth of industry and mechanization advanced, work hours were increased by factory owners who wanted the maximum productivity from their workers. A 60-hour to 70-hour, six-day workweek, which left little time for leisure, became commonplace. Festivals and sport were forbidden on Sunday, a relic of the Puritan era, and the number of holidays began to decline as demand for output increased. At the same time, open space within city limits, once available for recreational use, was being swallowed up by the ongoing construction of factories. Perhaps the only positive development during this period was the eradication of most blood sport.[2]

## Victorian Era

The reign of Queen Victoria from 1837 to 1901 is the longest in British history. During this era, a virtual revolution took place in recreation and leisure. The revolution was characterized by three factors. First was the acceptance of a clear distinction in everyday life between work and leisure. Second, free time began to be scheduled during nonworking hours and holidays. Third, a debate took place on the nature of "constructive leisure."[3]

At this time, British society was placing strong emphasis on morality. The heroes of the time were religious people such as African explorer Stanley Livingstone, soldier/philanthropist Charles Gordon, and Prime Minister

*Punting down the River Cam in Cambridge, England*

William Gladstone. Even agnostics such as poet Matthew Arnold and writer George Eliot were preaching the virtues of morality. Constructive leisure, as defined by the mores of the time, revolved around sport and games as endorsed by Britain's elite public schools (actually private schools whose purpose was to train the future civil servants of the British Empire). Constructive leisure clearly did not include such pastimes as gambling, drinking, and blood sport.

## Rise of the Middle Class

Spearheading the recreational revolution that took place during the Victorian era was the powerful rise of the middle class. The seeds for this development were planted early in the industrial revolution when the need arose to train a new professional and managerial class. Small shopkeepers and the owners of small farms also became part of this new class. According to one estimate, at the beginning of the 19th century the British population could be divided into an upper class (2%), the landed gentry (18%), a middle class (30%), and a laboring class (50%).[4]

The rise of the middle class in the Victorian era was manifested in two distinct ways. First, the members of that class attempted to emulate the behavior of the upper class and the landed gentry by buying houses in the country, by traveling during vacations, and by engaging in upper-class sports and other leisure pastimes. Second, as they became better educated, members of the middle class—particularly women—began to enjoy reading as a leisure pursuit. This trend increased the demand for books of all kinds, especially novels, and soon members of the lower classes also began to read. Traditional material from the oral popular culture provided authors a variety of themes and topics.

Traditionally a bastion of the male working class, public houses, or pubs, began to gain popularity among members of the emerging middle class, even admitting women during the day. On weekends many pub owners appealed to their middle-class customers by organizing family nights that offered simple leisure and recreational activities. Some pubs provided live entertainment on small stages, paving the way for the creation of music halls. In 1901 a film was shown in one such music hall, signaling a new era in leisure entertainment.

### A Sound Mind in a Sound Body

The Presbyterian Church adopted the concept of "muscular Christianity," in which fitness of the body was held to enhance fitness of the spirit. The Latin phrase for this idea is *mens sana in corpore sano*: "a sound mind in a sound body."

British educators and religious leaders, recognizing the growing importance of recreation and leisure, began to incorporate activities into their programs. Elite British schools for the sons of the aristocracy used sports to divert young minds from thoughts of drinking, gambling, and other unwholesome pursuits. The classic sports for the sons of the affluent were cricket and rugby. Cricket, a game that dates back to the 16th century, is played with a ball and a bat by two sides, each with 11 members,

on a large field centering on two wickets, each defended by a batsman. Rugby, named for the elite boys' school where the game originated in 1864, is a football game in which play is continuous, without timeouts or substitutions. Kicking, dribbling, lateral passing, and tackling are featured; interference and forward passing are prohibited.

### Rise of the Labor Movement

As the industrial revolution marched on, social reformers were earnestly attempting to improve conditions for factory workers, who were living in unsanitary if not filthy conditions and working excessively long hours. In 1847, workers in mechanized plants put in 10 hours a day while other workers worked 12 hours or more a day, six days a week. In 1886 unionists Keir Hardie, Tom Mann, and John Burns organized a labor union to seek better working conditions, including a shorter workday. They acted on behalf of all workers, particularly those who were not organized. Some social reformers, such as Randolph Churchill and Albert du Mann, asserted that workers could spend more time with their families if working hours were reduced. Others suggested that workers could use the added free time to enrich their lives.

Opposition to reduced working hours came from industrialists, who declared that such an action would kill the spirit of initiative for which British workers were known. Others were concerned that increased free time could lead to an increase in population and, thus, advance the spread of poverty. Despite protests and even strikes by industrial workers, it was not until 1919 that laws were passed to reduce the workday to eight hours.

### Popular Pastimes

Contemporary Britons enjoy a lifestyle that offers a variety of leisure pursuits. As noted earlier, fox hunting, horse racing, and yachting continue to be the sports of choice for the aristocracy and upper class; they also enjoy play-

*Victoria, British Columbia, was named after the former queen of England, and it offers a leisurely waterfront for residents and tourists.*

ing lawn tennis and badminton (originally called battledore and shuttlecock). For the country as a whole, attendance at museums and art galleries is strong, as are sales of recreational goods. The British Government conducted a longitudinal research study, called the General Household Survey (GHS). Despite criticism of this research tool, its data show a stable pattern in British leisure pursuits. For instance, the surveys show that home-based pursuits and socializing are the most popular leisure activities, that walking for pleasure is the favorite outdoor activity, and that the dominant indoor pursuits are darts and snooker (a variation of pool). By far the most watched sport, both live and on television, is soccer.[5]

Reading is an extremely popular pastime among Britons; the holdings of public libraries exceed 151 million volumes. This represents almost three books for each citizen, one of the highest ratios in the world. Some 113 daily newspapers are published in Great Britain, with a combined circulation of over 25 million.[6]

## France

In 600 B.C.E. the ancient Greeks established a colony called Massilia, today Marseilles.

During the reign of Julius Caesar, the Romans annexed the southern part of France, which was occupied by a Celtic people called the Gauls. The Gauls were protected by the Romans against the barbarians from the north, but not for long. In 486 C.E. the Franks, a West Germanic people, descended on the Gauls. The area was divided among several Frankish kings, but by 1328 France was unified under the rule of one king.

Ball games played in northern France were ancient rituals devised by the Gauls in honor of the sun. Some of these games were accepted by the Christian church to the extent that around 470 C.E. a ball game was played during Easter ceremonies in which "church officials formed a processional down the aisle of the church. Chanting a traditional liturgy, they danced to the music of an Easter hymn while passing a ball from person to person."[7]

As we learned in Chapter 2, the French monarchy and nobility were supported by the clergy and enjoyed a leisurely lifestyle of playing tennis and hunting on their vast country estates. One such estate eventually became the world-renowned Palace at Versailles, which was opened up to the common people after the French Revolution and which became one of Europe's most popular tourist attractions.

France continued to be mainly agrarian even after the establishment in the 12th century of the University of Paris, one of Christianity's most influential centers of learning. At this time the French began to have some contact with the Italian principalities to the southeast, which were experiencing some dramatic changes. A new popular culture was emerging, at the heart of which was the festival.

### Church-Sanctioned Debauchery

Although the festival was intended to mark a church event, many of its activities had pre-Christian elements. At the annual Carnavalesque, eating, drinking, and promiscuity predominated. The event was Italian in origin and was sanctioned by the Roman Catholic

Church; it also was celebrated by the Franks. This event allowed the participants to vent the high spirits they had stifled the preceding year. Many wealthy Italians opened up their huge estates for commoners to enjoy. Their French counterparts followed suit only after the French Revolution in 1789.

Fencing, considered by many as the national sport of France, was introduced in the 16th century by Italians. Under Italian masters, a guild of fencing masters was established in France in 1570.[2] Soon the French became the true masters of fencing with two innovations that helped transform the martial art of fencing into a sport. The first was the mask; the second was the *en garde* position with the head held back, indicating the chest as target.

Among France's many contributions to the sphere of recreation and leisure is the work of French-Swiss writer and philosopher Jean-Jacques Rousseau (1712–1778), who in his writings exalted the beauty of nature. Regarded by many as the father of naturalism, he suggested that the qualities of beauty and innocence found in nature also can exist in humans. Rousseau, who believed that the "natural man" is virtuous, was unhappy with the emphasis on producing modern conveniences to create more leisure time. These devices, he believed, became the yoke that modern people inadvertently imposed on themselves, as well as the first source of evil passed on to their descendants.[7]

### French Revolution

The French Revolution, which began in 1789, had a strong impact throughout Europe. Although the revolutionary motto was "Liberty, Equality, Fraternity", the revolution was not as generous to the common person as the monarchy had been. The monarchy had arranged with the church to grant everyone 52 Sundays off, 90 days of rest, and 38 holy days a year, for a total of 180 nonworking days per year. The revolutionary regime adopted a 10-day workweek, reducing the number of Sundays to 36 per year. It also reduced the number of holidays.

In post-revolutionary France the old elite of the monarchy and nobility gave way to a new elite of the wealthy and politically powerful. As the common people struggled for survival, the new elite class developed a lifestyle that included many leisure pursuits, chief among which were horse racing and gambling.

### After the Revolution

Not until the late 19th century did France recover from the shock of the revolution, with the ushering in of an era known as *la belle epoque* (the beautiful age), a period of high artistic and cultural achievement. A favorite leisure pursuit of the upper class was bicycling. Bicycle clubs flourished alongside tennis and croquet clubs, and women as well as men enjoyed the exhilarating new sport. Competitive cycling began in the 1880s with a race from Paris to Rouen, then Bordeaux to Paris. The Paris-Brest-Paris race (the world-famous Tour de France, still conducted today) attracted cyclists from all over Europe.

In the meantime, French workers were still seeking a shorter workday, but not until 1912 did the government reduce the workday to 10 hours, six days a week. As in Great Britain, the eight-hour workday did not become law until 1919. (In both countries the change was expedited by the governments' fear of communism, which had taken hold in Russia in 1917 after the Bolshevik Revolution.) In 1936 the government passed a law granting 12 days' vacation each year. The annual vacation was increased to 18 days in 1956 and to 24 days in 1969. In addition, French workers receive 10 paid holidays each year. Today France is the only industrial nation to call for 5 weeks vacation a year.

As in Great Britain, leisure research in France suffers from lack of adequate tools. Yet the data gathered there show an increase in participation in leisure pursuits, particularly in physical activities, due to the growing awareness of their importance to health.[8]

## Germany

The Germanic tribes that came under Roman rule in 9 B.C.E. retained their identity, even though they became Roman subjects and adopted Christianity when Rome did. Eventually, most of these tribal units disappeared and were replaced by larger political units. Many of the tribes became part of the Frankish Empire under Charlemagne in the seventh and eighth centuries.

A favorite game of medieval German monks and priests was *kegels*, a predecessor of modern bowling, in which wooden balls were rolled to knock down targets. The kegel (target) represented the devil, at which the bowler should aim. If successful in knocking it down, the player would be cleansed of his or her sins. Until a few decades ago, American bowlers often were referred to colloquially as "keglers."

In the mid-10th century, Otto I, the Holy Roman Emperor, consolidated the *Reich*, which displeased the Roman Catholic pope. The relationship with the Catholic Church continued to deteriorate until 1517. At that time, Catholic priest Martin Luther nailed his 95 theses protesting the actions of the church to the door of his Wittenburg church. Thus was born the breakaway denomination of Protestantism.

A devout and learned churchman, Luther did not discount the value of recreation and leisure. In fact, he urged his followers to pursue honorable and useful modes of exercise, such as dancing and the knightly sports of fencing and archery.[2]

Attempts to unify the Germanic peoples began as early as 9 B.C.E., just after the death of Roman emperor Julius Caesar. Such attempts were made again under Charlemagne in 800 C.E. During the Middle Ages, various towns formed unions that were in a continual state of flux until the early 19th century.

An important step toward unification was taken in 1815 when the princes of the German states met and decided not to revive the Holy Roman Empire, which had been dissolved by Napoleon in 1806. In its place, the princes formed what became known as the German Federation. A new spirit of German pride was born that was characterized by extreme nationalism revolving around physical strength and prowess.

### Patriotism and Fitness

A centuries-old German tradition is to equate physical fitness with national strength and pride. Johann Gutsmuth is considered by many to be the father of modern physical education. His book *Gymnastics for Youth* (1793) described a system of exercises that could be performed with simple equipment. From Gutsmuth's regimen emerged the discipline of gymnastics, which was championed by Friedrich Jahn. To Jahn the future of Germany was its youth, who could redeem it after its humiliating defeat by Napoleon in 1806. Jahn, who is known as the father of modern gymnastics, undertook a program whose aim was to build strong youth to serve Germany. The program was conducted on a playground that contained climbing poles, ladders, and ropes.

The tide of nationalism led to the restructuring of the German state in 1871 under Otto von Bismarck, a Prussian aristocrat and modern Germany's first chancellor. Less than half a century later, in 1914, Kaiser Wilhelm II led Germany into the disastrous conflict of World War I, which ended in the defeat of Germany and the loss of many of its colonies. Once again nationalism surged, this time to be exploited by the Third Reich, Adolf Hitler's fascist regime. A key tenet of Hitler's agenda was the use of sport and physical education to rebuild the German nation. In his famous book, *Mein Kampf* (My Struggle), Hitler wrote

Give the German nation six million bodies of flawless athletic training, all glowing with fanatical love of their country and inculcated with the highest aggressive spirit, and in less than two years if necessary the nation will have created an army.[2]

## Post-War Experience

Germany was defeated by the Allies in World War II and was partitioned into two states: West Germany (the Federal Republic of Germany), which was operated as an open society, and East Germany (the Federal Democratic Republic). East Germany was taken over by the Soviet Union and was ruled according to the communist belief that leisure should be controlled by the state. Leisure pursuits were viewed as mechanisms to foster the socialist spirit and to increase productivity. The result was the creation of athletes who were described by the French newspaper *Le Monde* in this way:

> Rarely has the comparison of a team to a machine been more appropriate: A steam-roller, the German Democratic Republic team seems to be composed of tireless human robots who can maintain the same rhythm for an hour. They are cast physically and mentally from the same mold: iron morale, nerves of steel, muscles of brass. It is almost as though one were talking about a team that is metallurgical in nature.[9]

The description above refers to East Germany's national handball team. Clearly, this and other sports undertaken in the communist regime were intensely serious and contained no element of relaxation or fun.

The reunification of Germany took place in 1989. West Germany is still struggling to absorb into its capitalistic system millions of East Germans accustomed to decades of communist support; the unified government continues to subsidize leisure pursuits such as the theatre, opera, ballet, and movies. The state also helps support Germany's many fine museums, including the famed Berlin Museum that since the end of World War II had been under communist control.

Although gymnastics is still popular in Germany, other sports are gaining ground. An umbrella organization called the German Sport Federation oversees competitive and recreational sports. Jogging is popular in Germany, but as in other European countries the unquestioned favorite of both spectators and participants is soccer.

Rituals and festivals play a major role in the lives of Germans. Oktoberfest, initially held in 1810 to celebrate a wedding in the ruling house of Bavaria (a state in southern Germany), originally lasted one day but now is held for 16 days and is essentially an agricultural fair. Today Oktoberfest is a favorite not only in Germany but also in the United States, where many Americans with no German heritage join in the festivities. Another important Bavarian ritual is Fasching, a festival featuring a procession of masked figures that for generations has been celebrated on Rose Monday and Shrove Tuesday (the days immediately preceding Ash Wednesday, the first day of Lent in the Christian calendar). Despite the passage of time since the reunification of Germany, the two states are treated seperately in the most recent data.[10] The data reveal a familiar pattern, characteristic of Western European nations for many years: home-based and social pursuits are much more popular than participatory activities.[10]

Before we continue our examination of recreation and leisure in western cultures, take some time out to raise your cultural conscience and do some armchair traveling by completing the Action Guide on pp. 150–151.

## Australia

Until 1788, when the British took possession of Australia in the name of the English crown, the continent was inhabited solely by its native population of about 350,000 aborigines. Today their numbers have dwindled to about 150,000, but they still engage in some of the ritualistic activities practiced by their ancestors. Their dancing, music, poetry, and art are all colorful rituals executed with great pleasure. The aborigines paint their bodies and decorate the grounds on which their dancing and singing take place. After two centuries of white domination, however, the aborigines have now absorbed much of that culture into their own.

The British government often exiled convicted felons to Australia, where they were settled on the east coast. The British did not begin to explore the rest of Australia until the mid-1800s, when self-government was established. Trade flourished, and the discovery of gold in 1851 added to the excitement.

Australia participated in both world wars, and in the 1950s the community center movement started as an offshoot of recreational services provided to enlisted men in World War II. In the 1970s the Australian government established the Ministry of Tourism and Recreation. The ministry developed a national recreation plan to achieve the development of leisure skills, the promotion of dynamic health and fitness, and the encouragement of self-expression and personal fulfillment. Because of a change in government, this plan was never implemented; however, it does indicate the importance accorded to recreation and leisure in Australian society.

### Sports and Public Parks

Australians play several games of British origin—cricket, tennis, and football (soccer)—and some that are unique to their culture. For example, Australian football is a combination of Gaelic rugby and soccer, played on an oval field.

According to at least one source, the concept of national parks originated not in America but in Australia, when in 1881 Port Hacking was designated a royal national park.[11] Demand for the protection of Australia's natural resources started with bushwalkers—hikers—who had begun to form walking clubs before the turn of the 20th century. In 1932 the government established the National Park and Primitive Areas Council to establish a policy on the use of open space. A conflict arose between recreational users and preservationists. Because of the Floral Reserve Act of 1948, a number of laws protect Australia's natural environment.

*Beautiful waterfalls are a major tourist attraction in Australia and New Zealand.*

Unlike the United States, where unsettled lands are owned by the federal government, in Australia such lands are owned by its six states, which designate areas for public parks and recreation.

Despite its small population (some 17 million in 1991), Australia has fared well in international athletic competition. One reason is that physical education is compulsory in schools. Australians have also become very sports minded, with strong emphasis placed on

## ACTION GUIDE

### "TRAVELING" TO ANOTHER CULTURE

Almost everyone loves to travel, and most American students probably would be delighted to have a chance to visit a foreign country and find out what it would be like to live in another culture. There's a way to enjoy this experience vicariously—and to check your own "multicultural IQ."

Find a friend, classmate, or neighbor who grew up in a country and culture outside the United States, and ask the following questions:

1. What are your nationality, ethnic heritage, and religion?

   _____

2. In your culture, what were considered appropriate and desirable forms of recreation and leisure for

   Boys _____

   Girls _____

3. What forms of leisure and recreation, if any, were forbidden or discouraged in your culture?

   _____

4. What is the favorite national sport in your country of origin? _____

5. Did you play this sport? Why or why not?

   _____

participation. Moreover, the country's urban centers are located in climates that are highly favorable for outdoor pursuits.

Data from the National Recreation Participation Survey reveal that watching television was the dominant pursuit (averaging over 90%), followed by listening to the radio (77%) and visitation (62%). Outdoor pursuits did not fare well; walking for pleasure was low (26%) and fishing was lower (4%).[11a]

Concept Check

- Give two examples of games that originally had a religious connection.
- Name two ways socioeconomic class influences opportunities for recreation/leisure.

## ACTION GUIDE

### "TRAVELING" TO ANOTHER CULTURE (cont'd)

6. How old were you when you came to the United States? _____

7. As a newcomer, what struck you as the most obvious differences between recreation and leisure in your native country and recreation and leisure in the United States?

   _____

   _____

8. What aspects of leisure and recreation, if any, do you like better in the United States than in your country of origin, and vice versa?

   _____

   _____

9. In the United States, do you tend to engage more in the recreation and leisure practices of your country of origin or in those of the United States? Why?

   _____

   _____

   _____

10. What forms of recreation and leisure enjoyed today in the United States originated in your native country?

    _____

    _____

## EASTERN BLOC

As we learned earlier, the nations of the former Eastern bloc are the countries of eastern Europe that came under Soviet domination after the end of World War II. Besides ideological differences with the nations of the Western bloc, each of the Eastern bloc countries has cultural characteristics that affect its citizens' attitudes toward and practices of leisure and recreational activities. A major point of difference between the countries of the East and the West is the influence of the Eastern Orthodox Church. Although it was

repressed by the Soviet regime, the church remains a powerful force in the lives of many eastern Europeans. In addition, the countries of the Eastern bloc lived under communism for many decades. Although communism fell in 1989, its policies and practices did not disappear. In fact, strong evidence suggests that the political structures of the communist bureaucracy are intact and that many average citizens continue to live under policies established by the communists.

As noted earlier, communist leaders believed that play, recreation, and leisure should be used both to increase productivity and to inculcate citizens with socialist dogma. These activities are not to be enjoyed for their own sake but done in service of the state.

## The Commonwealth of Independent States—Soviet Russia

Of the 15 original members of the Union of Soviet Socialist Republics (USSR), 11 decided after the fall of communism to remain in a loose federation called the Commonwealth of Independent States. The largest country in the group is the Russian Republic, formerly Soviet Russia, (earlier the Russian Empire).

Until the Bolshevik Revolution of 1917, which overturned the monarchy and ushered in communism, Russia was ruled by czars. Before the revolution, British engineers had introduced soccer[2] to the country, a move welcomed by industrialists who saw the game as an antidote to the social and political unrest gripping Russia at the time. After the revolution, soccer and other sports were encouraged by the Bolshevik government to build strong communist youth.

The communist regime prevailed in Russia for over eight decades. One of the positive outcomes of its otherwise corrupt and oppressive rule is the 40-hour workweek now enjoyed by most citizens, together with 21 days' paid vacation a year. Loyal workers spent their vacations in one of the inexpensive accommodations provided by the state: a house of rest for overworked employees, a sanatorium (health resort), a *pension* (hotel or boardinghouse), or a *dacha* (country estate). Under communism, some *dachas* were privately owned, the best being reserved for high party officials; others were administered by trade, labor, and professional unions.

Using sport to showcase communism's achievements, the Soviets organized a nationwide sports competition, the Spartakiad of the People of the USSR, following the Winter Olympics in 1956. The leaders chose the name

Spartakiad (feast of Sparta) because they were impressed by the devotion of the Spartans of ancient Greece to their city-state. Every town and province held qualifying events in sports such as gymnastics, swimming, and track and field. The final contests took place in Lenin Stadium, with its 104,000-seat capacity. The Soviet regime was preparing its athletes to compete in the 1956 Summer Olympics in Melbourne, Australia. Their success was noted:

> If the Olympic Games are a fair indication of athletic prowess, at Melbourne the Soviet Union emerged as the premier athletic nation on earth.[12]

Unfortunately, this success was a facade that concealed many serious social problems, including inadequate opportunities for recreation and leisure. One reason is that only a small part of Russia's vast territory is habitable. Moreover, the classification of land under the communist regime allowed no land to be designated for recreation. A positive sign is that in 1971 the Soviet government established Moose Island National Park near Moscow, a city of 10 million in dire need of recreational space.

August 1990 marked the beginning of a drastic change in Soviet society. The word *Soviet* disappeared with the collapse of communism and the surrounding republics, many of which broke away from the union.

In post-communist Russia, changes are taking place not only in the political and economic sectors, but also in the behavior of the common citizen, including leisure behavior. For instance, many of Russia's youth find it necessary to have a second job, which means lack of free time to pursue activities of choice. This change affects the level of health, which seems to be declining there.[12a]

In the meantime, the country is witnessing a marked decrease in the officially sponsored clubs that provide citizens with leisure opportunties. In fact, new private clubs cater to the new oligarchy, combining stylish relaxation and lavish surroundings.[12b]

## Poland

The history of the eastern European nation of Poland dates back to 963 C.E. when Mieszko, a leader of unknown background, tried to develop a united political community in an area surrounded by Slavonic tribes. To survive, the new entity in 979 C.E. made a pact with Otto I, the Holy Roman Emperor. Despite its efforts to forge alliances, Poland for centuries lived under threats. Most devastating was the German invasion in 1939 that launched World War II. By the war's end, Poland lay in ruins physically, economically, and politically and fell under Soviet domination.

Under communism, life and leisure in Poland were changed dramatically by Soviet efforts to narrow the gap between the wealthy and the poor. The new measures included,

(1.) free time for all workers;
(2.) annual holidays and vacations for all;
(3.) retirement plans for all;
(4.) equal cultural and recreational opportunities;
(5.) an increase in public recreational facilities and opportunities; and
(6.) public relations campaigns to inform citizens of recreation and leisure opportunities.[13]

### Leisure Pursuits

In Poland, the center of recreation and leisure is the home, where the most popular activities are visiting with family and friends, watching television, and gardening. Cafes serve as social centers where patrons drink and play table games such as cards, chess, and backgammon.[6] A survey conducted among the residents of Warsaw showed a great demand for more parks and green areas, better transportation to these facilities, and more swimming pools.[13] Many Poles take adult education courses offered by the Ministry of Culture and the Arts, trade unions, and general universities adult education.

### Solidarity

After the fall of communism in 1989, Lech Walesa, the leader of the Solidarity movement, which tried to improve conditions in Soviet-dominated Poland, was elected president of the newly liberated country. Although well intentioned, Walesa's changes were too radical and were implemented too quickly, forcing the country to undergo "shock therapy." Today the average workday in Poland is eight hours, and the workweek is six days.

Leisure services in post-communist Poland is limited to the elite. Many specialized private providers have emerged, but the general public cannot afford these leisure opportunities because of inflation and a budget crisis.[14]

Participation in leisure pursuits changed drastically when the Communist idealogy ended. Participation in fishing and hunting increased between the mid 1970s and mid 1990s, but a drastic decline occured in reading. Other acti-vities, such as going to shows, exhibitions, and circuses, also declined. Jung attributes these changes to the cultural vacuum observed in post-communist countries.[14a]

**Concept Check**

• How does communism view recreation and leisure?
• What are some benefits and drawbacks of this view for the average citizen?

## DEVELOPING NATIONS

The Third World is a term used to describe the developing nations that allied themselves with neither the East nor the West in the years of the Cold War between Soviet communism and Western democracy. These countries are called developing nations because their economies still are primarily agricultural, with very narrow commercial or industrial bases. The political ideologies of these countries vary significantly; some are closer to Western thought and others are more closely aligned with communist and socialist principles. In the sections that follow we will review the recreation and leisure scene in each of four developing nations: Mexico, India, Egypt, and China.

## Mexico

Geographically, Mexico is part of the North American continent, however its heritage and social and cultural systems are markedly different from those of its neighbors to the north, the United States and Canada. However, the state of its economy and the lifestyle of its citizens make it a Third World country rather than a Western nation.

When the Spanish *conquistadores* (conquerors) ventured into the land of the Aztecs in the 16th century, they found a cultural system that included many rituals that involved games. Among these games was *tlachtli* (see Chapter 2). This ball game was part of a ritual that portrayed a struggle between good and evil, light and darkness. The captain of the losing team was sacrificed because he represented evil.

The Spaniards continued their penetration into southern Mexico and subjugated most of the other Mexican tribes. Although the culture of Mexico and its neighbors was changed dramatically by the Spanish conquerors, many of its native customs and traditions have been incorporated into the country's adopted faith, Catholicism. Evidence of these colorful rituals can still be seen in the celebrations of local and national holidays.

### Religious Festivals

Although modern Mexico recognizes 14 secular holidays, religious events are commemorated by 20 national and 35 local fiestas and celebrations. Each of these fiestas honors a Christian event or personality, but traces of the old Aztec and Mayan cultures can be clearly seen. Not only do these celebrations take place on the same days that the old pagan ceremonies were held, but they also include many

songs and dances that pre-date Columbus. One ancient ritual featured in many fiestas is *el volador*, a flying pole performance in which four participants climb a pole, hook their feet to a rope, and jump off, each spinning around 13 times. The total of 52 spins represents the 52-week calendar of the Aztecs and Mayans. The fiesta begins at dawn with singing and lasts all day. Mass is celebrated at midday, followed by dancing the rest of the day. Each fiesta ends with a fireworks display.[16]

### Bullfighting and the *Paseo*

Mexico gained its independence from Spain in 1821, but the impact of centuries of Spanish rule remained. Many leisure pursuits and recreational activities in Mexico are of Spanish origin—most notably, bullfighting, which continues to be Mexico's most popular spectator sport. Bullfighting may have begun as "bull leaping." Traces of this activity are found in the ruins of the Minoan culture on the Mediterranean island of Crete, where images of acrobats leaping off the back of a bull were depicted on a clay container. Over time this activity spread to the Iberian Peninsula, where Spain is located. Originally restricted to the affluent, bullfighting in Spain later was opened to the commoners. Later, in Mexico, only the owners of large haciendas initially were permitted to attend bullfights, but the sport now is enjoyed by people of every socioeconomic class.

Wealthy Mexicans of the 19th century devised the *paseo*, a ritual in which they paraded their decorated carriages and elegant horses at dusk on a daily basis.

Small *rancheros* held contests in equestrian skills at *charreadas*, the forerunners of the rodeos of the American West. Another popular amusement of the 19th century was the *colear*, in which a skilled horseback rider chases a bull, grabs its tail, and flips it to the ground. The affluent also liked to attend cockfights, where they wagered large sums of money on their favorite roosters.

## Modern Leisure Pursuits

Mexicans love music, and even the smallest of villages has a music kiosk. Strolling musicians called *mariachis* entertain people in the streets; in plazas; and at fiestas, weddings, and virtually every other kind of celebration.

Despite the introduction of television and movies, the small village plaza still serves as the social and recreational center of the Mexican community. Young and old gather to talk, read newspapers, and play dominoes or chess while sipping coffee. The plaza is also the place to meet members of the opposite sex.

American movies and television unquestionably have had an impact on Mexican thought and culture. After bullfighting and soccer, the next most popular spectator sport in Mexico is baseball. Mexicans also enjoy watching *jai alai*, a game of Basque origin in which the players toss a ball against the walls of an elongated court using a curved basket (*pelota*) strapped to the wrist. Gambling on this sport and on horse and greyhound racing is a popular leisure pastime in Mexico.[15]

## Tourism in Mexico

In reviewing the impact of tourism on the Mexican economy during the past three decades, Clancy concluded that tourism has become an integral part of the country's economy. The tourism industry is the second largest employer and an important source of foriegn exchange.[16a]

## India

Modern India inherited a cultural system that centers on a hierarchy of Hindu deities and a rigid system of hereditary social classes, or castes. As we learned in Chapter 2, members of a given caste traditionally are restricted in their occupations and in their association with members of other castes. Despite many attempts to abolish castes or bridge the gaps, rigid social stratifications still exist.

Hinduism teaches that following the path to salvation requires mystical contemplation and ascetic practices. Traditionally, however, while ordinary citizens tried to follow this path, wealthy Hindus lived lives of luxury in ornate palaces, gambling and playing board games. Gambling is still an acceptable Hindu practice. The most famous board game, chess, originated in India (see A Closer Look, p. 156).

## Religious Rituals

Dancing was and still is an integral part of religious ceremonies in Hindu temples. Drama developed from ritual, mime, song, and dance. Hindu temples still organize processions led by musicians playing drums, trumpets, and conch shells. Idols are placed on massive carts and are adorned with garlands, green foliage, and dancing girls. The carts are pulled by 100 men followed by a group of people who pretend to be fighting.[17]

National religious festivals, for which Hindus are excused from work, are still numerous in India; there are 14 such festivals, compared with five secular holidays. Because India is home to many Muslims and some Christians, it recognizes eight Muslim and two Christian holidays. The Hindu festivals are special social and religious occasions involving whole families. For some festivals, Hindus must travel to sacred sites.

India's major contribution to recreation and leisure is yoga, practiced today by devotees all over the world. Yoga originated as a ritual for development of the will and achievement of complete control over one's body. Only a few yoga masters have truly achieved such control; the majority of practitioners use yoga as a form of relaxation and contemplative leisure.

## Agrarian Society

Despite the influence of Western education and technology, India continues to be a largely agrarian society whose huge labor force lives in the many villages of the subcontinent. The typical household consists of the patriarch and his wife, their married sons and families, and unmarried daughters. In essence, the young Indian is raised in a commune consisting of this

## A CLOSER LOOK

### CHESS: FROM VILLAGE GREEN TO WORLD CHAMPIONSHIP

Often called "the royal game" because of its pre-eminence among contests of intellectual skill, today chess is played by people of every background in every civilized country of the world.

Most scholars believe chess originated in about 500 C.E. in what is now Pakistan. It was an off-shoot of a Hindu game whose Sanskrit name was *chaturanga*, and it is thought to have a common origin with other board games such as backgammon, parcheesi, and cribbage. The word *chess* is derived from the Persian word *shah* (king), and checkmate comes from *shat mat*: "the king is dead." The Arabs learned the game when they conquered Persia in the seventh century, and they introduced it into Europe by way of Spain, Sicily, and Constantinople. A Byzantine form of the game may have been carried through Russia and Scandinavia, but western Europe ultimately adopted an Italian version derived from maritime association with the Arabs.

Chess today is played at the world championship level, with contests sometimes lasting several days or weeks. Russia has given the world some of its most brilliant chess players, and American Bobby Fischer, an erratic genius, became a virtual cult figure in the 1970s. In many parts of the world, chess clubs abound, and in some countries children begin to play at age 4. Whether played on an inexpensive cardboard surface or an elaborately carved board, with pieces roughly fashioned from wood or delicately carved in marble, chess today is a consuming passion among the people of many cultures.

large extended family. Incomes are pooled and used to provide food and other necessities to all household members. For the young rural Indian who does not attend school, the extended family is the only socializing agent. Children's play is unstructured; the two sexes do not mix.

The picture is different for city dwellers, who represent a very small percentage of India's population. Urban life has been affected by the technological developments of the 20th century. Today India produces almost 800 movies a year,[18] but the ratio of television sets to persons is extremely low: one set for each 375.5 persons.[6]

Controlled by Great Britain between 1857 and 1947, India owes some of its current leisure pursuits to that country. In October 1881, a petition to the British Government of Bombay defended the sporting rights of the Indians. While polo continued to be played by the colonizers, cricket was adopted by the natives.[18a] Patterned after British clubs, clubs in India are private enclaves where wealthy men can enjoy tennis, squash, badminton, and swimming. For the foreign tourist, the hill station offers a vantage point for observing rare Indian wildlife such as the tiger and the one-horned rhinoceros. Unfortunately, most natives cannot afford the luxury of either of these diversions.

### Egypt

Located in the northeastern portion of the African continent, Egypt is one of the world's most ancient civilizations, dating back to Neolithic cultures that lived along the Nile River as early as 6000 B.C.E. Egypt today is a predominantly Muslim country with a strong Arabic heritage. After some 500 years under the influence of Christianity introduced by the apostle Mark in the early years of the Common Era, the Arab/Muslim conquest in the mid-seventh century radically altered Egypt's cultural landscape. Variously taken over by the Turks, the French, and the British, Egypt today is a sovereign nation, having freed itself of British domination in 1952.

**Influences of Islam**

Islam, the dominant religion in Egypt, was founded by the prophet Muhammed, who did not frown on recreational activity but encouraged his followers to enjoy recreation and to participate in physical activities. Islamic rule began in 622 C.E. in Medina, in what is today Saudia Arabia, then was moved to other cities of the Middle East according to the dominant ruling dynasty. Although no entity ever achieved complete rule over all Muslims, a dominant cultural system unifies the people who live between the Atlantic Ocean in the west and the Arabian Gulf in the east. These people speak one language and are called Arabs. Other Muslims adhere to the faith but retain their identity as Turks, Iranians, Pakistanis, and Indonesians.

Early Muslim society, after its expansion into North Africa and western Asia, was composed of a large class of commoners and a very small ruling class that was supported by a cadre of soldiers and functionaries. Although the first set of caliphs who ruled from Medina was ascetic, the caliphs from the succeeding dynasties were truly members of the leisure class. Their palaces were huge, lavish edifices, and their gardens were designed to duplicate heaven on earth with pavilions, pools, and fountains.

### Traditional Pastimes

Among the pastimes of wealthy men were hunting, horseback riding, hawking, and playing chess. Well-to-do women were entertained at home by members of the harem, or women's section of the mansion. A household consisted of the master, his wives, his married sons and their families, his unmarried daughters, and servants. Some servants were trained in practical skills; others were trained to entertain in the harem by dancing, singing, or playing an instrument. The forms of entertainment once limited to the harem today are offered in nightclubs.

Both men and women of the upper and middle classes visited the public bath, or *hammam*, which originated with the Romans. Now obsolete, the *hammam* also was a social center and a place where women could perform beautifying rituals.

For generations an important public festival has been held throughout Egypt to celebrate the birth of the prophet Muhammed. Large tents are erected, in one of which men gather to perform *zikr*, a religious chant. The men stand in a circle holding hands and, accompanied by a flutist, chant, "There is no deity but Allah." The festival lasts 12 days and 11 nights. During the day people come to listen to poetry, buy sweetmeats, or watch *zikr*.[19]

### Modern Leisure Pursuits

A variety of traditional street entertainment is still performed in Egypt today, usually in the open spaces adjacent to mosques (Muslim houses of worship). Examples are dancing, sleight-of-hand tricks, tightrope performances, balancing acts, and monkey tricks.

The Muslim sabbath, which traditionally was a day of rest, begins on Friday at noon with a community prayer. After that, Muslims are free to do as they please. The most popular sport in Egypt is soccer, followed by team handball, basketball, and volleyball. Because of the high population density in urban centers, there is little open space for athletic fields. The same is true for park acreage, particularly in the older districts of Cairo and Alexandria.

Somewhat compensating for the lack of open space in cities is the 1,200 miles of Egypt's shoreline along the Mediterranean and the Red seas. Millions of Egyptians escape the summer heat by visiting the Mediterranean seacoast. The warmer temperature along the Red Sea makes that coast more attractive to winter visitors. In that same region, at the tip of the Sinai Peninsula, Egypt established its first wildlife preserve to protect the fragile coral reef and marine life there.

City dwellers and villagers alike watch television; there is one set for each 26 citizens, a reasonable ratio in view of Egypt's status as a developing nation.[6] Egypt dominates the Arab world in the production of movies, musicals, and plays.

## China

As we learned in Chapter 2, China is an

ancient civilization whose origins go back many thousands of years. Chinese tradition was based on the sanctity of the family, and this became the cornerstone of religious teaching under Confucianism. As a code of behavior and social relationships, Confucianism became the basis for China's educational system. In ancient and middle-era China, educational programs focused on training public officials who were recruited from the upper classes. These young men were trained in writing, mathematics, music, ritual, and charioteering. Before being granted an imperial office, they were required to pass an examination.

The Chinese masses, although not slaves, were poor peasants who suffered from epidemics of disease and natural catastrophes. Above them was the merchant class, which by the 11th century had become quite prosperous. They became the consumers of leisure pursuits that were introduced with the Mongolian invasion of China in 1215. The Mongols, for example, introduced boxing, which became a popular activity in the marketplace, where soldiers of the palace guard engaged in bouts. Audiences also were entertained by acrobatic stunts, traditional theatrical presentations, and operatic singing.

Before the Mongolian invasion a class of learned bureaucrats had been established to operate *hsien*, administrative units of the government. After the Mongolian conquest the system of *hsien* was abandoned, and these bureaucrats were forced to find another means of making a living. They began to write novels based on tales of the past, and novels became an important source of amusive leisure for China's growing middle class, followed by plays. Drama, puppetry, and music were performed and taught in the covered marketplaces that became known as "pleasure grounds."[20]

Shi writes that a number of parks were established in the early 20th century. They made an important impact on political, economic, and social life and helped in the emergence of a modern urban culture.[21]

**Pressure from Abroad**

During the 19th century, foreign powers became interested in China's vast untapped market, and China was either actually invaded by foreigners or controlled by them. First came the "Opium War" in 1839, when the British used force to put an end to the opium trade. In 1857 the British and French joined forces and invaded China, alleging the maltreatment of Christian missionaries. Next came demands from the Russians that China give up some of its territory. Japan in turn declared war on China in 1894 to force the Chinese government to relinquish its control over Korea and to cede Formosa. Public opinion in China attributed all these problems with foreign nations to the weakness of the Manchu dynasty. At the turn of the century, during what is known as the Boxer Rebellion, antiforeign sentiment ran high, and in 1912 the Republic of China was founded. A long-running conflict between Chinese nationalists and communists intensified over the next several decades, and in 1949 China fell to communism.

**The Communist Regime**

The communist regime seeks to achieve complete control over citizens' personal affairs. A key step in pursuit of this goal is socialization of the young. The first agent for socialization is *creches*, the day care/nursery centers that are part of every commune and factory. Supervisors even control the play of toddlers, who have very few toys and are encouraged to engage in useful pursuits such as planting seeds and pulling weeds. School authorities exert the same kind of control over children in elementary and secondary schools.

Like other communist regimes, China encourages its children to participate in sports as a means of achieving excellence and demonstrating the superiority of the communist system. The secondary school curriculum includes contemporary sports such as basketball, volleyball, gymnastics, and table tennis. Several organizations offer sports after school. An effort also is under way to revive traditional Chinese pursuits such as martial arts and breathing exercises. Many Chinese practice the ancient art of *tai chi chuan*—a series of slow, graceful movements executed each morning in public squares. *Tai chi* also has become a popular pastime among Westerners.

**Contemporary Leisure**

The communist regime pioneered a unique facility in which several leisure opportunities are available. These so-called cultural parks are an appealing combination of amusement park and athletic arena. For a minimal charge, people can participate in games and contests, watch a show, or see a display. Some parks have large television sets—an attractive feature for many visitors, given China's relatively low ratio of one television set for every 177 persons.[6]

A favorite traditional leisure pursuit in China is the opera, which now features themes of the communist revolution instead of productions that praise the emperor and promote upper-class ideals. Chinese theatres also present many live dramas. The communist regime controls movie production and the number and kind of festivals permitted. Of the holidays that existed before the revolution, only three are now celebrated: the spring, autumn, and dragon festivals. Another six secular holidays are added: New Year's Day;

*The market in Aberdeen near Hong Kong is always bustling.*

Labor Day; National Day; and children's, youth, and women's festivals.

The information and insights we have gained in this chapter into the recreational and leisure practices of other cultures provide the background for our exploration in Chapter 9 of the diversity of activities and participants in such activities to be found in contemporary America.

## Summing Up

◆ The countries of the former Western bloc tend to share a common cultural heritage influenced strongly by Christianity and by the Protestant work ethic. Several rituals combine elements of paganism and Christianity. In some of these countries, most notably Germany, athletic excellence is an important demonstration of national power and pride.

◆ Countries of the former Eastern bloc fell under the yoke of communism after World War II, and even after the collapse of communism in 1989 many people continue to live much as they did under Soviet domination. To showcase the virtues of communism, the Soviets instituted rigorous programs to develop top

athletes to represent the Soviet Union in international competitions. A strong traditional influence on eastern European countries is Eastern Orthodox Christianity, which was severely repressed during the eight decades of communist rule.

◆ Third World countries are developing nations with primarily agricultural economies that aligned themselves with neither East nor West during the Cold War between communism and free-market democracy. Most developing nations are located in Africa or Asia; a notable exception is Mexico on the North American continent. In addition to Christianity, influential religions in the Third World include Islam and Hinduism.

## Using What You've Learned

1. Read the United Nations Proclamation on Leisure Rights and write a short commentary on it.
2. Select a western European nation other than the ones you studied in this chapter. Conduct research to identify any recreational activities that are unique to this country and write a three-page paper on your findings.
3. Select a developing nation other than the ones you studied in this chapter. Conduct research about some of its rituals that

incorporate recreational activities and write a three-page paper on your findings.
4. Find a book on communist ideology. Learn the views of communist thinkers on play and leisure and write a two-page paper summarizing your findings.
5. Conduct research on the contemporary Olympic Games and write a three-page paper on why you do or do not believe the games can enhance international understanding.

## YOUR  Turn

1 How would you feel about having a foreign exchange student spend a year in your family's home? If you have had this experience, what did you like/dislike about it? What did the foreign exchange student like/dislike?

2 If you were hosting a foreign exchange student, how would you help him/her feel comfortable in your home, school, town, and with your friends?

3 How do you think you would benefit from the experience of having a foreign exchange student live with you? How might the student benefit from the experience?

4 Would you like to be a foreign exchange student in another country? If so, why? If not, why not? If you have had this experience, what did you like and dislike about it?

# REFERENCES

1. Strutt, J. (1970). *The Sport and Pastime of the People of England*. New York: Augustus Kelly, pp. viii, xxii.

2. Baker, W. (1982). *Sports in the Western World*. Totowa, NJ: Rowman & Littlefield, pp. 43–45, 48, 63, 73, 135, 247, 270.

3. Lowerson, J., & Meyerscough, J.C. (1977). *Time to Spare in Victorian England*. Hassocks, Sussex: Harvester Press, p. 53.

4. Golby, J.M., & Purdue, A.W. (1984). *The Civilization of the Crowd: Popular Culture in England 1750–1900*. New York: Schocken Books, p. 14.

5. Gratton, C.A. (1996). Britain. In G. Crushman, et al. (Eds.), *World Leisure Participation: Free Time in the Global Village*. Oxon, UK: CAB International.

6. Ibrahim, H. (1991). *Leisure and Society*. Dubuque, IA: Wm C. Brown Publishers, pp. 95, 99, 104, 122, 137.

7. Dare, B., Welton, G., & Coe, W. (1987). *Leisure in Western Thought*. Dubuque, IA: Kendall/Hunt. p.160.

8. Samuel, N. (1996). France. In G. Crushman, et al. (Eds.), *World Leisure Participation: Free Time in the Global Village*. Oxon, UK: CAB International.

9. Hoberman, J. (1984). *Sport and Political Ideology*. Austin, TX: University of Texas Press, p. 210.

10. Tokarski, W., & Michels, H. (1996). Germany. In G. Crushman, et al. (Eds.), *World Leisure Participation: Free Time in the Global Village*. Oxon, UK: CAB International.

11. Mosley, F. (Ed.) (1978). *Australia's Wilderness*. Hathorn, Victoria, Australia: Australian Conservation Foundation, p. 27.

11a. Darcy, S., & Veal, A.J. (1996). Australia. In G. Crushman, et al. (Eds.), *World Leisure Participation: Free Time in the Global Village*. Oxon, UK: CAB International.

12. Riordan, J. (1993). Leisure Policies in the Soviet Union. In P. Bramham, et al. (Eds.), *Leisure Policies in Europe*. Wallingford, Oxon: CAB International.

12a. Nazarova, I. (2000). Self-rated Health and Occupational Conditions in Russia. *Social Science and Health* 51:375.

12b. Azhgikhina, N., & Sutcliffe, B. (2000). Russia's Club Life. *Studies in Twentieth Century Literature* 24:169.

13. Olszweska, A. (1979). Leisure in Poland. In H. Ibrahim & J. Shivers (Eds.), *Leisure: Emergence and Expansion*. Los Alamitos, CA: Hwong, pp. 403, 405.

14. Riordon, J. (1993). Elements of Leisure in Post-War Poland. In P. Bramham, et al. (Eds.), *Leisure Policies in Europe*. Wallingford, Oxon: CAB International.

14a. Jung, B. (1996). Poland. In G. Crushman, et al. (Eds.), *World Leisure Participation: Free Time in the Global Village*. Oxon, UK: CAB International.

15. Horn, J. (1979). Leisure in Mexico. In H. Ibrahim & J. Shivers (Eds.), *Leisure: Emergence and Expansion*. Los Alamitos, CA: Hwong, pp. 373, 377–379.

16. Carlson, L. (1971). *Mexico: An Extraordinary Guide*. Chicago: Rand McNally, p. 38.

16a. Clancy, M. (2001). Mexican Tourism: Export Growth and Structural Change Since 1970. *Latin American Research Review* 36:128.

17. Basham, A.L. (1963). *The Wonder That Was India*. New York: Hawthorn Books, p. 204.

18. Armes, R. (1987). *Third World Film Making and the West*. Berkeley, CA: University of California Press, p. 95.

18a. Guha, R. (1998). Cricket and Politics in India. *Past & Present* November:155.

19. Lane, E.W. (1973). *An Account of the Manners and Customs of the Modern Egyptians*. New York: Dover.

20. Gernet, J. (1962). *Daily Life in China*. Stanford, CA: Stanford University Press.

21. Shi, M. (1998). From Imperial Gardens to Public Parks: The Transformation of Urban Space in Early Twentieth Century Beijing. *Modern China* 24:219.

We become not a melting pot but a beautiful mosaic. Different people, different beliefs, different yearnings, different hopes, different dreams.

JIMMY CARTER
*Speech, Pittsburgh, Pennsylvania, 1976*

# Diversity and Inclusiveness

## CHAPTER 9

## THE CHAPTER AT A GLANCE

Both the law and common morality require that equal opportunities be provided to all citizens, regardless of race, sex, age, national origin, creed, or level of mental or physical ability. In this chapter we focus on diversity and inclusiveness as they relate to recreational and leisure activities and to the people who participate in them. We explore the diverse American population and learn how recreation and leisure professionals must respond to its needs morally, practically, and legally. We also look at popular recreational and leisure activities: sports, fitness, outdoor recreation, hobbies, crafts, and cultural pursuits.

## Chapter Objectives

*After completing this chapter, you should be able to*

- ◆ Discuss population trends in the United States and identify key federal laws passed to ensure equal treatment for minorities.
- ◆ Outline changing trends in the American family structure and dynamics, and discuss family and intergenerational programs of leisure and recreation.
- ◆ Explain the ways in which women have experienced discrimination in sports and trace developments in the history of women's sports.
- ◆ Discuss the history of men's sports and recreation.
- ◆ Explain the significance and benefits of participating in sports, fitness activities, outdoor recreation, hobbies, crafts, and cultural pursuits.

## A World  of Difference

### MOTHERS AND DAUGHTERS TALK SPORTS

"Great game!" "Girls, you were terrific!" "Amy, that three-pointer was sheer brilliance!"

The mothers of junior varsity basketball players Stacia Saunders, Amy Whitney, and Maria Coletti gather around their daughters, dispensing congratulatory hugs and praise for their victory over the tough team from Forest Lake High. The girls, still amazed by Amy's last-second three-pointer swishing through the basket, are pounding each other on the back and yelling ecstatically.

"Come on, girls, we'll treat you to ice cream at The Scoop," says Maria's mother, Betty. Short and stocky, she's attractively dressed in a dark green dress and jacket and carries a bulging briefcase—her badge of office as a senior social worker for the county government. "Absolutely," chimes in Livonia Saunders. Small boned and slender, she looks elegant in a beautifully cut black suit—every inch the successful corporate lawyer she is. "Let's all go in our van," suggests Anne Whitney, her arm around Amy. A tall, slender blonde dressed in tailored casual clothes, she supervises the operation of the horse farm that's been in her family for 150 years. "We can bring you all back here afterward."

Laughing and talking, the girls and their mothers pile into the Whitneys' van for the short ride to The Scoop—the place to indulge in the ultimate ice cream fantasy.

After the remains of the last exotic concoction have been cleared away, the girls and their mothers linger over soda and coffee. "You know," Anne says, "it's almost unbelievable how much girls' sports have changed since I played. I'm 48, and, when I was in school, the girls took a back seat to the boys in all kinds of ways. The boys got to use the gym for practice every afternoon between 3:00 and 5:00; we had to get up at 5:30 in the morning so we could practice at 7:00 before school started. The school paid for the boys' uniforms; we had to buy our own. The boys' games always had advance publicity and programs, but the school didn't even post a schedule of the girls' games. It was pretty discouraging."

"You're kidding!" Stacia exclaims. "I wish I were," Anne says ruefully. "Our basketball team had some really good players, but all the attention and glory went to the boys. I'm happy to see how different things are for you girls."

## THE CHANGING FACE OF LEISURE PARTICIPATION

Leisure in America is no longer the domain of the elite. Barriers to participation in some activities still exist, but, as the white majority becomes a less dominant force, our society is moving toward a more inclusive approach to all leisure participants. Increasingly, members of all segments of society are being acknowl-edged and encouraged to retain their unique characteristics and cultures.

The leisure scene in the United States has been affected by three significant developments that have taken place over the past two centuries. The first is shifts in population composition; the second is the change in values that led to passage of the Civil Rights Act and related legislation; the third is the technological advances that have literally revolutionized the American way of life.

## A World of Difference

### MOTHERS AND DAUGHTERS TALK SPORTS (cont'd)

"I loved basketball, but my father wouldn't let me play," Betty Coletti says. "I know I'm short and sort of chunky, but I was a really good guard in the pickup games we used to play in the neighborhood. I was even chosen for the team in the tryouts in junior high. But my father was from the old country, and he believed that women belonged in the home. So I got to clean house and make pasta while my brothers played in all the games at CYO and at our parish school. I'm happy with my life, but I've always wondered if things might have been different if I'd been allowed to do the same things my brothers did."

"Papa wouldn't let you play basketball?" Maria says incredulously. She loves her stocky, affectionate grandfather, with his bellowing laugh and his still strongly accented English. She can hardly picture him being such a tyrant, although she knows her mother didn't go to college until after she was married and Maria had started first grade. "What a chauvinist!"

"What about you, Mrs. Saunders?" Amy asks Livonia. The handsome African-American woman shakes her head. "I grew up in southern Alabama, in cotton country," she says quietly. "There were 10 kids in our family, and my parents worked 14 hours a day in the textile mill to keep us in food and clothes. The school desegregation law had already been passed, but you couldn't tell it by the school we went to." She pauses, gazing back into a vanished world. "It wasn't much better than a shack, and it definitely didn't have a gym. There was a play yard outside covered with cracked asphalt and a splintery pole with a metal basketball hoop on it—no net. There was no gym teacher, so we all just took turns throwing a beat-up old basketball at the hoop. I never saw a gym until I went to college in Georgia."

As you study this chapter, think about the experiences of Betty Coletti, Livonia Saunders, and Anne Whitney and prepare to answer the questions in Your Turn at the end of the chapter.

## Population Dynamics

The United States today has a diverse population that claims ancestry from almost every geographic location and cultural background on earth. In contrast, the first U.S. Census in 1790 showed a population dominated by people of European descent, with those of English and Welsh heritage making up 82% of the white population. African-Americans represented 19% of the total population in 1790; in part because of the increased flow of immigration, by 1930 African-Americans made up only 10% of the population. For many years the population continued to be dominated by people of European origin, who shared a cultural heritage. For example, of the 49 million immigrants who arrived in the United States between 1820 and 1970, nearly three quarters were from Europe.[1]

The U.S. Bureau of the Census reports that roughly one third of the North American population is composed of diverse ethnic minorities, and that figure is climbing.[2] Nonwhites already comprise the majority of the population in all major cities, and mixed-race marriages are on the rise.[3] For a new century, one

African studies professor sees a promising future:

> What a gift it would be if we bring to it the cultural goal of eliminating racial hierarchy so that America might finally take advantage of the talents and skills of all its many and varied voices.[4]

For recreation and leisure professionals, the challenge of these dramatic demographic shifts is to continue to develop significant strategies that will enhance the effectiveness of programs for a clientele that is becoming more diverse.

## Toward Equality

For generations, minorities in the United States have been subjected to discrimination, both overt and covert, legal and illegal. The two groups that arguably have suffered the harshest discrimination are African-Americans, who were forced into slavery, and Native Americans, who were driven from their ancestral lands onto government-run reservations. The white, western European majority also meted out unfavorable treatment to a host of other ethnic minorities who emigrated to the United States: Irish, Italians, Poles, Hungarians, Hispanics, Asians, and Jews. Discriminated against in housing, employment, and education, these and other minorities often remained banded together in tightly knit communities, resisting assimilation in what seemed to be the hostile climate of the New World.

By the early 1960s, the African-American–led civil rights movement had become a powerful force in the United States. In 1964 President Johnson signed into law the landmark Civil Rights Act, which banned discrimination in voting, employment, public accommodations, and other areas. Other key federal legislation intended to prevent discrimination and protect the rights of minorities includes the Equal Pay Act of 1963, the Older Americans Act of 1965, the Rehabilitation Act of 1973, and the Americans

with Disabilities Act of 1990. The thrust of these laws is to ensure the provision of equal opportunities, including leisure services, for all Americans regardless of race, sex, age, national origin, creed, or level of mental or physical ability.

## The Global Village

In addition to population changes and the passage of civil rights legislation in the United States, technological advances are bringing the world together in what has been called a "global village," where people of virtually every culture are able to interact on a scale undreamed of only a few years ago. Such interaction is facilitated by improved telecommunications technology and powerful personal computers, which, equipped with modems, allow people to communicate efficiently and economically over the "information superhighway" opened up by the Internet. Communications that once took days to reach their destination now arrive in a matter of seconds. When the Asian market fell in 1997, the New York Stock Exchange reacted immediately. Sophisticated television and satellite technology brought the 1991 U.S. bomber attack on Baghdad, which opened the Gulf War, into millions of living rooms in America and all over the world. Of necessity, we humans are becoming citizens of the world, and it becomes increasingly important for us to understand each other's cultures and customs.

## Toward Diversity

The United States truly is a nation of immigrants who molded a uniquely American culture while retaining some of their native customs and traditions. Once referred to as a "melting pot," the United States today is thought of as a "salad bowl" or "mosaic," as former President Jimmy Carter observed in the chapter-opening quote. Whereas the melting pot image suggested that ethnic groups adopt new, "American" traits and leave old ones behind, the salad bowl and mosaic images emphasize an environment in which each culture retains its values and traditions while all cultures live together in mutual respect and acceptance.

America is becoming more diverse not only racially and ethnically but also in terms of gender, family structure, and lifestyle orientation. Over the past several decades the number and status of women in the workforce have increased dramatically. As we learned earlier, the rising divorce rate is causing a growing number of children to be brought up in single-parent homes or shared custody arrangements, and remarriages are creating "blended families" that include children of both partners. Many more people are choosing to remain single than in the past, and acceptance is increasing for children born out of wedlock and for gay and lesbian lifestyles. We will examine these important social trends in more detail later in the chapter.

All of these changes in laws and values give impetus to the effort to provide leisure services to everyone in America's increasingly diverse population. To ascertain the best way to serve each group, we must understand leisure behavior in terms of variables such as race, ethnicity, and physical and mental ability.

### Race

**Race** refers to a division of humankind possessing traits that are transmittable by descent and that are sufficient to characterize it as a distinct human type. Typically the world population is classified into three races: Caucasian (white), Mongol (Asian and Indian), and Negro (black). Race itself has no bearing on leisure preferences or services; the significant factor is the cultural system of each group within a race.

### Ethnicity

**Ethnicity** describes the affiliation of a large group of people classed according to a common racial, national, tribal, religious, linguistic, or cultural background. Public recreation has long been recognized for bringing people of different ethnic groups together and building constructive relationships among them. Today more than ever, recreation and leisure professionals must be prepared to work with people whose ethnic and cultural backgrounds represent a spectrum of diversity.

Culturally diverse recreation programming looks at differences among people as strengths to build on. Opportunities for interaction, cultural discovery, accessibility, and self-directed choices are critical ingredients of successful programming.

James Vasquez of the University of Washington in Seattle, who studied learning patterns among Hispanic, African-American, and Native American youth, found, for example, that Hispanic youth have a strong sense of loyalty to their family, which is their basic support group throughout life. They appreciate ethnic role models and tend to work more effectively in cooperative rather than competitive settings. African-American youth, he found, are noticeably person centered and are highly sensitive to the moods of others. They are especially receptive to multiple stimuli and variability. Native American youth prefer to have private experiences before engaging in public performances and are not strongly competitive.[5] Although not all members of a particular ethnic group are alike, these findings are useful to recreation and leisure professionals who plan programming for culturally diverse groups of people.

A noteworthy observation from the U.S. Commission on Civil Rights is that, although professionals with the same ethnic background

*race* a division of humankind possessing traits that are transmittable by descent

*ethnicity* the affiliation of a large group of people classed according to a common racial, national, tribal, religious, linguistic, or cultural background

as the population they serve do bring special qualities to the situation, they have not demonstrated a higher success rate than have professionals of other ethnic heritages.

### Persons with Disabilities

*Persons with disabilities* is the term used to describe individuals with some form of physical and/or mental disability. At least 54 million people in the United States have disabilities.[6] These individuals must be encouraged to be self-confident and to focus on what they *can* achieve, not on what they cannot do. Recreation programs have historically been segregated. More recently, however, people with disabilities have been integrated into programs in which the rest of the population participates (see Chapter 14).

For many people with disabilities, recreational and leisure activities not only may be part of a balanced life but also may be an integral component of rehabilitation.[7] Recreational therapists can also provide training for families with children with disabilities, including behavior modification, medication management, seizure management, and respiratory care.[8]

## Bridging Gaps Through Leisure

Over the past several decades, numerous efforts have been launched to promote harmony and understanding among America's wide variety of ethnic and cultural groups. In the late 1970s, realizing that the ethnic composition of the U.S. population was changing rapidly, the leadership of the Girl Scouts of the USA considered whether the organization should start to form separate troops for girls of different ethnic groups. Discarding this idea as unprogressive, the leaders instead focused on organizing troops that would welcome girls of all backgrounds.[9] Today the Girl Scouts actively recruit and welcome girls and adult leaders from diverse backgrounds, encouraging interaction with others who are different. They talk openly about diversity and promote tolerance, acceptance, and cooperation.

Anytown, U.S.A., camps were started in Arizona in 1957 by the National Conference of Christians and Jews. They offer teenagers a rustic camp experience that concentrates on weaving differences into community. For one week, high school students of diverse backgrounds from all around the country are immersed in a series of experiences that confront hatred and prejudice. They discuss various forms of discrimination and explore ways in which they have the power to right wrongs. Participants learn to see issues through the eyes of others before making judgments.[10]

The International Family Festival in Los Angeles is a cultural celebration of the arts that has been hailed for its success in bringing together people of all ages and many ethnic backgrounds. Celebrating the region's diverse cultural families, the multi-day special event features dance team competitions and an international marketplace and food court. Entertainment, sponsored by the Los Angeles Department of Recreation and Parks, includes a number of events such as Thai folk opera, gospel choruses, and Japanese puppet shows, to name just a few.

*The Los Angeles International Festival celebrates the city's diversity.*

- Name three pieces of federal legislation that are designed to prohibit discrimination against various minority groups.
- Briefly explain the rationale for culturally diverse recreation programming.

## THE FAMILY

Leisure plays an important role in the lives of most families, and family leisure is a major focus of the rapidly growing U.S. leisure industry. Nearly half of all Americans engage in outdoor recreation as a family at least once a month.[11] They go to recreation centers together, take family cruises, and participate in virtual-reality diversions. In planning family recreation, professionals understand the trends that shape family life and values in contemporary America.

In preindustrial societies, the typical family structure included not only parents and children but also other relatives such as grandparents and unmarried aunts and uncles—the extended family we learned about earlier in the text. In the post–World War II years of the 1950s and 1960s, the extended family gave way to the so-called nuclear family, consisting only of parents and children, with mom as homemaker and dad as breadwinner. As of 1991, however, nuclear families accounted for only 15% of U.S. families.[12] More typical now are dual-income households. In fact, the Census Bureau reports that in 1995 more than half of all mothers ages 15 to 44 had re-entered the labor force within a year after giving birth, compared with only 31% in 1976.[13]

Contributing to the increase in single-parent homes are divorce rates, which are expected to remain at about 50%,[14] along with the number of babies born out of wedlock. The latter trend is not confined to women who are poor, uneducated, or members of a minority group. Many unwed mothers are white, college-educated, and professional women.[15]

As a result of divorce and remarriage, so-called blended or reconstituted families are more common. In fact, the government estimates that stepfamilies will soon outnumber traditional nuclear families. More couples are deferring parenthood until their late thirties or early forties, and many are deciding not to have children at all. Among other structures are foster families, gay and lesbian families (some with children from previous marriages), families whose children were born through artificial insemination or in vitro fertilization, and communes. Moreover, in today's fast-paced society, any kind of family is far more subject to change than was the case in the years before World War II, which were characterized by family stability and a significantly slower pace of social and technological change.

### Family Leisure Programming

When parents and children share activities, they also share a sense of purpose, exhilaration, challenge, and accomplishment. Research consistently shows that families place a high value on time spent together and on leisure activities they can enjoy as a family. Moreover, home-based activities and family-oriented pursuits outside the home are the most common forms of leisure activity in the United States.[16] Most Americans look to their families first for meaning in their lives.[17] Nevertheless, one survey finds that 78% of the nation's younger workers (ages 15–31) work more than eight hours a day. As many as 56% of these respondents believe that they do not have enough time with their families.[18] Another survey indicates that, for many, recreational activities in which they take part with family members are among the peak experiences of their lives.[12] Studies also document increased marital communication and satisfaction resulting from participation in joint leisure activities and indicate a negative relationship between communication and participation in individual activities, including television viewing.[16]

*Effective family programming should promote communication, understanding, and harmony.*

1. Teach recreational skills to both child and parent
2. Teach skills for recreation at home
3. Encourage the parent to be a participant and a teacher, not a spectator
4. Do not assume the family knows how to interact or share a family experience
5. Provide inexpensive programming
6. Consider timing; for maximum benefit, centers should be open on weekends and during weekday evening hours

The major factors that affect the marketing of family leisure services in America are the strong and growing interest in such activities and the wide diversity of family structures. Providers of leisure services must use care in marketing family activities. Because the term *family* often conjures up memories of the traditional nuclear family, many people may exclude themselves from activities offered for "the family." Single parents and childless couples are more likely to be attracted to programs whose names use words and phrases such as *community* or *extended family*, or to the popular Parents Without Partners program. Programmers also must consider the different leisure needs of family members. Working mothers, for example, all too often suffer from overcommitment of time, and they may see family leisure activities as a burden rather than a release. Childcare programs can relieve some of this stress.

Another barrier to successful family leisure programming is lack of time, information, or interest in the programs. Programmers can seek to overcome these barriers by organizing drop-in centers, workshops, and self-directed programs; by conducting inclusive marketing and advertising through current participants; and by conducting surveys and experimental programs to determine the needs and preferences of prospective participants. The following guidelines can help leisure programmers meet family needs:[12]

Effective family programs promote communication, harmony, and understanding among family members. They serve as an antidote to stress and help build family strength and unity. They teach families the benefits of playing and working together. Some of the most popular family offerings are nature-related and outdoor activities; hobby evenings; programs in music, art, drama, and genealogy; foreign language classes; aquatics; coed sports; beach and trail cleanups; and barbecues. Fig. 9.1 shows a family fitness program that involves cooperation between parents and children.

## Intergenerational Programming

According to the Mayo Clinic, in 1993 over 70% of the U.S. population over 65 years of age were grandparents, and nearly half of those grandparents will become great-grandparents.[19] Many experts believe the bond between grandparent and grandchild is second in emotional power only to the parent-child relationship. Because grandparents do not have to play the disciplinarian role, the activities they enjoy with their grandchildren often are more relaxed than is the case with activities involving parent and child. Research shows that children benefit from close relationships with older relatives and that they feel more secure about themselves when they learn to work with different age groups.[19]

In contemporary society, distance and the decline of the extended family often create obstacles to the development of close relation-

**FIGURE 9.1** Family fitness contest

Become a family fitness team member, earn points, and get fit. Your team can earn points by enjoying any of the listed activities. For each 10 minutes that you do an activity, you will earn the points listed below. To earn points, the activity must be done by the participating child and at least one adult team member. The entire family can participate.

| ACTIVITY | TEAM POINTS (EVERY 10 MIN.) |
|---|---|
| Archery | 5 |
| Badminton | 6 |
| Baseball | 5 |
| Basketball | 6 |
| Bicycling | 8 |
| Calisthenics | 5 |
| Canoeing | 4 |
| Dancing | 4 |
| Football | 8 |
| Golf | 4 |
| Hiking | 7 |
| Horseback riding | 4 |
| Martial arts | 12 |
| Paddleball | 10 |
| Racquetball | 10 |
| Running | 14 |
| Sailing | 14 |
| Skating | 3 |
| Skiing | |
|    Downhill | 6 |
|    Cross-country | 12 |
| Soccer | 9 |
| Swimming | 9 |
| Tennis | 7 |
| Volleyball | 5 |
| Walking | |
|    Slow | 4 |
|    Moderate | 7 |

ships between grandparents and grandchildren. Moreover, as marriages become less stable, families tend to become smaller and more mobile, causing children to have less contact with relatives outside the immediate family.[20]

In these instances, the grandparent-grandchild bond can be kept intact through letters, telephone calls, audio and videotapes, and visits. Also beneficial to young people in this situation is recreational programming that links them to other older adults.

### Expanding Opportunities

For many years, members of Girl Scouts, Boy Scouts, and youth groups of religious organizations have visited senior citizens in retirement and nursing homes. Through intergenerational recreation programming, these services are being expanded. Children and elders garden together, read stories, share meals, and celebrate birthdays. One expert observed that children who participate in these programs receive loving attention and develop a more positive outlook toward growing older. Adults' lives are brightened; they feel needed; and they experience improved self-esteem, satisfaction, and memory. Patients with Alzheimer's disease also have responded well to children.[21]

The relationship between teenagers and older adults often is characterized by negative attitudes and stereotyping on both sides. Many teenagers assume all older people are old-fashioned, stodgy, judgmental, and out of touch; by the same token, many seniors view all teenagers as irresponsible, immoral, selfish, and disrespectful. Intergenerational recreation programming can help bridge this gap by allowing teens and seniors to get to know each other on a one-to-one basis. Particularly successful are nature and craft programs in which older adults serve as volunteer instructors and mentors to teenagers. Teens learn that older adults can be fun and that they have valuable insights and knowledge. Older adults learn that they can communicate with teenagers and that teenagers have many positive qualities.

### Successful Programming

Successful intergenerational programming involves frequent interactions between young people and older adults. Participants are kept busy with activities that promote learning, communication, and a sense of belonging. Competition is de-emphasized. One expert identifies the following benefits of intergenerational experiences:[22]

1. Enhanced sense of self-worth for people of all ages
2. Feelings of community
3. Improved educational achievement for young people
4. Preservation of older people's skills and experience
5. For youth, a sense of caring and being cared for
6. For older people, improved emotional and mental health
7. For troubled youth, a sense of being understood and prevention of delinquency
8. Transfer of knowledge to youth to promote social responsibility, economy, and more efficient use of limited resources

Concept Check

- Identify three specific trends that are changing the traditional American family structure.
- Name three challenges that face recreation and leisure professionals in developing family programming.
- Name three benefits of intergenerational leisure programming.

## THE SEX/GENDER FACTOR

The terms *sex* and *gender* often are used interchangeably to describe characteristics that differentiate males from females. For purposes of this text we will define **sex** as the physical characteristics that distinguish males from females and **gender** as the behavioral, cultural, and psychological traits typically associated with one sex. Interestingly, in the past 30 years

psychologists have published thousands of articles on the psychology of the sexes. In general, research shows that although predispositions in sex-based behavior exist at birth, they are not always clear-cut and in some instances may be overriden by cultural teaching.

Every society categorizes its members according to sex and expects some different behavior patterns from men and women.[23] When socially imposed gender-based roles predominate, neither males nor females have the choices that would be available in a society that valued individuals according to personal traits and achievements. Unrealistic assumptions about masculinity and femininity create difficulties for both men and women and may erode self-esteem.

### Androgyny

**Androgynous** is a term used to describe a person who has the characteristics of both male and female, or who is neither specifically feminine nor masculine. Originally used to describe the rare situation of a male who has the physical characteristics of a female, *androgyny* is now commonly used to describe persons of either sex whose behavior incorporates both masculine and feminine attributes. Such people can be decisive and assertive and at the same time tender and nurturing, without feeling any threat to their gender identity. Androgynous people may use more of their human potential and have the flexibility to respond to a wider variety of situations than do people who are locked into rigidly masculine or feminine sex roles.[24] One study found that people with a higher level of education are better able to view masculinity and femininity as flexible traits.[24]

### Changing Gender Roles

Until the early 20th century, American women were not allowed to vote, own property, or make contracts. They were not expected to pursue higher education or to contribute to public life; in fact, they were actively discouraged from becoming anything other than housewives and hostesses or, if unmarried, dutiful daughters. They were valued according to the status of the men in their lives, their physical appearance, their feminine accomplishments (piano playing, painting, needlework), and the extent of their deference to men.

Since that time, women's roles have changed dramatically, and gender roles for both sexes have become far more flexible. Men, who traditionally were pressured to be tough, domineering, striving, achieving, unsentimental, and emotionally inexpressive, now have more freedom to acknowledge and discuss their feelings, pursue careers that do not involve aggressive powermongering, and become involved in relationships where gender roles are flexible rather than rigid.

## Sports, Recreation, and Gender

In the United States, as in most other countries of the world, cultural pressures have restricted sports and recreation options for both males and females. In sports, boys or men who make mistakes or fail to win a game often are ridiculed by coaches and teammates who call them "sissies" or "girls." These epithets are two edged: they are demeaning to women, and they cause many boys to withdraw from sports. Similar damage is done when talented female athletes are called "tomboys" or are praised for being "almost as good as a man."

Table 9.1 provides statistics on male and female participation in sports and other recreational activities. Traditionally sports has been a male-dominated arena, where women have been deprived of opportunities to compete, build skills, and pursue professional careers. Moreover, other leisure activities, including hobbies and cultural pursuits, also have been effectively segregated by sex, with the result that many talented people withdraw from or fail to pursue certain interests because they fear criticism. In no form of endeavor, whether related to work or to leisure, should society sacrifice the contributions of dedicated and

accomplished people simply because they fail to adhere to accepted sex-role stereotypes.

Fortunately, in recent years the issue of gender equity in sports and recreation has begun to receive much-needed attention. One study found that the great majority of adults (97%) accept sport as an appropriate activity for girls, and 87% believe sport is as important for girls as it is for boys.[25] Throughout the 1990s women's sport has experienced notable growth as the U.S. Commission on Civil Rights has intensified its efforts to enforce federal laws against sex bias. In the 1960s and early 1970s, as women began to criticize publicly the inequality of sports opportunities, men started looking at their own relationship to sports and to identify training techniques that promoted excessive aggression and unwholesome levels of competition.[26] Today recreation and leisure professionals are challenged to provide programs that meet the needs of all participants and that strive to build leadership qualities in both males and females.

### Concept Check

- Define the terms *sex* and *gender.*
- State the benefits of androgynous behavior and attitudes in comparison with strict adherence to stereotypical sex roles.

*sex* the physical characteristics that distinguish males from females

*gender* the behavioral, cultural, and psychological traits typically associated with one sex

*androgyny* state of being specifically neither female nor male in terms of attitudes and behavior

**TABLE 9.1**   Participation in Sports Activities (by selected characteristics, 1995)*

| ACTIVITY | ALL PERSONS | | SEX | |
|---|---|---|---|---|
| | NUMBER | RANK | MALE | FEMALE |
| Number participated in: | | | | |
| Aerobic exercising | 23,052 | 11 | 4,302 | 18,750 |
| Backpacking/wilderness camping | 10,244 | 21 | 6,413 | 3,831 |
| Baseball | 15,729 | 16 | 12,087 | 3,642 |
| Basketball | 30,098 | 8 | 20,918 | 9,180 |
| Bicycle riding | 56,308 | 3 | 29,830 | 26,478 |
| Bowling | 41,898 | 6 | 21,142 | 20,756 |
| Calisthenics | 9,340 | 22 | 4,042 | 5,298 |
| Camping (vacation/overnight) | 42,818 | 5 | 22,835 | 19,983 |
| Exercise walking | 70,268 | 1 | 25,097 | 45,171 |
| Exercising with equipment | 44,328 | 4 | 20,583 | 23,745 |
| Fishing—fresh water | 39,282 | 7 | 26,444 | 12,838 |
| Fishing—salt water | 10,717 | 20 | 7,685 | 3,032 |
| Football | 8,270 | 24 | 7,366 | 904 |
| Golf | 23,959 | 10 | 18,016 | 5,943 |
| Hiking | 25,047 | 9 | 13,848 | 11,199 |
| Hunting with firearms | 16,253 | 15 | 13,968 | 2,285 |
| Racquetball | 4,699 | 25 | 3,343 | 1,356 |
| Running/jogging | 20,635 | 12 | 11,874 | 8,761 |
| Skiing—alpine/downhill | 9,261 | 23 | 5,623 | 3,638 |
| Skiing—cross-country | 3,429 | 26 | 1,757 | 1,672 |
| Soccer | 11,976 | 18 | 7,691 | 4,285 |
| Softball | 17,611 | 14 | 10,007 | 7,604 |
| Swimming | 61,531 | 2 | 28,944 | 32,587 |
| Target shooting | 11,193 | 19 | 9,019 | 2,174 |
| Tennis | 12,571 | 17 | 6,813 | 5,758 |
| Volleyball | 17,956 | 13 | 8,772 | 9,184 |

*Figures are referred to in thousands.

# HISTORY OF WOMEN'S SPORT AND RECREATION

Since the founding of the United States, women have participated in recreational and leisure activities. Today the arena for these activities is as wide as the world; in the preindustrial era most social interaction and leisure pastimes took place within the home or community. Although their lives were hard and dominated by work, early female settlers found time to participate in family card games, charades, quilting bees, and community celebrations. Women of the upper class, who had more time for leisure activities, ventured into fishing, boating, sleighing, ice skating, and horseback riding.[27] Eventually, dancing became the most popular and acceptable activity for women of all classes.

By the early 19th century, with the onset of industrialization and urbanization, a new middle class was beginning to emerge. Women of this class had more time for leisure activities than did women of the working class. During the Victorian era (1837–1901), American and British women of the middle and upper classes were considered too frail for strenuous exercise. Dancing continued to offer opportunities for both social interaction and exercise, and middle-class women accompanied men to sporting events.

During the Civil War (1861–1865) many women took on jobs to support the men at war, and following the period called Reconstruction (reorganization of the Southern states that had seceded from the Union) women began to engage in a wider variety of leisure activities. They joined clubs and other organizations and participated in sports tournaments offered by athletic clubs and other sponsors. Especially popular were fencing and outdoor sports such as lawn bowling, ice skating, archery, croquet, and baseball. By the early 1880s upper-class women were joining their husbands as members of country clubs and were participating in tennis, golf, and horseback riding.[27] The 1888 invention of the safety bicycle was a major factor in freeing women from their restrictive clothing. Amelia Bloomer's earlier innovation, the bloomer—full, loose trousers gathered at the knee—allowed women to cycle with much more freedom and enjoyment. Meanwhile, municipalities began to open public gymnasiums, where women participated in gymnastics, calisthenics, swimming, basketball, and volleyball.

## School-Sponsored Sports

With the opening of women's seminaries, academies, colleges, and universities, the demand increased for classes in physical education. Women now were encouraged to engage in regular physical exercise in the belief that healthy bodies would help them cope with academic challenges. Sports activities developed into competitions, and basketball became the most popular sport for women after the game was introduced at Smith College in 1892. Basketball clubs began to be formed, and in 1899 the Women's Basketball Rules Committee was organized to publish rules for a modified version of the game. By 1917 competition had expanded to the point that the Committee on Women's Athletics (CWA) was established. So popular were sports that graduates formed clubs for continued competition after graduation.

During the years of America's involvement in World War I (1917–1918), women successfully took over many of the physically demanding jobs vacated by men, clearly demonstrating that they had both the strength and the dexterity to succeed in competitive sports. After the war the economy flourished, allowing both more money and more time to be spent on leisure activities, and the women's sports movement continued to advance into the 1920s. As women's sports became more competitive, however, female physical educators began to protest the intense training regimens and exploitation of elite athletes. Lou Henry Hoover, president of the Girl Scouts, was asked to organize a division of the National Amateur Athletic Federation (NAAF) to study the matter. The newly formed division agreed with the protesting physical educators and discouraged female athletic competition in schools. Thus ended the golden era of expansion of women's competitive sports.

In line with the decreased emphasis on competition, in the 1920s a popular event for young female athletes was the playday, in which teams were formed from various schools.

These were essentially informal social events in which games were played with no preliminary practice and no announcement of scores. By the 1930s playdays had given way to sports days, in which individual school teams participated in minor competitions. In some areas of the country, varsity competition continued. At this point the desire for competition resurfaced and intensified, and women began to turn to recreational leagues and to the Amateur Athletic Union (AAU), which played a significant role in American women's participation in the Olympics.[28]

## "A League of Their Own"

During World War II the All-American Girls Baseball League (popularized in the hit movie *A League of Their Own*) was formed to entertain fans while male players were at war. Between 1943 and 1954 more than 600 women played a schedule of 110 to 116 games a year with nearly 1 million fans flocking to the games in 1948 alone.[27] Babe Didriksen dominated the fledgling Ladies Professional Golf Association (LPGA); the Women's Professional Bowling Association (WPBA) was established in 1959; and in 1950 Althea Gibson broke the color barrier in professional tennis, becoming the first African-American to compete in a Grand Slam event: the U.S. National Tennis Championships at Forest Hills, New York. In 1957 Gibson won the women's singles title at this event and thus became the first African-American to win a Grand Slam event.

## The Return of Competition

All of these developments reinforced the idea that women were physically capable of playing competitive professional sports. Schools once again allowed female athletes to take part in extramural competition, and two organizations were formed to govern them: the Girls Athletic Association (GAA) and the Women's Recreational Association (WRA). The National Section of Girls' and Women's Sports (currently the National Association for Girls

and Women in Sport) published strict guidelines for competitions.

In the 1960s, as pressure intensified to improve the performance of American female Olympic athletes, schools, colleges, and universities began to re-evaluate and upgrade their women's athletic programs. In 1971 the Association for Intercollegiate Athletics for Women (AIAW) was founded. In 1972 Congress passed landmark legislation to create equal opportunities for all persons who attend educational institutions that receive federal funding. Title IX of the Educational Amendment Act of 1972 reads in part[29]

> No person in the United States shall, on the basis of sex, be excluded from participation in, denied the benefits of, or be subject to discrimination under any educational program or activity receiving federal financial assistance.

## The Drive Toward Equality

The drive toward equality in sports continued to gather strength, and in 1973 Billie Jean King won the much-hyped "battle of the sexes" when she defeated Bobby Riggs, who claimed he could beat any of the top female tennis players. This groundbreaking event proved that women not only were fit for elite competition among themselves but also could meet—and defeat—some men in the professional sports arena. The next year, Little League baseball announced that its teams would be open to girls. More women competed against men in professional sports, women's professional teams expanded, records were broken, and the media became noticeably more attentive to women's athletics.

The impressive growth in women's athletic competitions came to the attention of the powerhouse in men's intercollegiate sports, the National Collegiate Athletic Association (NCAA). After the passage of Title IX, the NCAA lifted its ban against women, and in 1975 members voted to take over the governance of women's collegiate sports from the

*Weekend outrigger events allow these physically fit women to compete.*

AIAW. AIAW held firm until 1980, when the NCAA offered national championships for female athletes, free travel for qualified teams, and one institutional membership fee for men and women. Pressure from some of the member schools helped lead to the demise of the AIAW. In 1982, it lost a court battle to prevent the NCAA from sponsoring women's championships.

## The Challenges Ahead

The 1980s and 1990s saw a surge of activity among girls and women in sports, recreation, and fitness activities. Women's athletic participation has increased 250% since 1977,[30] and over 40 million girls and women participated in sports nationwide.[30a] For the first time, women represented more than 38% of the total number of athletes in the Sydney 2000 Olympic Games. These 4,069 women participated in 44% of all events.[30b]

Despite these impressive gains, about a third of U.S. women report participating in no leisure-time activity whatsoever,[31] and only about one third of the athletes in our nation's schools are female[32] (see the Action Guide on p. 178 and Table 9.1). An NCAA survey taken to coincide with the 25th anniversary of Title IX shows that men receive 62% of athletic scholarship money, account for 73% of recruitment money spent, disburse over three times as much on operating expenses, and receive 60% of the money allocated for head coaching salaries.[33,34]

Before Title IX was enacted in 1972, female administrators ran more than 90% of women's collegiate athletic programs and coached between 90% and 100% of the teams.[32] In 2000, only 18.5% of women's programs were administered by women, and the proportion of women coaches had declined to 45.6%. This is a decrease of 10% from 1994. Despite the growth of teams, this is the lowest representation of female head coaches.[34]

Since 1980, participation opportunities for women have increased, although the average number of sports offered has declined.[35] While coaching opportunities on women's intercollegiate teams have increased, fewer women are entering the coaching ranks due to desire or barriers.[35a]

One expert suggests that previously undervalued concepts such as "the women's way" and "sport for all" may be resurfacing. The women's way emphasizes sports participation for all women as a lifestyle rather than a competition only for those who excel. Sport for all simply means that every girl or woman participates in some sport. Incorporation of these concepts, the expert believes, might lead to "transformations of the meaning and value of the sport experience."[36]

### Concept Check

- What factors contributed to public acceptance of women's athletics around the time of World War I?
- What is the purpose of Title IX, and what developments in women's intercollegiate athletics are attributable to the passage of this law?

## ACTION GUIDE

### HOW "EQUAL" ARE WOMEN ATHLETES?

Find out for yourself how the passage of Title IX and the ongoing drive toward equality for women have affected the opportunities available to female athletes. Interview a top female college athlete and ask the following questions:

1. What is your major sport? _____

2. How old were you when you began to play it? _____

3. Were you able to play the sport at school, did you join a league, or did you take public or private lessons? _____

4. In high school, was your coach a man or a woman? _____

5. In what ways, if any, do you think the sex of your coach affected the quality of instruction you received and the attitude you developed toward practicing and competing?

   _____

   _____

6. Were college scholarships available for female athletes in your sport? _____

7. If so, how did the scholarships compare with those available to men?

   _____

   _____

8. Whether you are or are not attending college on an athletic scholarship, what, if any, differences can you perceive in the college administration's attitude toward women's athletics compared with men's athletics?

   _____

   _____

9. Is your sport played at the professional level? _____

10. If so, do you intend to embark on a professional career? In either case, why?

   _____

   _____

# HISTORY OF MEN'S SPORT AND RECREATION

Most of the early settlers of the American colonies were English, so the forms of leisure and recreation they enjoyed were of English origin. For men, preferred activities were horse racing, ball games, rowing, cockfighting, and gambling. Men's sports did not achieve significant growth until the nation became more urbanized during the industrial revolution that began in the early 19th century. Athletic clubs for men became popular in the mid to late 19th century, with some emphasizing one sport and others offering several. College students sponsored many athletic clubs until colleges and universities permitted the formation of athletic teams. The clubs were instrumental in promoting the growth of some professional sports, and members worked to form national organizations to sponsor championships. Beginning at this time and lasting until after World War II, athletic events for whites and blacks were strictly segregated. Full integration of men's sports was not achieved until after the passage of Title IX in 1972.

Largely controlled by students, college and university sport for men expanded rapidly until the late 19th century, when concern that athletics were hampering academic performance resulted in the loss of student control. The founding of the Intercollegiate Athletic Association (now the NCAA) in 1906 marked the beginning of school control of sport. In the 1920s, when women's competitive sport was restricted to playdays, men's intercollegiate athletics entered a golden age—and it began to encounter strong criticism for competitive excesses. By this time, however, the programs had become so entrenched that administrators were virtually powerless to bring about reform.

The 1930s brought the economic collapse known as the Great Depression, as well as revelations regarding abuses in sport. Athletic competition slowed, and recreational activities became more popular because of enforced leisure time resulting from an extremely high rate of unemployment during the depression. On the positive side, the federal government hired many workers to build new recreational facilities. During World War II, many sports activities, such as major league baseball, were curtailed, but at the same time sports teams were formed on military bases. Another sports boom followed the end of the war.

In the 1960s concern again began to mount over what were seen as excessive aggression and overemphasis on winning in men's intercollegiate sports. In an effort to put sports on a positive philosophical track, the NCAA Division of Men's Athletics in 1962 defined four broad areas of emphasis: physical fitness, skill development, social development, and recreation. By the 1970s, however, questions were arising about the character-building benefits claimed for sports participation and about the often-heard assertion that "a winner in sports is a winner for life." A Louis Harris survey conducted in 1990 found that 75% of the American public and 81% of the faculty in institutions of higher learning believed intercollegiate athletics were out of control.[37]

## A Rite of Passage

Sport for American men has become a rite of passage that is valued because it is supposed to teach competitiveness, self-discipline, sacrifice, dedication, and teamwork. Men are pressured to participate in sports, to be successful, and to develop desirable masculine traits. Team sports promote a model of masculinity, helping young men achieve recognition and establish identity and self-confidence. Some young men prefer to develop strength and skill by participating in individual sports, wilderness challenges, or noncompetitive activities such as weightlifting or in-line skating.

The traits that sports participation is supposed to develop in young men are admirable and should be emphasized by recreation and leisure providers. One expert, however, poses these questions: What are the effects of sports failure on boys and men? What are the

# A CLOSER LOOK

## WHEN A MAN HATES SPORTS

I can recall the moment as if it were yesterday, which it certainly was not, that warm and sunny afternoon in fifth grade when my best friends, Dick and Geoff, enacted one of the most singular acts of charity and fellowship I can remember in my life.

My family was moving soon, out of state, and my buddies escorted me to the empty school playground with a baseball bat to show me, once and for all, how to swing it correctly. No verbal sentiments passed between us—no "Don't forget to write" or "We're going to miss you," with those years of tree forts and sledding sweepstakes down Suicide Hill hanging in the air between us—but simply "Hold it here and stand like this and swing it there." Two unsubtle messages registered. Yes, I would be missed. And, yes, I needed all the help they could give; what they were trying to teach me would amount to a survival skill in the months and years to come.

My father, working punishingly long weeks and often away on business, hadn't had time to play catch or shag flies with me. But for his faint curiosity each year as to the outcome of the World Series, I cannot to this day connect his fatherly image with sports, played or viewed. Our weekend time together, when it came, ran to chores; his legacy to me would be a certain skill

with carpenter's tools, soldering irons and the like, for which I am eternally grateful. Perhaps bats and catcher's mitts were alien objects in his hands; they certainly were in mine, and no last-minute lesson from my worried friends as the movers emptied our South Jersey home would save me from ignominy in the faster-paced, jazzy suburbs of New York City.

I remember no subsequent acts of kindness having anything remotely to do with sports. I continued to have a happy childhood; all would have been perfect but for the constant procession of humiliations awaiting me on the softball diamond, the basketball court, the football field. To line up in the gym classes of elementary school and junior and senior high was to step miserably, forlornly, dependably, into hell. All of us unathletic geeks slumping in our clean T-shirts and unfaded gym shorts, too embarrassed and repelled even to look at each other! Always being the last picked for a team! (You take him! No, you take him!) And, always, when I came up to bat, the boys in the outfield taking one look at me, and all of them running into the infield, laughing, seeing no threat from me, even if he manages to hit it this time. May they all burn.

To my credit, I became a fairly good sprinter and even liked gymnastics, but, in our team-sports community,

consequences for intimate relationships of developing the traits of traditional masculinity? What happens to the identity of male athletes after they leave sport?[38]

The fact is that many boys do not succeed in sports (see A Closer Look, above). Because of the importance placed on success and the stigma attached to failure, these boys may experience strong feelings of shame, negative self-image, and problems with relationships. Trying to prove their masculinity, some boys even risk their lives by driving fast or drinking hard. According to one expert, boys who excel in sports may profit from the experience and

come to regard it as natural, but those who do not must come to their own terms with sport and find other ways to proclaim their masculinity to other males.[39]

Belief in the importance of sport in promoting masculinity and manliness dates back to at least the middle of the 19th century. At that time physical prowess became associated with moral strength: the courage to endure pain and make good judgments under pressure. Masculine power was established through skill and force. The popular sports of the day were football, lacrosse, hockey, track and field, and boxing. Some people believed that sports par-

## A CLOSER LOOK

### WHEN A MAN HATES SPORTS (cont'd)

such currency had no value. Our town—especially the high school—excelled in sports, all those champeen baseball teams strutting around in their letter jackets, and all the girls pining and swooning. When I broke a finger playing softball . . . [for God's sake] or when a rebounding football came up and bloodied my nose, no one was surprised, and no pity was wasted on me that I could see. Fortunately for my emotional health, there were other facets of my life to develop—music (after ninth grade, playing in a rock band rendered me suddenly cool) and writing, to which I've devoted my life.

Not surprisingly, I developed a profound aversion to games, even if they were on TV or radio being broadcast from a safe distance. I didn't memorize stats, as the twins across the street did. I didn't know the names of players or their positions. If you held a gun to my head, I couldn't confidently name even one team in the American League or the NFL. And, now, a secure adult with a career, I can be depended upon to offer a wisecrack when people begin to talk sports. Will the Cowboys win this year's World Series? How many home runs did they score at the Super Bowl? It may be obnoxious—but it's a defense mechanism right out of fifth grade, and who would argue with that?

Has it held me back? Well, yes, in one way, even now. You see, guys often can't verbally bond unless they set up this neutral territory—this . . . [damned] figurative playing field—between them, and start to talk sports. And I'd be quite a bit richer if I had a nickel for every social occasion when the guys all started talking about the big game yesterday, looking over to include, no, welcome me into the conversation that bonds them, the talk in which I have neither the vocabulary nor the interest, and the gulf starts to open between us and it's like they're running in from the outfield all over again. I have three or four friendships that will never be what they could, with whatever sustenance and fellowship they might supply, because of what is perceived as a hole in this guy's soul.

That's OK. I'm philosophical about it. But there's this new dilemma. Now I'm the father of two, a girl and a boy. They're both still much too young for team sports, but, before too long, my comfortable, nonsports life will be confronted by Little League, home and away games, etc. And, when I think of my kids' shining little expectant faces turned up to me, I know—with sinking heart but also undeniable resolve—that I will deny those children nothing—even me, glove in hand, shouting encouragement.

---

ticipation regenerated the body and allowed it to make more efficient use of sperm. Without sport, many thought, men would have difficulty controlling their sexual drives.[40] By the late 19th century, even spectating was thought to instill the values of sport in fans.

As women's political power increased in the late 19th century, many men used sport to help them reaffirm their masculine identity. At the same time, men feared that the closing of the frontier and changes in the workplace would feminize society. Sport became a validating masculine experience that represented a return to an

older, ascetic ideal of scrupulous conscience, strict discipline, and selfless dedication to duty.[41]

### Toward Redefinition

To minimize the sense of failure some boys and men experience when participating in sports, one option is to redefine *success*. Too often, American males have unrealistic and unattainable definitions of masculine success that when not reached cause feelings of emptiness and isolation. Success in sports and work do not translate to success in friendships and intimate relationships. One factor that inhibits

American males' achievement of intimacy is the socialization of men to be competitive. Rules and conventions often force athletes to treat one another as enemies, which is a serious barrier to the development and maintenance of close relationships. Although advocates of boys' sports say they promote friendships and connections, the less skilled athletes are alienated at an early age.

The rule-bound structure of sports allows for the development of superficial relationships while maintaining boundaries and separation. Praise and acceptance by peers, coaches, spectators, and the media come only after strong performances and victories. According to one expert, the successful athlete must develop a highly goal-oriented personality to defeat an objectified opponent. The athlete is likely to consider the public image of success more important than any of his personal relationships.[42]

The attention successful male athletes receive is difficult to replace in daily living. For some males the end of their athletic career introduces a major life transition. Retired professional athletes sometimes try to compensate for their sense of lost identity by overeating, by using alcohol or drugs to excess, or by engaging in other unhealthy behaviors intended to prove their manhood. In most cases professional athletes are disengaging from sports just as other men their age are becoming established in their careers.

For college stars who don't become professional athletes, the transition begins much earlier. They, too, may become disconnected until they can redefine success for themselves. Too many men, however, try to accomplish this task by throwing themselves into their work, believing they will be judged by their career success or failure. By midlife many such men realize that there is more to life than work, and they begin to understand the importance of personal connections and intimacy. Values become more important than material rewards, and former dreams of success begin to have less meaning.[42] Unfortunately, this new aware-

ness often comes to men when their children are teenagers seeking separation from their parents.

Enhanced awareness and acceptance of intimacy eventually lead men to live more balanced lives. One expert recommends that equality between men and women be a prerequisite for the humanization of men, sports, and society.[43] In this way boys and men would grow up to be more psychologically secure, balanced, and able to establish intimate relationships at an earlier age. Sports, particularly from a recreational standpoint, then could be enjoyed for the opportunities they provide for healthy exercise, pursuit of excellence, challenge, fun, and friendship.

### Concept Check

- Why is sports participation for men valued as a rite of passage?
- What aspects of sports participation have a negative effect on some boys and men, and what suggestions have been made to reduce or prevent these effects?

## ACTIVITIES FOR A DIVERSE POPULATION

Throughout the text we have discussed the historical, social, and cultural aspects of sports and have explored the benefits of participation in a wide variety of sports, both team and individual. In the sections that follow we address the need for various recreational and leisure programs that are suitable for the increasingly diverse U.S. population.

### Fitness

America is an increasingly health-conscious and fitness-conscious nation, with people of all ages and at all ability levels pursuing fitness through a variety of regimens. Commercial and corporate fitness centers and organizations such as the YM/YWCA and the

YM/YWHA offer broad menus of fitness programs that include aerobics, weight training, swimming, and yoga. Many hospitals sponsor fitness programs for seniors and for people who are recovering from heart attacks. More recently, recreation and park professionals are being asked to provide fitness activities. Many people develop their own fitness routines; others may employ a personal trainer to design a personalized health and fitness program.

## Youth Fitness

Since the end of World War II, researchers have been assembling information about the benefits of exercise for youth. A 1954 publication startled the nation with the revelation that American children were not as fit as their foreign counterparts.[44] In response, President Eisenhower in 1956 formed the President's Youth Council, now called the President's Council on Physical Fitness and Sports. As part of the U.S. Department of Health and Human Services, the Council administers the President's Challenge, which grants fitness awards to young people from 6 through 17 years of age, including children with special needs. The council also conducts several detailed surveys of fitness among American youth.

## A Need for Activity

Although some experts debate the validity of comparisons, most agree that the current state of physical fitness among American children leaves much to be desired. The percentage of young people ages 6 to 17 who are overweight has more than doubled in the past 30 years.[45] Contributing to this situation are several familiar factors: more hours spent watching television, an improper diet, and too little physical activity. The U.S. Surgeon General's 1996 report on physical activity stressed that almost 14% of the nation's young people do not engage in any form of physical activity. Inactivity is higher among black females than white females.[46] Research shows that activity level among adolescent females is related to their sense of self-worth and perceived physical appearance.[31] Clearly, our nation's youth need after-school programs that promote physical activity to help develop wellness and encourage activity later in life.[47]

One study showed that one third of all elementary school children and two thirds of all junior and senior high school students are unsupervised before and/or after school.[48] These "latchkey children" are both physically and psychologically at risk. They need the support of community and school leadership, and thousands of school-based after-school programs have since been developed or expanded.[48a]

## Reversing the Trend

Despite the recommendations of the American Academy of Pediatrics and the American College of Sports Medicine that children from kindergarten through 12th grade should engage in 20 to 30 minutes of vigorous physical exercise each day, only Illinois requires daily physical education classes for all students from kindergarten through 12th grade. Free play and traditional team sports competitions alone are not fulfilling children's fitness needs. Fitness programs are required that increase youth health awareness, provide appropriate fitness activities, and help children develop fitness habits for a lifetime.

Regular physical activity in childhood and adolescence helps to control weight, improve strength and endurance, build healthy bones and muscles, reduce anxiety and stress, and increase self-esteem, and it may also improve blood pressure and cholesterol levels.[45]

Some community fitness programs and camps offer young people a wide range of enriching experiences. (Table 9.2 shows how a fitness camp schedule for 8- and 9-year-olds can be set up.) As alternatives to traditional sports programs that are too competitive or time consuming for some young people, community programs may appeal to youth who prefer a less structured setting. Besides helping young people meet fitness objectives, these programs provide opportunities for creative self-expression, self-understanding, motor skill development, and overall enjoyment.

### Elements of a Successful Program

One expert recommends that fitness programs for young people include:[49]

1. *Intrinsic incentives.* These include enjoyable experiences and activities, skill improvement, and excitement, as opposed to extrinsic factors such as winning or prizes. Intrinsic incentives are difficult to measure but can be deeply rewarding and encourage a lifetime of healthy activity.
2. *The right kind of success.* Success must be redefined. Excellence in health is not measured in performance results. Poor performance can cause some young people to withdraw. Success is based on developing and maintaining appropriate lifestyle patterns. Goal setting that focuses on individual improvement helps youth adopt a more task-oriented focus.
3. *Appropriate reasons to be active.* Reasons for involvement in fitness activities change throughout the life course. Children under 10 years of age tend to be motivated by activities that provide immediate enjoyment. Activities for this age group should be fun, challenging, and exciting and should offer opportunities for success and socialization. Adolescents' motivations for engaging in activities include competition, mastery, affiliation, social recognition, improving appearance, health, flexibility, and agility, controlling weight, and experiencing an uplift in mental attitude.

Improving the fitness of youth should be a primary concern of all Americans. More partnerships are needed among recreation programs and churches and nonprofit organizations to expand fitness programs, particularly in the inner city. Family fitness opportunities should be increased, and community and business leaders are needed to help support and sponsor activities. Finally, adults must take the responsibility to be role models of health and fitness.

## Adult Fitness

Every year in the United States about 250,000 deaths are attributed to physical inactivity, according to the *Journal of the American Medical Association*. The Centers for Disease Control and Prevention and the American College of Sports Medicine recommend that all Americans exercise moderately for at least 30 minutes a day.[50] Physically active adults have a lower risk of anxiety, depression, osteoporosis, heart disease, high blood pressure, diabetes, and colon cancer.[51] However, the state of adult fitness in the United States is a study in contrasts. Even though most adults know that they should exercise,[52] about 25% of adults report taking part in no physical activity at all in their leisure time. This inactivity is more prevalent among women than men, among blacks and Hispanics than whites, and among the less affluent than the affluent.[46] Many adults attribute their sedentary lifestyles to a lack of motivation, but, more important, many adults simply do not know how to exercise properly.[51] For some, intervention has been successful in increasing physical activity in communities, worksites, and health care settings, as well as at home.[46] Others are seeking information on the Internet. One recent poll revealed that over 40% of web surfers are looking for health- and fitness-related material.[52]

Among American adults, the most popular fitness activities are walking and hiking (76%), swimming (39%), cycling (23%), and jogging (18%).[53] Adults also are turning more to low-impact and stretching exercises, yoga, and meditation.

### Programs for Seniors

Among the growing population of older

**TABLE 9.2**  Sample Fitness Camp Schedule

Schedule of Activities: KSU Sports Fitness School
Session II June 29–July 16       Age Group 8–9

| TIME | | MONDAY | | TUESDAY | | WEDNESDAY | | THURSDAY | |
|---|---|---|---|---|---|---|---|---|---|
| | | 29 | | 30 | | 1 | | 2 | |
| 8:30 9:10 | 1 | Names, Lockers, Shirts, Warm-up | FH | Warm-up Orienteering | MS/GY | Warm-up Course | FH | Warm-up Rhythms | FH |
| 9:10 9:40 | 2 | Organized Games | FH | Orienteering | MS/GY | Rope Activities | FH | Jumpnastics Folk | FH |
| 9:40 9:50 | 3 | BREAK | | BREAK | | BREAK | | BREAK | |
| 9:50 10:30 | 4 | Fitness Testing Jump & Flexibility | FH | Fitness Testing Flexed Arm Hang | FH | Fitness Testing Shuttle Run | FH | Fitness Testing Fifty-yard Dash & Sit-up | FH |
| 10:30 11:30 | 5 | Swimming | P | Swimming | P | Swimming | P | Swimming | P |
| | | 6 | | 7 | | 8 | | 9 | |
| 8:30 9:10 | 1 | Warm-up Floor Hockey | FH | Warm-up Frisbee Activities | MS/FH | Warm-up Ball Handling | FH | Warm-up Bowling | GY |
| 9:10 9:40 | 2 | Floor Hockey | FH | Frisbee Activities | MS/FH | Ball Skills | FH/MS | Bowling Skills | GY |
| 9:40 9:50 | 3 | BREAK | | BREAK | | BREAK | | BREAK | |
| 9:50 10:30 | 4 | Fitness Concepts | FH | Fitness Testing Mile Run | MS/FH | Fitness Concepts | FH | Fitness Concepts | P |
| 10:30 11:30 | 5 | Swimming | P | Swimming | P | Swimming | P | Swimming | P |
| | | 13 | | 14 | | 15 | | 16 | |
| 8:30 9:10 | 1 | Warm-up Track & Field | MS/FH | Warm-up Track & Field | MS/FH | Warm-up Rope Activities | GY | Parent Day Special Schedule | GY |
| 9:10 9:40 | 2 | Track & Field Activities | MS/FH | Track & Field | MS/FH | Organized Games | GY | | GY |
| 9:40 9:50 | 3 | BREAK | | BREAK | | BREAK | | BREAK | |
| 9:50 10:30 | 4 | Fitness Concepts | FH | Fitness Concepts | FH | Fitness Concepts | FH | | FH |
| 10:30 11:30 | 5 | Swimming | P | Swimming | P | Swimming | P | Swimming | P |

**KEY:**

| | | | |
|---|---|---|---|
| CL = Concepts Lab | DS = Dance Studio | GR =Gymnastics Room | FH = Field House |
| NFH = North Field House | SFH = South Field House | MS =Memorial Stadium | GY = Gymnasium |
| P = Pools | SF = South Field | WR = Weight Room | |

adults, popular health-related and fitness-related activities are light-impact and low-impact aerobics; stretching, toning, and strengthening exercises; water aerobics; chair exercises; weight-loss programs; and classes in healthy cooking. Research shows that about half of the physical decline in older adults is attributable to the muscle atrophy that results from lack of activity. Athletes between 55 and 80 years of age who engage in regular endurance training experience less physical decline than do those who are sedentary.[54] Ongoing research shows clearly that regular physical activity is a critical element in promoting older adult health, but, according to the Centers for Disease Control and Prevention, inactivity is more prevalent among older adults than among young adults.[55]

Programs such as "Fitness After 50" specifically target sedentary older adults with low-stress exercise regimens designed to improve fitness and health. Members of "Up with Movement" do regular walking and aqua aerobics. Water exercise is therapeutic and beneficial for people who are recovering from surgery or who have medical problems. Another appealing feature is that 30 minutes of water exercise can provide the same health benefits as about two hours of land exercise.[56]

**Fitness: A Necessity**

Fitness is essential for overall good health. The body is designed for movement, and regular exercise is necessary to prevent muscle atrophy and to achieve and maintain optimum health and fitness. In addition to improving physical health, exercise offers psychological benefits, including alleviation of stress and depression and enhanced self-esteem and self-image.

Almost as many Americans die of cardiovascular disease as from all other causes of death. Recreation and leisure service providers are now recognized as playing a major role in promoting Americans' physical and psychological well-being, and programs focusing on health and fitness must be enhanced and expanded to meet growing needs. With annual health care costs projected to reach $1.5 trillion by the year 2008, Americans must understand the need for regular, appropriate physical activity.

- Name three specific benefits of regular physical exercise.
- Give reasons for current concern about the fitness level of American children.

## OUTDOOR RECREATION

Outdoor recreation allows participants to focus on and interact with the natural environment through a wide range of activities—hiking, camping, fishing, boating, birding, rock climbing, horseback riding, snow skiing, and waterskiing. For some people, outdoor activities provide experiences that are emotionally and spiritually rewarding; for others the attractions are adventure, risk, challenge, and thrills.

In America the demand for outdoor and wilderness recreation began to grow after the end of World War II, when the economy was expanding and the birthrate was rising exponentially. As Americans took to the outdoors in increasing numbers, the integrity of public lands and of the environment began to be threatened, and governments at all levels enacted laws intended to strike a balance that would protect natural environments while allowing the public to enjoy the outdoors responsibly. In 1985 President Reagan established the President's Commission on Americans Outdoors, to look a generation ahead and determine what kinds of outdoor activities Americans would choose, with the intent of making the necessary facilities available. The commission found that nearly 90% of Americans look to mountains, seashores, lakes, pathways, and playgrounds for enjoyment, exercise, health, and fresh air. The demand for outdoor recreation, they found, was growing faster than the population.[57]

*Operation Challenge promotes the inclusiveness of people with physical disabilities.*

Americans who participated in outdoor recreation at least once a month grew from 50% to 78% from 1994 to 2000. Some of the most popular activities were walking (57%), driving for pleasure (41%), swimming (39%), picnicking (36%), fishing (26%), bicycling (23%), hiking (19%), campground camping (17%), outdoor photography (17%), bird watching (16%), wildlife viewing (16%), visiting cultural sites (16%), backpacking (9%), motor boating (9%), RV camping (9%), hunting (8%), wilderness camping (8%), off road vehicle driving (7%), canoeing/kayaking (5%), horseback riding (5%), mountain biking (5%), and personal water craft riding (5%).[53]

## Changing Trends

Because of time and money constraints, not all Americans are able to travel to distant sites to enjoy outdoor recreation. As a result, the need is increasing for access to attractive natural resources in and near cities.[58] A proposal by American Trails and the National Park Service called for providing a trail within a 15-minute drive of every home in America. The plan envisioned a network of interconnected private local, state, and federal trails. In 1991 and 1998 Congress passed the Intermodal Surface Transportation Efficiency Act and the Transportation Equity Act for the 21st century (TEA 21), which provides federal funding for trails, greenways, bicycle paths, and walkways.

## Risk and Adventure

Increasingly popular among Americans are outdoor activities that are characterized by exposure to real or perceived danger through interaction with the natural environment. Research has shown that participants in such activities show improvement in self-concept and modification of fear levels. Adventure-based programming also has been used to help delinquent and at-risk youth develop more socially acceptable behaviors.[59]

Popular outdoor adventure activities include backpacking, bicycle touring, canoeing, cross-country skiing, hang gliding, hiking, hot-air ballooning, kayaking, mountaineering, orienteering, rafting, rock climbing, ropes courses, sailing, scuba diving, skindiving, snowshoeing, spelunking (cave exploration), wilderness camping, and wilderness trekking.[60]

## Women's Participation

Traditionally, many women have avoided certain outdoor activities that were typically associated with males, such as rock climbing, rappelling, and tent pitching. The U.S. Census Bureau, however, reports that the number of women who participate in outdoor and physical activities sometimes equals or even exceeds the number of men, and women's rate of participation has often increased faster than that of men. As seen in Table 9.1, in 1995 about 26.5 million women rode bicycles, 20 million went camping, 15.9 million went fishing, and 5.3 million went downhill and cross-country skiing. Single-sex programs offer nonthreatening approaches for girls and women to learn new activities.

## People with Disabilities

Americans with disabilities are participating in a wide variety of outdoor activities and are

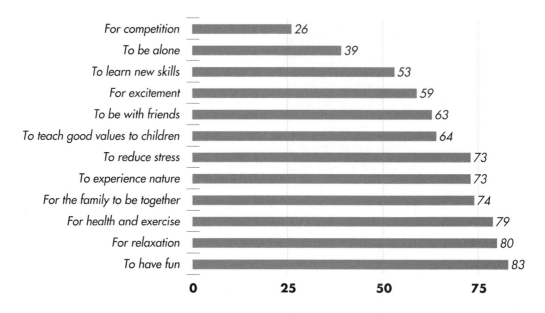

**Outdoor Recreation: Why Participate?**
% cited as important reason

| Reason | % |
|---|---|
| For competition | 26 |
| To be alone | 39 |
| To learn new skills | 53 |
| For excitement | 59 |
| To be with friends | 63 |
| To teach good values to children | 64 |
| To reduce stress | 73 |
| To experience nature | 73 |
| For the family to be together | 74 |
| For health and exercise | 79 |
| For relaxation | 80 |
| To have fun | 83 |

**FIGURE 9.2** Most important in outdoor recreation: fun, fitness, and family

eager to increase their participation. Through Operation Challenge, persons with physical disabilities can participate in windsurfing, waterskiing, sailing, rafting, kayaking, and mountain climbing. Special events include the U.S. National Disabled Waterski Championships, the Annual Bass Fishing Tournament for the Physically Disabled, the Annual Handicapped Riders Event, and the National Speed Skating Championships. (For further discussion, see Chapter 14.)

### Family Adventures

Traditionally, outdoor activities for American families have included camping, fishing, hiking, and horseback riding. Newer outdoor experiences are eco-vacations, llama treks, easy rafting, four-wheel driving, and a type of scuba diving, in which divers go down about 15 feet, breathing through a mouthpiece with air coming through a hose from a tank that is towed along the surface.

Adults can continue to enjoy their favorite outdoor activities while encouraging children to learn about the outdoors and test their abilities in new ways. External-frame baby packs hold both the baby and extra gear, making family backpacking a possibility. Small children can carry their lunches in a daypack. By 9 or 10 years of age, most children can carry the majority of their own gear in specially fitted packs. Older children enjoy walking the seashore, mountains, deserts, and woods. Cycling continues to be one of the most popular family activities. Adult bicycles can be fitted with trailers to carry children who are too young to pedal. Family camps are becoming increasingly popular and provide activities for people of all ages. Water sports from fishing to tandem kayaking help teach children about our nation's wilderness and water resources. Figure 9.2 points out important reasons for participating in outdoor recreation.

## HOBBIES AND CRAFTS

Each day Americans spend millions of dollars on hobbies and crafts. A survey conducted in 1994 by *Time* magazine showed that 59% of the respondents felt strongly about finding time for personal interests and hobbies. Hobbies expand knowledge and allow people to experience enjoyment, relief from stress, and a sense of achievement. In some cases hobbies are lifelong pursuits; in others they are of shorter duration. Hobbies can be done alone or with others. In the latter case they are an excellent way to bring people of various ethnic backgrounds together with a common purpose through clubs, exhibitions, and other gatherings. Enthusiasts and volunteers enjoy sharing and teaching others about the intricacies of their hobby, such as bonsai or ethnic cooking.

In the United States one of the most popular home-based hobbies is stamp collecting. More than 22 million philatelists spend an average of $150 per year on this hobby.[61] Collecting in general ranks high with Americans, and almost every specialty has an organization to which enthusiasts can belong. Some hobbies involve construction: woodworking, model building, toy making. Some science-based hobbies involve outdoor activity: observing insects; studying birds (ornithology), stargazing. Other popular hobbies are gardening, gourmet cooking, and creative writing. Unusual hobbies include activities such as enigmatology, the study of puzzles, and onomastics, the collection of unusual names of people.

Nearly 80% of U.S. households have at least one craft hobbyist,[61a] with needlework taking the lead as the most popular craft.[62] Many crafts originally were practiced out of necessity or as part of the daily routine and later evolved into art; examples are basketry, beadwork, cal-

ligraphy, ceramics, glassblowing, furniture making, jewelry design, leatherwork, metalcraft, quilting, weaving, and woodcarving. Crafts have wide appeal and can be presented at many levels: to children at camp, to adults on cruises, to participants in intergenerational programs, and to people who are physically or mentally challenged.

*Nearly 80% of U.S. households have at least one craft hobbyist, such as this wood-carver.*

Hobbies and crafts are educational tools, vehicles for creative self-expression, and a means of building self-esteem through personal accomplishment. Introducing hobbies to children can help them develop a lifelong interest while experiencing self-discovery and enhancing self-esteem. By working on hobbies, children learn to make decisions, solve problems, and work with others.[63]

Many adults (15%) have turned their interest in a craft into an entrepreneurial venture that has either augmented their regular income or replaced their career.[61a] Women who have chosen not to work outside the home often transform a craft into a profitable cottage industry. Likewise, new retirees may realize a lifelong dream by turning their hobbies into businesses. Crafters' guilds and the American Craft Council offer information about cottage industries and contemporary craft markets. The Small Business Administration publishes a wide variety of free and low-cost pamphlets that address the needs of new entrepreneurs.

## CULTURAL ACTIVITIES

Declining school support for the arts, the high cost of private instruction, and the increased prices of admission to many cultural events have made cultural pursuits economically impossible for many Americans. A positive development is the increased exposure to cultural activities being made available through public parks and recreation programming. Over the past several years, cultural programming has expanded to the point where it is provided by public recreation departments in almost every part of the country.

Increasingly, arts specialists are viewing recreation administration as a career choice, and recreation supervisors are learning the fundamentals of arts programming. Some state recreation departments have established arts sections and have developed training programs for both general managers and cultural specialists.

## Learning Opportunities

Mentally challenging and emotionally rewarding, arts instruction is beneficial for participants of all ages, backgrounds, and interests. Both children and adults find positive outlets by attending art camps and entry-level classes in music, voice, dance, painting, ceramics, sculpture, photography, film and video, pottery, weaving, and other arts.

## Cultural Events

Among the public venues for cultural events are amphitheatres, conventional theatres, and park green space. Performances include plays, musicals, operas, concerts, ballet, and films. Some recreation agencies stage their own productions, including children's theatre, dance recitals, instrumental and choral performances, and readers' theatre. Local amateur and professional performers may donate their services in exchange for the resulting public exposure. To generate broad public interest, many agencies organize ethnic festivals, local music award ceremonies, balloon races, and other events.

Successfully presenting and marketing public cultural events requires awareness and sensitivity, because audiences and participants

*Cultural arts programming is a vital part of public recreation programs.*

traditionally have tended to be well educated, upper income, and white. Administrators must offer and promote programming that responds to a culturally diverse audience and must set prices so that admissions and fees are within the reach of people at all income levels.

## "Park Art"

"Park art" has become a popular means of dressing up parks and jogging trails. Artists set up sculptures or paint murals to create visual appeal; students in park-sponsored art classes also may participate. Some states allocate funding for state park administrators to use for art purchases or to commission artists who work with architects and engineers to design outdoor spaces. Public and private donations fund art in city parks or promote summer art projects for inner-city youth. Mural design is particularly popular among teenagers.

## Making the Commitment

A commitment to cultural programming offers the public an enriching aesthetic experience while enhancing civic pride and accentuating the wholesome use of leisure time. The challenge is to develop public and private support for the arts so that cultural services become a permanent part of the public delivery of leisure services. A major step toward meeting this challenge was taken in 1985 when the National Parks and Recreation Association established the Dorothy Mullen National Arts and Humanities Award program, which rewards the most innovative and enriching cultural programs in the country.

In this chapter we have examined recreation and leisure activities and participants. Against this background, in the next chapter we consider the providers and resources of such activities, both public and private.

## Summing Up

- ◆ As the U.S. population becomes increasingly diverse, recreation and leisure programming must be designed for people with a wide range of interests, backgrounds, and ability levels.

- ◆ Family structures are changing. Family leisure is a strong and growing segment of the market for recreation and leisure goods and services. Even the youngest children can be part of many family adventures.

- ◆ As the senior population expands, intergenerational programming is on the increase. Both young people and older adults benefit from sharing meals, birthday celebrations, and activities.

- ◆ Since the passage of Title IX in 1972, amateur and professional sports for girls and women have experienced notable growth. At the same time, questions have arisen about the rationale for males' involvement in sports and about the techniques used to encourage aggression in competition.

- ◆ Fitness is a key pursuit in recreational programming; its popularity is increasing as a result of growing awareness of the physical, mental, and emotional benefits of staying fit.

- ◆ Outdoor recreation is growing in popularity among all age groups. Adventure activities such as backpacking and rafting can help improve participants' self-concept and modify fear.

- ◆ Hobbies and crafts can be mentally stimulating and emotionally satisfying, provide opportunities for social interaction, and in some cases be turned into successful business ventures.

- ◆ In recent years cultural programming has become a more frequent offering in public recreation departments. Key points in such programming are responding to the tastes of a diverse audience and setting prices at affordable levels.

## Using What You've Learned

1. Visit your local public recreation center and look at the flyers and other posted information about available activities. Do they appeal to diverse groups and to various family arrangements? Why or why not? Bring samples of flyers to class.

2. From your local newspaper, clip articles that cover various leisure activities and participants. Does the coverage appear to be inclusive of a variety of activities and participants? Why or why not? Bring the articles to class.

3. Interview someone who enjoys a challenging form of outdoor adventure activity. Discuss with this person the participants he or she has come to know. Has the person had an experience in which differences between people were bridged while participating in the activity? Prepare a written summary of your findings.

4. Interview someone who is actively involved in a hobby. Identify the various activities related to the hobby. How are this person's schedule, social needs, and satisfaction level influenced by participation in this hobby? Prepare a written summary of your findings.

## YOUR  Turn

1 Have you ever experienced discrimination in school sports based on your ethnic background or sex? If so, how did you feel? What, if anything, did you do in response?

2 If you haven't experienced such discrimination personally, have you ever been present when another person with whom you were playing a sport was being subjected to discriminatory treatment? If so, how did that person react? How did others react?

3 How would a person with a disability describe the benefits of inclusive leisure programs?

4 What benefits might result from programs intended to bring together participants of diverse ethnic backgrounds?

# REFERENCES

1. Lieberson, S., & Waters, M. (1988). In *Many Strands: Ethnic and Racial Groups in Contemporary America.* New York: Russell Sage Foundation, pp. 29, 38.

2. Cohn, D., & Fears, D. (March 13, 2001). Multiracial Growth Seen in Census. *The Washington Post*, p. A12.

3. Pugh, T,. & Arnett, E. (December 7, 1997). Interracial Unions Rise Despite Society's Same Old Prejudices. *The San Diego Union-Tribune*, p. A-29.

4. Toombs, D. (February 12, 1998). Racial Dialogue Form a Firm Foundation. *The San Diego Union-Tribune*, p. B-9.

5. National Council on Disability (September, 1997). *NCD Bulletin.* Washington, DC: National Council on Disability, p. 1.

6. Peniston, L. (December 1996). Hotel Accessibility and Accommodations for People with Disabilities. *Parks & Recreation* 31(12):24.

7. Devine, M., & McGovern, J. (1998). Inclusion. *Parks & Recreation* 33(7):69.

8. Cammack, E. (May 1996). In-Home Recreation Therapy Care: A Case Study of Dillon. *Parks & Recreation* 31(5):66.

9. Drucker, P. (1990). *Managing the Nonprofit Organization.* New York: HarperCollins, pp. 12, 121.

10. Dolbee, S. (June 26, 1993). Anytown, U.S.A. *The San Diego Union-Tribune*, p. B-7.

11. Roper Starch (1999). *Outdoor Recreation in America: The Family and the Environment.* Washington, DC: The Recreation Roundtable, p. 9.

12. McCormick, S. (1991). The Changing American Family at Play. *Parks & Recreation* 26(7):45-46, 47.

13. Armour, S. (December 29, 1997). Tight Job Market Squeezes Workers' Time with Kids. *USA Today*, p. 1-B.

14. .Smith, D. (October 1997). Strengthening Family Values in the Twenty-First Century—Home Centered Recreation. *Journal of Physical Education, Recreation and Dance* 68(8):39–40.

15. Herbert, W. (November 29, 1999). When Strangers Become Family. *U.S. News & World Report* 127(21):59.

16. Shaw, S. (December 1992). Family Leisure and Leisure Services. *Parks & Recreation* 26(12):13-14.

17. Peterson, K. (May 9, 1997). Mothers Drawing the Most Fulfillment from Family Life, *USA Today*, p. 4D.

18. Carey, A. and Mullins, M. (August 11, 1997). Putting Value on Family Time, *USA Today*, p. B-1.

19. The Mayo Foundation for Research and Education (1993). Grandparenting Time Can Be Free of Friction. *The San Diego Union-Tribune*, p. F-12.

20. Brock, B. (August, 1994). Recreation Programming for the '90s Family. *JOPERD* 65(6):64.

21. Weisburd, S. (April 1992). Grandpals: Link of Ages. *Health* 6(2):82–84.

22. Keller, J. (1992). Linking Generations. *Parks & Recreation* 27(3):60.

23. Robertson, I. (1987). *Sociology.* New York: Worth Publishers, pp. 314, 379.

24. VanHoose, W.H., & Worth, M.R. (1982). *Adulthood in the Life Cycle.* Dubuque, IA: Wm. C. Brown Co., pp. 104–105.

25. Sabo, D. (1993). Psychosocial Impacts of Athletic Participation on American Women: Facts and Fables. In D.S. Eitzen (Ed.), *Sport in Contemporary Society.* New York: St. Martin's Press, p. 379.

26. Messner, M., & Sabo, D. (1990). Toward a Critical Feminist Reappraisal of Sport, Men, and the Gender Order. In M. Messner & D. Sabo (Eds.), *Sport, Men, and the Gender Order.* Champaign, IL: Human Kinetics Books, p. 12.

27. Woolum, J. (1992). *Outstanding Women Athletes.* Phoenix: The Oryx Press, pp. 3–6, 15, 21.

## REFERENCES (cont'd)

28. Cordes, K. (November 1977). Then . . . and Now. *Courier*, p. 20.

29. Durrant, S. (1992). Title IX—Its Power and Its Limitations. *JOPERD* 631(3):64.

30. Women's Sports Foundation. (June 1997). Fair Game. *Women's Sports Fitness* 19(5):39.

30a. Everett, D. (1998). What a Difference a Day Makes. *GWS News* 25(3):1.

30b. International Olympic Committee (2000). Promoting Women's Sport in the Olympic Games. www.olympic.org/ioc/e/org/women/women _jo_e.html.

31. Henderson, D. and Winn, S. (August 1996). Females and Physical Activity. *Parks & Recreation* 31(8):28–34.

32. Carpenter L. and Acosta, R.V. (February 1997). Statistics on Females in Athletics. *Journal of Physical Education, Recreation and Dance* 68(2):10.

33. Wieberg, S. (April 29, 1997). Study NCAA Women Far from Equity. *USA Today*, p. 1C.

34. Wieberg, S. (April 29, 1997). Women's Groups Ask NCAA to Get Tough on Issues of Equity. *USA Today*, p. 2C.

35. Acosta, R.V., & Carpenter, L.J. (2000). Women in Intercollegiate Sport: A Longitudinal Study—Twenty-Three Year Update, 1977-2000. Brooklyn College.

35a. Lough, N. (2001). Mentoring Connections Between Coaches and Female Athletes. *Journal of Physical Education, Recreation, and Dance* 72(5):30.

36. Oglesby, C.A. (1993). Changing Times or Different Times—What's Happening with "Women's Ways" of Sport? *JOPERD* 64(3):60–62.

37. Lederman, D. (1991). Big Sports Programs are Out of Control, Most Say in Survey. *The Chronicle of Higher Education* 37(26):A35.

38. Eitzen, D.S. (Ed.). (1993). *Sport in Contemporary Society.* New York: St. Martin's Press, p. 373.

39. Wilson, D. (1990). Sport in Social Construction of Masculinity. In M. Messner & D. Sabo (Eds.), *Sport, Men, and the Gender Order.* Champaign, IL: Human Kinetics, p. 19.

40. Crosset, T. (1990). Masculinity, Sexuality, and the Development of Early Modern Sport. In M. Messner & D. Sabo (Eds.), *Sport, Men, and the Gender Order.* Champaign, IL: Human Kinetics, pp. 52–53.

41. Kimmel, M. (1990). Baseball and Reconstitution of American Masculinity, 1880–1920. In M. Messner & D. Sabo (Eds.), *Sport, Men, and the Gender Order.* Champaign, IL: Human Kinetics, pp. 57–59

42. Messner, M. (1993). The Meaning of Success: The Athletic Experience and the Development of Male Identity. In D.S. Eitzen (Ed.), *Sport in Contemporary Society.* New York: St. Martin's Press, p. 413.

43. Oglesby, C. (1990). Epilogue. In M. Messner & D. Sabo (Eds.), *Sport, Men, and the Gender Order.* Champaign, IL: Human Kinetics, pp. 242–243.

44. Griffin, K. (1992). Kids Gone Soft. *Health* 35(6).

## REFERENCES (cont'd)

45. Centers for Disease Control and Prevention. (1996). *Promoting Lifelong Physical Activity.* Atlanta: Centers for Disease Control and Prevention, pp. 1, 4–5.

46. Centers of Disease Control and Prevention. (1996). *Physical Activity and Health.* Atlanta: Centers for Disease Control and Prevention, p. 14.

47. National Association for Sport and Physical Education. (October 28, 1997). *Shape of the Nation Report.* Reston, VA: American Alliance for Health, Physical Education, Recreation and Dance, pp. 2, 9.

48. Long J. (March 1989). How Educators Can Help Latchkey Children. *Education Digest* (7):53.

48a. Ross, C. (March, 2000). No More Homes Alone. *West Virginia Family*, p. 8.

49. Fox, K. (1991). Motivating Children for Physical Activity. *JOPERD* 62(7):36.

50. ——— (Fall 1996). 30 Minutes a Day Can Help Keep Your Doctor Away. *Cigna Healthcare*, p. 4.

51. Thomas, D. and Quindry, J. (March 1997). Exercise Consumerism—Let the Buyer Beware! *Journal of Physical Education, Recreation and Dance* 68(3):56.

52. Reuters Health (January 4, 2000). More Americans Say Diet and Exercise Important to Health. *Inteli Health Inc.*, p. 1.

53. Roper Starch (2000). *Outdoor Recreation in America: Addressing Key Societal Concerns.* Washington, DC: The Recreation Roundtable, pp. 12, 16-17.

54. Harper, S. (1999). Building an Intergenerational Activity Program for Older Adults. *Journal of Physical Education, Recreation, and Dance* 70(2):68.

55. Mathieu, M. (1999). The Surgeon General's Report and Leisure Services for Older Adults. *Journal of Physical Education, Recreation, and Dance* 70(3):29.

56. Ekberg, J. (1990). Senior Fitness: Getting into the Swim of Things. *Park & Recreation* 25(2):47.

57. Ibrahim, H., & Cordes, K. (1993). *Outdoor Recreation,* Dubuque, IA: Brown & Benchmark.

58. Cordell, K., & Siehl, G. (July–September 1997). Did You Know . . . ? *Trailblazer* 12(3):4.

59. Robinson-Young, P. (March 1992). Recreation's Role in Gang Intervention. *Parks & Recreation* 27(3):54–55.

60. Kelly, J. (1987). *Recreation Trends Toward the Year 2000.* Champaign, IL: Sagamore Publishing, p. 85.

61. Roha, R. (1992). All-American Hobbies: The Sky's the Limit. *Kiplinger's Personal Finance Magazine* 46(1):70.

61a. Backer, N. (March, 1999). March is National Craft Month. *Crafts Report.* www.craftsreport.com/march99/ncm.html.

62. Siegel, E. (June 22, 1990). A Stitch in Time. *Publishers Weekly* 237(25):17.

63. Rosemond, J. (1991). Why Kids Need Hobbies. *Better Homes and Gardens* 69(2):27.

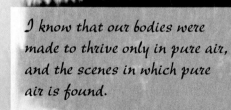

*I know that our bodies were made to thrive only in pure air, and the scenes in which pure air is found.*

**JOHN MUIR**
*The Wilderness World of John Muir, 1954
Edwin W. Teale (editor)*

# Providers and Resources

## CHAPTER 10

## THE CHAPTER AT A GLANCE

In this chapter we learn about the various providers of and resources for recreation and leisure services and opportunities. Among the providers we consider are federal, state, county, and municipal governments; quasipublic entities; private organizations; commercial enterprises; and specialized providers—employers, the military, and colleges and universities.

## Chapter Objectives

After completing this chapter, you should be able to

- Identify key federal providers of recreation and leisure services and describe their responsibilities.
- Explain the difference between the single-use and multiple-use concepts as applied to natural resources.
- Describe the kinds of recreational resources provided by state, county, and municipal governments.
- Distinguish among quasipublic, private, commercial, and specialized providers of recreational services and identify some of the offerings of each kind of provider.

## PUBLIC PROVIDERS

*A*bundant recreation opportunities exist throughout the nation's public lands. Outdoor-loving Americans can enjoy forests, mountains, desert and wildlife refuges, rivers, lakes, seashores, public parks, campgrounds, playgrounds, and open urban spaces. With appropriate development of natural resources, public lands also contribute to the nation's economy and enhance Americans' quality of life. Historical sites and landmarks preserve places and memories of the great individuals,

## A World  of Difference

### OLD TRADITIONS, NEW REALITIES

"World's Biggest Jackpot!" "You Play—We Pay!" "BingoRama—7 Days, 24 Hours."

These and a hundred other blazing neon signs suffuse the clear evening sky of southern Montana with an other-worldly glow, defeating even the spectacular descent of the sun into the mountains amid towering thunderheads. Rattling down the dusty highway in her father's ancient pickup, Jenny Rainwater feels the same mixture of sadness and apprehension that always visits her when she passes the Strip: her band's savior or destroyer, depending on one's point of view. People travel hundreds of miles to spend the weekend at bingo marathons in the reservation's huge halls. Motels and fast-food restaurants compete fiercely for tourists' attention; video arcades are crammed with bright, noisy games and excited kids; visitors laden with souvenirs elbow each other on the narrow sidewalks. The night air is rent by the metallic twang of an electronically amplified country-western band; people enter and leave the cluster of bars at the north end of the Strip; and the inevitable fights break out in the crowded parking lots.

*Just great,* Jenny thinks. She has nothing against bingo itself, nor does she object to moderate drinking or other forms of entertainment that many people find appealing. What she fears is the degradation of the culture of her people, the Crow, to the extent that many see this monument to commercialism as their only salvation from lives of poverty and deprivation. Jenny, a second-year student in the state university's highly acclaimed graduate program in microbiology, no longer comes home very often. Partly it's because she's so busy with school and work; another reason is that, every time she comes home, she and her father argue about the Strip.

"Listen, Jenny," Joe Rainwater tells his daughter. "You know we're proud of you and what you're doing. You're one in a million, and you have the brains and the grit to make a good life for yourself off the reservation. But what are the rest of us supposed to do? Finally the BIA [Bureau of Indian Affairs] lets us run bingo—look at all the jobs that have opened up here—including mine." Joe, who's assistant manager of the biggest bingo palace, gestures with an outflung arm to indicate the small community of trailer houses where the Rainwaters live. "If it weren't for the Strip, half of these people wouldn't have jobs—and I'd still be trying to feed five kids on what I could make doing day labor for McKenzie Brothers." Joe names the largest construction contractor in the area.

"I know, Dad," Jenny replies. "It's great that you have the job, and I know the benefits are important. But a lot more people have minimum-wage jobs where they earn just enough to go out and get drunk, or buy junk they don't need." Jenny's also disturbed that her brothers, 12-year-old Johnny and 14-year-old Sam, have begun to frequent the video arcades on the Strip, using all their spending money to play games that Jenny thinks are both mindless and a menace.

"Jenny, we finally have something that's our own," Joe says emphatically. "We run it ourselves—not the white men. There isn't much left of our culture, anyway, and people can't live on culture. We have to start somewhere—and who knows what we might be able to do after a few years?"

As you study this chapter, think about the disagreement between Jenny and her father and prepare to answer the questions in Your Turn at the end of the chapter.

cultures, events, and architecture that compose the fabric of our national heritage.

The public can enjoy these magnificent lands, waters, wildlife, and history, but these resources must be carefully managed to ensure that they will be available in perpetuity. All around the country, in both rural and urban areas, public and private resources have suffered from abuse and misuse. Beaches, roadsides, trails, and campgrounds have been littered; playgrounds and buildings covered with graffiti; signs and structures defaced and fences destroyed; wildlife poached; and archaeological sites bulldozed so that the "loot" could be stolen more easily.

Such actions foreclose opportunities for everyone to enjoy our public lands. In an effort to prevent such abuses, a group of committed public and private organizations in 1986 launched "Take Pride in America," a national public awareness campaign designed to encourage all Americans to make wise use of the resources that belong to everyone. "Take Pride in America" seeks to promote constructive activity on public lands and to reduce destructive behavior. People in every state are responding with activities that include outdoor stewardship and self-policing programs; archaeological resource protection awareness efforts; and watch programs or hotlines to report vandalism, wildlife poaching, theft, and other destructive activities. Many citizens help care for parks, trails, shorelines, campsites, and playgrounds by providing cleanup, maintenance, and general assistance when needed.

No other nation in the world has attempted to preserve and protect so much of its natural resources for public use and enjoyment. U.S. federal lands amount to more than 600 million acres—over 25% of the nation's entire land mass (Fig. 10.1). Because of the federal government's vast land holdings, it plays a crucial role in offering a broad range of opportunities for outdoor activities, including hiking, boating, hunting, fishing, camping, and photography.

As we will see later, state, county, and local governments also provide a myriad of recreational sites.

## Federal Providers and Resources

Several federal agencies and systems protect the nation's natural resources and provide recreational opportunities. Fig. 10.2 provides a breakdown of total recreational visitor hours in 1992 as recorded by six federal agencies. Appendix D lists relevant federal agencies with addresses.

A helpful way to categorize the federal agencies that are responsible for managing public lands is by the concept of land use they follow: *single use* or *multiple use.* The National Park Service practices the single-use or restricted-use concept, meaning that to the greatest extent possible national parks are to be preserved in their present state solely for the benefit and enjoyment of the public. Another single-use agency is the U.S. Fish and Wildlife Service. In contrast, the U.S. Forest Service practices multiple use, in which it seeks to balance conservation with economic use. The Forest Service administers national forests for simultaneous benefits such as timber, range, watershed, and outdoor recreation, while also promoting environmental awareness. Other multiple-use agencies are the Bureau of Reclamation, Army Corps of Engineers, Tennessee Valley Authority, and National Marine Fisheries Service.

### National Park Service

The National Park Service, a unit of the U.S. Department of the Interior, was established by Congress in 1916 to protect and preserve the nation's natural, historical, and cultural resources while providing opportunities for recreation. National Park Service holdings encompass nearly 84 million acres of land, and the service manages more than 380 national parks, battlefields, seashores, monuments, and historic sites located in the United States and in American trust territories. These areas offer Americans a diversity of outdoor experiences.[1,2]

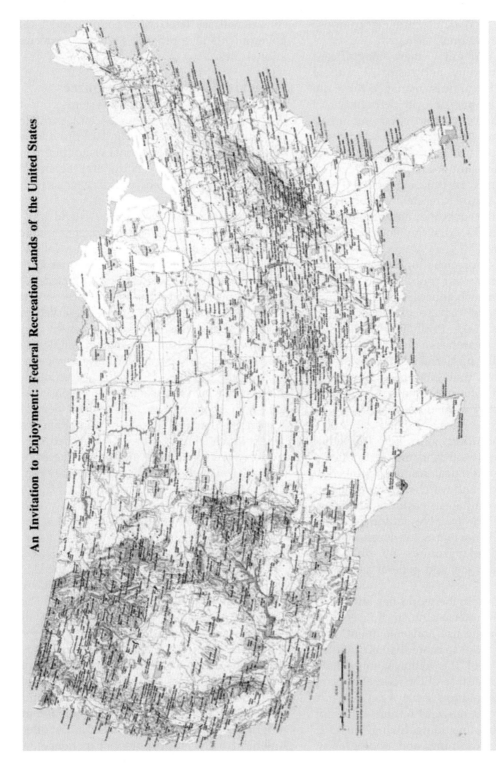

**An Invitation to Enjoyment: Federal Recreation Lands of the United States**

**FIGURE 10.1** U.S. federal lands. This map shows that most federal lands are located in the western United States. As indicated by the color key on the next page, the Forest Service (green) and Bureau of Land Management (yellow) areas dominate.

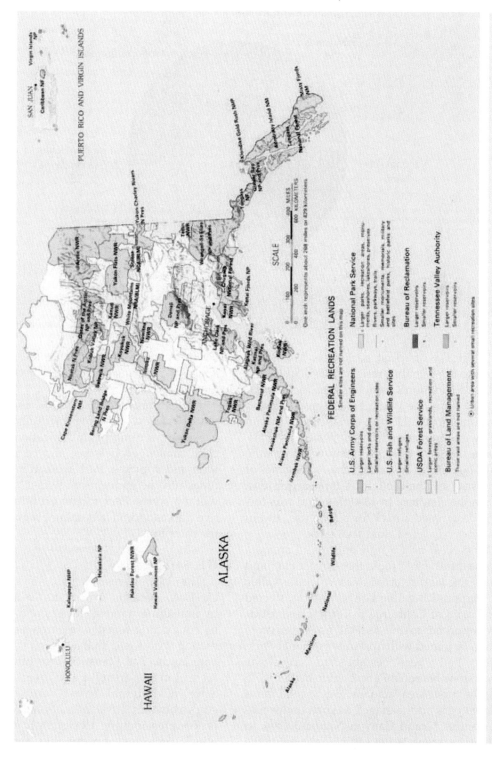

**FIGURE 10.1** (cont'd)  U.S. federal lands.

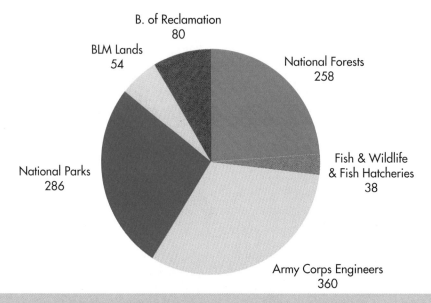

**FIGURE 10.2**  Annual visits to federal recreation areas (in millions of visitors).

Historically, the first parklands trace their origins to the 17 public reservations acquired in 1791 for the nation's capital. These include the National Mall, the White House grounds, and other units in the District of Columbia that in 1933 were transferred to the National Park Service. In 1832 Congress removed from the public domain an area called the Hot Springs of Arkansas (see the section on land acquisition later in the chapter). In 1880 this land was formally designated a park for public use, and in 1921 it was declared a national park.

The earliest action by Congress to create a large natural park took the form of a land grant.[3] The land referred to as Yosemite Valley and Mariposa Big Tree Grove was transferred to the state of California in 1864. These lands were returned to the federal government in 1906 to be joined with Yosemite National Park, which had been established in 1890. Yellowstone National Park, established in 1872, was the first area actually designated as a national park and managed as such under federal control. Grand Canyon National Park in northern Arizona is the setting for one of the Seven Wonders of the World: the magnificent and awe-inspiring Grand Canyon (see A Closer Look on p. 203).

The National Park Service offers some of the world's finest camping facilities, including backcountry camping, modifications for physically challenged persons, and concessions for food and supplies. Park recreational opportunities run the gamut from horseback riding to wildlife study. Park rangers conduct interpretive classes and offer evening programs around the campfire.

**U.S. Forest Service**

The U.S. Forest Service, a unit of the U.S.D.A., benefits Americans in many ways: by managing national forests and grasslands, by conducting forestry research, and by cooperating with forest managers on state and private lands. The Forest Service offers outdoor recreation opportunities on over 191 million acres of national forests and grasslands. Approximately 18% of national forest land is congressionally designated wilderness, which provides opportunities for recreation

# THE GRAND CANYON: A NATIONAL TREASURE

Among the truly awe-inspiring sights in the world is the vast and colorful Grand Canyon of the Colorado River. The 217-mile canyon is located in Grand Canyon National Park, which was established by act of Congress in 1919. The Grand View, opened in 1897, was the first hotel built in what is now the national park. At that time, stagecoach service was begun from Flagstaff. Four years later the Sante Fe Railroad opened its branch line from Williams, Arizona, to the South Rim and began passenger service to the canyon. Today Grand Canyon Village offers hotel accommodations, a variety of restaurants and shops, and a full-service visitor center.

Two excellent trails—Bright Angel and Kaibab—reach the bottom of the canyon (a journey of one mile) from the South Rim, and Kaibab continues to the North Rim. The trip on foot from either rim to the canyon depths is very strenuous; most people who descend into the canyon do so on muleback. The trip to the river and back from the South Rim takes a full day. A fascinating two-day trip takes the visitor to the Inner Gorge by way of the Bright Angel Trail, across the Kaibab Suspension Bridge, and to Phantom Ranch for dinner and shelter; the return the next day is made by the Kaibab Trail. Private concessionaires conduct rubber raft trips down the river through the canyon.

A modern visitor center, containing an extensive museum, is open year-round near Grand Canyon Village. During the summer on the North Rim (closed all winter), outdoor campfire programs, lodge talks on natural history, and geographical talks at Cape Royal are presented. During the heavy tourist season, the South Rim program is expanded to include the provision of information service at several points along the rim, nightly campfire programs, and exhibits on archaeology at Tusayan Ruin and Museum.

experiences amid spectacular scenery. Facilities are designed to protect the environment and ensure the safety and enjoyment of users.[1,2]

The National Forest System was established with passage of the Forest Reserve Act of 1891 and by the creation of the first forest reserves that same year by President Harrison. Even then, many Americans believed their country would suffer shortages of both timber and clean water if some land were not protected from exploitation. Other Americans, however, were convinced that supplies of timber and water were unlimited and therefore opposed the idea of placing large tracts of land under federal management. With the National Forest System moving through its second century, the controversy has intensified over the correct balance between use and preservation of the nation's forests and grasslands. Debates have centered on issues such as the spotted owl and other endangered or threatened species, old-growth forests, clear cutting, below-cost timber sales, roadless areas, and biodiversity.[4]

Amid the debates over these and other issues, the Forest Service has sought to chart a course for the future while continuing to manage the land in a way that balances Americans' growing interest in outdoor recreation, the need for traditional commodities such as timber and minerals, and the requirements of the fragile forest ecosystem.

National forests are used more heavily for recreation than are any other public lands. Together the forests have more than 133,000 miles of trails; about 7,700 miles of national scenic byways; and more than 10,000 recreation sites such as campgrounds, picnic areas, ski areas, and visitor centers. In addition, the Forest Service manages portions of 96 rivers as wild and scenic rivers and 37 national recreation areas, scenic areas, or monuments. Approximately 35 million acres of congressionally designated wilderness and almost all National Forest System lands are available for outdoor recreation.[5–8]

## Bureau of Indian Affairs

The Bureau of Indian Affairs (BIA) of the Department of the Interior was established in 1824 and is responsible for working with federally recognized Indian tribal governments and with Alaska Native village communities. The agency's main goal is to support tribes' efforts to govern their own reservation communities by providing programs, services, and technical assistance through area offices. One of the BIA's principal programs is administering and managing some 54 million acres of land held in trust for Native Americans by the federal government.[9] The BIA helps tribes protect and develop their forest, water, mineral, and energy resources. The BIA also provides training in environmental management and endangered species preservation.

Many reservations have spectacular scenery and may offer opportunities for hiking, horseback riding, boating, skiing, hunting, or fishing. Major reservations conduct motor tours to archaeological sites and areas of scenic interest. Powwows, ceremonial dances, museums, crafts, bingo, and gambling attract many visitors. Several tribes have created successful recreational developments.[10]

*The immensity and timeless nature of Monument Valley are shared in this Navajo tribal park in Utah and Arizona.*

## Bureau of Land Management

The Bureau of Land Management (BLM) of the Department of the Interior oversees the nation's largest federal land mass—more than 264 million acres—and offers virtually unlimited outdoor recreation opportunities such as camping, hiking, backcountry exploration, fishing, hunting, boating and other water activities, sightseeing and nature watching, off-road vehicles, cycling, and winter sports. Most of this land is located in the 11 Western continental states and Alaska. It includes 35 wild and scenic rivers, 15 national monuments, more than 5.3 million acres of wilderness, 4.1 million acres of lakes and reservoirs, 29 national trails, 58 backcountry byways, 726 developed and semi-developed recreation sites, and 22,366 family camping units. Once viewed as lands no one wanted, they have been rediscovered by millions of Americans looking for challenge, adventure, and open space.[11,12,13]

The BLM manages its lands according to the multiple-use concept, accommodating as many uses and activities as possible while working to protect natural historic and cultural resources for public use and enjoyment. BLM has moved to revitalize its outdoor recreation program, according it equal importance with other aspects of its mission.

## Bureau of Reclamation

The Bureau of Reclamation (BuRec), a unit of the Department of the Interior, is a multiple-use agency responsible for managing, developing, and protecting water and related resources in the interest of the American public. BuRec was created in 1902 to help develop and sustain the economy of the Western states by providing water and energy supplies where natural lakes are scarce. To achieve this goal, the Bureau built large storage reservoirs, canals, and hydroelectric power plants.

The management of recreational resources is a vital part of BuRec's multi-purpose water and power resource development programs. The majority of the 300-plus recreation areas at water resource management sites are operated in cooperation with other governments: federal, state, or local. Millions of Americans enjoy these sites and their variety of natural attractions.[1, 13]

**Tennessee Valley Authority**

The Tennessee Valley Authority (TVA), an independent multiple-use agency of the federal government, was established in 1933 to be responsible for flood control, navigation, and electric power generation in the Tennessee Valley, which includes all or part of Alabama, Georgia, Kentucky, Mississippi, North Carolina, Tennessee, and Virginia. The TVA's system of dams and reservoirs has become an increasingly popular resource for outdoor recreation. The system includes 50 lakes with more than 1,000 square miles of water surface and 11,000 miles of shoreline in its seven-state territory.[1,13] Recreation facilities are managed privately or by the federal, state, or local government. Thousands of acres of undeveloped land also are available for recreational use such as hiking, cycling, horseback riding, off-road vehicles, photography, nature study, and environmental education. Other popular activities at these sites are camping, picnicking, boating, swimming, fishing, and hunting.[14,15]

**U.S. Army Corps of Engineers**

The Corps of Engineers, a unit of the Department of Defense, operates more than 2,500 recreation areas in 463 projects in 43 states. Created in 1802, this multiple-use agency promotes the use of land and water while conserving the natural environment. Its National Resources Management Program includes forestry, fish, and wildlife management; archaeology; soil conservation; and other ecological disciplines.[3,16]

The corps was among the first federal government agencies to advocate protection of natural resources, and it was the first to explore and map Yellowstone. The corps also played an early role in surveying and protecting the Yosemite Valley; designed and supervised construction of the largest manmade harbor in the world at San Pedro Bay in California; built the tallest masonry structure, the Washington Monument; built the U.S. Capitol Building dome, one of the engineering wonders of the nation; and created the Panama Canal, one of the supreme human achievements of all time.[16]

Outdoor recreation opportunities are available at more than 4,000 parks on corps-managed land. Although the corps manages less than 2% of the federal estate, corps lands account for almost 30% of recreation visitation to federal lands. Visitors are attracted by the unique experiences offered by these water-oriented recreational resources, as well as by the opportunity to hike, camp, picnic, hunt, and fish. Because most corps projects are in locations convenient to large numbers of the public, they record visits from about 10% of the U.S. population each year.[1]

**National Oceanic and Atmospheric Administration**

The National Oceanic and Atmospheric Administration (NOAA) is an agency of the Department of Commerce. Its 13 national marine sanctuaries are the aquatic counterpart of our national parks, and its National Marine Fisheries Service (NMFS) manages the oceans' living resources between 3 and 200 miles off the nation's coasts. The NMFS is committed to promoting increased opportunities for recreational marine fishing. It shares with the U.S. Fish and Wildlife Service the administration of the Marine Mammal Protection Act.[17]

**U.S. Fish and Wildlife Service**

The U.S. Fish and Wildlife Service of the Department of the Interior manages a system of more than 500 national wildlife refuges that encompass over 94 million acres of land and water nationwide. The service's mission is to conserve, protect, and enhance fish, wildlife, and their habitats for the ongoing benefit of the American people.[1] Although the needs of wildlife come first, most refuges offer a variety of wildlife-oriented recreational opportunities, which attract an estimated 27 million visitors each year. Activities include wildlife observation, photography, nature study, hiking, boating, hunting, and fishing. Some refuges have visitor centers, interpretive trails and drives, wildlife observation towers, photography blinds, and other facilities.[18]

### National Wilderness Preservation System

The National Wilderness Preservation System spans more than 105 million acres.[19] Wilderness designation ensures that the land, supervised by the Forest Service, the National Park Service, the Fish and Wildlife Service, and the Bureau of Land Management, will be managed to retain its primeval character and influence without permanent improvements or human habitation. The first land designated as protected wilderness was the Gila National Forest in New Mexico in 1924. Protection of the nation's wilderness resources was formalized with the passage of the Wilderness Act of 1964, which protects designated wilderness lands from commercial enterprises; the use of mechanical transport; and the construction of structures, installations, and permanent roads. When using wilderness areas for recreation, visitors should practice the no-trace ethic described in Chapter 5.[20,21]

### National Wild and Scenic Rivers System

The National Wild and Scenic Rivers System was established by Congress in 1968 to preserve certain rivers with outstanding natural, archaeological, or recreational features in a free-flowing condition for the enjoyment of current and future generations. Rivers are classified as wild, scenic, or recreational. A wild river shows less evidence of human presence, is free of improvements (dams), and usually is inaccessible except by trail. A scenic river is relatively primitive and undeveloped but is accessible by road in some places. A recreational river is more developed, is accessible by road or railroad, and may have been dammed.[22,23] Recreational use of these 155

rivers must be compatible with preservation of wildlife and the environment.[24]

### National Trails System

The National Trails System was established in 1968 with passage of the National Trails System Act, which promotes enjoyment of and appreciation for trails and encourages greater access. The act established four classes of trails.[3,25]

1. *National scenic trails* are designated by Congress and are continuous, extended routes for outdoor recreation within protected corridors. Examples are the Appalachian and Pacific Crest trails.
2. *National historic trails,* also designated by

*The National Trails System scenic and historic distance trails also include the Pacific Crest, the Appalachian trail, and the Lewis and Clark trails.*

Congress, recognize past routes of exploration, migration, and military action. For example, the Trail of Tears marks the routes used for the forced removal of more than 15,000 Cherokees from their ancestral lands in four southeastern states to Oklahoma and Arkansas.

3. *National recreation trails* are managed by public or private agencies and are designated by the Secretaries of Agriculture and the Interior under authority of the National Trails System Act of 1968. They include a variety of trail types, uses, lengths, topography, histories, and physical challenges. Examples are Muscle Shoals in Alabama (administered by the TVA) and the Black Hawk Trail in Iowa (administered by the Burlington Parks Department). More than 800 national recreation trails are designated throughout the country, with a total length of more than 9,000 miles.[26]

4. *Side and connecting trails* provide additional access to and between components of the National Trails System.

Overall, the National Trails System is managed by the National Park Service, which encourages other public and private agencies to maintain and protect trails. The eight national scenic and 14 historic trails are managed by the National Park Service, the Forest Service, or the Bureau of Land Management.

## National Scenic Byways

The National Scenic Byways Program was established under the Intermodal Surface Transportation Efficiency Act (ISTEA) of 1991. As a result of the law, the Scenic Byways Advisory Committee recommended to the Federal Highway Administration that a program be established to designate a system of National Scenic Byways and All-American Roads. The law stipulated that each byway or road must have a community committed to its designation and management, and each is required to possess intrinsic qualities in one or more of six categories: scenic, historic, cultural, natural, recreational, and archaeological. Since September 1996, the U.S. Secretary of Transportation has named 81 National Scenic Byways and All-American Roads to represent the best of the previously designated state and federal land management agency scenic byways. National Scenic Byways—such as the Edge of the Wilderness Scenic Byway in Minnesota, Creole Nature Trail in Louisiana, and Seaway Trail in New York—exemplify outstanding regional characteristics. All-American Roads are recognized nationally and internationally.[27,28] These include Colorado's San Juan Skyway, North Carolina's Blue Ridge Parkway, and Alabama's Selma to Montgomery March Byway.

## State Providers and Resources

In accordance with the Tenth Amendment to the Constitution, all powers not vested in the federal government reside in the states. Under this mandate, each state provides recreational facilities and services by authorizing the establishment of local services and by rendering statewide services as necessary and appropriate. Most states specify the means by which counties and municipalities may conduct the following activities:

- Operate recreation programs
- Provide services to communities through state offices and staffs
- Provide land and facilities for recreational services through state parks, forests, nature preserves, and fish and wildlife areas
- Provide visitor facilities such as campgrounds and amphitheatres
- Protect both recreationists and national resources by enforcing health and safety standards, conducting inspections, and issuing licenses and permits
- Establish research and educational facilities
- Provide funding

- ◆ Cooperate with federal agencies
- ◆ Promote tourism
- ◆ Provide recreational services to state-maintained facilities such as hospitals, correctional institutions, and homes for orphans or senior citizens

As early as 1832 the federal government allowed the Arkansas Territory to withhold the Arkansas Hot Springs and Washita River Salt Springs from private ownership because of the waters' healing powers. In 1921 the Hot Springs was designated a national park. The first state park was established in 1864 when Congress committed the Yosemite Grant to California. Like the Hot Springs area, the Yosemite Valley was later taken over by the federal government and added to the nation's second national park in 1890. New York was the first state to make a lasting contribution to recreational activity when Congress, in 1885, placed Niagara Falls and its surrounding area in care of the state as the New York State Reservation of Niagara. Shortly thereafter the state designated the Adirondack Wilderness a forest preserve. In 1903 Illinois created the first state agency for state parks, which previously had been administered individually.

To further the development of state parks, the National Conference on State Parks was organized in 1921 under the guidance of the National Park Service. It is known today as the National Society for Park Resources and is an affiliate of the National Recreation and Park Association (see Chapter 11).

Many state parks were created during the Great Depression of the 1930s, when the federal government under President Franklin Roosevelt established a massive public works program to provide employment for thousands who had lost their jobs. Further expansion took place after World War II when attendance at state parks increased sharply and demand for recreation grew exponentially. States began to purchase recreation lands using bonds or earmarked taxes instead of acquiring them as gifts or as the result of federal land grants or tax delinquency. The Land and Water Conservation Act, passed in 1965, granted states matching funds to acquire land for recreation and for use as open space.

The states own approximately 78 million acres of land and water that can be used for recreational activities. This land is classified as state forests (26.5 million acres), fish and wildlife areas (9 million acres), state parks (5.5 million acres), and other areas (37 million acres), including nature preserves. The proximity of these lands to population centers makes them extremely popular resources for recreation. They offer developed roads, trails, swimming pools, beaches, picnic grounds, playgrounds, and campgrounds.[3] In 1999, state parks accommodated 767 million day and overnight visitors. Fees generated from these and other operating receipts totaled $651 million.[2] Appendix E lists state tourism offices that can provide information about state park facilities.

## Local Providers and Resources

The nation's 3,043 counties typically provide recreational facilities such as parks, picnic areas, horseback riding and hiking trails, athletic fields, campgrounds, beaches, lodges, and cabins. Some 18,000 municipal governments provide parks, playgrounds, and playing fields and offer programs that typically include games and sports, aquatics, outdoor and nature-oriented classes and activities, arts and crafts instruction, performing arts, social opportunities, festivals, and hobby groups. Local recreation and parks departments may team up with other community agencies to offer activities such as Little League baseball and youth soccer. Facilities also may be available for self-directed activities such as hiking, cycling, and picnicking. Some areas are designated as wildlife and waterfowl sanctuaries and offer facilities for water sports or winter sport activities. Large cities may have aquatic centers, zoos, aquariums, gardens, golf courses, museums, galleries, and facilities for the performing arts.

## History of City Parks

As far back as colonial times, American cities were setting aside squares, plazas, and gardens for public use and enjoyment. The most famous of these areas is the Boston Common, one of the first municipal parks in the United States, which is still in existence today. The Boston Common later was joined by four other "firsts." The Boston Public Garden,

*Wild Animal Park is a San Diego city park and receives support from the Zoological Society of San Diego, a nonprofit entity.*

located across the street from the Boston Common, was founded in 1852 and is the home of the nation's first public botanical garden and the first public arboretum. As we learned in Chapter 4, Boston also was the site of the nation's first playground, the Boston Sand Garden. Finally, the "emerald necklace" concept, introduced by landscape architects Charles Eliot and Frederick Law Olmsted, encouraged the development of green space around the city to provide convenient recreation areas for all citizens.[29]

Setting the standard for municipal parks in the United States was New York City's Central Park, the nation's first planned park. Authorized in 1853, Central Park was designed by Olmsted and another landscape architect, Calver Vaux. Planned to offer scenic vistas in a wooded setting, the park provided a refreshing change of scenery for urban dwellers. Facilities were available for walking, pleasure driving, ice skating, and boating.

Many other parks were built in the second half of the 19th century, but the greatest expansion occurred during the first half of the 20th century. During the Great Depression of the 1930s, growth in urban parks was assisted by public works programs established by the federal government. After World War II, Congress passed several laws that aided in the development of urban open space and recreational resources.

## Funding and Development

Before a local government can provide recreation services, it must be empowered by the state to do so. Enabling laws enacted by state governments allow localities to establish, maintain, and operate park and recreation systems; the laws also specify sources and methods of funding.

To a great extent, the availability of funds determines the scope and quality of local recreational opportunities. Current operating funds usually come from appropriations, recreation taxes, and user fees. Much of the funding for capital outlays is acquired through bond issues, assessments, donations, special events, and government grants.

The municipal government is best suited to provide appropriate recreation areas and facilities for the local community. Growth of urban areas, however, has increased the difficulty of acquiring and retaining sufficient lands for community needs. Additional funding is needed to develop and improve programs for inner-city residents and to develop waterfront facilities, nature paths, jogging and cycling trails, skating ponds, and cross-country ski routes. Public-private partnerships for facility development can maximize the benefits of tax dollars and expand opportunities for public recreation.

**Concept Check**

- Briefly state the responsibilities of the National Park Service, the Bureau of Indian Affairs, and the U.S. Army Corps of Engineers.
- Compare and contrast the recreational offerings of counties and municipalities.

## QUASI-PUBLIC PROVIDERS

The list of quasi-public providers of recreational services is extensive and covers a wide range of interests and activities. The quasi-public sector does not receive tax monies. Operating on a nonprofit basis, most such providers rely on funds from government grants, donations, or both acquired through fundraising and corporate sponsorship. Some providers also charge fees for certain services to maintain financial stability and subsidize services for those who cannot afford to pay for them. To remain tax exempt, nonprofit groups must adhere to Internal Revenue Service guidelines.

Often serving as major providers of recreational services, quasi-public providers frequently have broad overall goals that relate to social or moral values and may include, for example, the promotion of Christian fellowship, social welfare, or informal education for public benefit. The governing board or board of trustees of a quasi-public entity usually is composed of volunteers, but management and supervisory positions are held by full-time, paid professionals. Other employees may be hired on a part-time or seasonal basis.

In the sections that follow we describe the characteristics of various kinds of quasi-public providers of recreational services.

### Youth Organizations: Secular

Many secular nonprofit organizations offer recreational opportunities to young people. In the following sections we will learn about programs that are making important contributions to the lives of American youth.

**Boy Scouts of America**

The Boy Scouts was founded in England in 1908 by Lord Robert Baden-Powell and brought to America by William Boyce in 1910. The organization was granted a federal charter in 1916. Its purpose is to build character; foster good citizenship; and develop mental, moral, and physical fitness in boys through outdoor adventures and other meaningful learning experiences. Cub Scout dens and Boy Scout troops meet weekly, and Explorer Scouts help older, high school–aged boys explore career options.

**Girl Scouts of the USA**

Agnes Baden-Powell, sister of the founder of the Boy Scouts, became president of the Girl Guides in England. Juliette Lowe brought the movement to her native city of Savannah, Georgia, where she organized the first Girl Guide group in America. The organization's name was changed to Girl Scouts in 1913, and it received a congressional charter in 1950. The Girl Scouts' guiding principle is that girls can learn and grow through experience and discovery. Programs are developed for five age levels.

## Camp Fire Boys and Girls

Another prominent youth service organization is Camp Fire Girls and Boys. Founded in 1910 as Camp Fire Girls, this now-coeducational program focuses on camping; environmental education; and the development of decision-making skills, appreciation of diversity, and self-reliance.

## Boys and Girls Clubs of America

Established in 1906 as the Boys Clubs of America, this organization has expanded to include Girls Clubs. The clubs have an open-door policy and offer a variety of activities designed to teach self-reliance, good citizenship, and respect for others.

## Big Brothers and Big Sisters of America

In these programs, adult volunteers agree to spend a certain amount of time each week with a child who comes from an unstable family background or lacks a reliable same-sex role model. The adult may take the child on recreational or cultural outings or family gatherings, help with schoolwork, or just spend time listening to and talking with the child. The purpose of the program is to give children in need the opportunity to spend regular time with a safe, stable, reliable, and caring adult.

## Youth Organizations: Religious

One of every three organizations listed in the *Directory of American Youth Organizations* is church-affiliated, and many others exist that are not included in the directory. Between 30% and 50% of American young people report that they participate in a religious youth organization.[30] Church-affiliated entities such as the Congress of National Black Churches and the Fellowship of Christian Athletes attempt to instill both social and spiritual awareness, provide leadership training, and offer opportunities to engage in community service. Many religious youth organizations strive to reach underserved youth in high-risk environ-

ments and to meet the full spectrum of adolescent needs. Some also provide services for families, singles, seniors, and other groups with special needs.

## Young Men's Christian Association (YMCA)

The YMCA was established in London in the mid-19th century by George Williams and Matthew Young, who were concerned about moral conditions in the city. In 1881 Thomas V. Sullivan took the concept to Boston. The organization's purpose was to help young men enjoy Christian fellowship and to promote religious ideals and character building. Today YMCA programs are open to people of all faiths and both sexes, and the Y offers a choice of membership levels and options. Providing a wide range of services, the Y offers sports activities and clinics, fitness training, swimming, and other programs for infants, children, adults, and seniors. Some programs target at-risk and hard-to-reach youth and teen parents.

## Young Women's Christian Association (YWCA)

The YWCA was established in England in 1855 when Mrs. Arthur Kinnard brought together a group whose mission was to provide homes for young women in London. At about the same time, Emma Robart began a prayer union, and in 1877 the two groups merged. Similar groups were formed in the United States in the late 1850s; the first one to bear the name Young Women's Christian Association was established in Boston in 1866, and 10 years later it began to offer a class in calisthenics. Eventually, athletic programs were organized, and in 1884 the association moved into a new building with a gymnasium. Today the YWCA offers diverse programs for the general population: camps for children, activities for teens, child care, fitness, hiking, aquatics, and cooking. The YWCA also provides special programming for women: those in crisis, single parents, immigrants, and those in penal institutions.

### Young Men's and Young Women's Hebrew Associations (YM/YWHA)

The origins of the YM/YWHA can be traced to the 1840s, when Hebrew literary societies were established in several American cities. These societies ultimately would form the nucleus of the YM/YWHAs, which early in their existence employed physical fitness instructors. The YM/YWHA sponsors recreation centers, camps, outdoor activities, sports, fitness, and art and other cultural activities. Funded as a social service agency, the YM/YWHA offers programs for child care, teens, and citizenship.

### Catholic Youth Organization (CYO)

Established in 1930, the CYO focuses on the spiritual, social, and recreational needs of Catholic and non-Catholic youth. Relying for leadership on the parish priest and volunteers, the CYO offers retreats, religious education, seminars, sports programs, and social activities.

## Community Centers

Typically found in low-income urban communities, most of the nation's approximately 1,000 community centers were established in the late 19th and early 20th centuries. Usually regarded as social agencies, community centers provide counseling, cultural enrichment, health services, and recreational opportunities.[31] Examples are the American Youth Work Center and the Allied Youth and Family Counseling Center.

## Arts and Cultural Organizations

Many nonprofit organizations promote the arts and cultural activities. Museums, art centers, and civic centers often work closely with other nonprofit or public agencies to sponsor exhibitions or performances for both members and the general public. Some nonprofit groups organize art festivals that include folk music and ethnic dance. Art and civic centers may offer instruction in visual arts: ceramics, photography, drawing, painting; performing arts: dance, dramatics, music (vocal and instrumental); and literary arts: poetry readings, book clubs, storytelling. Some entities sponsor speakers, organize outings to foreign films and museums, and organize trips to sites of archaeological or anthropological interest.

## Preservation Societies

The main objective of preservation societies is to preserve natural areas and historical sites. Some societies own their own property; others do not own property but encourage other entities and individuals to preserve property for future generations. In most cases, specific outdoor pursuits are permitted on preserved property. Examples of preservation organizations are the National Audubon Society, The Nature Conservancy, and the National Trust for Historic Preservation.

### Concept Check

- What are the characteristics of a quasi-public provider of recreation and leisure services?
- Identify three quasi-public providers of recreation and leisure services in your home town.

## PRIVATE PROVIDERS AND RESOURCES

Private organizations provide a wide variety of recreational opportunities for their members. Membership in private entities such as country clubs is often costly and restrictive, whereas anyone with the interest and the modest membership fee can join a group such as the Sierra Club or the American Orchid Society. Like quasi-public organizations, private entities operate on a nonprofit basis and are governed by officers and directors elected by the membership, with paid employees managing day-to-day operations. In the following sections we will learn about several kinds of private providers of recreation and leisure services.

## Sport and Outdoor Clubs

Clubs in this category cater to a wide variety of active interests, and facilities range from lavish to modest. Country clubs typically have golf courses, tennis courts, and swimming pools and usually offer instruction in these sports. Typical amenities are a pro shop that sells and rents equipment and other merchandise; racquetball, squash, and handball courts; locker rooms, steam rooms, and sauna; one or more rooms where members can read, socialize, or play pool, cards, or board games; one or more bars; a dining room where lunch and dinner are served, and facilities for more casual dining; and a ballroom for dances and parties.

City athletic clubs cater to business people and typically offer most or all of the indoor recreational and social facilities mentioned above. Other private clubs may focus on only one sport, such as golf, racquetball, or tennis. Yacht clubs offer docking and marina services to members and provide many of the amenities available at country clubs, including facilities for dining and dancing. Private ski clubs may own their own slopes, lifts, and clubhouse. Also popular in North America are clubs for outdoor enthusiasts. Activities may take place on public, private, or leased land; some clubs operate their own lodging facilities.

## Social Clubs

Private social clubs run the gamut from small to large and from exclusive to inclusive. Country clubs, athletic clubs, and yacht clubs in reality are as much social clubs as they are recreational facilities. Other social clubs are organized by people who have a common ethnic or religious heritage, share political views, live in the same neighborhood, or belong to the same profession. Some clubs have their own facilities; others may rent quarters or meet in members' homes or at work.

## Special-Interest Groups

Thousands of organizations appeal to the special interests of people of all ages and backgrounds, from the American Orchid Society to the National Rifle Association. Many of these organizations offer local instruction and competitions for people who seek to enhance their skills in a given activity, from trapshooting to chess to model airplane building. Other activities may include workshops, demonstrations, exhibitions, and sales. Members receive regular bulletins and newsletters, often announcing social gatherings. Other common benefits are expert advice from paid staff members and discounts on equipment and services. Less formal groups may be organized by neighbors or officemates who share an interest such as walking, needlework, or reading. Members must pay dues to belong to private social clubs, which customarily are operated on a nonprofit basis.

## Adult Service Clubs

The members of adult service clubs (Kiwanis, Rotary, Optimists, Lions, Elks, Junior League) represent business, professional, and social groups in the community and volunteer their time to improve community life for all citizens. Members must qualify and pay dues. Service clubs operate on a nonprofit basis on income generated by dues, donations, and special events. Adult service clubs provide recreational opportunities for their members and often sponsor sports and other programs for local youth. Some organizations place a high priority on services for youth who live in low-income, high-risk neighborhoods. Others, such as the Shriners, provide activities for children with disabilities. The Shriners also operate national hospitals for crippled and burned children, where any child in need receives care at no cost.

### Concept Check

- Explain the differences between private and quasi-public providers of recreation and leisure services.
- What private club or organization do you belong to, if any, and what recreation and leisure services does it offer?

# COMMERCIAL PROVIDERS

Commercial providers of recreation and leisure services offer many popular and well-managed programs on a for-profit basis. In the United States and Canada, the market for such services is one of the fastest-growing sectors of the economy.[32] Commercial providers offer recreational opportunities through retail outlets; entertainment, hospitality, and leisure services in the natural environment; and travel and tourism. In the following sections we will present specific examples of such providers.

## Retail: Audiovisual

Among the key providers of entertainment in the United States are the manufacturers and distributors of televisions, videocassette recorders, stereos, video games, and other kinds of home entertainment merchandise, as well as the owners of video arcades. Approximately 98% of American homes have a television set,[33] and home viewers now can enjoy near-theatre quality reproduction with big-screen TVs, surround sound, and concert hall–quality sound. Although videotape rentals

*Cyber-recreational business is expected to boom.*

have increased at a phenomenal rate in recent years, movie attendance has not declined and in fact has showed solid gains, in part because of the immense popularity of blockbuster films that appeal to both adults and children.

One of the fastest-growing segments of the retail audiovisual market is electronic entertainment. This industry blossomed from the 1980s children's video games and evolved to professional online tournaments. In 1997 alone, arcade, console, and computer games grossed $16.5 billion, and the cyber-recreational business is expected to boom in the 21st century.[34] Some games are fashioned after sophisticated military simulation tools, and many are purchased for adult rather than child use.[35]

Although still extremely popular, video arcades have experienced a slight downward trend because of the increased realism and accessibility of home games. In response, several companies have developed virtual reality arcade games, and others are introducing bigger, faster, more sophisticated games made with multiple high-speed computers, laser disc players, strobes, large-screen projectors, and booming, discotheque-quality sound.

Ever since video games were first introduced, parents and manufacturers have debated the merits of this form of entertainment for children. Many parents, educators, and other concerned citizens object to the violent content, questionable values, and overstimulation of many video games, whereas manufacturers counter that the games can improve problem-solving ability, make learning more appealing, and build confidence and self-esteem.[36]

## Entertainment: Amusement and Theme Parks

Amusement parks offer thrill rides, games of chance, sideshows, and food and drink concessions. Theme parks evolved from these attractions but center entertainment around the family and invite attendees to experience a particular subject or historical era in a fantasy atmosphere.

"THESE AREN'T WORKING. CAN I EXCHANGE THEM FOR SOME OF THOSE, PLEASE?"

## Amusement Parks

Perhaps the best-known amusement park in the United States is the one at Coney Island in New York City. America's first permanent outdoor amusement facility, Jones Woods, also in New York, was built in 1857. Amusement parks with fun centers, rides, and shows flourished in the late 19th century, reached their zenith in the 1920s and 1930s, and then began to fade. Many people regarded them as disreputable, and aging equipment was sometimes the cause of serious injury and death. With government restrictions on the manufacture of rides and with skyrocketing premiums for liability insurance, many once-successful amusement parks were forced to close. Replacing them was a new concept that focused on providing entertainment in a family atmosphere: the theme park.

## Theme Parks

In the 1950s the famous animator, Walt Disney, began to design and construct America's first theme park. Opening in Anaheim, California, in 1955, Disneyland was built on 180 acres of land filled with orange and walnut groves. This new concept in entertainment was designed to be a fabulous playground, a colorful fair, a magical storyland, a metropolis of the future, and a source of both happiness and knowledge. Today "the happiest place on earth" offers eight "theme lands" and has expanded its 18 original attractions to 60. Within a few years of Disneyland's opening, no fewer than 30 more theme parks were built around the United States. These include Epcot Center, Disneyworld, and Busch Gardens in Florida, Six Flags in several midwestern and southern states, Knott's Berry Farm in California, and Great Adventure in New Jersey. Carrying the theme-park idea to what some would call an extreme, developers in 1993 alone opened three theme park-like hotels on the Las Vegas strip. MGM's 33-acre park, for example, offers rides, shows, and child care.

Theme parks have become travel destinations in themselves, and many have on-site hotels for tourists and business conventions. Owners cover their high operating costs by charging steep fees for admission and by setting high prices at food and souvenir concessions. As the theme park pioneer, the Walt Disney Company has acquired expertise in crowd management, high technology, and strategic planning. The Disney empire continues to develop plans for new domestic parks, and its success in America inspired it to create parks in France and Japan.

At the same time, European theme parks are coming to the United States. Denmark's successful Legoland cost some $130 million to build in Carlsbad, California. It employs 100 full-time administrative, professional, and technical personnel and approximately 600 seasonal workers. They expect 1.8 million people to visit the park each year, generating an estimated $76 million in annual revenue. Among the new projects proposed for Legoland is a 700-room luxury resort.

Theme parks offer the surrounding community important economic benefits: employment opportunities, increased sales revenue, and enhanced property values. For example, when Disneyland first opened in 1955, Anaheim had five hotels, two motels, and three restaurants. Today, during its busiest season Disneyland employs 12,000 people, and more than 50,000 students have augmented their college funds with Disneyland jobs. The marketing challenge in the theme park industry is to remain competitive by constantly upgrading attractions while maintaining a wholesome family environment. New interactive multimedia technology, for example, is influencing theme parks. Likewise, exploratory discovery through this medium is re-creating the way we receive information at many museums worldwide. With interactive technology, information is no longer received passively. Instead, visitors are invited to learn using a playful, hands-on approach. The visceral experience of discovery has, in essence, turned our museums into active "amusement parks of the intellect."[37]

## Entertainment: Malls and Restaurants

An emerging trend in indoor recreation is the shopping mall as entertainment venue. The Mall of America in Bloomington, Minnesota, which covers 78 acres, is the nation's largest combined retail and entertainment center and is now one of the top tourist attractions in the United States. In addition to retail outlets, the mall offers restaurants, sports bars, and nightclubs and showcases Gatlin Music City, which features live country music. Knott's Camp Snoopy, the country's largest indoor theme park, contains 26 rides and numerous other attractions. Other mall offerings are the three-level Lego Imagination Center, a five-level train track with 30 moving trains, and a golf mountain with a two-level miniature golf course.

Another popular family entertainment site is Chuck E. Cheese (created by the merger of Showbiz Pizza and Chuck E. Cheese Pizza Time Theatre). This nationwide chain of more than 379 restaurants features pizza, a salad bar, and cotton candy plus a variety of free child-oriented entertainment: live shows and animated robots on stage, video games, air hockey, kiddy rides, boats, spaceships, Ferris wheels, bulldozers, ball crawls, and baby ball baths.

Children can play skill games for 25 cents, and each child is a winner, earning at least one ticket that can be turned in for a prize.

## Hospitality: Commercial Campgrounds

Owned by individuals, families, small businesses, large companies, and franchises, commercial campgrounds account for close to 80% of the nation's individual campsites.[3] Camping continues to be an appealing activity for families and individuals, and it is expected to grow in popularity among adults of preretirement and retirement age.[38]

Commercial campgrounds that are located close to freeways cater to people who travel by car and who use recreational vehicles to make short stops. Other campgrounds are located near recreation sites for activities such as boating, hunting, and fishing. Commercial campgrounds usually have laundry facilities, a general store, gas pumps, and one or more restaurants. Some have swimming pools and tennis courts; some offer both day and evening activities and excursions.

Some commercial campgrounds sell memberships and allow members to purchase campsites on a time-share basis. In some cases members can trade for campsites in other areas. Condominium campgrounds sell specific lots. Appendix F lists sources of information about both public and private campgrounds.

## Leisure Services in the Natural Environment: Camps

For generations, attending camp has been a popular summer pastime for American young people. Some camps are sponsored by quasi-public agencies; others are privately operated or affiliated with a religious group; and a small number are sponsored by public or municipal entities. The great majority of camps are residential facilities; the remainder are day camps. About two-thirds of camps are coeducational; others are for boys or girls only; and a few are family camps.[39]

Traditionally, the summer camp experience has included water sports, archery, nature study, outdoor adventure programs, music, rhythm, drama, arts and crafts, and other activities, depending on the sex and age of the campers. In addition, many camps now cater to young people with special needs (youth at risk and children who have mental or physical disabilities, who want to lose weight, or who need academic tutoring) and special interests (tennis, sailing, horseback riding, baseball, hockey, figure skating, music, dance, music, drama, art, space study, or law).

The American Camping Association has developed national standards that apply to all kinds of camps: public, private, day, and resident. The American Camping Association accredits camps that meet its standards.

## Travel and Tourism

Between 1980 and 1990, pleasure trips taken by Americans increased from 342.8 million to 460.5 million.[40] According to the World Travel & Tourism Council, travel and tourism is the world's largest industry and will double in size between 1995 and 2005.[41] In 1996, travelers spent $473 billion in the United States and, according to the Tourism Works for America Council, tourism directly generated 6.8 million jobs and indirectly supported an additional 9 million jobs. That makes tourism the third largest sales industry in the nation.[42] Domestic travelers spent more than $380 billion, including $91.6 billion for food service, $89.5 billion for public transportation, $67 billion for lodging, $63.1 billion for auto transportation, $39.9 billion for recreation, and $31.4 billion for retail.[43] California, which collected $58.2 billion from tourists in 1996, generated more tourism dollars that year than any other state.[42] One survey conducted by *Travel & Leisure* magazine found that respondents believe personal travel should help them understand the culture and history of an area, assist them in working for an improved natural environment, or aid them in achieving a new perspective in their lives.[41] The advanced technology of today's clothing and equipment allows more people who are less fit to visit remote sites and participate in adventure and eco-tourism.[44]

### Rural Tourism

One area of growing interest to travelers is rural tourism. Many rural areas have experienced economic hardship as a result of declining revenue from farming, mining, and lumbering. Several rural communities are revitalizing their economies by catering to the growing number of tourists who are becoming attracted to leisure, country-style. Tourists increasingly are drawn to rural areas by their natural offerings: open spaces, pastoral countryside, lakes, streams, woods, and fresh air. Equally attractive are leisure pursuits such as fishing, hunting, horseback riding, hiking, canoeing, river running, rodeos, and country-western music and dancing. Profiting from this trend are hospitality providers such as the owners of hotels, motels, bed and breakfasts, restaurants, and bars; retailers of everything from food and camping equipment to souvenirs; and service providers such as horse and boat renters and guides, pack outfitters, and campground owners. Private property is leased for hunting or fishing. Tourists also are attracted by festivals that celebrate local history.

*The graceful, aerobatic maneuvers of the U.S. Navy's Blue Angels have entertained some 375 million fans since 1946..*

Working ranches and farms often are vacation havens for city dwellers attracted to country living. Guests help with the work while learning the various aspects of ranching or farming. Dude ranches, where guests do not work, provide a romanticized old-West atmosphere, offering lodging, meals, riding instruction, trail riding, swimming, tennis, cookouts, and special events. Once-abandoned mining towns in the West are reopening as tourist attractions, offering both entertainment and insight into a vanished way of life.

The growth of rural tourism was encouraged through initiatives of the now defunct U.S. Travel and Tourism Administration (USTTA), passage of the Rural Partnership Act of 1989, ongoing support from the Congressional Travel and Tourism Caucus, and actions of the National Governors Association and the Small Business Administration. Tourist facilities not only bring visitors to rural areas but also increase the availability of recreational opportunities to local residents. The growth of rural tourism also creates new career opportunities for recreation and leisure professionals. Increasingly, recreation planners and developers can be expected to recognize the appeal of rural life when planning activities for visitors and residents who seek a more relaxed pace and a simpler lifestyle.

**Concept Check**

- Identify three popular trends in commercial recreation.
- Explain the growing appeal of rural tourism.

## PROVIDERS OF SPECIALIZED SERVICES

The entities we will consider in this section are not in the business of providing recreational services to the public but instead offer such services to a select group of people. Such entities expect to profit indirectly from the improved health and morale of the people to whom they offer services.

## Employee Recreation

Employee recreation originated in the 19th century during the industrial revolution, when enlightened factory owners began to realize that their hardworking employees would be more productive and loyal if offered opportunities for company-sponsored leisure activities. Early offerings were simple: choirs, picnics, and other outings. Later they expanded to include calisthenics for office workers and bowling, basketball, softball, and baseball teams for men. A highly popular activity for many employees today is the company-sponsored golf tournament.

Today thousands of companies sponsor recreational activities for their employees; in 1995 the National Employee Services and Recreation Association (NESRA), founded in 1941, registered nearly 4,000 individuals and organizations as members.[45] Employee programs for recreation, health, and wellness come in all shapes and sizes, from modest walking clubs to million-dollar fitness complexes staffed by professionals. Many large companies have onsite facilities for some or all of the following: circuit training, weight training, aerobics, swimming, track, basketball, tennis, racquetball, baseball, and softball. Such companies may employ specialists in health and fitness or contract for such services. Some large industrial corporations, including Union Carbide and Lockheed, even offer employees designated areas for boating, hunting, and fishing.

Companies that do not have in-house recreational facilities for employees may pay part or all of the cost for employees to use commercial health and fitness centers. Participants may receive instruction, space, and equipment at company expense. In addition to providing facilities for physical fitness and recreation, many companies arrange trips and tours, outings to cultural and sporting events, discount movie tickets, hobby clubs, and choruses.

Companies that offer their employees recreational programs generally have the same goal: to improve employee health and fitness. Whether elaborate or simple, such programs help companies attract and retain good employees. Employee recreation programs are designed to improve health, build morale, reduce absenteeism, and help discourage drug and alcohol abuse. For many employers, the expense of health and wellness programs is justifiable as a means of controlling escalating medical costs and increasing productivity. For example, since Union Pacific started a job exercise program, it has been reported that 80% of participating employees have increased their productivity.[46]

## Military Recreation

Military recreation in the United States originated in the early 1900s. Some recreational programs were offered during World War I, but not until World War II did military recreation truly come into its own.

### USO

At the urging of U.S. Army General George Marshall, the USO (United Service Organizations) was formed in 1941 by the National Catholic Community Service, the National Jewish Welfare Board, the Salvation Army, the Travelers Aid Association of America, the YMCA, and the YWCA. Its mission was and is to provide social, welfare, and recreational services to members of the U.S. armed forces and their families. USO is a nonprofit social service agency supported by private donations.

By the summer of 1941, USO service clubs and recreation centers had begun to open, and by November of that year USO Camp Shows, Inc., was taking celebrity entertainers to Veterans Administration hospitals at home and to military commands overseas. Particularly popular was the annual Christmas show conducted overseas by Bob Hope for troops who fought in World War II, the Korean War, and the Vietnam War. In 1944 the number of USO recreation centers peaked at 3,035. The organization was disbanded after World War II, but it was reactivated when the United States became involved in the Korean conflict in 1951.[47]

Today the USO maintains 160 locations around the world. In addition to celebrity entertainment, it offers counseling, drug abuse programs, and other social services for military personnel.[45]

### Contemporary Facilities

Military recreation programs and facilities are operated by the Morale, Welfare and Recreation Program of the Department of Defense. Standard programs today include physically challenging activities, fitness routines, sports, spectator events, participation in performing arts events, arts and crafts, libraries and recreational reading, movies, and a wide variety of social opportunities. Other offerings are leadership seminars and classes in computers, cosmetics and fashion, marriage enrichment, financial planning, gardening, and smoking cessation. Indoor recreational activities include pool, bingo, bowling, basketball, and chess. For outdoor recreation, participants can choose from archery, swimming, cycling, tennis, golf, softball, rugby, soccer, in-line skating, horseback riding, fishing, boating, scuba diving, and camping.

Many bases offer Little League baseball and Youth Soccer programs for children. At military bases both at home and abroad, Camp Adventure, a nonprofit youth service organization, offers day and residential camp experiences to children of military personnel. In 1992, for example, Camp Adventure served more than 300,000 children while supporting the overall objectives of military morale, welfare, and recreation programs for youth.[48]

At military bases, separate recreational facilities may be provided for officers and enlisted personnel. For example, an officers' club may have tennis courts and a swimming pool, whereas these facilities are not available to enlisted personnel. On board a ship or submarine, however, all personnel use the same recreational facilities. Submarines, aircraft carriers, and destroyers have workout facilities that include weights, treadmills, and exercise bikes. On any large ship with a helicopter landing pad, personnel can play volleyball and basketball. On carriers, personnel can play touch football on the hangar deck and flight deck.

### Sports and Music

Each branch of the military has men's and women's teams in a wide variety of sports; two examples are bowling and boxing. These teams train rigorously under professional coaches and compete within their own branch of service and in interservice matches.

Each branch of the service also has bands, orchestras, jazz combos, and other music groups. Recruits who pass an audition receive both military training and instruction at the Armed Forces School of Music.

### Success of Military Recreation

The success of military recreation has been based on its contribution to the mission of national defense, which includes:[49]

1. Contributing to the readiness of the armed forces by enhancing physical fitness, leadership, military skills, unit cohesion, and high morale
2. Essential morale-building and recreational activities for deployed military personnel
3. Activities that enhance the community and assist in the recruitment of outstanding young people to the Army, Navy, Air Force, and Marines
4. Recreation programs that support the retention of quality military personnel

In recent years military recreation has been significantly affected by the downsizing of the various service branches that began in the early

1990s. In response, some military bases are forming partnerships in their local communities to offer recreational activities (other than those associated with combat readiness) to both civilians and military personnel.

## Campus Recreation

Colleges and universities offer the campus community a broad spectrum of extracurricular activities; theatres, gymnasiums, and student unions are just a few examples. Students are the primary focus of these activities, but opportunities are offered to faculty, staff, alumni, and members of the surrounding community.

Campus recreation programs enhance the school's image and assist in the recruitment and retention of quality students. Today a major focus of campus recreation managers is to develop a more holistic approach to programming that considers students' psychological and social needs. As a result, more offerings are available in fitness, outdoor recreation, and dance, which serve as alternatives to the highly competitive sports competitions that take place on many campuses.

Unquestionably, a major area of student activity is participation in and observation of intercollegiate sports competitions. For students who enjoy sports but who want low-key competition, intramural sports offer a wide range of choices and provide opportunities for social interaction. Many students enjoy participating in plays, musicals, choirs, bands, and orchestras. Campuses often have special-interest clubs for students with hobbies such as chess, stamp collecting, ecology, and debating. Journalism, English, and creative writing majors can work on the school magazine, newspaper, and yearbook; communications and broadcast majors can refine their skills by assuming various duties at the campus radio station.

Many campuses present lectures by noted authorities in fields related to the social sciences: anthropology, sociology, psychology, political science. Some campuses sponsor debates between candidates for political office, sometimes at the presidential level. All of these activities offer students opportunities to widen their intellectual and social horizons and to connect their academic learning with real-world situations.

Outdoor recreation programs offer students a chance to learn new skills, meet others with similar interests, and become environmentally aware by attending clinics, symposiums, and conferences. Activities may include backpacking, camping, day hikes, canoeing, kayaking, rafting, sailing, sailboarding, bike touring, cross-country and telemark skiing, nature photography, and other wilderness activities.

Fraternities and sororities offer members opportunities to learn social and leadership skills (see the Action Guide on p. 222). Lifetime friendships often develop, and members serve the campus and community through philanthropic endeavors. On the negative side, some fraternities and sororities have been charged with violent hazing rituals, alcohol abuse, and discriminatory behavior. Some campuses now prohibit hazing and many fraternities and sororities have taken steps to improve both their conduct and their image in this regard.

## Elder Care Recreational Services

Not-for-profit nursing homes, continuing care retirement communities, assisted living and senior housing facilities, and community service organizations help meet the recreational needs of millions of older persons across the country. Increased demand for these recreational services has occurred due to the burgeoning senior population. Chapter 14 addresses this topic.

In this chapter we have learned about the various providers of and resources for a wide range of recreation and leisure services. In the next chapter we turn our attention to the various professionals who pursue careers in the field of recreation and leisure.

# ACTION GUIDE

## WHAT'S YOUR CLUB IQ?

Do you belong to an organization, club, fraternity, or sorority? Do you not belong but wish you did? Were you invited to join but chose to decline? Whatever your situation, you can raise your consciousness about clubs by taking the following quiz.

1. Do you currently belong to a school-sponsored organization? _____

2. If so, for what specific reasons did you choose to join?

   _____

   _____

3. If you don't belong, why?

   _____

   _____

4. If you do belong to an organization, did you undergo hazing as a pledge? _____

5. If so, what did the hazing involve, and how did you feel about it?

   _____

   _____

6. If you belong to an organization, how if at all has membership affected your social life, your academic performance, and your involvement in extracurricular activities?

   _____

   _____

7. If you don't belong, how if at all has not belonging affected your social life, academic performance, and involvement in extracurricular activities?

   _____

   _____

8. Whether you do or do not belong to an organization, club, fraternity, or sorority, if you had the chance to make the choice again, would you make the same choice? Why or why not?

   _____

   _____

## Summing Up

- The federal government owns nearly 25% of the land in the United States and plays a significant role in recreation.
- The National Park Service administers more than 380 sites.
- The U.S. Forest Service administers more than 191 million acres of land in a multiple-use fashion that accommodates the interests and needs of diverse groups such as recreationists, loggers, ranchers, and miners. Other federal agencies contribute significantly to the administration and use of public lands.
- State systems hold 78 million acres of land for recreational purposes and are authorized to operate through enabling laws.
- New York City's Central Park, designed in the 1850s, set the standard for municipal parks in the United States.
- Federal, state, and local governments cooperate in several ventures related to the recreational use of public lands; one example is the National Trails System.

- Nonprofit or quasi-public providers of recreation services depend financially on government grants, donations, and fees for services. These providers include youth service organizations, community centers, special-interest groups, arts and cultural organizations, and preservation societies.
- Private providers have restrictive memberships and include sports and outdoor clubs, social clubs, special-interest groups, and adult service clubs.
- Commercial providers are profit-oriented entities and include wholesale and retail outlets, entertainment facilities, hospitality providers, and travel and tourism. Popular attractions and activities are home entertainment, video games and arcades, amusement and theme parks, camps and campgrounds, and tourism.
- Specialized recreation services are offered by employers, the military, and colleges and universities.

## Using What You've Learned

1. What is the most recent legislation that has been proposed in your state to protect wildlife habitats or to protect public land for future generations? Describe the provisions of the legislation, what it is intended to achieve, and who supports it.
2. Identify 10 parks and public recreation areas in and around your community. For what outstanding feature is each site known? How many visitors does each site have in a year? What measures do the managers of each facility take to lessen the impact of visitors?
3. Identify a public or private recreation area that is being planned in your municipality, county, or state. Describe the features of the plan. What is its anticipated impact on the land itself? On the economy?

## YOUR Turn

1. What are some benefits and drawbacks of Jenny's band's decision to start a bingo operation on their reservation?

2. Do you agree or disagree with Jenny's belief that gambling on her reservation is degrading to her band's culture?

3. What steps can Jenny and her father take to try to reconcile their differences?

4. What steps might parents take to discourage their children from spending too much time and money in the video arcades?

## REFERENCES

1. *Outdoors America* (pamphlet) (1998). Washington, DC: National Park Service; USDA Forest Service; Bureau of Land Management; Bureau of Reclamation; U.S. Fish & Wildlife Service; U.S. Army Corps of Engineers; Tennessee Valley Authority; U.S. Geological Survey; and Office of the Outdoor Recreation Initiative, U.S. Department of the Interior.

2. *Statistical Abstract of the United States*, 2000. Lanham, MD: Bernam Press, pp. 251-253.

3. Ibrahim, H., & Cordes, K. (1993). *Outdoor Recreation*, Madison, WI: Brown & Benchmark.

4. *The National Forests: Ending Their First Century*. (1990). Washington, DC: U.S. Forest Service, FS-495.

5. Williams, G.W. (2000). *The USDA Forest Service— The First Century*. Washington, DC: USDA Forest Service.

6. *America's Great Outdoors* (1992). Washington, DC: U.S. Forest Service, PA-1403.

7. USDA Forest Service (2001). *National Forest Visitor Use Monitoring National and Regional Project Results*. Washington, DC: USDA Forest Service.

8. *Celebrating an American Treasure* (1991). Washington, DC: U.S. Forest Service.

9. Hirschfelder, A., & Dreipe de Montaño, M. (1993). *The Native American Almanac*. New York: Prentice Hall General Reference, p. 40.

10. *American Indians Today* (1991). Washington, DC: U.S. Department of the Interior, MS 2620-MIB.

11. *Fish and Wildlife Resources on the Public Lands* (1994). Washington, DC: Bureau of Land Management.

12. *Public rewards from Public Lands* (2000). Washington, DC: Bureau of Land Management.

13. Smith, D. (Ed.)(1995) *Parks Directory of the United States*. Detroit, MI: Omnigraphics, Inc., pp. 84, 681–682, 700.

14. *Recreation on TVA Lakes* (brochure) (1992). Washington, DC: Tennessee Valley Authority.

15. *TVA Reservoir Recreation Areas* (2001). www.tva.com/river/recreation.

16. *Services for the Public U.S. Corps of Engineers* (2001). www.usace.army/mil/public.html

17. *NOAA'S National Marine Sanctuaries* (2001). www.noaa.gov/ocean.html

18. *The U.S. Fish and Wildlife Service* (brochure). Washington, DC: U.S. Fish and Wildlife Foundation.

19. Hendee, J. & Pitstick, R. (1995). The Use of Wilderness for Personal Growth and Inspiration. In V.G. Martin & N. Tyler (Eds). *Arctic Wilderness*. Golden, CO: North American Press, pp. 65–73.

20. Landres, P., & Meyer, S. (2000). *A National Wilderness Preservation System Database: Key Attributes and Trends, 1964-1999*. USDA Forest Service General Technical Report RMRS-GTR 18-Revised Edition. Ogden, UT: Rocky Mountain Research Station.

21. *Twenty-Five Years of Wilderness Preservation* (1990). Washington, DC: The Wilderness Society.

22. *Rivers, Trails, and Conservation Programs* (1992). Washington, DC: U.S. Department of the Interior, National Park Service.

23. *An Introduction to Wild and Scenic Rivers* (2001). Washington, DC: Department of the Interior, BQ-NA-05M-00.

24. National Parks and Conservation Association (May/June 1997). Legal Victory Protects River. *National Parks* 5(6):15..

25. Cordes, K.A. (1999). *America's National Historic Trails*. Norman, OK: University of Oklahoma Press.

26. *Cordes, K.A. (1999). America's National Scenic Trails.* Norman, OK: University of Oklahoma Press.

## REFERENCES (cont'd)

27. U.S. Department of Transportation (2000). *America's Byways.* Washington, DC: Federal Highway Administration, HEPM 700(300K).

28. Cordes, K., Olson, J., Draper, R., Petty, K. (2001). Millennium Trails and Scenic Byways: Recreation in the 21st Century. *Journal of Physical Education,Recreation, and Dance* 72(1)

29. Knudson, D. (1984). *Outdoor Recreation.* New York: Macmillan.

30. Carnegie Council on Youth Development (1992). *A Matter of Time.* New York: Carnegie Corp.

31. Kraus, R. (1990). *Recreation and Leisure in Modern Society.* Glenview, IL: Scott, Foresman.

32. Edgington, C., Hudson, S.D., Lankford, S.V. (2001). *Managing Recreation, Parks, and Leisure Services: An Introduction.* Champaign, IL: Sagamore Publishing.

33. Kraus, R. (2000). *Leisure in a Changing America.* Glenview, IL: Addison-Wesley.

34. Business Communications Company (1999). *RG230 The Electronic Entertainment Industry.* Norwalk, CT: Business Communications Co., Inc.

35. Lindstrom, B. (1992). The Gaming Globe. *Compute* 13(1), Issue 125.

36. White, W. Jr. (1992). What Value are Video Games? *USA Today* 120(2562):74.

37. Ebisch, R. (Aug 1997). Amusement Parks of the Mind. *Sky.*

38. Kelly, J. (1987). *Recreation Trends.* Champaign, IL: Sagamore Publishing.

39. Meir, J., & Mitchell, A. (1993). *Camp Counseling.* Madison, WI: Brown & Benchmark.

40. *Statistical Abstract of the United States 1994* (1994). Lanham, MD: Bernam Press.

41. Majesky, S. (April 29, 1993). Travelers of the 90's Look for Substance. *Travel Weekly.*

42. ———— (November 23, 1997). Industry News. *The San Diego Union-Tribune,* p. F–3.

43. ———— (February 14, 1998). Business Fact. *The San Diego Union-Tribune.* p. C-2..

44. Older, W. (Oct 1997). Pay Per View. *Women's Sports & Fitness* 9(8):38–40.

45. Edginton, C., et al. (1995). *Leisure and Life Satisfaction.* Madison, WI: Brown & Benchmark.

46. Mainella, F. (Oct 1996). The Benefits Are Endless. *Parks & Recreation* 31(10):2..

47. *The New Encyclopedia Brittanica* (1995). Vol. 12, Chicago: Brittanica.

48. Edginton, C., & Luneckas, L. (Oct 1993). Magic of Camp Adventure. *Parks & Recreation.*

To love what you do and feel
that it matters—how could
anything be more fun?

KATHARINE GRAHAM
*in an article by Jane Howard,*
*Ms., October 1974*

# The Profession

## CHAPTER 11

THE CHAPTER AT A GLANCE

The recreation and leisure services sector of the economy is vast, and the occupations in this field are numerous and surprisingly diverse. In this chapter we discuss the profession from a historical perspective. We learn about academic preparation in the United States and Canada and discuss the work of professional organizations in the United States. We then explore diverse career opportunities in the field and learn the importance of leadership and adherence to high standards of professional ethics.

## Chapter Objectives

*After completing this chapter, you should be able to*

- Outline the history of the recreation and leisure services profession.
- Identify and describe the work of the major U.S. organizations for recreation and leisure professionals, as well as organizations in Canada, Great Britain, the Netherlands, and international organizations.
- Identify the various career opportunities in the field of recreation and leisure services and describe the academic preparation required for each.
- Describe the leadership skills required for recreation and leisure services professionals and the ethical standards to which they should adhere.

## A World of Difference

### CLASHING OVER CAREERS

"Hi, son—back from the big woods, I see."

At the sound of his father's voice, Tim Mrazek immediately straightens up from his comfortable sprawl on the living room couch. Casting a dismayed glance at the disorderly heap of camping gear on the floor, he braces himself for his father's inevitable next words.

"This stuff belongs in the basement—not on the living room floor," Jack Mrazek says with a familiar critical edge in his voice.

"Yes, sir." Tim scoops up the gear in a clumsy bundle and hurries to the basement. *Guess I should have saluted when I said "Yes, sir,"* he thinks ruefully. *It would be a waste of time to tell him I was up all night helping take care of an injured fawn.* Tim stows his canteen and messkit on a shelf, pulls dirty clothes out of his duffel bag and puts them in the washing machine, and carries his sleeping bag outside to air it on the clothesline. *Just once if he'd show some interest in what I'm doing,* he

thinks as he spreads out the sleeping bag. *Just once if he wouldn't act like I'm playing stupid kid games in the woods.*

At 17, Tim Mrazek is a high school junior with a 3.5 GPA, a slot on the varsity track and field team, and an enthusiastic trombone player in the school's jazz combo. Although he has another year to go, he's already set his sights on the college he wants to attend: a respected institution in Colorado that offers one of the country's best four-year programs in wildlife management. As long as he can remember, Tim has been trying to help sick and injured animals he finds in the woods. He's part of a regular patrol that hikes through a nearby state forest looking for animals who need help, and he volunteers at the local wildlife shelter. When the shelter's director, a woman Tim greatly admires, told him he could actually make a career out of what he loves doing most, he was both incredulous and ecstatic. Ever since then he's

## FROM OCCUPATION TO PROFESSION

Historically, the people employed in the field of recreation and leisure services have not been professionals because they were not formally trained for positions in the field. Over the years, however, the leaders of recreational activities began to amass a body of knowledge about their field and to disseminate it among others, either formally through college and university courses or through less formal means such as workshops and in-service training sessions. The original recreation and leisure professionals came from diverse fields, including social work, physical education, and religious studies.

The first recreation courses were offered primarily by college and university physical edu-

cation departments. At its first national meeting in 1907 the Playground Association of America recommended that professional training courses be provided at three levels:

1. *The normal course in play.* This course, designed for future playground directors, would cover both the theory and the conduct of recreational activities.
2. *Play for grade school teachers.* This course was intended to help elementary school teachers lead play activities in school.
3. *Institute course in play.* This course was designed for playground supervisors.

As municipalities and agencies began to increase the number of their recreational offerings, the need for well-trained administrators became apparent. In 1926 the Playground

## A World of Difference

### CLASHING OVER CAREERS (cont'd)

focused on his objective: acceptance at the college he believes will be perfect for him.

Tim's father, however, has other ideas. A hard-driving, self-made man who grew up in Pittsburgh's tough Polish district near the steel mills, Jack Mrazek was the only person in his large family to attend college. He did it the hard way, working nights in the mill, studying every spare hour, keeping himself awake with super-strong coffee and caffeine pills. Now a supervisor in a local paper company, Jack has the lined face and scarred forearms of a man who had to fight for everything he got. To him, nothing counts but hard work—and he finds it impossible to see Tim's passion for working with injured animals as anything but a frivolous and self-indulgent hobby. Jack can't believe his son can make a respectable living as a wildlife manager—and he's not inclined to let him try.

In their last confrontation, Jack told Tim, "You can forget about that place in Colorado.

You don't have four years to waste on that nonsense. You'll go to the state university like your sister and brother, and you'll work the way I did—not wander around the woods looking for sick animals."

Replaying this conversation in his mind one more time, Tim feels frustrated and despairing all over again. With his good grades he's reasonably confident he can win at least a partial scholarship to the college of his choice—and he knows he can get paying work in his field on weekends and over the summer. Still, he loves and respects his father and hates the idea of defying him. Jack Mrazek loves his children with a silent, unsmiling passion—but he doesn't tolerate defiance. *If I could just find some way to show him what I really do, Tim thinks, why it's so important . . . why I love it . . . .*

As you study this chapter, think about Tim's situation and prepare to answer the questions in Your Turn at the end of the chapter.

---

Association of America (by this time renamed the National Recreation Association) began to offer a one-year program of graduate study through its National Recreation School. In 1937 the University of Minnesota offered the first specialized curriculum in recreation. Soon other colleges and universities that had developed clusters of recreation courses in their physical education curricula began to offer undergraduate degrees in recreation. At the end of World War II in 1945 only 37 such degree programs were available; by 1960 the number had nearly doubled.[1] Today hundreds of institutions in the United States and Canada grant undergraduate and graduate degrees in this field and in therapeutic recreation. Recreation, park, and leisure curricula are offered in at least 270 two-year colleges and 320 four-year institutions. In addition,

more than 100 graduate programs are available. Of these, about 125 have master's programs and 31 offer doctoral programs.[2]

In the early 1980s, educators and practitioners were concerned about a decline in the numbers of students majoring in recreation, park resources, and leisure services, but by the end of the decade the trend had reversed.[3] During the period of declining enrollment, the variety of career opportunities increased, which most likely will force traditional employers to compete for quality students.[4]

The college curriculum in recreation and leisure studies is constantly under review. For example, in a report on higher education based on a 1990 survey conducted by the Society of Park and Recreation Educators, 61% of the respondents said that within the past two years new courses had been added to their curriculum. The study identified seven categories of program emphasis:

1. Leisure studies
2. Therapeutic recreation
3. Administration/management
4. Outdoor/natural resources
5. Program/leadership
6. Commercial/tourism
7. General recreation

Table 11.1 shows the concentration of majors in these areas of emphasis.

As curriculum offerings increased in the fields of recreation and leisure, the National Recreation and Park Association (NRPA), in cooperation with the American Association for Leisure and Recreation (AALR), attempted to establish an accreditation process to ensure that courses and programs met certain standards of quality. When these two organizations established the National Council on Accreditation in 1974, the leisure service profession was recognized by the Council of Post-secondary Accreditation—the only body that certifies professional accreditation in the United States. As of 1998 nearly 100 four-year undergraduate programs were accredited by the NRPA-AALR Council on Accreditation.

## Becoming a Professional

According to one authority, a profession must meet five criteria:

1. Systematic body of knowledge
2. Professional authority based on that body of knowledge
3. Approval of the society in which it functions
4. Code of professional ethics
5. Professional culture based on shared values and traditions[5]

The recreation and leisure profession satisfies these criteria. The field has become increasingly complex and sophisticated by drawing from both applied and conceptual knowledge in many disciplines to form a systematic body of knowledge found in books, research journals, and popular literature. Persons who seek employment in the field must undergo highly specialized academic preparation and must obtain credentials by registering with a professional organization or by becoming licensed or certified by either a professional organization or a government agency. For example, to work in the area of correctional recreation, one must meet certification standards established by the American Correctional Association. Other examples of qualifications are those required for employment in civil service, the YM/YWCA or YM/YWHA, and the Boy Scouts and Girl Scouts.[6] The many career opportunities available for recreation professionals at the local, state, and national levels are evidence of society's acceptance of the recreation and leisure profession.

**TABLE 11.1** Percentage of Students in Areas of Emphasis, 1990 (N=164)

| EMPHASIS | ASSOCIATE'S | BACHELOR'S | MASTER'S | Ph.D. |
|---|---|---|---|---|
| General /Administrative | 21% | 32% | 36% | 32% |
| Therapeutic Recreation | 29% | 28% | 27% | 37% |
| Commercial/Tourism | 11% | 13% | 11% | 11% |
| Outdoor | 18% | 16% | 14% | 21% |
| Program/Leadership | 21% | 10% | 10% | ——— |

Based on the key values of the leisure profession, a code of ethics was developed by the American Recreation Society (a forerunner to the National Recreation and Park Association) in 1960. A number of leisure service organizations have developed specific codes of ethics.[7] The NRPA code of ethics is found on p. 247, at the end of this chapter. In addition to the value system that guides the roles and conduct of recreation professionals, a traditional hierarchy among those roles is observed. For example, supervisors and directors manage staffs of other recreation professionals.

## Professional Identity and Role

Professionals also must be able to identify with a certain mission and with acceptable values, which provide the direction needed to preserve unity—essential to the survival of a profession. Several goals were established by the Commission on Goals for American Recreation, formed in 1964 by the American Association for Health, Physical Education and Recreation. Anyone who is considering entering the recreation and leisure profession should become familiar with these goals. Condensed descriptions follow.

1. *Personal fulfillment.* To enrich life by contributing to the fulfillment of others so that they might enjoy success in their search for self-esteem.
2. *Democratic human relations.* To contribute to qualities of good citizenship by seeking social, moral, and ethical values that will preserve and strengthen democracy. This is an outcome that moves beyond fun, relaxation, and immediate fulfillment.
3. *Leisure skills and interests.* To contribute to the development of skill and interest in wholesome activity, which is fundamental to well-rounded development and to a good life.
4. *Health and fitness.* To contribute to participation in pleasurable pursuits that are important for the release of tension and mental stress and to challenge individuals through physical activity that promotes good health and fitness.
5. *Creative expression and aesthetic appreciation.* To contribute to the depth and richness of life by stimulating and guiding creativity that otherwise might never surface.
6. *Environment.* To contribute to preserving the environment for present and future enjoyment and for all life forms.

## Rethinking Professional Status

Some people question the rationale for professionalizing the provision of recreation and leisure services. These people believe professionalism tends to encourage conformity and group thinking because the values of the profession are institutionalized and thus not subjected to outside influences. The result could be protection of the status quo because the professional would tend to regard himself or herself as the sole expert and would try to control the process, thus preventing participants from collaborating in development of the program. This line of thinking raises a critical question: who will determine what is wholesome in recreation and leisure programming—the professional or the consumer? There is general agreement that the granting of powers and privileges through accreditation, certification, and licensing should be for the benefit of consumers.[8]

Another concern is that play and spontaneity could be sacrificed through professional organization and institutionalization of leisure time. Unquestionably, professionals can create inequitable social hierarchies. Health care in the United States, for example, focuses not on prevention and wellness but on the treatment of illness, and access to care is determined by economic status rather than by need. Given their control over health care, have health care providers become an industry rather than a profession?[9]

In contemporary American society, the professional in any field occupies a privileged position. Professionals cannot be simply the isolated owners of their expertise or view their clients as commodities. They must be leaders who develop standards based on an ethic of service (discussed later in the chapter).

## U.S. Professional Organizations

Organizations represent the profession, serve as advocates for its services, and improve the standards of those who practice and identify with the profession. The first two organizations that represented park and recreation professionals were the National Recreation Association (NRA; formerly the Playground Association of America) and the American Institute of Park Executives (AIPE), formed in 1898, whose members were executives of various government park systems and of groups such as the Sierra Club, representing the public's interest in conservation. The National Conference on State Parks (NCSP) was organized in 1921 to advance the state park movement. The American Recreation Society (ARS), founded in 1937, represents recreation workers.

In 1966 the NRA, AIPE, NCSP, and ARS merged to form the National Recreation and Park Association (NRPA), which developed a structure to accommodate both professionals and interested members of the public. The association also formed branches for professionals with particular specialties:[10]

- ◆ American Park and Recreation Society (APRS)
- ◆ Armed Forces Recreation Society (AFRS)
- ◆ Citizen Board Members (CBM)
- ◆ Commercial Recreation and Tourism Section (CRTS)
- ◆ Leisure and Aging Section (LAS)
- ◆ National Aquatic Section (NAS)
- ◆ National Society for Park Resources (NSPR)
- ◆ National Therapeutic Recreation Society (NTRS)
- ◆ Society of Park and Recreation Educators (SPRE)

- ◆ Student Branch (SB)
- ◆ Friends of Parks and Recreation

The NRPA, along with the American Association for Leisure and Recreation (AALR) of the American Alliance for Health, Physical Education, Recreation and Dance (AAHPERD), serves the public and enhances the status of the professionals who provide leisure services. Appendix G lists the names and addresses of professional organizations in the field of recreation, and in the following section we briefly describe the work of several of these organizations.

### American Alliance for Health, Physical Education, Recreation and Dance (AAHPERD)

AAHPERD was founded in 1885 to advance professional education at all levels through services such as consultation, periodicals and other publications, leadership development, standards, and research. AAHPERD maintains biographical archives, supports placement services, and sponsors scholarship programs. It publishes the *Journal of Physical Education and Recreation,* the *Research Quarterly for Exercise and Sport,* and publications in the specialties of its diverse membership. AAHPERD is the largest and most influential organization that serves as an advocate for professionals in the fields identified in its title. The alliance consists of six national associations and six district associations for its 54 state and territorial affiliates.

### American Association for Leisure and Recreation (AALR)

AALR, which formerly was the division of recreation of AAHPERD, is now a separate organization that serves recreation and leisure professionals and educators. AALR publishes *Leisure Today* in the *Journal of Physical Education and Recreation* and *AALReporter,* as well as many publications in the fields of recreation, leisure, and parks. Since its founding in 1938, AALR has been committed to advancing the recreation profession and enhancing the quality of life of all Americans by promoting creative and meaningful recreation experiences.

## American Camping Association (ACA)

ACA was founded in 1910 to advance the welfare of children and adults through organized camping as an educational and recreational experience. The ACA provides assistance to camps through its 32 geographical locations; educational programs; monthly publication, *Camping Magazine;* and summer crisis hotline.

## Association of College Unions (ACU)

ACU was founded in 1914 for the providers of services to college unions. Its 950 members receive current information on trends and events in their field, including activities, facilities development, programming, and management techniques. The ACU's publications include the *Union Wire* and the *Bulletin of the Association of College Unions.*

## American Therapeutic Recreation Association (ATRA)

ATRA was established in 1984 to meet the needs of therapeutic recreation professionals in health care and human services. ATRA publishes the *ATRA Annual in Therapeutic Recreation.*

## National Employee Services and Recreation Association (NESRA)

Established in 1941 as the National Industrial Recreation Association, NESRA represents the interests of people who are responsible for planning employee recreation and leisure activities. In addition to its magazine, *Employee Services,* the association publishes several specialized manuals and research reports.

## National Intramural-Recreation Sports Association (NIRSA)

Founded in 1950, NIRSA is dedicated to the establishment and development of quality recreation and sports programs and represents a worldwide network of highly trained professionals. It is the leading advocate for excellence in recreational sports. NIRSA publishes the *NIRSA Journal* and provides research and resource materials to institutions that conduct programs in intramural sports, campus recreation, and community recreation.

## Travel and Tourism Research Association

This international organization promotes travel and tourism through research and marketing. It offers conferences each year on travel topics, operates a travel reference center, and publishes *The Annals of Tourism and Research.*

## National Recreation and Park Association (NRPA)

As we learned earlier, NRPA is the successor to the NRA, AIPE, NCSP, and ARS. NRPA attempts to enhance the human environment through the improvement of park facilities and the provision of satisfying recreation and leisure opportunities. In pursuit of its objectives, the association works closely with national, state, and local recreation and parks agencies, corporations, and citizens' groups. NRPA publishes *Parks & Recreation* and *Inside P & R,* a monthly membership newsletter, as well as books and pamphlets dealing with parks and recreation. The association conducts an annual Congress for Recreation and Parks each October. To serve the special needs of its members, NRPA has several branches, which are described below.

**American Park and Recreation Society (APRS).** This is NRPA's largest professional branch. APRS is composed primarily of professionals who are involved in local park, recreation, and leisure services. APRS members represent diverse park and recreation interests in government, private agencies, and commercial organizations. It publishes *Keeping You Current,* a quarterly newsletter.

**Armed Forces Recreation Society (AFRS).** This branch of NRPA serves professionals,

The National Recreation and Park Association provides leadership in the field.

technicians, and others involved with armed forces morale, welfare, and recreation (MWR) programs (see Chapter 10). The AFRS mission is to provide a common forum to promote communication, networking, and professional development and to serve as a strong advocate for armed forces MWR services. It publishes the quarterly *AFRS Newsletter*.

**Citizen/Board Member.** This branch of NRPA is for past or present appointed or elected citizen members of public policy bodies that deal with parks and recreation. Any interested citizen can belong to this branch. Its quarterly newsletter is called *Branching Out*.

**Commercial Recreation and Tourism Section.** This branch serves professionals who are involved in the management, operation, and programming of theme parks, tour and travel businesses, campgrounds, health and fitness clubs, country clubs, corporate employee service programs, and resorts.

**Friends of Parks and Recreation.** This branch has a membership of community volunteers, active participants at local parks and community recreation centers, legislative advocates, and individual citizens all over the country who support recreation and parks through tax-deductible gifts. Participants receive a quarterly newsletter, *Friends of Parks and Recreation.*

**Leisure and Aging Section.** This section brings together professionals who provide recreation and leisure services to older adults through municipal park and recreation agencies and retirement communities. Members receive *L & A Today*, a quarterly newsletter.

**National Aquatic Section.** This branch of NRPA is for people who provide aquatic programs for facilities such as swimming pools, marinas, beaches, water parks, water slide parks, and sailing programs.

**National Society for Park Resources.** This branch of NRPA is for park, forest, and natural resources professionals at all levels of government who are involved in planning, maintaining, interpreting, and administering resources of national, historical, and cultural value. The membership is committed to advocating and promoting a sound environmental ethic through research-based recreation and education programs. This branch publishes the quarterly *Recreation and Park Law Reporter* and, in cooperation with the National Park Service, the quarterly *Trends, Grist and Design.*

**National Therapeutic Recreation Society.** This branch of NRPA consists of professionals and organizations involved in providing therapeutic recreation services that help people with disabilities achieve maximum rehabilitation and independence. In cooperation with NRPA, NTRS publishes the *Therapeutic Recreation Journal* and the *NTRS Report.*

**Society of Park and Recreation Educators.** This organization was founded in 1966 by educators in the fields of parks, recreation, and leisure. SPRE publishes the NRPA's *Journal of Leisure Research,* the biennial *Curriculum Catalog,* and *Schole,* a referred publication.

**Student Branch.** This branch of NRPA was organized for college and university students enrolled in parks and recreation curricula. It produces *Cornerstone,* a quarterly publication.

### Concept Check

- State the goals of the founders of AAH-PERD.
- Explain the arguments for and against professionalization in the field of recreation and leisure services.

## THE PROFESSION IN OTHER COUNTRIES

As technological advances cause our world to become ever smaller, we must become knowledgeable about the work of recreation and leisure professionals in other countries with whom we share interests and needs. Approximately 25 organizations around the world represent the professional and technical interests of recreation and leisure service personnel.[11] In the following sections we will describe organizations in Canada, Great Britain, and the Netherlands and an international organization.

### Canada

Over the past 25 years the field of recreation and leisure in Canada has experienced consid-

erable growth. The first formal education programs were launched in the early 1970s, with the majority of growth occurring in the 1980s. Canada offers a two-tier system of study: the college-level curriculum teaches practical skills for the technician, and the university program takes a more philosophical approach to the study of leisure.

As of 1993, 44 Canadian colleges were offering recreation and leisure programs in 10 areas of concentration: recreation leadership, tourism, recreation management, recreation facilities management, therapeutic recreation, older adult recreation, parks and recreation, resort management, recreation for special populations, and recreation technology. At the graduate level, seven universities offer studies beyond the bachelor's degree.[12]

The Canadian Parks/Recreation Association (CPRA) is Canada's major professional organization. It is partially funded by the Canadian government. The association publishes *Recreation Canada* five times a year; sponsors an annual conference; and offers consultation and technical assistance to agencies concerned with parks, recreation, and leisure. CPRA's national office is located in the province of Ontario. In addition, each province has its own professional society and other specialized organizations that provide services and conduct research in the field.

### Great Britain

Formed in 1982 by the merger of four national groups representing various sectors of the British leisure industry, the Institute of Leisure and Amenity Management (ILAM) promotes effective management of recreation and leisure facilities and supports continuing professional development. ILAM works closely with other British organizations and is establishing links with similar groups in other countries of the European community.[11]

### The Netherlands

As the name suggests, members of the Netherlands Association of Heads of Municipal

*Professionals from North America and South America meet to share learning experiences at the Universidad de Los Andes in Venezuela.*

Parks and Gardens are the heads of municipal parks and garden organizations and their staffs. Municipal parks and gardens occupy 132,500 acres in the towns and villages of the Netherlands and 170,000 acres in surrounding areas. The association's six districts interact through the General Committee, which concentrates on national and international policy, public relations, and research and education.[11]

## International Organization

The purpose of the World Leisure and Recreation Association is to aid organizations in all nations that seek to provide recreation services to their citizens. The association provides education, information, consultation, and research. Founded in 1956, it publishes the *WLRA Journal* bimonthly.

**Concept Check**

- Briefly explain Canada's two-tier system of academic preparation for a career in recreation and leisure services.
- Identify and briefly describe the functions of three organizations for parks and recreation professionals outside the United States.

## RECREATION AS A CAREER

The broad range of providers of recreation and leisure services discussed in Chapter 10 offers a diversity of employment opportunities. Some positions require a wide range of expertise, whereas others are narrowly focused specialties. The aim of every position is to satisfy human interests and needs. Most positions require the ability to organize, plan, promote, and motivate. Virtually all positions require a sincere interest in and enjoyment of working with others of various ages and backgrounds. Recreation and leisure careers can be divided into four major areas:[13]

1. *Recreation services:* Leadership of organized activities in a variety of settings, including therapeutic recreation
2. *Recreation resources:* Planning, development, maintenance, and protection of resources
3. *Tourism:* Services related to travel for pleasure
4. *Amusement and entertainment:* Operation, supervision, and management of games, rides, and surrounding facilities

Overall, careers in leisure services have been identified as promising for Americans.[13] In 2000, the U.S Department of Labor projected double the rate of growth for amusement and recreation services due to Americans' increasing leisure time, income, awareness of health benefits, and retirement population.[13]

Because the field covers a broad spectrum of leisure opportunities, employment is available to people of diverse backgrounds. Women represent at least 50% of the students seeking degrees in the field, and they are moving into higher levels of administration.[13a] Colleges are challenged to recruit more minorities, both to respond to the demand for their services and to satisfy federal and state equal employment opportunity requirements.[4] Furthermore, more career opportunities are opening for people who are physically challenged as facilities are built or remodeled to accommodate these people.[14]

*In the past decade, many new entrepreneurial recreational opportunities have emerged.*

## Careers and Requirements

Detailed information about careers in recreation and leisure services can be obtained from the AALR and the NRPA. Two books are highly recommended for the interested student: the AALR publication *Careers in Recreation* [15] and the NRPA's *National Job Bulletin*. Each can be purchased from the organization (see Appendix G). In the following sections we present an alphabetical listing of some of the many career opportunities and requirements for professionals with degrees in recreation and leisure services. To help you check out careers, take the self-test in the Action Guide box on p. 238.

### Adventure/Risk Recreation

Employers look for people with outdoor leadership experience and technical training. In addition to college/university curricula, such training is provided by private organizations such as the National Outdoor Leadership School, Outward Bound, and the Wilderness Education Association. Employers may require certification and advanced first aid, CPR (cardiopulmonary resuscitation), EMT (emergency medical technician), or certification as a Wilderness First Responder.

### College/University Teaching

Teaching at the junior or community college level requires a master's degree. Four-year universities and four-year colleges generally prefer a doctorate or completion of the degree before tenure or promotion is granted. Continuing education is essential for recreation and leisure instructors, as is registration, certification, or both where applicable. Just before 2000, there were 111 college or university teaching positions open in the field and only 41 students graduating with doctoral degrees.[15]

### Commercial Recreation

Recreation is big business. According to one source, employment in commercial recreation is expected to continue growing through the year 2005.[2] Students who seek careers in this field take courses in leisure behavior, recreation leadership, program management, facility design, marketing, business law, risk managment, budgeting, and finance. Often some coursework in business is required. Supervisory and management opportunities are available in travel agencies, resorts, casinos, amusement and theme parks, professional sports, theatres, campgrounds, and sales of recreation-related merchandise such as indoor and outdoor equipment, clothing and shoes, and recreational vehicles.

### Community Education

Recreation and adult education are now provided under the broader umbrella of community education, which in turn is part of the

## ACTION GUIDE

### CAREERS IN RECREATION: HOW DO YOU MATCH UP?

Whether or not you plan to pursue a career in recreation and leisure services, you can benefit from taking this self-assessment quiz to identify your preferences and priorities.

1. List and briefly describe your top three career priorities.

_____

_____

2. List and describe three things you do *not* want to be part of your career.

_____

_____

3. What kinds of leisure and recreational activities do you enjoy?

_____

_____

4. Do you enjoy teaching or showing others how to engage in your favorite activities? Why or why not?

_____

_____

overall delivery of school services. A community education director needs an understanding of public education, an expansive view of diversified services, and the ability to work with a variety of local groups. Many states have not prescribed minimum degree standards for community education, but some state departments of education are considering certification requirements.[15] Professionals who aspire to increased responsibility will need a minimum of a bachelor's or a master's degree. Majors come from many backgrounds, including recreation, parks, and leisure studies.

### Community Recreation

In this field, professional careers are available in administration, public information, park management, planning and development,

garden and grounds maintenance, golf course management and maintenance, recreation supervision, aquatics, therapeutic recreation, athletics, interpretive and outdoor program management, cultural arts programming, and various support and paraprofessional positions.[15] Certification is mandatory or preferred for many positions. Most support and paraprofessional positions require an associate's degree in recreation. An advanced degree in recreation generally is required for management and administrative positions.

### Convention Management

The growing popularity of mixing business with pleasure at recreation-oriented sites has significantly changed the structure of meetings and conventions. The successful convention

## ACTION GUIDE (cont'd)

### CAREERS IN RECREATION: HOW DO YOU MATCH UP? (cont'd)

5. Based on your career likes and dislikes, do you think you would like to pursue a career in recreation and leisure services? Why or why not?

_____

_____

6. If you would like to pursue a career in this field, which particular career do you find most appealing? Why?

_____

_____

7. Which career do you find least appealing? Why?

_____

_____

8. In this chapter you will learn not only about the academic background required to be a successful recreation and leisure services professional but also about the personal traits and skills this work requires. Do you think you have the requisite traits and skills to succeed in this field? In either case, give reasons for your answer.

_____

_____

manager is highly organized, responsive, creative, people oriented, a good communicator, and a skilled negotiator. Some college and university curricula offer courses in travel management, tourism, managing special events, and hospitality and resort management; internships in these fields may be available. A recreation/leisure services major also should consider taking courses in accounting, business law, human resource management, food and beverage management, computer basics, public relations, photo communication, and marketing.

### Corporate Fitness

Some colleges and universities offer degree programs that prepare students to handle the administrative, programming, and evaluation tasks involved in managing a corporate fitness program. Training in exercise science or certification by professional organizations such as the American College of Sports Medicine improves employment possibilities.[15] Corporate fitness directors have a variety of academic backgrounds ranging from an associate's degree to a doctorate. (See also Employee/Industrial Recreation.)

### Correctional Recreation

The American Correctional Association (ACA) has established certification standards for recreation managers in the areas of programming, facilities, equipment, staffing, and inmate participation. The ACA requires a minimum of a bachelor's degree in recreation, physical education, or leisure service or the equivalent combination of education and experience.

Working with various levels of criminals has inherent risks and rewards (see Appendix G). Courses taken in public services and administration of justice are helpful.

### Cultural Arts

This professional should have a bachelor's degree in recreation with a strong arts emphasis or component. Other areas of study include public administration or business administration. Cultural arts directors should be able to select and interact with artists and be knowledgeable about current arts-related issues. Positions are available in supervision, management, and direction of cultural arts in recreation programs at the local, state, and federal levels.

### Employee/Industrial Recreation

Responsibilities in this field vary with the facilities available. Salaries are often slightly higher than those for other positions, and benefits may include reduced prices for company products and country club memberships. Employers look for a four-year degree in recreation, parks, and leisure studies, plus courses in business management. This professional has knowledge of facility management, broad programming experience, and a strong background in health and physical fitness. For more information about this career field, contact the ESMA (see Appendix G and Corporate Fitness).

### Entertainment and/or Sports Law

Professional opportunities abound in this growing field. A law degree is essential, and a strong background is provided by a bachelor's degree in recreation, leisure, or physical education. Also recommended are courses in business and sports administration, political science, and communications. Employment opportunities exist with professional sports teams, entertainers, theme parks, wholesalers, and retail chains.

### Facility Management

Recreational facilities run the gamut from bowling alleys and skating rinks to elegant spas and exclusive yacht clubs. They also include golf pro shops, sports complexes, country clubs, resorts, marinas, theatres, theme parks, aquatic facilities, and industrial recreation facilities. People who have completed a bachelor's degree in recreation, parks, and leisure studies and who have some experience may qualify as supervisors or assistant managers in this field. Some positions require a master's degree and extensive experience. The creation of more facilities and continuing expansion in the public, private, and commercial sectors should create opportunities for rapid advancement for well-trained and qualified professionals.[15]

### Intramural/Recreation Sports

A director in this field should be able to organize, administer, and supervise intramural recreational activities; manage facilities; and supervise subordinates. An important personal requirement is strong human relations and communication skills. Most positions require a minimum of a four-year degree with a major in recreation, intramural administration, physical education, student services, or a related field; at the college or university level, a graduate degree is generally required. Graduate assistantships are available. For more information, contact the NIRSA (see Appendix G).

### Leisure Counseling

Because leisure influences and is influenced by every aspect of life, leisure counselors can offer useful guidance by testing and assessing individuals' interests, needs, preferences, attitudes, and limitations. Counselors are often entrepreneurs who establish their own business, work for a small business, or consult for other businesses. This position requires several years' experience and a combination of graduate degrees in recreation/leisure studies and psychology or counseling. Counseling preretirees and retirees is a growing business.

## Military Recreation

In the armed forces, leisure service programs generally are referred to as morale, welfare, and recreation. Such programs are designed to promote mental readiness and physical fitness among service personnel. Competition is strong for entry-level positions due to downsizing. It is not necessary to be in the military to become a military recreation specialist. Although the rate of pay is the same, positions are classified as civil service (CS) or unappropriated (UA). Military recreation positions are listed in the *Federal Jobs Bulletin* under Recreation Services #188.[15] The best sources of information about careers in this field are the local Civil Service Commission office, the division of special services of the particular military branch, and the AFRS of the NRPA (see Appendix G).

## Outdoor Recreation/Education

This field offers a wide variety of career opportunities: camp director, tour guide, nature leader, museum director, park ranger, resort owner/operator, sailing instructor, river trip guide, ski lodge operator, radio/TV program consultant, children's zoo leader, interpretive naturalist, nature center programmer, and youth or adult programmer.[15] To prepare for professional positions in this field, students need a bachelor's degree in recreation and leisure studies and should take a variety of courses related to people, natural resources, and outdoor activities. The best source of information about careers in this field is the director of the Outdoor Education Project of AAHPERD (see Appendix G).

## Park Ranger

Park rangers at the state and federal level help protect and maintain parks, serve as guides and interpreters, ensure the safety of park visitors, and enforce laws and regulations. Rangers also are involved in conservation efforts, landscaping, construction, and maintenance. Positions are available through national, state, county, and municipal parks. Employment as a ranger generally requires a bachelor's degree in

*A ranger at work in Glacier National Park.*

parks and recreation management or forestry. Further studies in history, ornithology, and other natural sciences are helpful. Certification for eligible candidates is available through the National Recreation and Park Association. Federal job information testing centers are located in many large cities and are listed under U.S. Government in the telephone white pages. See also state and county listings in your area.

## Recreation Forester

The Forest Service offers a variety of career opportunities in administration, research, and state and private forestry. Entry-level positions require a bachelor's degree with at least 24 semester hours in the specialized fields of forestry, outdoor recreation, or landscape management.[15] Experience in forest management or conservation work can be acquired by attending summer school camps or through summer employment with federal, state, or private forestry and conservation organizations or forest industry firms. Federal job information testing centers are located in many large cities and are listed under U.S. Government in the telephone white pages. See also state and county listings in your area.

### Resource and Park Management

Positions in this field include management, development, and protection of wildlands; wildlife, fishery, and soil conservation; and timber, watershed, and recreation management. Students interested in this field are encouraged to obtain a bachelor's degree in forestry or recreation management and to take courses in natural resource management, wildlife management, biology, environmental interpretation, and outdoor systems management. For more information, contact the Soil Conservation Service, the Department of the Interior, and the U.S. Forest Service. (See also Park Ranger, Recreation Forester, and Wildlife Manager in this section.)

### Rural Recreation

Efforts are increasing to provide recreational activities to residents of rural areas. The recreation director in a small town must be able and willing to do many tasks, be proficient in planning programs for a diverse group, have strong organizational ability, and have effective communication and public relations skills. Academic requirements may range from an associate's to a master's degree in recreation and leisure services. For more information, contact the Travel and Tourism Research Association, the Travel Industry Association of America, and the Commercial Recreation and Tourism Section of NRPA (see Appendix G).

### Senior Centers

Employment opportunities in senior centers are strong because of the commitment of government at all levels to provide recreational services for the growing number of older Americans. Potential employers are camping programs; day care centers; homes for older adults; and retirement centers, including apartment communities and communal living arrangements. Full-time employment normally requires a bachelor's degree in recreation, education, sociology, or gerontology plus two years' experience.[15] For more information, contact the Leisure and Aging Section of the NRPA (see Appendix G).

### Student Unions

These campus leisure centers, also known as "the Commons," "campus center," or "activity center," are major business operations that provide a wide range of facilities, services, and programs designed to meet the needs of students, faculty, staff, and their guests. Management of campus leisure centers requires managerial and technical skills to develop and operate indoor and outdoor programs and competence in building operations, labor relations, culinary arts, advertising, marketing, budgeting, and accounting. Employers seek graduates in recreation, parks, and leisure studies who have a strong background in programming, administration, and finance. Coursework is recommended in business administration, speech, writing, and art and music appreciation.[15]

### Therapeutic Recreation

Therapeutic recreation has been one of the fastest growing fields in recreation and leisure services. Professionals in this field design programs to meet the recreation needs of special populations—people with physical or developmental disabilities and people with temporary or permanent psychiatric disorders—and to facilitate their optimal functioning. Professionals work in children's hospitals, mental health institutions and psychiatric hospitals, rehabilitation clinics, nursing homes, medical care facilities, sheltered workshops, transitional living facilities, group homes, camps, community-based programs, and community residential agencies. To learn about a highly successful program of therapeutic recreation, see A Closer Look, at right.

The field of therapeutic recreation offers many educational programs, from associate's degrees through doctorates. A bachelor's degree is the entry-level requirement, and certification by the National Council for Therapeutic Recreation Certification can be obtained with appropriate academic and experience credentials and by passing a national examination. The profession is served by two national organizations: the National Therapeutic Recreation Society (NTRS) and the American Therapeutic Recreation Association (ATRA) (see Appendix G).

### Travel and Tourism

In almost every state tourism ranks as one of the top three industries.[14] Because tourism is one of the largest industries in the world, it offers a wide range of employment opportunities: travel agencies, resorts, cruise ships, the airline industry, amusement and theme parks, campgrounds, hotel-motel management, and public and private organizations that promote tourism. Many entry-level positions offer only modest remuneration but provide attractive fringe benefits such as free travel. Some institutions have curriculum tracks that concentrate on travel and tourism; also useful is coursework in geography, psychology, sociology, economics, computer applications, and business administration. The state office of tourism can provide information on local statistics, trends, and career opportunities (see Appendix E).

### Volunteer Agencies/Youth Organizations

This work is a mix of recreation, education, social work, and camping supervision. Examples of organizations in this category are Girls Incorporated, which serves girls between 6 and 18 years of age; the 4-H program, intended for youth between 9 and 19 years of age in

## A CLOSER LOOK

### THERAPY ON HORSEBACK

From apathy to enthusiasm . . . from frustration to pride . . . from despair to exultation: those are some of the remarkable changes that are taking place in people with disabilities who participate in a highly successful program known as therapeutic horsemanship. Conducted under the auspices of the North American Riding for the Handicapped Association (NARHA), the program is serving close to 27,000 children and adults with mental or physical disabilities or both.

Many children who seemed to have no hope of enjoying physical activity are showing remarkable responses to the horseback riding experience. In addition to producing exhilaration, some experts say that bobbing along on horseback helps a child's physical and physiological development. Because a horse's motion closely mimics a "normal" human gait, riding allows children with disabilities to have experiences their own bodies cannot provide. Riding also can enhance coordination, balance, and muscle tone for children with muscular dystrophy, spina bifida, or cerebral palsy. Children with mental retardation or learning or other cognitive disabilities can improve their concentration and attention span.

Therapeutic horsemanship is available at more than 450 NARHA-accredited centers in the United States, Puerto Rico, and Canada. Facilities range from several loaned horses, one paid instructor, and dozens of volunteers to a network of eight stables. Some facilities employ full-time physical therapists; others can afford only part-time or volunteer consultation. To obtain NARHA certification, instructors must have at least 120 hours' experience in teaching riders with disabilities.

Whether the goal in horseback riding is to help an autistic child accept contact with a horse or to improve the torso strength of a child paralyzed by injury, the benefits are often more than physical. For a girl who wears leg braces and has friends at school with track trophies, knowing how to groom and trot her favorite Appaloosa can be an incredible equalizer.

rural areas but now being extended to suburban and urban areas; and Campfire Girls and Boys, whose programs are designed to give youth from kindergarten through grade 12 an opportunity to realize their potential.

The workweek is long and includes night meetings and occasional weekends. Professional employees are expected to support the goals of the organization both personally and philosophically, and they need skills in program planning, human relations, and fundraising. The applicant should have a bachelor's or a master's degree, usually in social work, recreation, or physical education, although specific fields are not always demanded.

### Wildlife Manager

State and federal wildlife managers protect animals and their habitats, monitor animal populations, provide treatment for injured animals, set hunting guidelines, enforce regulations, and sometimes plan and supervise construction of shelters and other facilities. Particularly for management-level positions, the applicant will be required to have a bachelor's degree in parks and recreation management, forestry, or biology. Further study in the natural sciences is helpful. Certification for eligible candidates is available through NRPA (see Appendix G). Federal job information testing centers are located in many large cities and are listed under U.S. Government in the telephone white pages. See also state and county listings in your area.

### Youth Sports

Positions are available for coaches, administrators, and officials in school-based or agency-sponsored programs. Most employment opportunities are in municipal recreation departments. The director of recreation who is responsible for youth sports generally will have a bachelor's or a master's degree in recreation and leisure studies or physical education. A bachelor's degree in physical educa-

*Outfitters are a dynamic segment of the tourism industry.*

tion with teaching certification may be required to coach interscholastic sports. Athletic administration may require a master's degree in sports management. Officiating often requires competence on a written examination. Most coaching and officiating positions in agency-sponsored sports are volunteer. Hours are long, frequently extending into evenings, weekends, and vacations, but aspiring coaches and officials can gain valuable experience.

**Concept Check**

- Briefly describe the responsibilities and requirements for careers in community education, therapeutic recreation, and travel and tourism.
- Of the careers described in the preceding section, which three appeal to you most? Why? Which three appeal to you least? Why?

## LEADERSHIP AND ETHICS

The development of excellent leadership skills and a strong ethical position is essential to maintain the integrity of the recreation and leisure services profession. Professional leaders not only guide participants and clients but also influence the direction of the profession. For example, a goal of every organization should be to earn recognition as an asset to the community. The leader must represent the organization's values regarding ethical and legal codes of conduct and must communicate them to others in the organization.

## Leadership Characteristics

To be an effective manager, one must first be a leader. A true leader is ultimately more effective than a manager who lacks leadership skills. Recreation, park, and leisure service professionals are faced with the challenge of becoming effective leaders and managers.[16] Former President and U.S. Army General Dwight D. Eisenhower illustrated the art of leadership with a simple demonstration. After placing a string on the table he would *pull* it and it would follow wherever he led it. But, when he *pushed* it, it would go nowhere. Eisenhower, who commanded the allied forces in World War II, believed that the same principle applied in leading people. By understanding people's basic needs for belonging, self-esteem, achievement, and recognition, leaders strive to help people meet those needs and thus pull society in a desirable direction. Leaders aspire to motivate, energize, and inspire others. To lead effectively, leaders must recognize the value and respect the dignity of all others.

Professionals need certain essential leadership characteristics,[14] including

- Ability to work effectively with others
- Insight into leisure trends
- Ability to develop interest and appreciation in others
- Sincere interest in public service
- Cooperative attitude and strong sense of dedication
- Common sense

- Ability to enjoy life
- Administrative skills
- Creativity
- Personable manner
- Trustworthy and respectful style
- Strong sense of values

These skills are becoming increasingly important to respond to the rapid pace of change in society at large and in the recreation and leisure field in particular. Proactive leadership is needed to monitor changes, assess their implications, and shape goals and structure programs that will meet the changing needs of diverse participants and clients.

In times of change, competent professional leadership is invaluable because such leaders identify patterns and interrelationships that help them understand trends and events. They use this information to create visions and develop strategies that are appropriate for new situations and needs. In the recreation and leisure field, leaders must be able to plan carefully and boost staff morale in the face of challenges such as declining federal and state support, conflicting demands of special-interest groups, privatization, liability concerns, and park crime.[17] At the same time, leaders must maintain their responsiveness to individual and community needs, especially during stressful times of change.

Before seeking to bring a vision into reality, a leader must ensure that everyone involved understands the vision. Then the leader can begin to motivate and inspire others to embrace the future and meet the challenge. To encourage others to move in the desired direction, effective leaders empower them to be active participants in the decision-making process.[16] Through empowerment, leaders give others the authority, tools, and information they need to make wise decisions and solve problems. People also need to feel secure enough to take risks and even make some mistakes. By empowering others, leaders give them a sense of control and an opportunity to grow professionally. In this way, leaders invite others to lead and thus nurture new leadership. In the long run, greater productivity, loyalty, and commitment can be expected from subordinates and clients or participants who feel appreciated and valued.

The need is increasing for leaders to develop human relations skills.[18] Leaders must be particularly sensitive to women, to members of diverse ethnic and cultural groups, and to members of special populations. One study found that each year up to 25% of all workers experience some form of intimidation based on race, religion, or ethnicity. If gender is added, the figure increases considerably.[19] Leaders need to develop and implement a policy of inclusiveness that calls for hiring women, minorities, persons with disabilities, and others who have not been dominant or visible in the organization. Inclusiveness should be a key principle in the organization's code of ethics and standards of practice.

## Professional Ethics

Ethics is generally described as the aspect of philosophy that is concerned with moral issues and judgments. This includes the study of standards of conduct and moral judgments and of why one state of affairs is morally superior to another. An ethical or a moral person is one who attempts to distinguish between right and wrong in conduct and acts accordingly. A code of ethics represents a moral philosophy based on the principles of a particular person, religion, profession, or other group.

Since ancient Greek philosopher Socrates sought to enlighten others concerning the need to rationally criticize beliefs and practices, abundant scholarly discourse has taken place on the entire spectrum of ethics. Most of the human services professions have spent considerable time examining the ethical issues faced by their practitioners and trying to reach reasonable conclusions to guide behavior. The recreation and

leisure profession is no exception.

By establishing a code of ethics, a profession makes contracts with society. These contracts embody the moral imperatives that pledge to assist society to the degree society will consent. Even with a code, however, questions of ethics are complex. The study of personal freedom provides some guidance to the profession in formulating a code of ethics. An individual's freedom is limited to the extent his or her actions infringe on the rights of others. Some outcomes of leisure behavior are both destructive and immoral.

Consider the following example. A group watches football on television and drinks beer all afternoon. Two from the group decide to go out for more beer. While they are driving, their car strikes another vehicle. A child is thrown from the other vehicle and is killed instantly. By driving while intoxicated, these two people grossly infringed on the right of others to a safe roadway. Their action was not only legally wrong but morally wrong.

This example shows clearly that the public must be continually educated not to drink and drive. Do recreation and leisure professionals have a moral obligation to help educate adolescents and others about drinking and driving? Should partnerships be formed with liquor distributors, bars, or others to help raise public awareness? Should the profession embark on moral teaching? Can it? Certainly professionals have a moral duty to address obvious wrongs and to lead society in participating in wholesome activities.

The recreation and leisure profession also faces ethical questions such as conflicts of values between human desires and environmental concerns, the extent of competition for natural resources, and the appropriate degree of exposure to risk. By integrating an ethical component into each activity, leaders can enhance the quality of the experience while protecting the natural and manmade resources involved.

Recreation and leisure are much more than simple activities or spontaneous experiences, and they are much more than rest or pleasure. Through recreation and leisure we can express our moral convictions by pursuing activities that not only bring happiness but also help us create a good life for ourselves and others. A key moral imperative for recreation and leisure professionals is to teach participants to enjoy activities and protect natural resources while respecting the rights of others. One expert suggests that the ideal of leisure is at the core of the recreation, park, and leisure services fields.[20] Leisure, as the embodiment of collective and individual freedom, creative expression, and the development of human potential, represents the virtue of professional action.

---

## National Recreation and Park Association Code of Ethics

Members of the National Recreation and Park Association (NRPA) have special responsibilities to the general public and to the specific communities and agencies in which recreation and park services are offered. These obligations are set forth in the following NRPA Code of Ethics:

*As a member of the National Recreation and Park Association, I accept and agree to abide by this Code and pledge myself to:*

- Adhere to the highest standards of integrity, truthfulness and honesty in all public and personal activities to inspire public confidence and trust.
- Strive for personal and professional excellence and encourage the professional development of associates and students.
- Strive for the highest standards of professional competence, fairness, impartiality, efficiency, effectiveness, and fiscal responsibility.

- Avoid any interest or activity which is in conflict with the performance of job responsibilities.
- Promote the public interest and avoid personal gain or profit from the performance of job duties and reponsibilities.
- Support equal employment opportunities.

## Summing Up

- Early workers in the field of recreation and leisure services were amateurs rather than professionals because they lacked formal training. Today undergraduate curricula in recreation, parks, and leisure studies are offered at hundreds of colleges and universities; several institutions also have master's and doctoral programs.
- A profession must possess a systematic body of knowledge, professional authority based on that body of knowledge, approval of the society in which it functions, a code of professional ethics, and a professional culture based on shared values and traditions.
- In the United States, influential organizations in the recreation and leisure services profession include the AAHPERD, the AALR, and the NRPA. Similar organizations exist in countries throughout the world.
- Diverse employment opportunities exist in the field of recreation and leisure services. Some require a wide range of expertise, whereas others are narrowly focused specialties. Most positions require at least a bachelor's degree and the ability to organize, plan, and motivate others.
- Recreation and leisure services professionals must develop strong leadership skills because they not only guide participants and clients but also can influence the direction of social attitudes and trends.
- Leaders should adopt a policy of inclusiveness by employing women, minorities, people with disabilities, and others who have not been dominant or visible in the organization.
- Through a code of ethics, a profession makes contracts with society. These contracts embody the moral imperatives that pledge to assist society to the degree society consents.
- Leisure is more than human activity or experience, more than rest or pleasure. Through leisure we can express our moral convictions by pursuing activities that allow us to enjoy a good life while respecting the rights of others.

## Using What You've Learned

1. Read and study the mission statement, the standards of professional practice, and the code of ethics of one of the professional organizations described in this chapter. Explain specifically how society benefits if members follow these guidelines.
2. Interview three professionals in different branches of the recreation and leisure field. Ask each one to identify occupations he or she believes are promising for the future, and why. Ask each individual what professional journals he or she recommends. Finally, ask each one to suggest appropriate elements in a code of ethical conduct for the recreation and leisure profession.
3. Think of someone you know who demonstrates the ability to lead others effectively. Identify the characteristics that contribute to this ability and give examples of those characteristics in action.

## YOUR  Turn

1. Have you ever faced parental opposition to your career choice? If so, what did you do? If not, what do you think you would do?
2. What do you think is Jack Mrazek's real reason for objecting to his son's career choice?
3. If you were in Tim's situation, how would you try to change your father's mind? Name some specific steps you could take.
4. If you were Tim and you did not succeed in changing your father's mind about your career choice, what would you do?

## REFERENCES

1. Kraus, R., & Bates, B. (1975). *Recreation Leadership and Supervision: Guidelines for Professional Development.* Philadelphia: W.B. Saunders, p. 72.
2. Houghton, J. (February 19, 1998). Ashburn, VA: Accreditation Coordinator, National Recreation and Park Association.
3. Bialeschki, D. (1994). What's Happening to Our Curricula in Recreation, Park Resources and Leisure Services. *Parks & Recreation* 29(5):24.
4. Bialeschki, D. (1992). The State of Parks, Recreation and Leisure Student Curricula. *Parks & Recreation* 27(7):76.
5. Hartsoe, C. (1973). Recreation: A Professional Transition. *Parks & Recreation* 8(6).
6. Murphy, J., et al. (1991). *Leisure Systems: Critical Concepts and Applications.* Champaign, IL: Sagamore Publishing, p. 135.
7. Edgington, C., Jordan, D., DeGraaf, D., & Edgington, S. (1995) *Leisure and Life Satisfaction.* Dubuque, IA: Wm. C. Brown, p. 326.
8. Witt, P. (1991). Gaining Professional Status: Who Benefits? In Thomas Goodale & Peter Witt (Eds.), *Issues in an Era of Change.* State College, PA: Venture Publishing, pp. 271–273.
9. Lord, J., Hutchison, P., & VanDerbeck, F. (1991). Narrowing Options: The Power of Professionals in Daily Life and Leisure. In Thomas Goodale & Peter Witt (Eds.), *Issues in an Era of Change.* State College, PA: Venture Publishing, pp. 276–277.
10. Sessoms, H.D. (1991). The Professionalization of Parks and Recreation: A Necessity? In Thomas Goodale & Peter Witt (Eds.), *Issues in an Era of Change.* State College, PA: Venture Publishing.
11. Barber, A. (1989). Associations Abroad: A Sample of Missions and Means. *Parks & Recreation* 24(4):39–41.
12. Gagnon, N., Ostiguy, L., & Sedburg, R. (1993). The Ivory Tower Syndrome *Recreation Canada* 51(2):27–29.
13. Bureau of Labor Statistics (2000). *Occupational Outlook Handbook.* Washington, DC: U.S. Department of Labor.
13a. Anderson, D.M. (2001). The Current Status of Women in the Parks and Recreation Profession. *Parks & Recreation* 36(5):22.
14. Jensen, C., & Naylor, J. (1990). Recreation and Leisure Careers. Chicago, IL: VGM Career Horizons.
15. Coles, R. (2000). *Careers in Recreation.* Reston, VA: American Association for Leisure and Recreation.
16. Ibrahim, H., & Cordes, K. (Jan 1996). Leader or Manager? *Journal of Physical Education, Recreation and Dance* 67(1):41.
17. Foley, J. (Spring 1988). The Human Factor in Managing Leisure Human Services. *California Parks & Recreation* 44(1):12.
18. Walker, B. (October 31, 1993). Managing Cultural Diversity, *The Sun,* p. H4, Redlands, CA.
19. Gaines, T. (October 31 1993). Age of Diversity, *The Sun,* p. H1–H3, Redlands, CA.
20. Fain, G. (1991). The Promise and Wonder. In Gerald Fain (Ed.), *Leisure and Ethics.* Reston, VA: American Alliance for Health, Physical Education, Recreation and Dance, p. 316.

You can never plan the future by the past.

EDMUND BURKE
1791

# Planning and Management in Recreation and Leisure

## THE CHAPTER AT A GLANCE

In this chapter we explore the processes of planning in general and in recreation, parks, and leisure services in particular. We review national planning for recreation from its inception in the 1970s until it was discontinued. We also consider planning on both the state and local levels. We examine the management of leisure services and the financing and evaluation of those services.

### Chapter Objectives

*After completing this chapter, you should be able to*

- Define *planning* and explain the difference between planning at the macro and micro levels.
- Describe the planning process and the planning document.
- Trace the history of planning for recreation and leisure services at the national level.
- Explain the considerations and steps in recreation and leisure planning at the state and local levels.
- Describe the factors involved in managing recreation and leisure services.

## PLANNING LEISURE SERVICES

Planning involves the assessment and establishment of desired objectives and the development of a course of action to achieve them. Strategic planning describes the steps to be taken in this regard.[1] Planning is based on and proceeds from a common understanding of the planning exercise. For example,

## A World  of Difference

### WHEN PUBLIC RECREATION BECOMES PRIVATE

"Man, it's hot—I can't wait till we get to the lake!" Jamal Jeffers wipes his face with his trademark blue bandanna and leans out the window of his friend Michael's old van to catch a breeze. In the back of the van three more friends—Antoine, Marco, and Dwayne—are sprawled on the big truck innertubes the boys use to float on the lake at the county park. Two more tubes are lashed to the top of the van, which is snaking its way slowly up the road to the park, caught in a long line of vehicles full of people who have the same idea: to find relief from the oppressive heat by cooling off in the big manmade lake.

"Why is it taking so long to get to the entrance?" Dwayne wonders. "It never goes this slow."

"Who knows—maybe some car broke down or overheated," Marco replies. "We'll get there."

Half an hour later, the old blue van does get there, and the boys learn the reason for the long wait. Posted prominently by the entry gate to the park is a large, carefully lettered sign:
SWIMMING BADGES:
ADULTS 18/OVER 18, $5; CHILDREN 5–17, $3; CHILDREN UNDER 5 FREE.

"*What?*" Jamal exclaims incredulously. "Since when do they charge you to swim? This is a public park—we're not supposed to have to *pay!*" He digs in his pocket and comes up with some crumpled bills and change. "Man, I've only got four bucks after we kicked in for gas. If I swim, I can't eat!"

"I don't even have *three* bucks," Dwayne puts in. "I don't get paid at the gas station till Monday, so I brought a sandwich—but now I can't afford to swim."

Michael pulls the van to the side of the road, and all five boys arrange their money on the front seat. They have $21 and change between them—enough for everybody to get in, but definitely not enough to buy lunch for the four boys who will need it.

"This is crazy," Antoine says. "This was the only decent free place to swim, and now we can't get in. Everything else is fancy private clubs, or that scummy pool at the city rec center."

"Yeah, with all the broken bottles and dead bugs and crack dealers," Michael says sardonically. "That place is no better than a cesspool."

Marco, who has left the van, comes back with a pamphlet in his hand. Under the logo of the county park service, the title reads: *Serving You Better*. "This is supposed to explain why they're charging for swimming and other stuff," he tells his friends. "They say it's costing them a lot more to take care of the lake and pay lifeguards, and that insurance has gotten really expensive. Basically they're saying that they had to make a choice between charging for swimming and maybe shutting down in another year."

"Yeah, right, it's always something," Jamal says bitterly. "Money didn't stop them from building that zillion-dollar convention center for rich businesspeople, but, when it comes to swimming for ordinary people, all of a sudden they're out of dough."

As you study this chapter, think about the dilemma faced by these five friends and about the challenges that confront the county park system managers and prepare to answer the questions in Your Turn at the end of the chapter.

in planning a trip, one should first consider its purpose then take into account it cost, its duration, and the appropriate accommodions.

Planning for recreation and leisure services takes place on a much larger scale than does the planning of a personal trip. For purposes of this chapter we will consider such planning on two levels: macro and micro. At the macro level we deal with planning both public and private services at the national, state, and local levels; at the micro level we examine the planning of individual recreational programs and personal leisure pursuits.

## Macro Planning

As we learned in earlier chapters, the history of public planning for recreation and leisure services in the United States dates back to the establishment of public commons by the first settlements in the American colonies in the early 17th century. The 19th century witnessed the opening of Yellowstone, America's first national park, and of New York's vast Central Park; ever since that time the public recreation movement has been gaining momentum.

Today planning for recreation and leisure services takes place at all levels of government—federal, state, and local—and among the many private enterprises that offer these services. Planning for public recreation services is political as well as financial in nature and must consider the input of various interest groups, whereas private commercial entities must plan not only to meet consumer demand but also to make a profit. Despite differences in the nature and level of services these various entities offer, however, they have many common objectives and goals. Several years ago the AALR appointed a commission to study the goals of American recreation. Below is a summary of the commission's recommendations.[2]

♦ The role of leisure in people's lives has broadened in this time of economic constraint and new social needs.

♦ Planners of leisure services must accept, refine, and integrate alternatives if access and improvements are to be responsive to the new realities.

♦ Planners of leisure services must develop and maintain natural resources and provide programs for their proper use and appreciation.

♦ Leisure planners must encourage participation in health and fitness programs because they have a direct impact and positive influence on physical and psychological well-being.

♦ Leisure planners should try to increase public awareness of the significance of leisure activities in their lives.

♦ Planners of both public and private leisure services should establish relationships that will enhance the role of recreation in light of economic and social realities.

♦ Leisure and recreation curricula should be structured to produce adaptable generalists who will be able to meet the public's changing needs.

### Balancing Supply and Demand

The guidelines presented above form a general framework for the planning of recreation and leisure services. We now need to consider three specific factors that affect planning.

*Demand* is generated by individuals and groups who express a desire for or interest in a particular activity, such as tennis.

*Supply* refers to the resources available to meet demands, such as private and public tennis courts, instructors, and equipment.

*Consumption* is the extent to which individuals and groups actually use the available resources (supply); consumption, thus, measures the adequacy of the supply with respect to existing demand.

This equation states the true objective of planning: to serve consumers by supplying them with the resources and programs that meet their demands.[3]

## Identifying Needs

To provide an adequate supply of recreation and leisure services, planners must obtain information about what consumers are demanding. Although many public and private entities engage in long-range planning, the rapid pace of change requires that plans be flexible. The variables that planners must consider are the following:

◆ *Demographic changes.* The market for recreation and leisure is expanding as the U.S. population increases. Furthermore, the ethnic composition is changing significantly and the proportion of older people is increasing.

◆ *Economic changes.* Corporate downsizing and advances in computer technology are causing a decline in middle management positions as well as technical and manufacturing jobs. The number of low-paying service positions will continue to increase. These trends are constraining the ability of many Americans to pay for recreation and leisure services.

◆ *Social changes.* American society is undergoing profound changes in morals, values, and political orientation. The influence of conservative thought is expanding, and many people are seeking a return to traditional family values.

◆ *Diminishing resources.* Open space in the United States is becoming scarce, and many public recreation facilities are overcrowded to the point of saturation. In addition, the high cost of fuel affects the travel and leisure decisions of many people.

## Planning Process

The process of planning recreation and leisure services involves the following three steps:[4]

1. *Policy statements.* First, planners should formulate several general statements that guide the decision-making process and can be used to implement the entity's goals and objectives.

2. *Goals and objectives.* Second, planners should develop goals and objectives that support the entity's stated policies. An environment-oriented agency, for example, might have the goal of preserving nature, whereas a commercial health club would seek to enhance its members' physical fitness. Planners also must establish standards for the maintenance of facilities.

3. *Decision making.* Finally, planners need to decide on specific courses of action that will help them to achieve their goals and objectives. In addition, they should identify alternative strategies in case they are needed.

## Planning Document

The planning document should contain the following elements:

1. A statement of goals and objectives
2. A recreation resources inventory
3. An analysis of geographic and demographic factors
4. A consumer needs analysis
5. A statement of financial resources
6. Recommendations

**Concept Check**

• What are the three steps in the recreation and leisure planning process?
• What factors should planners consider in seeking to identify users' needs?

## NATIONAL PLANNING FOR RECREATION AND LEISURE

Although the federal government began to provide recreation facilities to Americans at the end of the 19th century, not until the 1950s did the government take any meaningful steps to develop formal plans for the resources under its jurisdiction.

*A prehistoric cliff dwelling, built around 1100–1300 C.E., is preserved at Montezuma Castle National Monument in Northern Arizona.*

## Outdoor Recreation Resources Review Commission (ORRRC)

In 1958 President Eisenhower appointed the Outdoor Recreation Resources Review Commission and charged it with responsibility to

1. Determine the outdoor recreation needs of Americans at that time, again in 1976, and finally in the year 2000
2. Conduct an inventory of the national recreation resources available to meet those needs
3. Identify the policies that should be implemented and the programs that should be offered to meet those needs

Several outside experts served as consultants to the commission, which in 1962 presented to Congress a summary document titled *Outdoor Recreation in America.*[5]

The commission's report established a framework for the federal government's policy on recreation based on the following statements:

1. The basic responsibility for providing recreation opportunities lies with state and local governments.
2. Individual and private groups should be encouraged to preserve land and to provide recreation programs and services.
3. The federal government should provide the states financial and technical assistance in developing recreation opportunities.
4. The federal government is responsible for preserving areas of national significance.

At that time, Congress acted on two of the commission's recommendations. First, it established the Bureau of Outdoor Recreation in 1963, whose mandate was to develop comprehensive national outdoor recreation plans and to coordinate the recreation-related efforts of the National Park Service, the U.S. Forest Service, the Bureau of Land Management, and other agencies. The bureau also worked closely with state and local agencies that provided recreation services. Renamed the Heritage Conservation and Recreation Service in 1978, this agency was absorbed by the National Park Service three years later as a cost-cutting measure. Most of the federal programs that assisted state and local agencies in acquiring open spaces and developing recreational facilities vanished in the 1990s.

Second, in 1965 Congress passed the Land and Water Conservation Fund Act. This law allowed the federal government to raise funds for conservation from entry and user fees at federal recreation areas, from sales of federal property, and from a special tax on motor fuel. Administered by the Bureau of Outdoor Recreation, this fund was to be shared with any state that submitted a State Comprehensive Outdoor Recreation Plan (SCORP).

## Public Land Law Review Commission (PLLRC)

Another milestone in national recreation planning was the establishment of PLLRC to study federal land policies and laws. Its report, completed in 1970, was titled *One Third of the Nation's Land*[6] and contained 452 recommendations.

Broad in scope, it identified the federal government as the custodian of one-third of the nation's land and defined the government's role in providing recreation services this way:

1. The federal government should be responsible for sites of national significance, be they primitive, historical, or natural. These lands should be managed in a way that considers their recreational use along with other essential uses.
2. The states should be encouraged to play a pivotal role in providing outdoor recreation opportunities through acquisition, development, and provision of facilities.
3. Local governments should be assisted in their efforts to provide outdoor recreation services, with particular emphasis on open space around metropolitan areas.
4. Individual and private efforts to provide similar services should be encouraged.

The PLLRC was concerned about overuse of public lands and recommended the adoption of rigorous standards for their use. The commission's report received little attention because its recommendations covered all phases of the management of federal lands, and because finding a rallying point was difficult.[7]

## Nationwide Outdoor Recreation Plan, 1973

The federal act that established the Bureau of Outdoor Recreation stipulated that the agency submit to Congress every five years a nationwide plan for outdoor recreation. The first such plan was prepared in 1968 and in 1970 was revised under the title *The Recreation Imperative*.[8] This second report in turn was modified in 1973 to create a new publication called *Outdoor Recreation: A Legacy for America*.[9] The report stated that, although participation in leisure pursuits had increased significantly in the United States, outdoor recreation resources had not expanded at the same rate.

The report called for federal, state, and local governments to become involved in providing recreation resources and opportunities. It also pointed out the deteriorating condition of America's natural resources from overuse.

In an effort to expand outdoor recreation opportunities for Americans, the report recommended that the federal government assume the following responsibilities:

1. Identify, select, and plan for the acquisition of land
2. Open to the public seldom-used federal lands that are of recreational value
3. Accelerate the establishment of national trails, wild and scenic rivers, wilderness areas, wetlands, and historic sites
4. Transfer surplus underused federal land to state and local governments for recreational use
5. Promote development of recreation facilities by private entities on or near federal lands
6. Coordinate planning for recreational land use with state and local agencies

## Nationwide Outdoor Recreation Plan, 1979

To prepare this plan, the Heritage Conservation and Recreation Service formed several task forces to study specific issues related to outdoor recreation in America. Each task force produced a report that was submitted for review to both government and private agencies. The task forces used this feedback to revise their reports. The reports also contained responses to surveys about Americans' participation rates and preferences in outdoor recreation and leisure pursuits. After assessing Americans' needs and existing facilities to meet those needs, the final report identified nine areas for federal government action:[10]

1. Acquisition of new federal lands and protection of existing lands
2. Establishment of guidelines for the use and protection of wild and scenic rivers

3. Development of new trails and maintenance of existing trails under the National Trails System, in coordination with state and local agencies
4. Disbursement of grants to study the possible use of federal waters along with revitalization of urban waterfront projects
5. Development of programs to enhance energy conservation on federal, state, and local lands
6. Development of programs in environmental education by agencies of the Department of the Interior
7. Improvement of access to recreation facilities of persons with disabilities and encouragement of special populations to use these facilities
8. Exploration of the feasibility of involving the private sector in managing natural resources and offering recreation opportunities
9. Preparation of a comprehensive agenda for national outdoor recreation

At the end of the 20th century, the National Park Service focused on its challenges and strategies for the 21st century, with these objectives: resources stewardship and protection, access and enjoyment, education and interpretation, proactive leadership, science and research, and professionalism.[10a]

**Concept Check**

- What were the responsibilities of the Bureau of Outdoor Recreation?
- Identify key provisions of the Nationwide Outdoor Recreation Plans (1973, 1979).

## STATE PLANNING

The Tenth Amendment to the U.S. Constitution specifies that all powers not delegated to the federal government and not pro-hibited to the states are reserved for the states. This amendment gives states the authority to provide services, including those related to recreation and leisure. Over the years the states have performed the following functions:[11]

1. Enact legislation that enables local authorities to fund recreation resources and provide activities
2. Provide technical services and financial aid to local recreation agencies
3. Establish recreational facilities such as parks, forests, and beaches and develop programs for their use

*Hearst Castle near San Simeon, California, is managed as a state park. Fees are charged for tours of the grounds.*

4. Manage plants and wildlife through reforestation and improvement of habitats
5. Conduct research on social and scientific concepts and strategies that enhance recreational opportunities
6. Promote tourism in the state
7. Set standards and establish regulations to protect typical citizens in their recreational pursuits
8. Cooperate with federal authorities in matters related to service, research, and education

Early efforts by the states to manage their natural resources focused on preserving those resources rather than on developing them for recreational use. With help from the federal government, many areas within states were given special status that protected them from commercial development: in Arkansas, the Hot Springs and the Washita River Salt Springs; Yosemite in California; the area surrounding Niagara Falls in New York. In 1892, 3 million acres of mountains and lakes in New York's Adirondack wilderness were designated a state park, and three years later another vast wilderness, the Catskills, was added to New York's list of "forever wild" areas.

In 1893 Minnesota established Itasca State Park in an effort to protect the headwaters of the Mississippi. Illinois was the first state to establish a state park agency. By 1928 every state had established an agency to deal with outdoor recreation resources. After passage of the Park, Parkway and Recreational Study Act of 1936, the National Park Service became involved in analyzing the resources of the various states. The results of this research helped the states plan the management of those resources on the basis of current and future needs.[12]

Two pieces of federal legislation helped the states acquire land for recreation purposes: the Surplus Property Act of 1944 and the Recreation and Public Purposes Act of 1954. As we learned earlier, Congress passed the Land and Water Conservation Fund Act in 1965, which stipulat-

*The California coastline drive, known as Big Sur, is one of the most beautiful in the world.*

ed that, for a state to receive financial assistance, it must develop a comprehensive plan for how it would meet the recreational needs of residents. From the mid-1960s through 1980, each state developed SCORP every five years. The Bureau of Outdoor Recreation/Heritage Conservation and Recreation Service administered the fund; when this agency was merged into the National Park Service in 1981, some states stopped developing such plans.

Many states continued to develop their own plans.[12a] Their role with respect to recreation relates largely to the abundance of natural resources and how they are managed. Alaska leads with 3,291,209 acres followed by California with 1,412,825 acres and New York with 1,015,911 acres.[12b] Overall, states have experienced a drastic increase in demand for the use of these resources. The Closer Look box below explains how one state established a policy and a plan to provide recreational opportunities for its residents.

**Concept Check**

• Identify three functions states perform that are related to recreation and leisure.
• Describe three ways in which the federal government supports the states in providing recreation facilities and opportunities for their residents.

## A CLOSER LOOK

### THE CALIFORNIA PLAN: BLUEPRINT FOR SUCCESS

In 1962 California became one of the first states to establish a policy on recreation and a plan to provide recreation services. The California Public Outdoor Recreation Plan was based on the input of providers of organized recreation, legislators, and interested members of the public. The plan acknowledged serious problems with recreation in the state and suggested they arose from three sources:

1. Tremendous deficiencies in recreational lands, facilities, and services to meet the needs of the state's growing population
2. Increased competition for land among both recreational and nonrecreational users
3. Confusion about what level(s) and agency(ies) of state government could best meet recreation needs with the fewest overlaps or gaps in services

The plan outlined its solutions to the problems in the form of recommendations to the state legislature:

1. Conduct inventories of recreation areas and facilities
2. Determine residents' recreation needs for the next 20 years
3. Establish and assign responsibilities for the delivery of recreation services
4. Coordinate the roles of the various levels of government

The plan recommended that the legislature adopt the following elements in establishing a state policy on recreation:

1. Provide a variety of recreation opportunities to serve all population groups
2. Recognize the human values of the activities that make up recreation in its broadest sense
3. Increase recreation opportunities commensurate with the growth in need
4. Accelerate programs to supply those recreation areas, facilities, and opportunities that clearly are the responsibility of the state
5. Assume new leadership by encouraging all government agencies, volunteer and commercial entities, and citizen groups to cooperate and coordinate their efforts

To implement this policy, the governor directed all state agencies that provided public recreation to develop long-range plans based on an analysis of the public's recreation needs. The governor assigned the state's department of parks and recreation, with advice from the state parks and recreation commission, responsibility for establishing realistic goals and creating a program that would coordinate recreation efforts at all levels of government. The two agencies were to give due attention to intercounty recreation needs and to the preservation of open space, particularly near urban centers.

## LOCAL PLANNING

Local recreation and leisure services are provided through agencies of a city or county or through a special district. In incorporated areas the city government typically offers recreation programs, whereas the county government provides this service in unincorporated areas. Sometimes the state forms a subdivision, known as a parks and recreation district, that provides recreation services to a designated area.

Regardless of which administrative structure meets the recreation needs of local residents, it must develop a plan to provide both facilities and programs. A short-term recreation service plan for a locality usually covers up to five years, whereas a long-term plan might cover up to 20 years. Among the factors to consider in developing a plan are

- *The demographic profile* of the community: ages, income levels, numbers of males and females, ethnic heritage, family structures, and predominant lifestyle
- *Needs, preferences, and interests* of members of the community
- *Existing local facilities* operated by public, private, and quasi-public agencies: playing fields, auditoriums, parks, swimming pools, indoor facilities
- *Programs and activities* offered by public, private, and quasi-public agencies in art, music, drama, sport, and other areas of interest
- *Location* of recreation areas and facilities and accessibility to users

### Development of Local Facilities

Leisure pursuits and recreational activities occur in several local facilities:

1. *The neighborhood playlot.* This small play area should be designed for children of preschool age. It usually includes swings, seesaws, slides, and a small family picnic area.

2. *The neighborhood playground.* This facility is designed to serve children of school age. It usually includes a playlot equipped as described above, a paved area for games, restrooms, and a small administration building.
3. *The neighborhood park.* This area adds playing fields to the facility listed above.
4. *The community park.* This is a large facility that includes all the features described above and has enough open space for a golf course, riding trails, or both. A small pond often enhances the park.
5. *The regional park.* This area is designed for use by people of several communities. In addition to all the features mentioned above, it usually has additional enhancements such as a lake or a large amphitheatre.
6. *Special areas.* This category includes beaches, historical sites, public plazas, community centers, public golf courses, and other facilities.

Table 12.1 presents the recommendations of NRPA for planning the areas and facilities described above. Standards are in place that serve as guides to planners in determining the appropriate acreage for specific recreation areas and the capacity of facilities that are intended to serve the public. A commonly used ratio for calculating the amount of open space for a given population is 10 acres per 1,000 population. This means that a city of 100,000 persons should have 1,000 acres of parks, playing fields, and other open spaces. Another standard calls for designating 10% of a community's total acreage as open space. A third standard is the maximum service radius for each type of facility as shown in Table 12.1. Still other standards are recommended for specific facilities, as shown in Table 12.2.

### Program Development

Earlier we learned that a key factor in the success of community recreation services is identifying the needs and desires of the residents to be

## TABLE 12.1 Recreation Space Standards Recommended by NRPA

| | ACRES/1,000 POP. | SIZE RANGE | POPULATION SERVED | SERVICE AREA |
|---|---|---|---|---|
| Playlots | NA | 2,500 ft²–1 acre | 500–2,500 | Subneighborhood |
| Vest pocket parks | NA | 2,500 ft²–1 acre | 500–2,500 | Subneighborhood |
| Neighborhood parks | 2.5 | 5–20 acres | 2,000–10,000 | 1/4–1/2 mile |
| District parks | 2.5 | 20–100 acres | 10,000–50,000 | 1/2–3 miles |
| Large urban parks | 5.0 | 100+ acres | One park per 50,000 | Within 1/2 hour driving time |
| Regional parks | 20.0 | 250+ acres | Entire smaller community; distributed throughout larger metro areas | Within 1 hour driving time |
| Special areas and facilities | NA | No standard applies: includes parkways, beaches, plazas, historical sites, floodplains, downtown malls, small parks, and free lawns | | |

## TABLE 12.2 Standards for Specific Facilities

| TYPE OF FACILITY | RECOMMENDED STANDARD |
|---|---|
| Baseball diamonds | 1 per 6,000 |
| Softball diamonds (and/or youth diamonds) | 1 per 3,000 |
| Tennis courts | 1 per 2,000 |
| Basketball courts | 1 per 500 |
| Swimming pools (25-meter) | 1 per 10,000 |
| Swimming pools (50-meter) | 1 per 20,000 |
| Skating rinks (artificial) | 1 per 30,000 |
| Neighborhood centers | 1 per 10,000 |
| Community centers | 1 per 25,000 |
| Outdoor theatres (noncommercial) | 1 per 20,000 |
| Shooting ranges | 1 per 50,000 |
| Golf courses (18-hole) | 1 per 25,000 |

served. As a first step in obtaining this information, planners should conduct constituency surveys to find out what activities residents would like the community to offer. (The Action Guide on p. 262 presents a quiz you can take to find out how effectively your community recreation department is meeting your needs.) Because the demographics of most areas are continually shifting, planners also should conduct needs projections to guide them in planning future services. Once a proposed program has been developed, planners should retain a private consultant to conduct a feasibility study to evaluate the program in terms of both cost and effectiveness.

## ACTION GUIDE

### LOCAL RECREATION: HOW DOES YOUR TOWN MEASURE UP?

If designed correctly, local recreation and leisure facilities meet the needs and desires of residents as identified by surveys and other techniques. How good a job is your local recreation department doing in meeting the needs of you and your family and friends?

1. How often, if at all, do you and your family and friends use local recreation facilities and programs? _____

2. If you do use local facilities, what do you like about them? Be specific.

   _____

   _____

3. If you don't use local facilities, why not? What do you dislike about them?

   _____

   _____

   _____

4. In your opinion, how effective is your local recreation department at providing facilities, programs, and activities you and your family and friends enjoy? Be specific.

   _____

   _____

**Concept Check**

- Describe three factors that must be considered in developing a community recreation plan.
- Describe three kinds of local recreation facilities.

## MANAGEMENT OF RECREATION AND LEISURE

Management of recreation and leisure is both an art and a science, the principles of which are based on human experience and scientific research. These principles apply equally to the manager of a small local recreation program or a modest boat rental business and to the manager of a huge national forest or a vast and complex theme park. The literature abounds with management styles and strategies, some of which may be better suited than others to the management of recreational facilities and programs. One example is management by objectives (MBO), which usually is described as a four-step process:[13]

1. *Agreement.* At regular intervals a manager and each subordinate agree on the

## ACTION GUIDE (cont'd)

### LOCAL RECREATION: HOW DOES YOUR TOWN MEASURE UP?
#### (cont'd)

5. What specific improvements, if any, do you think need to be made in your local recreation facilities and programs?

_____

_____

6. Have you or anyone in your family or circle of friends been asked to complete a survey about their recreation needs and preferences? _____

7. If so, are such surveys conducted on a regular basis? _____

8. If you and others you know have completed such a survey, did you subsequently see any changes in local recreation facilities and programs in response to your comments?

_____

_____

9. If changes weren't made, do you know why?

_____

_____

results that the subordinate will try to achieve during the next period. The subordinate *participates* actively in spelling out the meaning and feasibility of the assignments he or she accepts.

2. *Delegation.* The supervisor then makes a high degree of delegation to the subordinate. During this period the main role of the supervisor is to *assist* the subordinate in fulfilling the agreement.

3. *Evaluation of results.* At the end of the period, actual results are measured, and the supervisor and subordinate discuss reasons for success and failure. This evaluation becomes the basis for making another agreement (perhaps at a later meeting) for the next period.

4. *Associated activities.* The evaluation of results often serves as the basis for setting salaries and bonuses and for planning personal development. Also the negotiation of agreements may lead to modifications in organization, procedures, policies, and controls. But these associated activities are not essential parts of MBO.

### Areas of Responsibility

Whatever strategy or system a recreation and leisure manager uses, he or she will be required to make decisions or provide input for decisions in several key areas:

*Carrying capacity.* The manager must estimate the number of people and the kinds of activities an area or a facility can accommodate before it begins to deteriorate.

*Use rates.* The manager must estimate how often a given area or facility is used. Three standards are used to measure use rates. A *recreation visit* is the entry of one person into an area or a facility. A *recreation visitor hour* is a 60-minute recreation visit. A *recreation activity hour* describes one person's participation in a specific activity for 60 minutes. Estimates are based on general observation or are obtained by a sampling method or by counting heads.

*User fees.* This issue concerns the managers of both private and public recreation facilities. For private facilities, fees must be set at appropriate market rates to attract the desired clientele while allowing the provider to make a reasonable profit. On the public side, however, many people believe that no fees should be charged for the use of recreation facilities. Others believe that charging fees will enhance the quality of services provided as well as restrict access to threatened natural resources. The managers of public recreation facilities have important input into the decision of whether or not to charge fees.

*Rock climbing challenges the physical and mental boundaries of the individual.*

*Visitor management.* The purpose of visitor management is to make each person's or group's visit as pleasant as possible while at the same time maintaining the quality of the setting. Clearly worded, appropriately placed signs should direct visitors to the sites of information and education programs, and personnel at these sites should be courteous and well informed. Outdoor interpreters should also be cordial and knowledgeable, as should security personnel and the staffs of shops, restaurants, and other facilities. To the greatest extent possi-

ble, facilities should be accessible to persons with disabilities. A key aspect of visitor management is the prevention of undesirable actions such as vandalism and graffiti.

*Risk management.* Injuries and fatalities can occur in even the best-managed recreational facilities, and the facility may be found liable in a court of law. Large facilities employ risk managers, who arrange insurance coverage and develop comprehensive programs to prevent or reduce both personal injury and property losses through safety inspections, staff training, and the development of emergency procedures. Smaller facilities can obtain similar assistance from the loss control department of their insurance company. Systematic record keeping and reporting of incidents will help managers identify important trends in this area.

## Recreation, Leisure, and the Law

Providers of recreation and leisure facilities and services must become acquainted with the legal principles that govern their relationships with participants. Here we briefly describe some of the most important principles.

- *Tort* is the legal term for a civil (as opposed to criminal) wrong inflicted on a person other than a breach of contract. (In some cases, such as assault, an act may be both a tort [a civil or private wrong] and a crime [a public wrong].)[14]
- *Liability* is responsibility or obligation under the law.
- *Act of God* is the legal term used to describe a sudden interruption by a natural cause (such as a flood or an earthquake) of the usual course of events that experience, knowledge, or care cannot reasonably foresee or prevent. The owner/manager of a recreation facility would not be held liable for a death or an injury on his or her premises that resulted from an act of God.
- *Negligence* is failure to use at least the degree of care in a given situation that a reasonable person in similar circumstances would exercise to avoid harming others. Negligence is an unintentional tort.[14] A fitness club manager might be held liable for negligence in failing to maintain exercise equipment in a reasonably safe condition when that failure caused injury to a client who was using the equipment in the prescribed manner and had no knowledge that the equipment was unsafe.

- *Contributory negligence* is conduct on the part of an injured person that falls below the standard required for his or her own protection.[14] In the fitness club example, contributory negligence might describe a situation in which a client who knew the correct, safe way to use a piece of equipment chose instead to use it in an obviously unsafe way and as a result sustained an injury. A finding of contributory negligence usually prevents an injured person (plaintiff) from recovering any damages from the defendant (person the plaintiff alleges caused the injury). In determining contributory negligence, courts use the reasonable person test; that is, how a reasonable person would behave in these circumstances.[14]
- *Comparative negligence* is a legal doctrine that asserts that, when both the plaintiff (party claiming to be injured) and the defendant (party alleged to have caused the plaintiff's injury) are at fault, the damages will be apportioned between them according to one of several formulas. Whereas contributory negligence is usually a complete bar to recovery on the part of the plaintiff, comparative negligence prevents the plaintiff from recovering only that proportion of damages for which he or she was responsible.[14]
- *Assumption of risk* describes a situation in which a person assumes the risk of harm by another's negligence when the person voluntarily exposes himself or herself to potential harm with full knowledge of the danger. An example is choosing to attend a baseball game where the attendee knows he or she may be injured by a ball hit into the stands. Assumption of risk requires knowledge and deliberate choice, whereas contributory negligence involves lack of care and therefore the absence of deliberate choice.[15]

- *Trespasser* is one who enters the property of another without the possessor's knowledge or consent. To an adult trespasser the possessor of property owes the duty of only slight care—that is, refraining from intentionally harming a discovered trespasser or setting traps for undiscovered trespassers.[15] In the case of children who trespass, the possessor owes a higher degree of care under the doctrine of *attractive nuisance.* Under this doctrine, if the possessor of land has something artificial on the land that is likely to attract children (for example, a swimming pool), it is construed as an implied invitation for a child to enter onto the land. In this case the possessor is required to keep the premises in a suitable and safe condition and to use ordinary care to protect trespassing children from harm.[14]

- *Licensee* is a person who enters another's premises with implied or expressed permission but who does so only for his or her own benefit. In this case the owner owes the duty of reasonable care: to remove known hazards or to post adequate warnings of those hazards. Examples of licensees are door-to-door sales representatives, persons seeking shelter from inclement weather, and those seeking help in an emergency.[15]

- *Invitee* is a person who enters another's premises with permission and for the mutual benefit of the possessor and the invitee. To invitees the possessor owes the duty of great care: to make a definite effort to discover hazards that may endanger others and to remove those hazards or post suitable warnings. Invitees include customers and prospective customers, representatives of government bodies (other than police officers and firefighters, who are considered licensees), representatives of public utility firms, and others whose entry directly or indirectly benefits the possessor.[15]

- *Sovereign or governmental immunity*, a doctrine created over time by the courts, held that the states and the federal government could not be sued without their consent. The doctrine also applied to municipalities for acts they performed when functioning in a governmental (not proprietary) capacity. In recent years this doctrine has been eroded by both judicial and legislative action,[14] and sovereign immunity no longer protects governments and their agencies from civil lawsuits.

- *Waivers and releases* are attempts to avoid liability. Many business owners either require patrons to sign waivers or release agreements or simply state, on signs or ticket backs, that the proprietor is not responsible for injury to patrons. Such documents and statements, however, frequently do not hold up in court. A prime example is the "ride at your own risk" warning commonly printed on the backs of tickets for amusement park rides. Such warnings do not shield the owner from liability for injuries or deaths caused by faulty maintenance, overcrowding, negligent operation, or mechanical failure of rides.

## Financial Aspects of Recreation Management

In Chapter 7 we learned that the U.S. Bureau of the Census estimated that recreation spending by individuals and nonprofit organizations rose from 116.3 billion dollars in 1985 to close to 500 billion dollars in 2000. These statistics do not include travel for pleasure, which has risen dramatically in recent years, nor do they consider government spending on recreation and leisure facilities and programs. In this section we examine the financial aspects of management in recreation and leisure with special emphasis on the public sector, which is oriented toward providing a service rather than making a profit.

*The popular tourist attraction of Sedona, Arizona, was incorporated as a city in the 1980s, which greatly improved its tax base. Red Rock Crossing on the Oak Creek attracts and enchants many visitors.*

### Financing Public Recreation

The primary source of funding for public recreation is taxes. Three kinds of taxes are used to support public recreation. Federal income tax revenue is used to maintain and operate national recreation resources. State income tax and sales tax revenue are used to acquire and develop state recreation areas and facilities, and local property taxes are used to finance recreation and leisure programs for residents of communities.

Projects that require major capital outlays, such as stadiums and sports/entertainment arenas, are financed by bond issues. Bonds are debt instruments purchased by individuals and businesses and repaid with interest by the bond issuer over long periods, usually between 10 and 30 years.

Another important source of revenue for public recreation facilities, particularly on the local level, is fees and charges. Despite opposition to this practice from some providers and consumers, local recreation departments have been imposing fees and charges for many years. It is accepted practice to charge concessionaires a fee for operating in a public recreation facility. Users of a facility may be required to pay fees for entry, parking, and special-use permits (for example, camping or fishing).

Once a major source of funding for local recreation facilities, state and federal grants have been drastically reduced in recent years. Local authorities now are seeking and acquiring funds from foundations and corporations that support public programs in art, music, drama, and sport. To obtain a share of these funds, community recreation and leisure managers must acquire expertise in fundraising.

### Concept Check

- What is management by objectives?
- Briefly describe the terms *tort* and *negligence.*

## EVALUATION OF RECREATION AND LEISURE PROVIDERS

Evaluation is a process by which a manager assesses the effectiveness of a recreation or leisure facility in achieving its objectives as stated in its plan. The evaluation encompasses each unit of the agency or facility, each employee, and each program offered. On the basis of the evaluation, the manager decides whether to maintain, modify, or discontinue certain programs or to introduce new ones. Evaluation must be an ongoing process conducted in a thorough, systematic way.

## Agency Evaluation

The NRPA has published a manual that can be used to evaluate recreation and leisure service agencies. The manual explains how to measure the effectiveness of the agency's philosophies and goals, administrative structure, resources, programs, personnel, and even its evaluative procedures. Following the manual's guidelines, a team of experts gathers the needed information by conducting interviews and making observations.[16] A manual published by the now-defunct Bureau of Outdoor Recreation suggests criteria such as ratings by users, numbers of visitors, upkeep of facilities, helpfulness of staff, hours of operation, safety practices, accessibility of facilities, and variety of offerings.[9]

## Facility Evaluation

Using a checklist of standards prepared in the planning process, the manager or a subordinate physically inspects all recreation areas and facilities. Items on the list include level of cleanliness, state of repair, condition of equipment, effectiveness of lighting, noise level, existence of fire and other safety hazards, and accessibility.

## Personnel Evaluation

This one area that is most neglected in the public sector of park, recreation, and leisure service.[16a] Evaluation of personnel concentrates on quality and quantity of work, effectiveness in achieving agreed-upon objectives, relationship with others, punctuality and reliability, and compliance with instructions. In a qualitative evaluation the manager uses a word or phrase to describe the employee's performance, such as *outstanding, satisfactory,* or *needs improvement.* In a quantitative evaluation the manager assigns the employee a numerical grade for his or her performance in each category, usually on a scale of 1 to 5 or 1 to 10, with 1 being the lowest grade and 5 or 10 the highest. In each case the manager discusses the evaluation with the employee, listens attentively to the employee's comments, then asks him or her to suggest ways to improve performance in weak areas. The manager may unilaterally establish interim timetables for completion of certain items or may invite the employee to help set such deadlines.

## Program Evaluation

Although its programs and activities are the reason for a recreation agency's existence, they often are not evaluated because their features are not easily measured.[4] One expert identifies several techniques that can be used to assess program effectiveness:[17]

- *Discrepancy evaluation* reveals the extent to which the program has *not* achieved its objectives.
- *Professional judgment* is direct observation by recognized outside experts.
- *Socioeconomic evaluation* uses demographic information for purposes of comparison.
- *Standards-based evaluation* uses established or suggested standards, such as number of acres of land per 1,000 population.
- *The decision-oriented model* compares the input, process, and output of the program.
- *Cost-benefit evaluation* compares the benefits gained by users of the program with the costs incurred in providing the program.
- *Importance-performance evaluation* measures both the importance of the program to participants and their satisfaction with it.

## Summing Up

◆ Planning is a process that involves establishing desired objectives and developing a course of action to achieve those objectives.

◆ In the United States, recreation and leisure planning takes place at all levels of government and in the quasi-public and private sectors.

◆ Effective recreation and leisure planning considers three factors: demand, supply, and consumption.

◆ The Nationwide Outdoor Recreation Plans developed by the Bureau of Outdoor Recreation (now part of the National Park Service) defined the responsibilities of federal, state, and local governments and the private sector in providing recreation and leisure services.

◆ With respect to recreation and leisure services, the role of the states is largely related to the management and protection of natural resources.

◆ Local recreation facilities usually include neighborhood playlots, playgrounds, and parks; a community park; a regional park; and one or more special facilities, such as a community center, public golf course, or historical site.

◆ The planning of local recreation is based in part on standards for how much open space and how many specific facilities are needed to accommodate a given population.

◆ Management in recreation and leisure is both an art and a science whose principles are based on human experience and scientific research. Managers must instruct, guide, and evaluate personnel. With respect to the facility itself, managers are responsible for risk management and visitor management; for ascertaining carrying capacity and use rates; and for recommending or discouraging the imposition of fees and charges for use of the facility.

◆ Important legal principles affect the owners and operators of both public and private recreation and leisure facilities. Managers must understand the concept of negligence and its different degrees; they also must know the differences among a trespasser, a licensee, and an invitee and recognize the special duty owed to child trespassers under the doctrine of attractive nuisance.

◆ The major source of funding for public recreation and leisure facilities at the federal, state, and local levels is tax revenue. To obtain funds for a project that requires a major capital outlay, a city or county may sell a bond issue. Other sources of funds are government grants (although these have declined drastically over the years), donations from foundations, and fees and charges for the use of facilities.

◆ In evaluating the effectiveness of recreation and leisure programs, managers must assess the administrative structure, the physical state of facilities, the performance of staff members, and the success of programs.

## *Using What You've Learned*

1. Attend a meeting of the planning commission in your community. Write a one-page report about what took place in the meeting and how you reacted to it.
2. Make an appointment with the superintendent of parks and recreation in your community. Discuss with him or her the department's plans for the future.
3. Write to your state department of parks and recreation and ask for information about its plans for the future, or if possible obtain this information from your local library.
4. From the federal depository in your library, obtain a copy of the current plans of the U.S. Forest Service and the National Park Service. Write a one-page report on the plans of each agency.

## YOUR  Turn

1. Have you ever been in a situation where you were expected to pay for public recreation services? If so, how did you react, and why?
2. Under what circumstances, if any, should public recreation facilities be permitted to impose user fees and charges?
3. If public recreation facilities want to impose charges, what proof, if any, should they be required to offer of their need to impose such charges? Should a proposal to impose charges be put to a public vote?
4. If public recreation facilities are permitted to charge users, what, if any, exceptions or exemptions do you think should be made?

# REFERENCES

1. Bannon, J. (1999). *911 Management: A Comprehensive Guide to Leisure Managers.* Champaign, IL: Sagamore Publishing.

2. Dunn, Diane (Ed.) (Oct 1986). Aims of American Recreation. *Leisure Today,* p. 1.

3. Mitchell, Leslie (1983). Future Directions of Recreation Planning. In S. Leiber & D. Fesenmaier (Eds.), *Recreation Planning and Management.* State College, PA: Venture Publishing, p. 323.

4. Murphy, James, et al. (1991). *Leisure Systems: Critical Concepts and Applications.* Champaign, IL: Sagamore Publishing, p. 326.

5. Outdoor Recreation Resources Review Commis-sion (1962). *Outdoor Recreation in America.* U.S. Government Printing Office, Washington, DC.

6. Public Land Law Review Commission (1970). *One Third of the Nation's Land.* U.S. Government Printing Office, Washington, DC.

7. Knudson, Douglas (1984). *Outdoor Recreation.* New York: Macmillan, p. 332.

8. Bureau of Outdoor Recreation (1970). *The Recreation Imperative.* Washington, DC: Senate Committee on Interior and Insular Affairs.

9. Bureau of Outdoor Recreation (1972). *How Effective Are Your Community Services?* Washington, DC: Department of the Interior.

10. Heritage Conservation and Recreation Service (1979). *The Third Outdoor Recreation Plan.* U.S. Government Printing Office, Washington, DC.

10a. National Park Service (1991). *The Vail Agenda.* Washington, DC: U.S. Government Printing Office.

11. McLean, J., Peterson, J., & Martin, D. (1985). *Recreation and Leisure: The Changing Scene.* New York: Macmillan, pp. 104–106.

12. Fazio, James (1979). Parks and Other Recreational Resources. In H. Ibrahim & J. Shivers (Eds.), *Leisure: Emergence and Expansion.* Los Alamitos, CA: Hwong, p. 214.

12a. Planning Division (2001). *Planning Milestones: California State Park System.* Sacramento, CA: Department of Park and Recreation.

12b. National Association of State Park Directors (2001). *The 2001 Annual Information Exchange.* Tucson, AZ: NASPD.

13. Newman, W., et al. (1982). *The Process of Management,* ed. 5. Englewood Cliffs, NJ: Prentice-Hall, p. 45.

14. Lorimer, J., et al. (1981). *The Legal Environment of Insurance,* ed. 2, vol. II. Malvern, PA: American Institute for Property and Liability Underwriters.

15. Williams, C., et al. (1978). *Principles of Risk Management and Insurance,* vol. II. Malvern, PA: American Institute for Property and Liability Underwriters.

16. van der Smissen, B., et al., editors (1999). *Management of Park and Recreation Agencies.* Ashburn, VA: NRPA.

16a. Kraus, R., & Curtis, J. (2000). *Creative Management in Parks, Recreation and Leisure Services.* St.Louis, MO: McGraw-Hill.

17. Theobald, W. (1979). *Evaluation of Recreation and Park Programs.* New York: John Wiley & Sons.

The moral and spiritual forces of our country do not lose ground in the hours we are busy on our jobs; their battle is leisure time. We are organizing the production of leisure. We need better organization of its consumption.

**HERBERT HOOVER**
(U.S. President, 1929–1933)
1950

# Issues and Challenges in Recreation and Leisure

### THE CHAPTER AT A GLANCE

In this chapter we explore issues and challenges in contemporary recreation and leisure. Among these are the apparent inequality in the time allotted for leisure among different groups; the adverse consequences for leisure of excessive emphasis on sex and violence, as well as substance abuse and other social problems; and the apprehension in some quarters that public recreation is becoming more commercialized.

## Chapter Objectives

*After completing this chapter, you should be able to*

◆ Identify groups who have less time than do others to devote to leisure pursuits.
◆ Describe the impact on leisure of problems such as a sedentary lifestyle; high-risk activities; overemphasis on sex in the popular media; abuse of alcohol and drugs, including steroids; gambling; violence; delinquency; and vandalism at leisure sites.
◆ Explain the reasons for and effects of charging fees for various forms of public recreation.

## INEQUALITY IN RECREATION AND LEISURE

E quality in recreation and leisure requires that free time be provided for all, regardless of sex, race, ethnic background, or socioeconomic status. Moreover, free time should be coupled with accessible facilities and equal opportunities to use them. Unfortunately, despite praiseworthy efforts to achieve these goals, many segments of society continue to experience inequality in recreation and leisure.

### A CITY BOY IN A COUNTRY PARK

"Yo, Ramon! Come on out!"

Running out to the balcony of his apartment in the projects, Ramon sees his best friend, Joey, waving his blue Yankees cap and motioning to Ramon to join him. Grabbing his own Los Angeles Angels cap, Ramon pounds down five flights of stairs to the street, barely conscious of the bullet holes in doors and walls and the lights shot out by drug dealers. He runs up to Joey, glad to see his friend after being gone for four days.

"So how was it at your cousin's?" Joey demands. A stick-thin boy in his older brother's bike shorts and a too-big tank top, he talks rapidly and radiates nervous energy.

Ramon takes a breath. Where to begin? How to describe the way his cousin Ric and his aunt and uncle now live since they left the city last year for a small town in the suburbs? Now that he's back in the city, he can scarcely believe the reality of what he experienced on his visit to Elm Grove.

"Well? What did you see? What did you *do*?" Joey asks insistently. "Or did you make the whole thing up and you were really here all the time, hiding out and watching "Power Rangers"?"

Ramon shakes his head and begins. "You won't believe this, but Ric and Uncle Tomas and Aunt Maria have a whole house, all to themselves, just like on those reruns of "Leave It to Beaver." And get this—about half a mile down this road with hardly any cars on it, there's this huge park." Joey is staring at him incredulously. "No, really," Ramon says, reading Joey's eyes. "It has zillions of trees, and a treehouse we climbed into, and this neat rope swing. We walked on a trail, and Ric said to be real quiet, and we saw a mother deer and her baby drinking out of a pond. It was way cool!"

"You're telling me you saw a *real deer*?" Joey says in disbelief. "You mean like Bambi?"

"I swear it," Ramon says solemnly. "I couldn't believe it myself, but I really saw them. Then my parents and my aunt and uncle came and got us, and we had a picnic right there under the trees. There was a barbecue grill and a table with benches, and we fed crumbs to the squirrels. After we ate, my uncle took me and Ric to the playground. There was all this great stuff made of wood and ropes, and places you could climb and swing. Wow, Joey, I wish you could see it." Ramon's brown eyes become unfocused as he gazes back into what now seems more like a dream than reality.

"Yeah," Joey replies dispiritedly. "Be a big change from what they call a park around here." He extends his arm to indicate the city park across the street from the project. Full of rusted, dangerous old playground equipment, it has long since been abandoned as a recreation site. Its unforgiving asphalt surface is riddled with cracks and glittering with shards of broken bottles. The former snack shack has been taken over by drug dealers, and their customers are often seen sprawled under the few spindly trees, sleeping off their hits. Ramon, Joey, and their friends have been ordered by their parents to keep out of the park, and it's a rule they're not remotely tempted to break. They prefer to take their chances playing kickball in the street and running to the sidewalk when cars come.

As you study this chapter, think about the differences between the park in Ramon's neighborhood and the park he visited with his cousin Ric and prepare to answer the questions in Your Turn at the end of the chapter.

Even in the most advanced democracies, women, minorities, and the poor traditionally have less leisure time and fewer opportunities than do men and more affluent people.

## Women

The old rhyme "A man works from sun to sun, but a woman's work is never done" illustrates a major constraint on women's leisure time. Whether or not women work outside the home, in most cases they continue to do the bulk of the work inside the home: child care, cooking, cleaning, laundry, shopping. As attitudes and values shift, particularly in the United States and Canada, the women's situation is beginning to improve, but inequities persist in some countries of Europe and the third world.[1–4]

## Underprivileged Persons

Inequality of time for and access to recreation and leisure also is seen among underprivileged persons. For example, a 1984 report in the *Los Angeles Times* described the parks in an impoverished section of the city as "dead parks" because they were used by gangs, drug dealers, and alcoholics, a situation the city's parks and recreation commission was supposed to have rectified. Nonetheless, the report said, a recreational "apartheid" still existed in the city because two systems of leisure existed that were separated by income in addition to race and ethnicity. One expert asserted that the decline of leisure services in certain sections of Los Angeles attests to the decline of those residents' "leisure rights."[5]

A study of the public recreation opportunities in central Los Angeles compared with those available in the suburbs supports the assertion of the loss of "leisure rights":

1. The inner-city communities have less public recreation land than do the suburban communities.
2. The suburban public recreation staff works 59% more time per week than does the inner-city staff.

3. Community support is minimal in most inner-city recreation areas, whereas the suburban areas enjoy volunteer support.
4. To a considerably greater extent than the suburbs, the inner-city areas seem to suffer from the problems of gangs and vandalism.[6]

In Chicago a four-year legal battle between a public interest group and the city park district ended when the district agreed to allocate $60 million over six years to renovate old parks and build new ones in poor neighborhoods. A study of Detroit city parks showed that poor maintenance was the reason for underutilization of inner-city parks. Although the park acreage appeared to be adequate, residents viewed the parks as unsafe because of stray dogs, gang activities, and vandalism.[7]

Access to leisure opportunities also is rendered inequitable because of the location of facilities. In the United States, for example, most national parks and forests are located far from most populated areas. Fig. 10.1 showed the locations of national recreation resources compared with areas of population concentration. Although by no means intentional, this factor certainly restricts access to such facilities to those who have the time and money to travel to them.

### Concept Check

- Briefly explain why women traditionally have had less time than men for leisure pursuits.
- Identify three factors that restrict underprivileged people's use of recreation and leisure facilities.

## SEDENTARY LIFESTYLES

As we learned earlier, the human body is designed for an active lifestyle. In earlier times human beings depended on foraging and hunting for survival, activities that required a fit, agile body.

In today's post-industrial, pushbutton culture, however, most people no longer have to exert themselves to obtain food or erect shelters. Although many people pursue fitness through regular exercise and many others play sports, by far a greater number are spectators of rather than participants in sports, either in person or on television.[8,9]

As we learned earlier, fully 98% of American households have a television and thus have instant, free access to a vast array of entertainment options. Today the average American watches television between 2.24 and 3.97 hours per day.[10]

One expert estimates that, for every individual who watches a game in person, between 100 and 500 people are watching it on television.[11] With the advent of the remote control, viewers no longer even have to walk a few steps to change the channel or adjust the volume. We seem to be on the way to becoming a nation of couch potatoes.

One assessment of the physical activity level of American adults between 25 and 65 years of age concluded that no more than 17% met the minimum requirements deemed necessary to combat the current leading cause of death in the United States, which is cardiovascular disease.[12]

**Concept Check**

- What effects do energy-saving devices have on our lifestyle?
- How does excessive television viewing affect health and fitness?

## HIGH-RISK RECREATION

At the opposite end of the spectrum from the couch potatoes described above are the people for whom recreation means engaging in various risky activities: bungee jumping, hang gliding, whitewater rafting, ballooning,

and an emerging trend known as "extreme sports" (see A Closer Look on p. 277). These adventurers have what one researcher has identified as a "type T" personality that is characterized by a low arousability threshold that causes the individual to become a sensation seeker.[13]

Clearly, participation in the kinds of activities that appeal to type T personalities carries the risk of serious or even fatal injury. For example, one study showed that, whereas 64% of the hang gliders surveyed had been injured, some seriously, only 4% of bowlers reported injuries, and these were minor. The sensation seekers themselves perceived their activities as high risk: the same study found that 67% of hang gliders considered their activity to be high risk, while none of the bowlers characterized their sport that way.[14] Most sensation seekers are men in their early twenties and thirties, although an increasing number of women are participating in high-risk activities.[15]

The question arises: should a leisure service program, whether public or private, include high-risk activities and assume the legal liability for injuries or deaths? Insurance coverage for such activities is costly and may not be available at all. Although the participant inherently assumes some of the risk, a lawsuit will seek evidence of contributory negligence on the part of the provider. For this reason the provider of any high-risk activity must ensure that all staff members have been thoroughly trained, systematically inspect all equipment, implement and follow stringent safety procedures, carefully screen prospective participants, and prepare appropriately for emergencies.[16]

**Concept Check**

- What is a "type T" personality?
- Name two high-risk recreational activities in addition to those identified in this section.

## A CLOSER LOOK

### GOING TO EXTREMES TO LURE THE HOTDOGS BACK

You'd think that, at 55, Carole Brownson would be skiing gentler runs. But not this former New York City chef. She rides to the end of a ski lift at Breckenridge, Colorado, then hikes up the mountain for a 20-minute trek she likens to climbing to the top of the Empire State Building. After pausing at the summit of Peak 7 to admire the view, she's off through deep powder, flying down an ungroomed mountain bowl with a 1,200-foot, 35-degree drop. "It's like free-falling. I laugh all the way down the hill. Yes! Yes!" says Brownson, owner of a bed and breakfast in town. "If this is as close to heaven as I get, that's OK. It's pretty close."

Brownson isn't the only one seeking nirvana in the backcountry. Searching for ever greater thrills, expert skiers are schussing macho, or "extreme," slopes at winter resorts all over America. Using standard downhill equipment, they are pressing the hunt for what Telluride ski patrol director Norman Gray calls "the ultimate challenge."

Extreme sports' biggest enthusiasts, however, may be owners/managers of ski resorts, which have been battling a decade of stagnant growth. Resorts must now market to specific niches: kids, oldsters,

Europeans. Snowboarders accounted for 11% of resort visits in 1994, a 17% increase over the previous season. Extreme skiing may not see that pace of growth, but it's part of an overall strategy to "offer a range of activities for the destination visitor—snowshoeing, dogsledding, extreme skiing," says Michael Berry, president of the National Ski Areas Association.

There are no hard numbers on extreme skiers because they buy the same tickets and ride the same lifts as downhillers, but enrollment in Ski Schools of Aspen's extreme clinics was up 50% in 1995 over the previous year. Across the mountains at Telluride, extreme skiing was up 100% in 1995 over 1994.

Extreme slopes are popular with resorts because they're cheap. Readying Peak 7 costs less than 10% of what Breckenridge would have spent to cut runs and build a ski lift for a traditional downhill slope. And, because the terrain is left in its natural state, there's little grooming cost.

Who are these hotshots? They're mostly Generation X thrillseekers, men and women, plus baby boomers out to prove they haven't lost it. After a run down Peak 7, a 40-something dentist says, "I'm 33 and sneering at everybody."

## SEX AND LEISURE

The impact of sex on all aspects of modern life is unquestioned. For some people the sex act seemingly has become neither an expression of love nor a means of procreation but rather a recreational activity. One author claims that humans tend to play a sexual game with an opponent much as one plays tennis. "The satisfaction from a sexual encounter, like tennis, combines elements of pleasure, physical sensations, skill, diversion from the required aspect of life, and an opportunity to be with and communicate with another person."[7] Indeed, if one sets aside the emotional aspects

and consequences of a sexual encounter, and, if one considers the high rate of effectiveness of modern contraceptives, one can see the possibility of sex as recreation.[17]

Sex also affects recreation and leisure through the many sexual images and acts conveyed by the popular media, particularly television and movies. The effort begun in the 1960s to liberate sex from the stigma imposed on it by a Puritan/Victorian morality was indeed welcome, but many people believe sexual liberation has gone too far and is having a disruptive effect on the social order. Authorities increasingly are scrutinizing television shows and

*Tours of Dolly's House in Sitka, Alaska, commemorate the popular house of prostitution during the Gold Rush era.*

**Concept Check**

- What is meant by sex as recreation?
- Name some ways in which society is affected by pornography and "sex for sale."

movies for content that features excessive violence and sexual content. Sex itself is not a social problem; what causes concern is the behavior that often surrounds it: prostitution, pandering, promiscuity, illegitimacy, abortion, the risk of disease, drug use, and homicide.

A third area in which sex and leisure intersect is the commercialization of sex and pornography. In the United States, pornography is close to a $10 billion business, despite innumerable legal battles, zoning restrictions, and community censorship. Houses of prostitution, call-girl rings, "adult" bookstores, massage parlors, X-rated movies, and topless/bottomless bars are on the increase in many parts of the world.[16] Are these forms of entertainment a part of the leisure scene? Such activities frequently are controlled by figures in organized crime, and far too often minors are involved. Moreover, violence is a typical companion of the sex business. "Sleaze" tourism is a term that describes traveling to countries where prostitution is readily available.[17] The activities described above may constitute leisure for a small segment of the population, but they are far from the mainstream of wholesome leisure and recreation.

## LEISURE AND SUBSTANCE ABUSE

The increasing "recreational" use of alcohol and drugs has become a major concern worldwide and is the focus of many efforts to reverse what many experts view as an alarming and destructive behavior pattern. No legal venues exist for the consumption of street drugs; however, bars, taverns, pubs, saloons, cocktail lounges, and other establishments dedicated to drinking are almost too numerous to count.

### Alcohol

In an effort to understand the relationship between drinking and leisure behavior, a researcher interviewed 1,706 Canadian nationals from all 10 provinces to find out why they frequented drinking establishments, how often, and with whom they drank. Of the sample, 78% drank alcoholic beverages, and 68% of those drank in a public place. The first reason given for going to a drinking establishment was companionship, followed by entertainment and eating.[18]

Another study showed that social drinking is second only to television watching as America's favorite pastime. This researcher believes the two activities are mutually reinforcing because so many people drink beer while watching TV and because breweries often are major sponsors of televised sports.[19]

Whether or not it is a leisure activity, alcohol consumption has produced close to 20 million addicts in the United States. Furthermore, alcohol has been identified as a factor in 500,000 murders, suicides, and accidental deaths in this country.[16]

## Drugs

For decades the use of street drugs has had devastating effects on individuals, their families, and society in general. The concept of recreational drug use came into being when the National Commission on Marijuana and Drug Abuse identified "recreational" as one of five types of drug abuse; the other four are experimental, situational, intensive, and compulsive. Some people use drugs to relax, ease tension, or sleep; others seek a thrilling trip to another dimension or a "high" that will let them party all night. Some users want to escape from reality; others strive to heighten it. Drug use is commonly seen at many sports and recreation events, at concerts, and at car and motorcycle races, among other places—often in combination with alcohol. Worse yet, many drug users endanger themselves and others by driving cars, piloting boats, flying planes or balloons, or engaging in other high-risk behavior while under the influence of drugs.

### Performance-Enhancing Drugs

For many years the sport scene, both amateur and professional, has been plagued by athletes' use of drugs to enhance performance. Athletes use two kinds of drugs: restorative and additive. Restorative drugs are intended to help heal injuries, whereas additive drugs are designed to enhance performance. Sometimes

*Cigarette smoking is often considered substance abuse. Where do you stand on tobacco use?*

athletes use these drugs on their own initiative, in other cases on the insistence of trainers or coaches.[20] The most commonly used additive drugs are amphetamines and anabolic steroids. Amphetamines are stimulants; anabolic steroids are male hormones that help build bulk. They also provide an unfair advantage to the user, so their use in most competitions is prohibited. Canadian Olympic runner Ben Johnson was stripped of his gold medal in 1988 when a drug test revealed he had used steroids to enhance his performance.

Anabolic steroids have been shown to produce extreme aggressiveness and mood swings in many users—the so-called roid rage effect—and they may have adverse physical consequences that include liver cancer, kidney and heart damage, severe acne, hair loss, shrunken testicles, impotence, sterility, and enlarged breasts in men. Women who use steroids are at risk for masculinizing effects such as permanent deepening of the voice and increased body hair.[21]

### Concept Check

- What are some dangers of drug and alcohol abuse?
- Why do some athletes use anabolic steroids, and what are some of the possible adverse consequences of using them?

## VANDALISM AND GRAFFITI AT LEISURE SITES

Vandalism—the deliberate destruction of property—is a growing problem at leisure sites throughout the United States. Visitors to natural sites cause damage while removing signs, rocks, and plants; others break down doors and windows to gain entry to buildings, strip bark from trees, or damage animal shelters and feeding stations. Concert patrons and sports spectators may break seats, throw bottles and cans, and grab souvenirs such as a piece of Astroturf or a piece of the stage curtain.

Another practice that damages property is the traditionally popular pastime of defacing it with graffiti. Prime targets are buildings; walls; train stations; and subway stations, cars, and tunnels. Once done in chalk and relatively harmless, graffiti now is permanently affixed with acrylic spray paints that are difficult or impossible to remove. Gang members announce their presence on a street or in a neighborhood by spraying their symbols on the walls of buildings. In southern California a great deal of graffiti vandalism is done by so-called taggers, groups that compete with each other to mark the greatest number of buildings. Although not in the mainstream of leisure pursuits, inscribing graffiti continues to be a source of enjoyment for young people in both urban and suburban areas.

**Concept Check**

- How might graffiti artists be encouraged to use their skills in ways that do not deface property?

## GAMBLING, LEISURE, AND SPORT

Once satisfied to visit Las Vegas once or twice a year, dedicated gamblers in many parts of the country now scarcely have to leave home to play the slots or try to beat the house at "21." For gamblers on the East Coast there is the glittering array of casinos along the Jersey shore in Atlantic City. Midwesterners are revisiting the days of riverboat gambling: the Mississippi and Missouri rivers are home to an increasing number of riverboat casinos. The cities that host these enterprises benefit from increased tax revenue, but the downside is the rising rate of alcoholism, absenteeism, and even suicide among gamblers. Gambling for some years has been recognized as an addiction, and many gamblers desperate to quit seek the support of Gamblers Anonymous, which follows the principles of Alcoholics Anonymous.

*Las Vegas, one of the gambling meccas, has diversified as a tourist destination and now offers theme park adventures for families.*

Sports betting, although illegal in all states but Nevada and New Jersey, is big business in the United States with a reported $24 billion in circulation.[22] Bookmaking (sports betting) is often linked to organized crime: some "bookies" are themselves organized crime figures, whereas others may seek protection or loans from such figures.

The media bear some responsibility for the increase in sports betting in the United States. Point spreads and predictions of outcomes are commonly given in newspapers and on radio and television. This "handicapping" may actually encourage more people to bet on sports. It has also been suggested that betting on the outcome of a game may lead to point shaving, a practice that has plagued basketball, where it is easier than in other sports to manipulate points. Furthermore, some players may use the payoff for point shaving to support a drug habit.[23]

**Concept Check**

- Identify some consequences of the increase in legalized gambling.

## VIOLENCE IN SPORT AND THE MEDIA

Many sport scientists believe that sport serves as a safety valve through which aggressive feelings can be discharged. Events that have occurred at soccer matches in several countries, however, show that violence often is more rampant among spectators than among players. In Great Britain the media use the term *football hooliganism* to describe the extreme aggressiveness of some soccer fans that has led to injuries and even deaths. In Ankara, Turkey, a shooting battle over the outcome of a soccer match led to the deaths of 42 people. In Buenos Aires, Argentina, burning newspapers thrown from the top of a stadium stairway caused the deaths of 71 persons. In Turin, Italy, 38 persons were crushed to death in a stadium melee. In 1994 a Colombian soccer player was murdered when he returned home after inadvertently kicking a ball into his own goal during a World Cup match against the United States.

Spectator violence in the United States has not reached the level seen in other parts of the world. Nonetheless, injuries and fatalities plague American sports, particularly football. These incidents occur despite the use of sophisticated protective gear such as pads, masks, and helmets.

Another disturbing phenomenon is the rising tide of violence on television and in movies. Increasingly, these media are being blamed for causing violent behavior among viewers, particularly children. In one instance a 5-year-old

*Rodeo clowning is one of the most dangerous and high-risk activities.*

boy was alleged to have torched his family's mobile home in imitation of his television hero, a cartoon character who plays with fire. In another case in which a 15-year-old boy murdered his 85-year-old neighbor, the boy's lawyer tried to show that he was influenced by a murder scene he saw on television a few minutes before committing the crime.

The producers of movies, television shows, and newscasts realize that, the more violence people are exposed to, the more they seemingly become numb to it and the more violence it takes to excite them. (See the Action Guide on p. 282.) This fact explains the escalation of violence on the screen, as producers try to retain existing viewers and capture new ones by offering increasingly violent fare. As noted earlier in the text, excessive violence in the media is coming under increasing scrutiny not only by parents and educators but also by government authorities.

## THE COMMERCIALIZATION OF PUBLIC RECREATION

Leisure and recreation have been part of the North American scene for as long as the continent has been inhabited by human beings. For at least 150 years, leisure and recreation opportunities in the United States and Canada have been provided as a public service through parks and children's playgrounds.

Between 1922 and 1940, public recreation in the United States moved through five stages. First the playground movement became a recreation movement; next it involved both the state and federal governments; then the organization of recreational activities expanded beyond urban centers to rural areas; next public schools began to provide recreational activities; finally, such activities shifted from the quasi-public to the public sector.[24]

With the establishment of Yellowstone as the first national park in 1872, the federal government became involved in providing outdoor recreation opportunities to Americans. The federal government of Canada followed suit, later followed by state and provincial governments.

# ACTION GUIDE

## HOW DO YOU RESPOND TO VIOLENCE?

In today's world it's difficult if not impossible to avoid all incidents of violence, whether in real life, on television, or in the movies. It's also easier than many people think to become so accustomed to some kinds of violence that one stops being excited or horrified by them. By taking the quiz that follows, identify your personal patterns of response to violence.

1. Have you ever attended a spectator event (sport, concert, rally, race) where some fans either became violent or threatened to become violent? _____

2. If so, how did you feel, what if anything did you do, and why did you act (or choose not to act)?

   _____

   _____

3. Have you ever participated in violent behavior at a spectator event? _____

4. If so, why? What happened as a result? If not, why not?

   _____

   _____

5. What is your definition of violence on TV and in the movies?

   _____

   _____

6. Do you tend to like or dislike violence on TV and in the movies? _____

7. In either case, why?

   _____

   _____

8. In what ways, if any, do you think or know you are personally influenced by the violence you see on TV and in the movies?

   _____

   _____

Governments at all levels accepted donations of land and money, but they depended primarily on public funds. In the 1970s, however, some well-publicized tax revolts, particularly the one in California, signaled the unwillingness of many people to pay increasingly high property taxes. As tax revenues dwindled, local and state governments began to look for money from other sources, both public and private. Those unable to obtain adequate funds then began to charge fees for the use of recreational facilities. In 1979 the Heritage Conservation and Recreation Service supported the collection of fees, indicating that the typical citizen is both willing and able to pay the fees.[25] Despite strong opposition, fees continue to be charged and even raised.

The chief argument against charging fees is that public recreation no longer will be public. A second objection is that people who need recreation the most are the least able to pay for it. Many people believe that recreation should be provided as a public service, as are police and fire protection and sanitation. The sad reality is that in many cases public recreation is becoming less public and less inclusive.[4]

## Crowding and Carrying Capacity

Although crowding and carrying capacity are issues that concern large outdoor resources on the national, state, and regional levels, they are being seen in urban recreational sites as well. Carrying capacity addresses the physical aspects of a site (how many persons it can hold); crowding, on the other hand, has a psychological, subjective meaning to the participants. Solutions include imposing carrying capacity limits and zoning certain areas of the site to avoid conflicting use.[25a]

---

*Summing Up*

- Despite progress, leisure is still less accessible to women, minorities, and the underprivileged than to other groups.
- People are living an increasingly sedentary lifestyle dominated by TV viewing.
- High-risk recreational activities appeal to a segment of the population identified as having a "type T" personality that drives them to seek thrills and excitement.
- The increasing effectiveness of contraceptives and the loosening of old moral strictures have caused some people to view sex as recreation. Serious social and health problems are caused by "sex for sale" via pornography, prostitution, X-rated movies, and other means.
- For some, the abuse of alcohol or street drugs has become a leisure pastime. The use of performance-enhancing drugs by athletes has severe emotional and physical consequences.
- Vandalism of recreation and leisure sites is costly and destructive, as is the increasingly popular leisure-time activity of spraying property with graffiti.
- Legalized gambling has brought new revenue to many municipalities and has been blamed for increases in alcoholism, absenteeism, and suicide.
- Spectator violence is a serious problem in some countries, and violence on television and in the movies is the focus of increasing scrutiny by parents, educators, and government authorities.
- Short of funds because of declining tax revenue, some state and local public recreation facilities have started to charge fees to cover their operating costs.
- Outdoor recreation resources are reaching their maximum capacity. There have been attempts to find solutions to crowding in these sites.

## *Using What You've Learned*

1. Interview four people of both sexes and different ages and occupations. Ask them what leisure pursuits, recreational activities, and forms of play they like to engage in. Submit a paper in which you compare their answers.

2. Bring to class four different definitions of *recreation*. Your instructor will lead a discussion of these definitions.

3. Interview four women and four members of minority groups. Find out what barriers, if any, they experience to recreational activities, facilities, or both.

4. Watch the programs on a particular television network for four hours. Write down every incidence of sex or violence that takes place during this time and how long it lasted. Bring your findings to class for a discussion.

5. Interview five people from your community who use local public recreation facilities. Find out their reaction to the charges imposed for use of the facilities. If no charges are imposed, ask the people how they would feel about being charged to use public facilities.

## YOUR  Turn

1 What might be some of the effects on children such as Ramon and Joey of not having a safe, pleasant place to play?

2 If you were the director of recreation in Ramon's city, what steps would you take to try to improve facilities such as the park in his neighborhood? How could you involve members of the community?

3 What kinds of recreational activities might be beneficial to children such as Ramon and Joey? Why?

4 Do you consider Ramon and Joey to be youth at risk? Why or why not?

# REFERENCES

1. Szalai, A. (Ed.), (1972). *The Use of Time: Daily Activities of Urban and Suburban Population in Twelve Countries.* The Hague: Mouton.
2. Ibrahim, H., et al. (1982). Leisure Behavior Among Contemporary Egyptians. *Journal of Leisure Research* 13(2):89–104.
3. Russell, R. (1996). *Pastimes: The Context of Contemporary Leisure.* Madison, WI: Brown & Benchmark, p. 320.
4. Edgington, C., et al. (1996). *Leisure and Life Satisfaction.* Madison, WI: Brown & Benchmark, pp. 402–403.
5. Foley, Jack (1989). *Leisure Rights Policies for Los Angeles Urban Impact Parks.* A paper presented to the People of Parks Conference, Griffith Park.
6. Lawrence, D. (1984). *The Recreation Gap.* Los Angeles: University of Southern California.
7. Marans, R., & Fly, J. (1981). *Recreation and the Quality of Urban Life.* Ann Arbor, MI: Institute of Urban Research, University of Michigan.
8. Bammel, G., & Burrus-Bammel, L.L., (1992). *Human Behavior and Leisure.* Madison, WI: Brown & Benchmark, p. 339.
9. Godby, G. (1997). *Leisure & Leisure Services in the 21st Century.* State College, PA: Venture Publishing, p. 214.
10. Kelly, J.R., & Freysinger, V.J. (2000). *21st Century Leisure: Current Issues.* Boston: Allyn and Bacon, p. 187.
11. Kelly, John (1990). *Leisure.* Englewood Cliffs, NJ: Prentice Hall, pp. 194, 375–376.
12. Brooks, C.M. (Apr 1987). Leisure Time Physical Activity Assessment of American Adults Through an Analysis of Time Diaries Collected in 1981. *Journal of Public Health*, pp. 455–460.
13. Farley, F. (May 1986). The Big T in Personality. *Psychology Today*, pp. 44–50.
14. Straub, William (1982). Sensation Seeking Among High and Low Risk Male Athletes. *Journal of Sport Psychology* 4:246–253.
15. Mills, J. (Mar 1986). Living on the Edge. *Women's Sports and Fitness*, p. 24.
16. Kraus, R. (1990). *Recreation and Leisure in Modern Society.* New York: HarperCollins, pp. 293, 344.
17. Kraus, R. (2000). *Leisure in a Changing America: Trends and Issues for the 21st Century.* Boston: Allyn and Bacon, p. 263.
18. Cosper, R., Okraku, I., & Neuman, B. (1985). Public Drinking in Canada: A National Study of a Leisure Activity. *Society and Leisure* 8(2):709–715.
19. Gross, L. (1983). *How Much Is Too Much: The Effects of Social Drinking.* New York: Random House.
20. Eitzen, D.S., & Sage, G. (1989). *Sociology of North American Sport.* Dubuque, IA: Wm. C. Brown, p. 119.
21. Du Puy, N., & Mermel, V. (1995). *Focus on Nutrition.* St. Louis: Mosby, pp. 12–28.
22. Phillips, J. (1993). *Sociology of Sport.* Boston: Allyn & Bacon, pp. 243–245.
23. Plesser, D., et al. (1986). *Gambling: Crime or Recreation?* Plano, TX: Information Aids.
24. Hjelte, G. (1940). *The Administration of Public Recreation.* New York: Macmillan.
25. Heritage Conservation and Recreation Service (1979). *Fees and Charges Handbook.* Washington, DC: Department of the Interior.
25a. Manning, R., et al. (2000). Crowding in Parks and Outdoor Recreation: A Theoretical and Managerial Analysis. *Journal of Park and Recreation Administration* 18(4): 57-72.

Life is either a daring adventure or nothing. To keep our faces toward change and behave like free spirits in the presence of fate is strength undefeatable.

HELEN KELLER
*Let Us Have Faith*
1940

# The Changing Scene

## CHAPTER 14

THE CHAPTER AT A GLANCE

A major challenge for professionals in the recreation and leisure field is to anticipate and respond constructively to change. In this chapter we examine the potential effect of three changes in society: the Americans with Disabilities Act, the homeless population, and fluctuation in the crime rate. Other societal trends that affect recreation, such as partnerships, enviro-ethics, and changing attitudes toward work, are also discussed. Finally, we examine emerging trends and projections that are relevant to recreation and leisure, emphasizing the need for professionals to take a proactive approach to change.

## Chapter Objectives

*After completing this chapter, you should be able to*

- Explain what is meant by "leisure as a human right."
- Describe the key components of the Americans with Disabilities Act and identify earlier legislation intended to facilitate access by persons with disabilities.
- Discuss the special needs of homeless and unemployed persons and explain how recreation and leisure professionals can help meet those needs.
- Explain the problem of violent crime in contemporary American society and describe the role of recreation and leisure services in rehabilitating persons in penal institutions.
- Describe the purposes and benefits of partnerships of recreation and leisure providers and give examples of successful partnerships.
- Identify key concerns with respect to environmental pollution, dwindling natural resources, threats to wilderness, and threatened and endangered animal species. Describe Aldo Leopold's environmental code of ethics. Explain how recreation and leisure professionals can be leaders in the effort to safeguard the environment.

*Continued*

## A World  of Difference

### WHO HAS TIME FOR LEISURE?

"Okay, guys, hop in quick. We need to get home and have dinner so I can meet Mrs. Kantor for tennis." Naomi Rosen pulls open the van's big door and her three chattering sons clamber in, hauling backpacks and their soccer ball.

"Tennis?" says 10-year-old Aaron. "You're playing tennis tonight?"

"Yes indeed," Naomi replies, glancing in the mirror to be sure the 7-year-old twins, Josh and Michael, have fastened their seatbelts. "I've had to break my last two dates with Mrs. Kantor, but I'm definitely keeping this one. Terri will come over and stay with you while I'm gone, and when I get back maybe we can go for ice cream."

"But Mom," Aaron says, "tonight's our game with Marshfield. We've been practicing all week, and I have to be there. I *have* to. I told you last week, after practice—remember?" A glance at Aaron shows pleading brown eyes and a brow wrinkled in distress. "Anyway, don't you want to see me play?"

Naomi feels like sighing, but she doesn't. As a single parent with a demanding job and three boys to raise, she's increasingly aware that her life has become a high-stress juggling act—job, kids, activities, school, housework—in which relaxation and leisure for her always end up at the bottom of the list. Not until the boys go to visit their father for

a month in California each summer does Naomi feel she can take any time for herself, and even then she spends most of her time doing things such as painting the twins' room or putting up shelves in the garage—tasks she has no chance to do while the boys are at home. She loves her job as a clinical nursing supervisor, but sometimes she just wants to shut out the sights and sounds of human misery and the endless frustrations of dealing with the hospital bureaucracy. As a health care professional, she knows the importance of living a balanced life that includes time for unwinding and enjoying things just for their own sake, yet it's been months since she went to her aerobics class at the Y, the garden that was once her pride and joy is choked with weeds, and now she's faced once again with the prospect of having to call her closest friend, Sheri Kantor, and tell her she has to break their third tennis date in a row.

"Okay," Naomi says to Aaron, who's watching her anxiously. "We'll get you to your game—and of course I want to see you play, soccer hero. Actually," she says, half to herself, "I'd kind of like to get out on the field myself."

As you study this chapter, think about Naomi Rosen's situation and prepare to answer the questions in Your Turn at the end of the chapter.

*Chapter Objectives (cont'd)*

◆ Describe current trends that affect the time people have available for recreation and leisure, and discuss the problems of stress, burnout, and heart disease.

◆ Identify important emerging trends in the workplace, family structure, demographics, and public attitudes and explain how these trends will affect the future demand for recreation and leisure services.

# LEISURE: A HUMAN RIGHT

In the U.S. Constitution our founding fathers declared that the pursuit of happiness is an inalienable right of all citizens. Because engaging in leisure activities can lead to improved health and enhanced self-esteem, these activities clearly contribute to our pursuit of happiness. Unfortunately, many people consider recreation to be simply a reward for hard work, without giving thought to the specific intrinsic and extrinsic benefits they derive from their activities.[1] An important challenge facing recreation professionals, then, is to teach people the well-documented personal, sociocultural, economic, and environmental benefits of recreation.

Unlike entrepreneurs, public agencies cannot simply offer programs for niche markets. Instead they must continually search for ways to provide shelter, transportation, day care, playgrounds, inner-city programs, senior center programs, and outreach programs. Public providers have an obligation to serve the rapidly growing minority cultures in the United States, as well as the migrant population, the homeless, the unemployed, the disabled, substance abusers, persons in penal institutions, and other special populations.

To serve these varied groups, public providers are challenged to develop strong fundraising skills, seek corporate and foundation sponsorships, and form partnerships with other providers. They must seek ways to make their resources available to everyone who needs them. For example, a public recreation center might offer recreation and leisure services during the workday, when attendance otherwise would be low, so that these services can be enjoyed by people with large amounts of discretionary time and by people in need. The growth of the underclass of the poor and uneducated, the burgeoning homeless population, and the ongoing corporate downsizing that continues to cause layoffs are all trends that must be addressed by recreation and leisure professionals who work in the public sector. Many experts believe that people who are not receiving support for constructive use of free time may turn instead to crime.

# Disability: Access and the Law

When the Americans with Disabilities Act (ADA) was signed into law in 1990, a new era began in the quest to integrate people with disabilities into the mainstream of society. Not since passage of the Civil Rights Act of 1964 had such sweeping legislation been enacted to secure the rights of a specific class of persons. Before ADA became law, however, other legislation—the Architectural Barriers Act of 1968, the Rehabilitation Act of 1973, and the Disabilities Education Act of 1974—led the way to improved accessibility and removal of barriers for persons with disabilities.

The Rehabilitation Act of 1973 contains a major provision that prohibits discrimination on the basis of physical or mental handicap on the part of every federally assisted program or activity in the country. Section 504 of the Act states:

> No otherwise qualified handicapped individual in the United States . . . shall, solely by reason of his handicap, be excluded from participation in, be denied the benefits of, or be subjected to discrimination under any program or activity receiving federal financial assistance.[2]

In 1977 a Section 504 regulation was issued to all recipients of funds from the U.S. Department of Health, Education, and Welfare (now the Department of Health and Human Services and the Department of Education), including social service agencies, schools, and hospitals. The regulation provided that the programs of all such entities must be accessible to persons with disabilities. It did not, however, require that every building be accessible.

## The Americans with Disabilities Act

The Americans with Disabilities Act (ADA) picks up where the Rehabilitation Act of 1973 left off by extending access requirements to employers who are not federally funded. ADA also covers access to government facilities and the delivery of services and programs by government agencies. To the nation's over 54 million people with disabilities, ADA represents

an unprecedented mandate to eliminate barriers to independence and productivity. Modeled after the Civil Rights Act of 1964 and Title V of the Rehabilitation Act of 1973, ADA's purpose is to extend to people with disabilities the same rights those earlier acts granted on the basis of race, sex, national origin, and religion. ADA prohibits discrimination on the basis of disability in the private sector and in state and local governments and requires that these entities provide reasonable access to buildings, transportation, and public facilities.

Under the law, persons with disabilities are entitled to equal access to employment, including recruitment, hiring, promotion, and any other benefits and privileges of employment, provided they satisfy the job requirements in terms of education, experience, and skills and provided they are able to perform the essential functions of the job with or without a reasonable accommodation. Such accommodations include modifying existing facilities to make them accessible, acquiring or modifying equipment, restructuring the job, part-time or otherwise modified work schedules, and changing policies unless doing so imposes an undue hardship on the employer. Accessibility also applies to new construction and to the alteration of existing facilities.

### Who Is Disabled?

Under ADA, a person is considered to have a disability if he or she has a mental or physical impairment that substantially restricts a major life activity such as walking, talking, breathing, sitting, standing, or learning. A person also is considered to have a disability if he or she has a record of such an impairment or is perceived or regarded as having an impairment. Family members who need special support in caring for a disabled person also may be entitled to some protections.[3] Persons with temporary conditions are not usually found to have a disability under the law.

### Jurisdiction

Jurisdiction over ADA is divided between the Department of Justice, which enforces the requirement that public facilities make achievable changes to ensure access, and the Equal Employment Opportunity Commission (EEOC), which oversees the portion of the law that bans discriminatory employment practices and requires reasonable accommodations for workers. Although the public access provisions took effect in January 1992, many businesses chose to defer compliance until enforcement procedures imposed on others provided more guidance as to what is required. As a result, thousands of businesses have been sued for failing to make accommodations for disabled persons by altering physical facilities. Confusion, lack of knowledge, absence of specific standards, and lack of enforcement have been cited as reasons that many park areas lack appropriate access. In addition, many organizers, although well intentioned, created separate facilities and programs for disabled persons instead of bringing those persons into the mainstream as the law requires.

### ADA and Recreation

The law requires that all programs, services, and activities of a parks and recreation department be available to persons with disabilities. Agencies also must remove architectural, communication, and transportation barriers and must provide auxiliary aids and services. Among the facilities affected by ADA are municipal and county parks and recreation programs such as senior centers, gymnasiums, fitness centers, golf courses, places of public gathering, and other sites where recreational activity takes place.

Examples of required accommodations are

- ◆ Persons with physical limitations should be able to enter a facility through a front door and should not be forced to use a side or rear door.
- ◆ Inside a building, furniture should be moved or services relocated to provide easy access to facilities.
- ◆ Locker areas must be designed with wide aisles, lockers placed low, and extra-wide benches.
- ◆ Racquetball and tennis courts and gymnasiums should have doors wide enough to accommodate wheelchairs.
- ◆ Lifts should be provided at swimming pools.
- ◆ Auxiliary aids and special equipment should be provided when needed.

For recreation and leisure professionals, ADA compliance begins with evaluation of existing policies, practices, programs, and facilities. It is helpful and appropriate to invite persons with disabilities to serve on planning committees. Changes should be introduced as needed, with the aim of making facilities not only accessible but inviting. Professionals also must educate and train employees so they are prepared to accommodate persons with disabilities. Professionals also are well suited to provide leadership in the community to encourage acceptance and inclusion of persons with disabilities.

Recreation facility planners can obtain helpful input about the needs of persons with disabilities by consulting recreational therapists, who use recreation and leisure to help people with limitations live rewarding lives, and physical therapists, who can offer advice on how to integrate persons with disabilities into programs. Planners also can benefit from consulting representatives of companies that specialize in adaptive recreation equipment for physically challenged persons. Major sources of accessibility criteria for recreation facility planners are outlined in *Minimum Guidelines and Requirements for Accessible Design, Uniform Federal Accessibility Standards* and *The Americans with Disabilities Act Accessibility Guidelines* (see Appendix H for more information). Agencies also must comply with any state or local building code whose provisions exceed federal requirements.

## Leisure Services for the Homeless and Unemployed

Homelessness is described by the Department of Housing and Urban Development as a "condition of being without a regular dwelling place. This person or family lives on the streets, tries to find a public or private shelter at night, or sleeps in a makeshift dwelling such as a car or train station."[4] Homeless people are found in virtually every American community. Some estimates suggest that as many as 2.5 million persons may be living on the streets, with perhaps one half to two thirds of them being drug abusers or mentally ill.[5] The majority of the homeless are male, and they are more likely to be white than black or Hispanic.[4] Some of the homeless are persons with severe mental impairments who have been discharged from institutions and left without community services; others are veterans, many with physical disabilities, the poor, and the elderly. Recent years have seen even greater diversity in the homeless population. Unemployed persons, middle-aged homemakers,

younger people, and children are added to the homeless statistics each year. Most single-parent homeless families are headed by women. In many cases, divorce has left these women and their children without support.[6]

Research shows that Americans as a whole are seriously concerned about the increasing numbers of homeless persons. In one survey, 84% of the respondents believed the homeless could be helped to re-enter society, and 82% percent said homeless persons should not be prohibited from entering public places such as libraries, parks, and mass transit systems.[6] Often lacking family or community support, homeless people face alienation and loneliness that can be helped and even overcome through the intervention and support of leisure service providers. One expert identifies steps providers can take to improve the condition of the homeless:[4]

- Integrate homeless persons into community recreation as equal participants
- Develop and participate in task forces that help define the responsibility of the recreation and leisure profession in a comprehensive delivery system
- Develop links that cover the full range of services for the homeless
- Collaborate with other professions in addressing illiteracy, stress, family problems, lack of independent living skills, and social isolation
- Become part of a local referral network to identify homeless persons and refer them to appropriate services

How can recreational opportunities help the homeless and the unemployed? Persons in these situations have no fixed structure of external obligations and therefore have an abundance of time they have difficulty filling. As a result they often become withdrawn, apathetic, or depressed. Recreation services help them overcome social isolation and develop self-awareness, enhanced self-esteem, a sense of community, and appropriate social behavior.[4] Integrated recreation programs and community outreach efforts extended to homeless shelters, welfare hotels, hospital-based day treatment programs, and drop-in centers can help homeless and unemployed people develop trust, express themselves, alleviate stress, set priorities and goals, and build self-confidence.

## Correctional Recreation and Rehabilitation

From 1950 to 1990, the number of guns on our streets increased from 54 million to 201 million. Incidents of violent crime jumped 371% between 1960 and 1992, with more youth arrested for crimes at younger ages.[7] Statistics released in 1994 showed that over 80% of our country's population could expect to become victims of violent crime at least once during their lifetime.[8] As a result, many Americans feel cheated of their ability to move about freely without fear.[9] An increasing number of individuals, communities, and governments are adopting get-tough policies, strong new anti-crime programs, longer prison sentences, fewer paroles, and fewer frills for prisoners.

Perhaps as a direct result, crime rates began to drop. According to the crime victimization survey developed by the Bureau of Justice, the largest decreases have been among less-serious crimes.[10] Experts advance many theories to explain violent crime.[11] They blame unstable home and neighborhood environments that create stress and promote violence, crack and cocaine use, availability of weapons, layoffs and unemployment among unskilled workers, single-parent families, and sharply rising spouse and child abuse. Countering these influences are citizen advocates, public policy-makers, and professionals who provide recreational services that diminish the likelihood of crime. However, continuing public debate reveals serious disagreements among policy-makers, legislators, and advocates about which strategies are effective in reducing crime. While most agree that preventing crime is preferable to bearing the high social and economic costs of dealing with it after the fact, a consensus has not been reached on when and how to invest in prevention through social strategies.[12]

One crime expert credits several factors for the improved climate: expanded community policing efforts, increased use of incarceration, and more effective youth crime-prevention programs.[10] Despite mounting evidence of the benefits of recreation programs, one of the main challenges we continue to face is the need to prove that wholesome recreational activities prevent or reduce crime.[12] Midnight basketball, for example, has taken thousands of young people off the streets and has placed them in healthy, productive environments.[13] NRPA documents 21 initiatives that explain why public recreation programs successfully reduce crime, gang involvement, and substance abuse. However, more statistics and data are needed to continue to generate revenue to keep crime-prevention programs alive.

### Need for Recreation and Leisure

Now more than ever, correctional facilities must offer prisoners rehabilitation programs that truly work. As part of such an effort, appropriately structured recreation and leisure services do make a difference. As one member of Project CULTURE (Constructive Use of Leisure Time Under Restricted Environments) observed, "one of the reasons people are in prison is because they fail to use their leisure constructively and instead use it destructively."[14]

Initially, leisure experiences were included in correctional rehabilitation programs only to serve as an outlet for inmates' tension, frustration, and anger. Over time, however, it has become clear that incarcerated persons need appropriate guidance to help them make constructive use of their free time. Without leisure counseling, recreation programs for inmates may be either ineffective or actually destructive. As one criminal justice educator commented, "Prisoners come in, pump iron, and go out stronger than ever, often committing the same crimes." Moreover, taxpayers increasingly are opposed to subsidizing "health clubs" for inmate body building. They want programs

that deter crime rather than indirectly promoting it.[15]

### Restructuring Time with Leisure

Using leisure as a restructuring device requires the participant to assess his or her needs and goals. This process begins with leisure education. The inmate first learns about available options and how these options enhance the quality of life. In the second step the inmate is guided in clarifying personal values and defining his or her identity. The third step involves testing and counseling. Here the inmate is guided to identify personal needs, likes, and dislikes and then is encouraged to explore ways to use free time in balanced and satisfying leisure activities. Finally, the inmate is given opportunities to acquire new skills.[16] Inmates can learn basic skills through a wide range of programs and activities, including library use; physical activity; classes in crafts, drama, and social etiquette; and rehabilitative services such as art and music therapy and therapeutic recreation.

### Programs for Juvenile Offenders

Community-based programs for juvenile offenders are proving to be successful in combating delinquency. In Detroit, for example, the recreation and parks department and the county juvenile court formed a partnership called the Detroit Youth Restitution Program. Its purpose is to discourage young people 14 to 17 years of age from using free time destructively by guiding them in redirecting their lives, family relationships, and future prospects. To make restitution for their infractions, offenders are assigned to community service projects in the city recreation department. They also participate in leisure counseling; family support activities; seminars on drug abuse, teen sexuality, college and career planning, mental health, and self-motivation; and tutoring in basic study skills. Bringing a new dimension to their lives, the program has retained 80% of the teens in center activities after they have met their community service obligation. Even more impressive, the recidivism rate among participants is only 3%.[17]

The success of the Detroit program and others like it demonstrates the profound impact that leisure activities can have on at-risk youth when coupled with appropriate counseling. In 1994 the then chairman of the House of Representatives Natural Resources Committee's National Parks, Forests, and Public Lands Panel reported that urban recreation and sports programs are a proven commonsense, cost-effective means of preventing crime and delinquency. Not surprisingly, studies show that crime tends to be higher in areas that have no parks or recreation facilities. In response to these findings, a conservation group in San Francisco called The Trust bought 1,000 properties to protect for future use as parks and recreation areas for inner-city residents.[18]

### Concept Check

- Explain how legislation that asserts the rights of disabled persons affects the delivery of recreation and leisure services.
- Describe problems faced by homeless and unemployed persons and explain how these persons can benefit from recreation and leisure services.
- How can leisure counseling benefit both incarcerated persons and society as a whole?

## TRENDS IN LEISURE

The term *trend* has several meanings. It is a prevailing tendency or inclination, a line of development, and the general movement in the course of time of a statistically detectable change. *Trend* also is popularly defined as a current style or preference. Recreation and leisure professionals must observe and study trends carefully so they can develop intelligent, proactive strategies that will contribute to a better future. As we have learned throughout this text, professionals also must understand the needs, traditions, and characteristics of an increasingly diverse population. To heighten the challenge of this task, the nature,

magnitude, and pace of change today are unprecedented in our history.

In this section we examine three significant trends and learn how they relate to recreation and leisure. We then offer some projections about the future of recreation and leisure based on specific trends.

### Partnerships

The importance of leisure in American life has grown, and the public demand for leisure programs and services has both increased and broadened. To respond constructively to this demand, recreation and leisure professionals must find ways to reach all segments of the population with meaningful and cost-effective programming. One way that is proving both economical and effective is forming partnerships with other agencies to deliver services.

Through joint efforts it is possible to meet goals that otherwise would be unattainable and to reach more members of the community than otherwise would be served. By forming partnerships with other community agencies, recreation and leisure service providers can strengthen their program offerings and expand their user base. Partnerships reduce duplication of effort and allow more specialization. Goals, risks, and rewards all are shared, and the community's quality of life and economic vitality are enhanced. Shared resources and facilities save money and prevent environmental damage from unnecessary construction. A partnership also can work to preserve and protect landscapes and sites of cultural significance and to build trails and greenways. Several successful partnerships are discussed next.

The Bay Area Ridge Trail Council in San Francisco provides an excellent model for how a regional goal can be accomplished through public-private teamwork. For more than 30 years, residents in counties that surround the San Francisco Bay envisioned a trail around the bay. After several public agencies, private nonprofit groups, and interested citizens formed a partnership, the dream began to unfold. Within four years a large section of the trail was dedicated. The Trail Council received funding through a federal appropriation administered by the National Park Service Rivers and Trails Conservation Assistance Program. Additional support was provided by a substantial grant from a local foundation, and donations from local corporations support specific projects to keep the dream alive.[19]

At the national level, the Partnership for the National Trails System (PFNTS) is emerging as an effective force in assisting public and private partners in the preservation, development, commemoration, and promotion of the National Trails System. By representing the collective interests of the organizations of trail volunteers such as the Santa Fe Trail Association, who cooperate with federal agencies, the PFNTS gives the organizations a forum to discuss shared issues. It also coordinates communication among the trail organizers, promotes support for the National Trails System, and organizes leadership and other training programs that enable the volunteers and staffs of the member organizations to work more efficiently on behalf of their respective trails. Through coordinated efforts in the partnership, annual appropriation from Congress has increased by several million dollars, with specific yearly funding for almost all 22 trails.[20,21]

Another example of a successful partnership is one formed by agencies in Tucson, Arizona. Recognizing the complexity of local social issues, the city government brought together four agencies—recreation, public housing, social services, and police—in a program whose goal is to increase community involvement in social issues and to provide recreation programming that will help eliminate drug dealing in a high-risk area of the inner city. Each agency contributes its expertise and commitment to help resolve the problem.[22] Working together through the partnership, the agencies are encouraging community involvement and enhancing local quality of life in ways that would be impossible without teamwork.

The U.S. Forest Service has formed partnerships with groups in many states to inform Americans about the recreational opportunities in our national forests, many of which are just a day's drive from home.[23] In the Tonto National Forest in Arizona, for example, volunteer partners are making recreation areas more accessible to people with disabilities, children, and the elderly. In Alaska, Forest Service interpreters are paid by private cruise lines to provide a full range of information about natural resources.

## Enviro-Ethics

As we move into the 21st century, both our nation and the world must develop creative strategies to deal with the twin challenges of population expansion and depletion of natural resources. Perhaps no profession is better suited than recreation and leisure to promote environmental awareness. Once on the fringe, environmental issues are now a leading concern of recreation and leisure professionals. When national park employees were asked to rank current issues and concerns in order of importance, they ranked environmental threats first and the impact of visitors second.[24]

Environmental threats are all too common and can be seen in national parks throughout the country.[25] Efforts are being made to save the polluted Florida Everglades from the flow

*Seaway Trail, incorporated partners with local organizations along the 454-mile National Scenic Byway which is primarily in New York.*

of water tainted with phosphorus-containing fertilizer from Lake Okeechobee. Olympic National Park in Washington is bordered by a line of clear-cut forests with topsoil runoffs that clog essential spawning beds for trout and salmon. In California's Sequoia National Park, brochures warn hikers to avoid strenuous exercise throughout the summer months because of hazardous air pollution. The Grand Canyon is affected by air and noise pollution, and fluctuating releases of water from the Glen Canyon Dam are eroding the canyon floor. The Great Smoky Mountains National Park in Tennessee shows signs of foliage injury and growth suppression from ozone. The "smoke" is now actually a haze of natural hydrocarbons and water vapors interacting with the sunlight above the humid forest. Highway construction, proposed dams, and gravel mining threaten Petroglyph National Monument in New Mexico, Zion National Park in Utah, and Sleeping Bear Dunes National Lakeshore in Michigan.

The first Earth Day was held in 1970 to call attention to worldwide environmental concerns. Long before that, however, thoughtful scholars were reflecting on the challenges of humankind's interaction with nature.

Conservation philosopher Aldo Leopold, father of modern game management and promoter of wilderness preservation, proposed

*A balance between immediate and long term needs is necessary in order to wisely use natural resources.*

that everyone extend his or her concept of ethics to include the natural world by calling for a "land ethic," or set of attitudes, to lessen the degree of strife between humans and nature. In his best-known work, *A Sand County Almanac,*[26] published in 1949, he cautioned that there was "as yet no ethic dealing with man's relation to the land and to the animals and plants which grow upon it . . . . The land-relation is still strictly economic, entailing privileges but not obligations." Leopold urged humans to seek harmony with nature by examining environmental questions ethically and aesthetically, advising, "A thing is right when it tends to preserve the integrity, stability, and beauty of the biotic community. It is wrong when it tends otherwise."[26]

If we consider the plight of endangered species, we may gain some perspective on why environmental conscience is appropriate. In fact, all other environmental problems might pale beside the ongoing crisis of extinction, in which fully a third of the Earth's species could vanish forever within the next two decades.[27]

Aside from any altruistic desire to help save species, we must realize that plants and animals have important uses, known and unknown, in the fields of science, medicine, agriculture, and industry. Certainly species that face extinction because of environmental threats can warn humans that they, too, may be endangered by such threats. In an unprecedented move that environmentalists hailed as a remarkable political and economic innovation, negotiators from around the word agreed on a global-warming pact that they would take back to their governments for ratification. The 1997 pact would legally obligate industrialized countries to cut emissions of industrial gases that scientists say are warming the Earth's atmosphere, a phenomenon that many believe is causing irreparable harm to the environment.[28]

An environmental code of ethics, as Aldo Leopold suggested, places limits on individuals to promote the well-being of society and the natural world. Recreational activities, for example, are personal choices that affect the environment to a greater or lesser degree, depending on the nature of the terrain, the activity, the participants, and the equipment used. For example, many people oppose the use of all-terrain vehicles (ATVs) and snowmobiles because of the air and noise pollution they cause. The Closer Look box at right describes one country's approach to creating an environmentally friendly venue for the Winter Olympics.

## The Environment and the Leisure Professional

An environmental ethic demands a world view that encourages certain behavior for the benefit of others. U.S. industries that clean the air, water, and land resources employ nearly 3.5 million people, and environmental protection laws actually boost the nation's economy by encouraging companies to invest in innovative technology for which world demand is growing.[29] Ultimately, however, adoption of and adherence to an effective environmental ethic will depend on the commitment of individuals.

Recreation and leisure professionals today are called on to be stewards of nature. Those who manage natural resources must help achieve balance between preservation and enjoyment. They can use their knowledge and training to teach others to tread lightly by applying the no-trace ethic (see Appendix I). They can protect natural resources by encouraging the use of sites other than the best-known parks and recreation sites and by explaining the benefits of using sites in the off-peak seasons. Professionals can encourage people to pursue healthy recreational activities that do not place an undue burden on the natural environment and to find appropriate locations for activities that have more detrimental effects. They should consider the environmental impact of construction and facility development and make recommendations as appropriate. Recreation and leisure professionals also

### A CLOSER LOOK

#### NORWAY'S EARTH-FRIENDLY OLYMPICS

When the Norwegians were planning the 1994 Winter Olympics, they saw it as an opportunity to promote the values of environmentalism. Seeking to minimize environmental impact to the greatest extent possible, they built unobtrusive facilities that blended harmoniously with the natural surroundings. One planned facility was shifted to a new site to save a wetland sanctuary. A mountain was rebuilt to hide a hockey rink inside, the bobsled and luge tracks were designed to run through forest land but not to be seen from the highway below, the ski jumps were fitted into the natural rocky contours of the mountain, and new technology was used to make all facilities 30% more energy efficient.

In addition, plates used for food were designed to be recycled into plant and animal feed; the Olympic torch burned with ethanol, a renewable energy source made by local potato farmers; the number of billboards was restricted to prevent visual pollution; and contractors were fined $7,000 for needlessly chopping down a tree. At the close of the games, Norway's message to future sponsoring nations was to follow its lead and do better. Other nations are responding positively to Norway's impressive example, and some are eagerly testing these innovations, attracting bright economic prospects in response to their environmentally sensitive investments.

can support and help influence important environmental decisions that can bring about a better future for all species.

## Leisure and Time

We should be able not only to work well, but to use leisure well, for the first principle of all action is leisure. Both are required, but leisure is better than work and is its end.

This is how Greek philosopher Aristotle described the relationship between work and leisure.[30] Workers today seem to be caught in a struggle between popular portrayals of "the good life" and economic realities that require them to work extra hours or even take a second job. Surveys indicate that an ever-increasing number of American workers want to devote less time to work and more time to family, community, and fun. One scholar reports, however, that, while most people want to work less, they will do so only if they think they can afford it. A U.S. News/Bozell survey shows that only 17% of Americans polled, including 20% of the managers, say they are willing to take a 5% pay cut in exchange for a 5% cut in work hours. Even so, a cultural shift may be in the making. The same survey reveals that 30% of respondents, including 46% of the managers, say they have seriously considered cutting back on hours. Another 30% believe that they are likely to take this option in the next decade. Of these, 54%, including 76% of the managers, say it will happen because they will personally take steps to cut their hours. In addition, the Opinion Research Corporation indicates that 49% of Americans today, compared with only 28% in 1986, say that society places too much emphasis on work and does not give enough attention to leisure.[31]

As a result of automation and labor-saving technology, the American workweek became shorter over several decades. One set of statistics indicated that weekly hours of work declined approximately 35% from 1850 to 1930. A continual decline at this rate would have reduced the workweek to 42 hours in 1959, 40 hours in 1979, and 37 hours by the year 2000. Another study's projections, if fulfilled, would have reduced the workweek to 28 hours by the year 2000.[32] Furthermore, experts testifying before Congress in 1967 said that by 1985 people could be working 22 to 27 hours per week, working 27 weeks a year, or retiring at age 38.[33]

Partly because of America's shift into a post-industrial economy and partly because of significant changes in social values and behavior, these optimistic projections have not been achieved.

The 1997 Steelcase Workplace Index reports that nearly half of workers surveyed say they are working more hours than they did five years ago.[34] Robert Reich, former Secretary of Labor in the Clinton administration, commented, "For the last 15 years, more and more Americans have been earning less and working harder."[35] (Raise your own work consciousness by completing the exercise in the Action Guide box on p. 299). The Closer Look box on p. 300 describes the newest wrinkle in the American work ethic: workaholics.

After decades of steady decline in the length of the workweek, one expert believes, people simply failed to notice the gradual increase in work time that began in the 1940s and continued until leisure time for the average American worker was only 16.5 hours per week. In addition, the decade of the 1980s saw workers lose 3.5 days per year of vacation time, holidays, and other paid absences, reversing 30 years of progress in terms of paid time off.[36]

A study conducted by Primark Decision Economics shows that the average U.S. worker receives 11.37 days a year in paid vacation, a steady decline from 12.17 days in 1987. Indeed, the amount of vacation time available to American workers compares unfavorably with that in most other advanced countries. America is also the only major industrialized nation in which vacation time is a reward for seniority rather than a basic job benefit.[37]

### Looking Ahead

The trend toward shrinking vacation time is only expected to gather momentum, even though workplace psychologists warn that reduced vacation time is a recipe for a national case of job burnout.[37] A poll of American workers revealed that 40% of respondents felt stress and tension at the end of each day,[38] and throughout the 1990s Americans consistently ranked their jobs as the number one source of stress in their lives.[39] One expert reports that stress is much higher in occupations in which employees must work overtime, and too much

# ACTION GUIDE

## CHECKING OUT THE WORK ETHIC

As a college student, you may be working part-time or even full-time, or you may do so over breaks and holidays. If you do work, you can respond to the following questions yourself; if you're not currently working, ask a friend who does work to take the quiz.

1. What job do you hold? Briefly describe the workplace and your duties.

   _____

   _____

2. What were your reasons for taking this job?

   _____

   _____

3. How many hours a week do you work? _____ Do you regularly work nights and/or weekends? (Specify) _____

4. What is your weekly salary or hourly rate of pay? _____

5. What are the advantages to you of working this job?

   _____

   _____

6. How are the duties of the job and your hours of work affecting your life in terms of
   (a) School and studies
   (b) Physical health (diet, exercise, sleep/rest)
   (c) Mental and emotional well-being
   (d) Social life
   (e) Recreation and leisure (sports, hobbies, indoor and outdoor activities)

   _____

   _____

   _____

   _____

   _____

Of all the forms of compulsive behavior, the most accepted—and even encouraged—is compulsive overworking. People who are obsessed by their jobs are called *workaholics.* Although most workaholics say they value their families above all else, they continue to neglect spouses and children and fail to meet their own physical, social, and spiritual needs. They frequently cite the demands placed on them by their jobs as valid reasons for their addiction.

The problem of addiction to work among Americans is so severe that in 1983 a self-help group called Workaholics Anonymous was established, based on the 12-step program created by Alcoholics Anonymous. Also formed was a companion group, Work-Anon, for people who have relationships with workaholics. Workaholics Anonymous recommends the following steps to recovery: listen, set priorities, substitute, underschedule, play, concentrate, pace, relax, accept, ask, meet, telephone, balance, serve, and live in the now.

overtime work causes stress in the family.[40] Job stress harms physical and mental well-being and contributes to dozens of health problems. Statistics indicate that job stress costs the United States at least $200 billion a year in the form of stress-related absenteeism, lowered productivity, increased compensation claims, health insurance, and direct medical expenses.[39]

Besides working longer hours, Americans are also expected to retire later. After a century of retiring earlier and earlier, retirement ages are expected to creep back up. Between 1995 and 1997, the number of workers ages 55 to 64 rose about 400,000 more than predicted. The trend toward later retirement is expected to continue because of higher eligibility ages, lengthening life span, and anxiety about adequate savings. One researcher found that more men plan for retirement than women, and they expect to retire earlier, between the ages of 61 and 64. Women, in comparison, expect to be nearly 65 before they retire.[41] A poll taken by the Employee Benefit Research Institute indicates that two thirds of Americans would like to retire before age 65, but 72% of them plan to work after retirement.[42]

**Women in the workforce.** As the number of women in the workforce continues to increase, employers will need to accommodate their concerns about flexible hours and child care. In 1950 about one in three women participated in the labor force. By 1998 nearly three in five women were in the labor force. A PBS poll shows that 48% of mothers say that finding a job with a flexible schedule is a problem.[43]

**Flextime.** Many companies offer *flextime* so employees can choose their hours of work, usually based on a schedule of "core hours." For example, if core hours are 9:00 A.M. to 5:00 P.M., flextime hours might run from 6:00 A.M. to 7:00 P.M. One employee might start the workday at 6:30 A.M. and leave at 2:30 P.M., whereas another might begin at 10:00 A.M. and leave at 6:00 P.M..

**Flexplace.** As computer technology advances, more companies are discovering the benefits of *flexplace,* an option that lets certain employees work at home and exchange data with the office via modem. The company saves overhead and benefits from the increased productivity that results when employees can spend more time working and less time commuting, socializing, and "dressing for success." Employees benefit from the reduced stress and tension, from the security of their home environment, and from the freedom from workplace constraints.

**Leaves of absence.** Maternity leave, paternity leave, and time off to care for elderly parents are helping many employees lead more balanced lives. Some experts recommend that employers offer employees the option of being paid for overtime not in money but in extra vacation time. Having this choice would help employees gain greater control over their circumstances and would take some of the sting out of mandatory overtime. Other organizations are offering sabbaticals to their employees. In a survey of its members, the Society for Human Resource Management found that 23% of companies offer unpaid sabbaticals and 5% offer paid sabbaticals.[44]

## How Will We Use Leisure?

The question for the future is, If more free time becomes available, how will people use it? Given the statistics we have seen thus far, the likely answer is that most people would use the time to be with their families and to explore new personal, social, and cultural vistas. For many people, however, more free time poses problems. They may not realize that what they do during free time can make them happier, healthier, wiser, more tolerant, and less isolated.[45] People must learn about the leisure options available to them and how to use leisure time for their greatest benefit and enjoyment.

Leisure counselors help people learn wholesome ways to use their free time. For example, television viewing, one of Americans' most popular leisure pursuits, has become so routine that, according to one expert, most people no longer think of it as a true leisure pastime.[46] These people and others often need to be led back to family rituals and dinners; introduced to new hobbies and classes; encouraged to exercise; persuaded to participate in arts-related activities that stimulate intuition and creativity; or simply shown how to relax, meditate, and have fun.

## The Future of Recreation and Leisure

Overworked and overstressed as they may be, research shows that Americans spend more than $462 billion a year in the leisure market.[47] A *Wall Street Journal* survey provides valuable information on current and future trends in leisure and recreation.[48] The survey shows that Americans have the following goals:

*Enjoying a tropical sunset may relieve work stress.*

| | |
|---|---|
| Spend time with family and friends | 77% |
| Improve intellectually, emotionally, or physically | 74% |
| Have free time to spend any way desired | 66% |
| Save money | 61% |
| Make money | 61% |
| Travel or pursue hobbies or personal interests | 59% |

The results of this survey might indicate that Americans are turning away from materialism and toward simpler pleasures. Although many wish to make and save money, they also want to spend money on travel and hobbies. Because

*Zoos, aquariums, and parks are becoming environmental education centers.*

having free time outranks earning or saving money, Americans may be seeking a more balanced life that allows time to enjoy leisure pursuits. The desire for balance also is reflected in the wish to improve intellectually, emotionally, or physically. Participating in activities in natural settings might help people achieve their goals and enable them to spend more time with family and friends.

As we have learned in this text, statistics show that our society is aging and becoming more diverse, crime is an ever-present concern, the environment and wildlife need concern and protection, and most working Americans want more free time. Without question, flexible, imaginative, enjoyable, and wholesome recreation programs can greatly enhance the balance and richness of our society.

## Summing Up

- Both public and private providers of recreation and leisure services are required to address the needs of an increasingly diverse population that, in addition to persons of various ethnicities, includes persons with mental and/or physical disabilities, homeless and unemployed persons, persons in correctional facilities, and juvenile offenders.

- The formation of partnerships (public-private, public-public, or private-private) among providers and agencies permits the development of creative and cost-effective solutions to community challenges such as drugs, crime, and gang activity. Other such partnerships can achieve environment-oriented goals, such as building trails, or share valuable information about nature and wildlife.

- Environmental threats to our nation's natural resources are on the increase. Many national parks are experiencing air, water, and noise pollution, disruption of wildlife habitats, and damage from overbuilding.

- According to one prediction, fully one third of the Earth's living species could be extinct by the year 2020. Preservation of species is vital to maintaining ecological balance and helps humankind because many plants and animals have important uses in science, medicine, agriculture, and industry.

- Recreation and leisure professionals are called on to be stewards of nature and to teach others respect for our environment.

- Many Americans appear to be working more, enjoying it less, and expressing the need and desire for more leisure time. For respondents to one survey, the desire to improve oneself intellectually, emotionally, or physically outranked by 13 percentage points the desires to make and save money.

- Options such as flextime, flexplace, and job sharing are some of the creative ways employers are responding to workers' needs for more control over their lives and more hours to spend with family and in leisure activities.

- As Americans seek to restore balance and meaning to their lives, recreation and leisure professionals will play a key role in helping people identify interests and needs and find recreation and leisure pursuits that promote physical, emotional, and spiritual well-being.

## *Using What You've Learned*

1. Identify a program or facility that accommodates one of the special needs you learned about in this chapter. Describe the program or facility. What is its goal or purpose? Is the program or facility successful? On what facts or observations do you base your opinion?

2. Does your community have an environmental problem that affects, or is affected by, leisure activities? Describe the problem. Explain what efforts have been made to correct the problem or minimize its impact. What recommendations would you make to individuals or the community in this situation? Why?

3. Select two people, one of each sex, who are steadily employed. One person should be in his or her thirties, the other in his or her fifties. Ask both persons what job they hold, how long they have had the job, what hours they customarily work, and how working this job affects their mental, emotional, and physical health. Ask both persons to state their personal work ethic, and compare and contrast the statements. Ask both persons whether they would prefer more time off or a higher salary, and why.

## YOUR  Turn

1  Identify the key stressors in Naomi Rosen's life.
2  How might these stressors be affecting her emotionally and physically?
3  What steps can she take to reduce job burnout and restore some balance to her life while still continuing to fulfill her responsibilities as a mother and a professional?
4  How might Naomi benefit from consulting with a leisure counselor?

## REFERENCES

1. Cappel, M.L. (1997–1998) The Benefits of Recreation. *California Association for Health, Physical Education, Recreation and Dance,* p. 3.

2. U.S. Department of Health, Education and Welfare (July 1977). *Section 504 of the Rehabilitation Act of 1973 Fact Sheet.* Washington, DC: U.S. Government Printing Office, p. 2.

3. Rubin, P. (Sept 1993). *The ADA and Criminal Justice: An Overview.* Washington, DC: U.S. Department of Justice, pp. 1–2.

4. Kunstler, R. (1992). Forging the Human Connection: Leisure Services for the Homeless. *Parks & Recreation* 27(3):43.

5. Sessoms, D., & Orthner, D. (1992). Our Growing Invisible Population. *Parks & Recreation* 27(8):64.

6. Clement, M. (January 9, 1994). What Americans Say About the Homeless. *Parade,* pp. 4, 5, 42.

7. Minerbrook, S. (1994). A Generation of Stone Killers. *U.S. News & World Report* 116(2):24, 33.

8. Collins, S. (1994). Cost of Crime: $674 Billion. *U.S. News & World Report* 116(2):40.

9. Gest, T., Witkin, G., Hetter, K., & Wright, A. (1994). Violence in America. *U.S. News & World Report* 116(2):24.

10. Kim, E. (November 16, 1997). U.S. Violent Crime Rate Fell in 1996, Justice Survey Finds. *The San Diego Union-Tribune,* p. A-2.

11. Zuckerman, M. (1994). War on Crime, by the Numbers. *U.S. News & World Report* 116(2):68.

12. Tice, R.D. (Mar. 1996) Programs That Work! *Parks & Recreation* 31(3):2.

13. Mainella, F. (Oct 1996). The Benefits Are Endless. *Parks & Recreation* 31(10):2..

14. Nicolai, S. (1981). Rehabilitation and Leisure in Prisons. *JOPERD* 52(4):33.

15. Hull, J. (1994). Building a Better Thug? *Time* 143(15):47.

16. McCall, G. (1981). Leisure Restructuring. *JOPERD* 52(4):38–39.

17. Kirchbaum, D., & Alston, M. (1991). Youth Restitution and Recreation: A Successful Mix. *Parks & Recreation* 26(3):43-45.

18. Report Says More Parks and Recreation Reduce Crime. (June 9, 1994). *Escondido Times-Advocate*, p. A-7.

19. Rice, B., & McNally, M. (1992). The Bay Area Ridge Trail Council: A Model in Community Recreation. *Trends* 29(2):18-22.

20. Marshall, R. (Winter 1998). Partnership Key to Succes of National Trails. *Pathways Across America*, pp. 2, 11.

21. _____. (April 15, 1997). *Partnership for the National Trails System*, pp. 1–2.

22. McCormick, S. (1991). Social Change = The Future. *Parks & Recreation* 26(3):33–34.

23. *America's Great Outdoors* (1988). Washington, DC: Forest Service and American Forestry Association, USDA Program Aid 1423.

24. Taylor, J., & Thompson, J. (January 2, 1994). Park Service Needs to Emulate Its Zealous Past. *The San Diego Union-Tribune*, p. F5.

25. Satchell, M. (July 21, 1997). Parks in Peril. *U.S. News & World Report* 122(8):24.

26. Leopold, A. (1949). *A Sand County Almanac.* New York: Oxford University Press, pp. 224–225.

27. Fetter, T. (2001). Message from the President. *ZooNooz* 74(6):6..

28. Watson, T., & Weisman, J. (July 16, 2001). 6 Ways to Combat Global Warming. *USA Today*, pp. 1A-2A.

29. Cannon, F. (June/July 1993). Economic Growth and the Environment. *Economic and Business Outlook*, p. 1.

30. VanHooses, W., & Worth, M. (1982). *Adulthood in the Lifecycle.* Dubuque, IA: Wm. C. Brown Publishers, p. 172.

31. Saltzman, A. (October 27, 1997). When Less Is More. *U.S. News & World Report* 123(16):79–84.

32. Lance, L. (1988). Leisure Time of U.S. Adults—A Look into the Future. *JOPERD* 59(4):43.

33. Gibbs, N. (April 24, 1989). How America Has Run Out of Time. *Time* 133 (17):58-59.

34. Armour, S. (December 29, 1997). Tight Job Market Squeezes Workers' Time with Kids. *USA Today*, p. 1B.

35. We Can Save Jobs (May 21, 1995). *Parade*, p. 4.

36. Schor, J. (1991). *The Overworked American.* New York: HarperCollins, p. 32.

37. Kinssley, M. (1990). You Must Be Very Busy. *Time* 136 (8):82.

37a. Neuborne, E. (March 21, 1997). Firms Today Less Willing to Pay for Play. *USA Today*. p. 1B.

38. Winik, L. (July 11, 1999). Let Go Of Stress. *Parade Magazine*, p. 4.

39. Hales, D., & Hales, R. (March 17, 1996). You Can Beat Stress on the Job. *Parade*, pp. 22–24.

40. Sixel, L. (February 23, 1998). For Many Workers Reward of Overtime Can Be Bittersweet. *The San Diego Union-Tribune*, p. C-2.

41. _____. (February 23, 1998). Planning for Retirement. *The San Diego Union-Tribune*, p. C-1.

42. Samuelson, R. (November 11, 1997). Working Longer and Retiring Later. *San Diego Union-Tribune*, P. B-7.

43. Peterson, K. (May 9, 1997). Mothers Drawing the Most Fulfillment for Family Life. *USA Today*, p. 4D.

44. Ravo, N. (November 17, 1997). Time Well Spent. *New York Times News.*

45. Weissinger, E. (1994). Recent Studies About Boredom During Free Time. *Parks & Recreation* 29(3):33.

46. Shrieves, L. (1994). Is Leisure-Time Problem Having Too Many Choices? *The San Diego Union-Tribune*, p. D-7.

47. _____. (2000). *U.S. Leisure Spending thru 1997.* Big Picture Publ. Inc. www.resonator.com/stad/content/spending.htm.

48. "Goals of the 90s," *Health Net News*, vol. 5, no. 1, Van Nuys, CA: Health Net, 1993.

# APPENDIX A
# Playground Safety Tools

For information on the necessary playground safety tools:

ASTM--F1487-97
*Standard Consumer Safety Performance Specification for Playground Equipment for Public Use*
American Society of Testing and Materials (ASTM)
100 Bar Harbor Dr
West Conshohocken, PA 19428-2959
www.astm.org

*Handbook for Public Playground Safety*
U.S. Consumer Product Safety Commission (CPSC)
Washington, DC 20207-0001

National Playground Safety Institute
National Recreation and Park Association (NRPA)
22377 Belmont Ridge Rd
Ashburn, VA 20148-4501
www.nrpa.org

National Program for Playground Safety
School of HPER
WRC 205, University of Northern Iowa
Cedar Falls, IA 50614-0618
www.uni.edu/playground/home.html

# APPENDIX B

# Organizations with Sport Activities for Individuals with Disabilities

Adapted Physical Activity Academy
American Alliance for Health, Physical
Education, Recreation and Dance
1900 Association Dr
Reston, VA 22091
www.aahperd.org

American Association on Mental Retardation
444 North Capitol St NW, Suite 846
Washington, DC 20001-1968

American Blind Bowling Association
411 Sheriff
Mercer, PA 16137

American Red Cross
17th and D Streets NW
Washington, DC 20006
www.redcross.org

American Wheelchair Bowling Association
2912 Country Woods Ln
Palm Harbor, FL 34683
www.awba.org

The Arthritis Foundation
1330 West Peachtree St
Atlanta, GA 30309
www.arthritis.org

Asthma and Allergy Foundation of America
1233 20th St NW, Suite 402
Washington, DC 20036
www.aafa.org

Canadian Association for Health, Physical
Education, and Recreation
403-2197 Riverside Dr
Ottawa, Ontario, Canada K1H 7X3
www.cahperd.ca

Canadian Deaf Sports Association
4545 Ave. Pierre-DeCoubertin
Montreal, Quebec, Canada H1V 3R2

Canadian Wheelchair Sports Association
2460 Lancaster Rd, Suite 200
Ottawa, Ontario, Canada K1B 4S5
www.cwsa.ca

Council for Exceptional Children
1110 N. Glebe Rd, Suite 300
Arlington, VA 22201-5704
www.cec.sped.org

Council for National Cooperation in Aquatics
901 W New York St
Indianapolis, IN 46223

Deaf Athletics Canada
708-85 Emmett Dr
Toronto, Ontario, Canada M6M 5A2

Disabled Sports U.S.A.
451 Hungerford Dr, Suite 100
Rockville, MD 20850
www.dsusa.org

Dressage for Disabled
U.S. Dressage Federation
PO Box 6669
Lincoln, NE 68506-0669
www.usdf.org

Dwarf Athletic Association of America
418 Willow Way
Lewisville, TX 75077
www.daaa.org

International Foundation for Wheelchair
Tennis
2203 Timberloch Pl, Suite 126
The Woodlands, TX 77380
www.itftennis.com

International Paralympic Committee
Adenauerallee 212-214
53113 Bonn, Germany
www.paralympic.org

International Wheelchair Road Racers Club,
Inc.
30 Myano Ln
Stanford, CT 06902

Joseph P. Kennedy, Jr. Foundation
1325 G St NW, Suite 500
Washington, DC 20005-4709
www.familyvillage.wisc.edu/jpkf/

Muscular Dystrophy Association
27th Floor
810 Seventh Ave
New York, NY 10012
www.mdausa.org

National Center for Therapeutic Riding
PO Box 42501
Washington, DC 20015
www.narha.org

National Foundation of Wheelchair Tennis
940 Calle Amanecer, Suite B
San Clemente, CA 92672

National Disability Sports Alliance
25 Independence Way
Kingston, RI 02881
www.uscpaa.org

National Information Center on Deafness
Callaudet University
800 Florida Ave NE
Washington, DC 20002
www.clerecenter.gallaudet.edu

National Sports Center for the Disabled
PO Box 1290
Winter Park, CO 80482

National Multiple Sclerosis Society
733 Third Ave
New York, NY 10017
www.nmss.org

National Wheelchair Basketball Association
110 Seaton Bldg
University of Kentucky
Lexington, KY 40506
www.nwba.org

National Wheelchair Racquetball Association
535 Kensington Rd, Apt 4
Lancaster, PA 17603

National Wheelchair Shooting Federation
PO Box 18251
San Antonio, TX 78218
www.wsusa.org

National Wheelchair Softball Association
1616 Todd Ct
Hastings, MN 55033

North American Riding for the Handicapped
Association
PO Box 33150
Denver, CO 80233
www.narha.org

President's Committee on Mental Retardation
Washington, DC 20201
www.acf.dhhs.gov

Ski for Light
1455 West Lake St
Minneapolis, MN 55408

Special Olympics International
1325 G St NW, Suite 500
Washington, DC 20005
www.specialolympics.org

U.S. Association of Blind Athletes
33 N Institute St
Colorado Springs, CO 80903
www.usaba.org

U.S. Les Autres Sports Association
1101 Post Oak Blvd, Suite 9-486
Houston, TX 77056

U.S. Organization for Disabled Athletes
143 California Ave
Uniondale, NY 11553

USA Deaf Sports Federation
3607 Washington Blvd, #4
Ogden, UT 84403-1737
www.usadsf.org

United States Quad Rugby Association
1605 Matthews St
Fort Collins, CO 80525
www.quadrugby.com

U.S. Swimming, Inc.
1 Olympic Plaza
Colorado Springs, CO 80909

VWW Sports Program
Rehabilitation Institute of Chicago
PO Box 1461
Los Gatos, CA 95031-1461

Wheelchair Sports, USA
3595 E Fountain Blvd, Suite L-1
Colorado Springs, CO 80910
www.wsusa.org

# APPENDIX C

# Resources for Older Adults

Alliance for Retired Americans
888 16th St NW
Washington, DC 20006
www.retiredamericans.org

American Association for International Aging
(AAIA)
1133 20th St NW, Suite 330
Washington, DC 20036
www.unm.edu/~aging/AAIAwelc.html

American Association for Retired Persons
(AARP)
601 E St NW
Washington, DC 20049
www.aarp.org

American Society on Aging (ASA)
833 Market St, Suite 512
San Francisco, CA 94103
www.asaging.org

Center for the Study of Aging (CSA)
706 Madison Ave
Albany, NY 12208-3604
www.rand.org/labor/aging

Elder Craftsmen (EC)
610 Lexington Ave
New York, NY 10022
www.eldercraftsmen.org

Gerontological Society of America
1030 15th St NW, Suite 250
Washington, DC 20005

Gray Panthers (GP)
733 15th St NW, Suite 437
Washington, DC 20005
www.graypanthers.org

International Institute for Health Promotion
4400 Massachusetts Ave NW
Washington, DC 20016
www.healthy.american.edu

International Federation on Aging (IFA)
425 Viger Ave West, Suite 520
Montreal, Quebec, Canada H2Z 1X2
www.ifa-fiv.org

International Senior Citizens Association
(ISCA)
1102 S Crenshaw Blvd
Los Angeles, CA 90019

Jewish Association for Services for the Aged
(JASA)
40 W 68th St
New York, NY 10023

National Alliance of Senior Citizens (NASC)
2525 Wilson Blvd
Arlington, VA 22201

National Association of Area Agencies on
Aging (NAAAA)
927 15th Ave NW, 6th Floor
Washington, DC 20005
www.n4a.org

National Association for Human
Development (NAHD)
1424 16th St NW, Suite 102
PO Box 100
Washington, DC 20036

National Association of Nutrition and Aging
Services Programs (NANASP)
1101 Vermont Ave NW, Suite 1001
Washington, DC 20005
ww.nanasp.org

National Caucus and Center on Black Aged
(NCCBA)
1424 K St NW, Suite 500
Washington, DC 20005
www.ncba-blackaged.org

National Center on Arts and the Aging (CAA)
c/o National Council on Aging

National Center on Rural Aging (NCRA)
c/o National Council on Aging

National Council on Aging (NCOA)
409 3rd St SW
Washington, DC 20024
www.maturityworks.org

National Hispanic Council on Aging
(NHCOA)
2713 Ontario Rd NW
Washington, DC 20009
www.nhcoa.org

National Indian Council on Aging (NICOA)
10501 Montgomery Blvd NE, Suite 210
Albuquerque, NM 87111-3846
www.nicoa.org

National Institute on Aging
c/o U.S. Department of Health and Human
Services

National Voluntary Organization for
Independent Living for the Aging (NVOILA)
600 Maryland Ave SW
West Wing 100
Washington, DC 20024

U.S. Department of Health and Human
Services, Administration on Aging
330 Independence Ave SW
Washington, DC 20201
www.aoa.dhhs.gov/directory/toc.html
(resource directory for older Americans)

# APPENDIX D
# Public Lands Information

## DEPARTMENT OF AGRICULTURE

**USDA Forest Service**
PO Box 96090
Washington, DC 20090-6090
www.fs.fed.us

**Regional Offices**
Alaska Region
PO Box 21628
Juneau, AK 99802-1628

Eastern Region
310 W Wisconsin Ave, Room 500
Milwaukee, WI 53203

Intermountain Region
Federal Building
324 25th St
Ogden, UT 84401

Northern Region
Federal Building
PO Box 7669
Missoula, MT 59807

Pacific Northwest Region
PO Box 3623
Portland, OR 97208

Pacific Southwest
630 Sansome St
San Francisco, CA 94111

Rocky Mountain Region
PO Box 25127
Lakewood, CO 80225

Southern Region
1720 Peachtree Rd NW
Atlanta, GA 30367

Southwestern Region
Federal Building
517 Gold Ave SW
Albuquerque, NM 87102

## DEPARTMENT OF THE ARMY

**U.S. Army Corps of Engineers**
Attn: Lakes Information
20 Massachusetts Ave NW
Washington, DC 20314-1000
www.usace.army.mil

**Local Offices**
Lower Mississippi Valley Division
Attn: CELMV-CO-R
PO Box 80
Vicksburg, MS 39181-0080

Missouri River Division
Attn: CEMRD-CO-R
PO Box 103, Downtown Station
Omaha, NE 68101-0103

New England Division
Attn: CENED-OD-P
424 Trapelo Rd
Waltham, MA 02254-9149

North Atlantic Division
Attn: CENAD-CO-P
90 Church St
New York, NY 10007-9998

North Central Division
Attn: CENPD-CO-R
PO Box 2870
Portland, OR 97208-2870

Ohio River Division
Attn: CEORD-CO-R
77 Forsyth St SW, Room 313
Atlanta, GA 30335-6801

South Pacific Division
Attn: CESPD-CO-O
630 Sansome St, Room 1216
San Francisco, CA 94111-2206

Southwestern Division
Attn: CESWD-CO-R
1114 Commerce St
Dallas, TX 75242-0216

For information about recreation opportunities on military lands, write to
Deputy Assistant Secretary of Defense (Environment)
400 Army-Navy Dr, Room 206
Arlington, VA 22202-2884

# DEPARTMENT OF COMMERCE

14th and E St NW
Washington, DC 20240
http://home.doc.gov

**National Oceanic and Atmospheric Administration (NOAA)**
National Marine Fisheries Service
1335 East-West Hwy
Silver Spring, MD 20910
www.noaa.gov

# DEPARTMENT OF THE INTERIOR

Office of Public Affairs
Washington, DC 20240
www.doi.gov

**Bureau of Indian Affairs (BIA)**
Office of Public Affairs
1849 C St NW
Mail Stop 4542-MIB
Washington, DC 20240
www.doi.gov/bureau-indian-affairs.html

**BIA Area Offices**
Aberdeen Area Office
115 4th Ave SE
Aberdeen, SD 57401

Albuquerque Area Office
615 First St NW
PO Box 26567
Albuquerque, NM 87125

Anadarko Area Office
WCD—Office Complex
PO Box 368
Anadarko, OK 73005

Billings Area Office
316 N 26th St
Billings, MT 59101

Eastern Area Office
1951 Constitution Ave NW
Washington, DC 20245

Juneau Area Office
Federal Building
PO Box 3-8000
Juneau, AK 99802

Minneapolis Area Office
Chamber of Commerce Building
15 S Fifth St, 6th Floor
Minneapolis, MN 55402

Muskogee Area Office
Old Federal Building
Muskogee, OK 74401

Navajo Area Office
PO Box M
Window Rock, AZ 86515

Phoenix Area Office
No. 1 North First St
PO Box 10
Phoenix, AZ 85011

**Bureau of Land Management**
Office of Public Affairs
1849 C St NW, MS 204 LS
Washington, DC 20240
www.blm.gov

### State Offices
Alaska State Office
222 W 7th Ave #13
Anchorage, AK 99513-7599

Arizona State Office
PO Box 16563
Phoenix, AZ 85011

California State Office
2800 Cottage Way, E-2841
Sacramento, CA 95825

Colorado State Office
2850 Youngfield St
Lakewood, CO 80215-7076

Eastern States Office
350 S Pickett St
Alexandria, VA 22304

Idaho State Office
3380 Americana Terr
Boise, ID 83706

Montana State Office
PO Box 36800
Billings, MT 59107

Nevada State Office
PO Box 12000
Reno, NV 89520-0006

New Mexico State Office
PO Box 27115
Santa Fe, NM 87502-7115

Oregon State Office
PO Box 2965
Portland, OR 97208-2965

Utah State Office
CFS Financial Center Building
324 S State St, Suite 301
Salt Lake City, UT 84111-2303

Wyoming State Office
PO Box 1828
Cheyenne, WY 82003

**Bureau of Reclamation**
Office of Public Affairs
1849 C St NW, Room 7640
Washington, DC 20240
www.usbr.gov

### Area Offices
Great Plains Region
PO Box 36900
Billings, MT 59107-6900

Lower Colorado Region
PO Box 61470
Boulder City, NV 89006-1470

Mid-Pacific Region
2800 Cottage Way
Sacramento, CA 95825

Pacific Northwest Region
PO Box 043
Boise, ID 83724

Upper Colorado Region
PO Box 11568
Salt Lake City, UT 84147

**National Park Service**
Office of Public Inquiries
1849 C St NW, Room 1013
Washington, DC 20240
www.nps.gov

### Regional Offices
Alaska Region
2525 Gambell St
Anchorage, AK 99503-2892

Mid-Atlantic Region
143 S Third St
Philadelphia, PA 19106

Midwest Region
1709 Jackson St
Omaha, NE 68102

National Capitol Region
1100 Ohio Dr SW
Washington, DC 20242

North Atlantic Region
15 State St
Boston, MA 02109-3572

Pacific Northwest Region
83 S King St, Suite 202
Seattle, WA 98104

Rocky Mountain Region
12795 W Alameda Pkwy
Denver, CO 80225-0287

Southeast Region
75 Spring St SW
Atlanta, GA 30303

Southwest Region
PO Box 728
Santa Fe, NM 87504-0728

Western Region
600 Harrison St, Suite 600
San Francisco, CA 94107-1372

**U.S. Fish and Wildlife Service**
Office of Public Affairs
1849 C St NW, Mail Stop NCTC
Washington, DC 20240
www.fws.gov

**Regional Offices**
Alaska Regional Office
1011 E Tudro Rd
Anchorage, AK 99503

Mountain Prairie Regional Office
Box 25486, Denver Federal Center
Denver, CO 80225

North Central Regional Office
Federal Building, Fort Snelling
Twin Cities, MN 55111

Northeast Regional Office
1 Gateway Center, Suite 700
Newton Corner, MA 02158

Pacific Regional Office
911 NE 11th Ave
Portland, OR 97232

Southeast Regional Office
75 Spring St SW
Atlanta, GA 30303

Southwest Regional Office
PO Box 1306
Albuquerque, NM 87103

## INDEPENDENT AGENCIES

**Land Between the Lakes**
100 Van Morgan Drive
Golden Pond, KY 42211-9001
www2.lbl.org/lbl

**Tennessee Valley Authority**
Communications and Employee Development
400 W Summit Hill Dr ET 6B
Knoxville, TN 37902
www.tva.com

**U.S. Geological Survey (USGS)**
www.usgs.gov
Although the U.S. Geological Survey does not
manage federal lands, it does produce one of the
principal tools for understanding and enjoying
those lands: maps! The USGS has covered the
country with the most detailed topographical
maps available from any source, including special maps for national parks and monuments,
which are available from many dealers all over
the country. The maps and information about
them, such as available scales and date of last
revision, can also be obtained from the following
USGS Earth Science Information Centers:

345 Middlefield Road
Mail Stop 532
Menlo Park, CA 94025-3591

PO Box 25046 Federal Center
Mail Stop 504
Denver, CO 80225-0046

507 National Center
Reston, VA 22092

# APPENDIX E

# *State Lands Information*

Alabama Bureau of Tourism & Travel
PO Box 4927, Dept TIA
Montgomery, AL 36103-4927
205-242-4169
Toll-free: 1-800-ALABAMA
www.touralabama.org

Alaska Division of Tourism
PO Box 110801, Dept TIA
Juneau, AK 99811-0801
907-465-2010
Toll-free: 1-800-862-5275
www.dced.state.ak.us/tourism

Arizona Office of Tourism
2702 N 3rd St, Suite 4015
Phoenix, AZ 85007
602-230-7733
www.arizonaguide.com

Arkansas Tourism Office
1 Capitol Mall, Dept 7701
Little Rock, AR 72201
501-682-7777
Toll-free: 1-800-NATURAL
www.arkansas.com

California Office of Tourism
PO Box 1499, Dept TIA
Sacramento, CA 95812-1499
916-322-2881
Toll-free: 1-800-TOCALIF
http://gocalif.ca.gov

Colorado Tourism Board
PO Box 38700
Denver, CO 80238
303-592-5410
Toll-free: 1-800-COLORADO
www.colorado.com

Connecticut Department of Economic
Development, Tourism Division
505 Hudson St
Hartford, CT 06106
860-270-8080
Toll-free: 1-800-CTBOUND
www.state.ct.us/tourism

Delaware Tourism Office
99 Kings Hwy
PO Box 1401, Dept TIA
Dover, DE 19903
302-739-4271
Toll-free: 1-800-441-8846
www.visitdelaware.net

Florida Division of Tourism
126 W Van Buren St, FLDA
Tallahassee, FL 32399-2000
904-487-1462
Toll-free: 1-888-7 FLAUSA
www.flausa.com

Georgia Department of Industry, Trade, &
Tourism
PO Box 1776, Dept TIA
Atlanta, GA 30301
404-656-3590
Toll-free: 1-800-VISITGA
www.georgia.org

Hawaii Department of Business, Economic
Development, & Tourism
PO Box 2359
Honolulu, HI 96804
808-586-2423
Toll-free: 1-800-353-5846
www.visit.hawaii.org

Idaho Division of Tourism Development
700 W State St, Dept C
Boise, ID 83620
208-334-2470
Toll-free: 1-800-635-7820
www.visitid.org

Illinois Bureau of Tourism
100 W Randolph, Suite 3-400
Chicago, IL 60601
312-814-4732
Toll-free: 1-800-223-0121
www.enjoyillinois.com

Indiana Department of Commerce
Tourism and Film Development Division
1 N Capitol, Suite 700
Indianapolis, IN 46204-2288
317-232-8860
Toll-free: 1-800-289-6646
www.ai.org/tourism

Iowa Division of Tourism
200 E Grand, Dept TIA
Des Moines, IA 50309
515-242-4705
Toll-free: 1-800-345-IOWA
www.state.ia.us/tourism

Kansas Travel & Tourism Division
700 SW Harrison St, Suite 1300
Topeka, KS 66603-3712
913-296-2009
Toll-free: 1-800-252-6727
www.kansascommerce.com

Kentucky Department of Travel Development
500 Mero St
22nd Floor, Dept DA
Frankfurt, KY 40601
502-564-4930
Toll-free: 1-800-225-TRIP
www.state.ky.us/tour/tour.htm

Louisiana Office of Tourism
Attn: Inquiry Department
PO Box 94291, LOT
Baton Rouge, LA 70804-9291
504-342-8119
Toll-free: 1-800-33-GUMBO
www.louisianatravel.com

Maine Office of Tourism
189 State St
August, ME 04333
207-289-5711
Toll-free: 1-800-533-9595
www.visitmaine.com

Maryland Office of Travel & Tourism
217 E Redwood St, 9th Floor
Baltimore, MD 21202
410-767-3400
Toll-free: 1-800-543-1036
www.mdisfun.org

Massachusetts Office of Travel and Tourism
100 Cambridge St, 13th Floor
Boston, MA 02202
617-727-3201
Toll-free: 1-800-447-MASS
(for ordering vacation kit only, U.S. only)
www.mass-vacation.com

Michigan Travel Bureau
PO Box 30226
Lansing, MI 48909-7726
517-373-0670
Toll-free: 1-888-78-GREAT
www.michigan.org

Minnesota Office of Tourism
121 7th Place East
St. Paul, MN 55101
612-296-5029
Toll-free: 1-800-657-3700
www.exploreminnesota.com

Mississippi Division of Tourism
PO Box 849
Jackson, MS 39205
601-359-3297
Toll-free: 1-800-647-2290
www.visitmississippi.org

Missouri Division of Tourism
PO Box 1055, Dept TIA
Jefferson City, MO 65102
573-751-4133
Toll-free: 1-800-877-1234
www.missouritourism.org

Travel Montana
Room 259
Deer Lodge, MT 59722
406-444-2654
Toll-free: 1-800-541-1447
http://travelmontana.state.mt.us/

Nebraska Division of Travel and Tourism
PO Box 94666
Lincoln, NE 68509
402-471-3796
Toll-free: 1-800-228-4307
http://visitnebraska.org

Nevada Commission of Tourism
Capitol Complex, Dept TIA
Carson City, NV 89710
702-687-4322
Toll-free: 1-800-NEVADA-8
www.travelnevada.com

New Hampshire Office of Travel and Tourism
Development
PO Box 1856, Dept TIA
Concord, NH 03302
603-271-2343
Toll-free: 1-800-FUNINNH
www.visitnh.gov

New Jersey Division of Travel and Tourism
20 W State St, CN 826, Dept TIA
Trenton, NJ 08625
609-292-2470
Toll-free: 1-800-JERSEY-7
www.state.nj.us/travel/

New Mexico Department of Tourism
491 Old Santa Fe Trail
Santa Fe, NM 87503
505-827-0400
Toll-free: 1-800-545-2040
www.newmexico.org

New York State Department of Economic
Development
One Commerce Plaza
Albany, NY 12245
518-474-4116
Toll-free: 1-800-CALLNYS
http://iloveny.state.ny.us/

North Carolina Division of Travel and
Tourism
301 N Wilmington St
Raleigh, NC 27601-2825
919-733-4171
Toll-free: 1-800-VISITNC
www.visitnc.com

North Dakota Tourism Promotion
Liberty Memorial Building
604 E Blvd
Bismarck, ND 58505
701-224-2525
Toll-free: 1-800-HELLOND
www.ndtourism.com

Ohio Division of Travel and Tourism
PO Box 1001, Dept TIA
Columbus, OH 43266-0101
614-466-8844
Toll-free: 1-800-BUCKEYE
(Continental U.S., Ontario, Quebec)
www.ohiotourism.com

Oklahoma Tourism and Recreation
Department
Travel and Tourism Division
500 Will Rogers Bldg, DA92
Oklahoma City, OK 73105-4492
405-521-3981
Toll-free: 1-800-652-6552
(information requests only)
www.otrd.state.ok.us/

Oregon Economic Development Department,
Tourism Division
775 Summer St NE
Salem, OR 97310
503-373-1270
Toll-free: 1-800-547-7842
www.traveloregon.com

Pennsylvania Bureau of Travel Marketing
Room 453, Forum Bldg
Harrisburg, PA 17120
717-787-5453
Toll-free: 1-800-VISITPA
www.experiencepa.com

Rhode Island Tourism Division
1 West Exchange St
Providence, RI 02903
401-222-2601
Toll-free: 1-800-566-2484
www.visitrhodeisland.com

South Carolina Division of Tourism
PO Box 71, Room 902
Columbia, SC 29202
803-734-0235
www.discoversouthcarolina.com

South Dakota Department of Tourism
711 E Wells Ave
Pierre, SD 57501-5070
605-773-3301
Toll-free: 1-800-732-5682
www.travelsd.com

Tennessee Department of Tourism
Development
320 Sixth Ave N
5th Floor, Rachel Jackson Bldg
Nashville, TN 37243
615-741-2158
Toll-free: 1-800-491-TENN
www.state.tn.us/tourdev/

Texas Department of Commerce, Tourism
Division
PO Box 12728
Austin, TX 78711-2728
512-462-9191
Toll-free: 1-800-88-88-TEX
www.state.tx.us/travel/

Utah Travel Council
Council Hall/Capitol Hill
Dept TIA
300 N State St
Salt Lake City, UT 84114
801-538-1030
www.utah.com

Vermont Travel Division
6 Baldwin St, Drawer 33
Montpelier, VT 05633-1301
802-828-3236
Toll-free: 1-800-VERMONT
www.vermont.com

Virginia Division of Tourism
1021 E Cary St, Dept VT
Richmond, VA 23219
804-786-4484
Toll-free: 1-800-VISITVA
www.state.va.us

Washington, DC Convention and Visitors
Association
1212 New York Ave NW
Washington, DC 20005
202-789-7000
Toll-free: 1-800-422-8644
www.washington.org

Washington State Tourism Development
Division
PO Box 42500
Olympia, WA 98504-2500
206-586-2088
Toll-free: 1-800-544-1800
www.tourism.wa.gov/

West Virginia Division of Tourism & Parks
2101 Washington St E
Charleston, WV 25305
304-348-2286
Toll-free: 1-800-CALLWVA
www.callwva.com

Wisconsin Division of Tourism
201 West Washington Ave
Madison, WI 53703
608-266-2161
Toll-free in state: 1-800-372-2737
Out of state: 1-800-432-TRIP
www.travelwisconsin.com

Wyoming Division of Tourism
I-25 at College Dr, Dept WY
Cheyenne, WY 82002
307-777-7777
Toll-free: 1-800-225-5996
www.wyomingtourism.org

Puerto Rico Tourism Company
666 Fifth Ave, 15th Floor
New York, NY 10103
Toll-free: 1-800-866-STAR, Ext. 17
www.prtourism.com

U.S. Virgin Islands Division of Tourism
PO Box 6400, VITIA
Charlotte Amalie, St. Thomas
USVI 00801
809-774-8784
Toll-free: 1-800-372-8784
www.usvi.net

# APPENDIX F

# Camping Resources

Bureau of Land Management
Department of the Interior, MIB
1849 C St NW, Room 5600
Washington, DC 20240
(for camping information)
www.blm.gov
www.doi.gov
www.recreation.gov

Department of the Army
U.S.A.C.E.
Regional Brochures, 1M-MV-N
3909 Halls Ferry Fr
Vicksburg, MS 39180
(U.S. Army Corps of Engineers Projects has
53,000 campsites. For a list, write to the
address above.)
www.usace.army.mil

Go Camping America Website
www.gocampingamerica.com
(for more information on public and private
campgrounds as well as a free vacation planning guide)

Kampgrounds of America
PO Box 30558
Billings, MT 59114
(offers a free directory, *Road Atlas and Camping
Guide,* at any of its over 500 locations or by
sending $3.00 to the address above)
www.koakampgrounds.com

National Association of RV Parks and
Campgrounds (ARVC)
113 Park Avenue
Falls Church, VA 22046
(offers free brochures on private campgrounds
at www.gocampingamerica.com)

*National Wildlife Refuges—a Visitor's Guide*
U.S. Fish and Wildlife Service
Publications Department
4040 N Fairfax Dr, Room 130 (WEBB)
Arlington, VA 22203
www.fws.gov

USDA Forest Service
Public Affairs Office
PO Box 96090
Washington, DC 20090
1-800-280-2267 for reservations
(offers a free list, *National Forest
Campgrounds,* of its over 4,000 campgrounds
in its 155 forests)
www.fs.fed.us

# APPENDIX G

# Selected Professional and Service Organizations

American Alliance for Health, Physical Education, Recreation and Dance (AAHPERD)/American Association for Leisure and Recreation (AALR)
1900 Association Dr
Reston, VA 22091
www.aahperd.org

American Alpine Club
710 10th St, Suite 100
Golden, CO 80401
www.americanalpineclub.org

American Association of Museums
1575 Eye St NW, Suite 400
Washington, DC 20005
www.aam-us.org

American Association of Zoological Parks & Aquariums
8403 Colesville Rd, Suite 710
Silver Spring, MD 20910-3314
www.aza.org

American Camping Association
Bradford Woods
5000 State Rd, 67 North
Martinsville, IN 46151-7902
www.acacamps.org

American Correctional Association
4380 Forbes Blvd
Lanham, MD 20706-4322
www.corrections.com/aca/

American Federation of Arts
41 E 65th St
New York, NY 10021
www.afaweb.org

American Forestry Association
1516 P St NW
Washington, DC 20005

American Recreation Coalition
1225 New York Ave NW, #450
Washington, DC 20005
www.funoutdoors.com

American Society of Landscape Architects
636 Eye St NW
Washington, DC 20001-3736
www.asla.org

American Therapeutic Recreation Association
1414 Prince St, Suite 204
Alexandria, VA 22314
www.atra-tr.org

American Youth Hostels, Inc.
733 15th St NW, Suite 840
Washington, DC 20005
www.hiayh.org

Association of Outdoor Recreations and Education
PO Box 1319
Boulder, CO 80306
www.aore.org

Boy Scouts of America
1325 Walnut Hill Ln
PO Box 152079
Irving, TX 75015-2079
www.bsa.scouting.org

Camp Fire USA
4601 Madison Ave
Kansas City, MO 64112
www.campfire.org

Conservation Foundation
1800 N Kent St, Suite 1120
Arlington, VA 22209
www.theconservationfoundation.org

Employee Services Management Association
(ESMA)
2211 York Rd, Suite 207
Oak Brook, IL 60523
www.esmassn.org

Girl Scouts of the United States of America
420 Fifth Ave
New York, NY 10018-2798
www.gsusa.org

Hobby Industry Association of America, Inc.
319 E 54th St
Elmwood Park, NJ 07407
www.hobby.org

International Association of Amusement Parks
& Attractions
1448 Duke St
Alexandria, VA 22314
www.iaapa.org

Izaak Walton League of America
707 Conservation Ln
Gaithersburg, MD 20878
www.iwla.org

National Association of County Park &
Recreation Officials
c/o National Association of Counties
440 First St NW, Suite 800
Washington, DC 20001
www.nacpro.org

National Association for Interpretation
PO Box 2246
Fort Collins, CO 80522
www.nai-link.org

National Association of Professional Forestry
Schools & Colleges
3325 Rose Ln
Falls Church, VA 22042
www.napfsc.org

National Audubon Society
700 Broadway
New York, NY 10003
www.Audubon.org

National Intramural Recreation Sports
Association (NIRSA)
4185 SW Research Way
Corvallis, OR 97333
www.nirsa.org

National Parks & Conservation Association
1300 19th St NW, Suite 300
Washington, DC 20036
www.npca.org

National Recreation and Park Association (its
branches & sections)
22377 Belmont Ridge Rd
Ashburn, VA 20148-4501
www.nrpa.org

National Spa and Pool Institute
2111 Eisenhower Ave
Alexandria, VA 22314
www.nspi.org

National Therapeutic Recreation Society
22377 Belmont Ridge Rd
Ashburn, VA 20148-4502
www.nrpa.org/branches/ntrs.htm

National Trust for Historic Preservation
1785 Massachusetts Ave NW
Washington, DC 20036
www.nationaltrust.org

Presidents Council on Physical Fitness and
Sport
Department W
200 Independence Ave SW, Room 738-H
Washington, DC 20201-0004
http://phs.os.dhhs.gov/ophs/pcpfs.htm

Resort and Commercial Recreation
Association
PO Box 1208
New Port Richey, FL 34656-1208
www.r-c-r-a.org

Sierra Club
85 Second St, 2nd Floor
San Francisco, CA 94105-3441
www.sierraclub.org

Society of American Foresters
5400 Grosvenor Ln
Bethesda, MD 20814
www.safnet.org

Travel Industry Association of America
1100 New York Ave NW, Suite 450
Washington, DC 20005
www.tia.org

Travel and Tourism Research Association
PO Box 2133
Boise, ID 83701
www.ttra.org

Wilderness Society
1615 M St NW
Washington, DC 20036
www.wilderness.org

Wildlife Management Institute
1101 14th St NW, Suite 801
Washington, DC 20005
www.nwi.org

World Leisure Secretariat
Site 81C Comp O
118 Big Horn Trail
Okanagan Falls, BC, Canada V0H 1R0
www.worldleisure.org

Young Men's Christian Association of the
United States of America—National Council
101 N Wacker Dr
Chicago, IL 60606
www.ymca.net

Young Women's Christian Association of the
United States of America
Empire State Building
350 5th Ave, Suite 301
New York, NY 10118
www.ywca.org

# APPENDIX H

# ADA-Related Resources

*Accessing ADA Resources* (directories by geo-graphical region)
Mainstream Inc.
Takoma Business Center
6930 Carroll Ave, Suite 240
Takoma Park, MD 20912
www.mainstreaminc.org

The Architectural and Transportation Barriers
Compliance Board
1331 F St NW, Suite 1000
Washington, DC 20004-1111
www.access-board.gov

The Association for Retarded Citizens of the
United States
1010 Wayne Ave, Suite 650
Silver Spring, MD 20910
www.thearc.org

Disability Rights Education and Defense Fund
2212 Sixth St
Berkeley, CA 94710
www.dredf.org

Equal Employment Opportunity Commission
1801 L St NW
Washington, DC 20507
www.eeoc.gov

National Center on Accessibility
Indiana University
2805 E 10th St, Suite 190
Bloomington, IN 47408-2698
www.ncaonline.org

National Center on Physical Activity and
Disability
1640 W Roosevelt Rd
Chicago, IL 60608-6904
www.ncpad.org

National Conference of States on Building
Codes and Standards
505 Huntmar Park Dr, Suite 210
Herndon, VA 20170
www.ncsbcs.org

Office of the Americans with Disabilities Act,
Civil Rights Division
U.S. Department of Justice
PO Box 66738
Washington, DC 20035-6738
www.usdoj.gov/crt/ada/adahom1.htm

Pacific Disability and Business Technical
Assistance Center
2168 Shattuck Ave, Suite 301
Berkeley, CA 94704-1307
www.pacdbtac.org

The President's Committee on Employment of
People with Disabilities
1331 F St NW, Suite 300
Washington, DC 20004
www.pcepd.gov

U.S. Department of Justice
Coordination and Review Section
Civil Rights Division
PO Box 66118
Washington, DC 20035
www.usdoj.gov/crt/cor

# APPENDIX I
# No-Trace Camping

Following are ways to enjoy nature and the outdoors and leave the land as it was originally so that other campers can enjoy the environment.

## Leave a No-Trace Campsite
Pick up and pack out every trace of litter.
Erase all signs of a fire.
Replace rocks and logs where they were originally.

## Plan Ahead to Avoid Impacts
Travel and camp in groups of four or fewer.
Avoid *popular* holidays and weekends.
Re-package food to reduce containers.
Take a litterbag to carry out all refuse.
Carry a stove and foods requiring little cooking.
Check with BLM offices for low-use areas.

## Travel to Avoid Impacts
Walk in single file in the center of the trail.
Stay on the main trail even if it is wet or snow-covered.
Never short-cut switchbacks.
Travel cross-country only on rocky or timbered areas, not on fragile vegetation.
Look at and photograph; never pick up or collect.

## Make No-Trace Camps
Camp away from trails, shorelines, and fragile plant communities.
Do not dig holes or drainage ditches.
Wear soft, "no-trace" hiking boots.
Avoid trampling vegetation.
Remove natural trail blockages; do not create a new trail around them.
Wash at least 100 feet from natural water sources.
Use biodegradable soap that will not contaminate the water.
Place campsites in well-drained, sandy, or rocky areas.
Build small, efficient fires (with wood about two fingers wide) on soil. Do not blacken nearby stones or pits.
Carry in small firewood or use fallen deadwood. Never cut standing trees.
Bury human waste at least 6 inches deep; pack out all other waste.
Speak softly, avoid playing music, and leave with only memories.

# Glossary

**activity**
performance of a specific deed or act

**activity theory**
suggests that successful aging depends on remaining active and socially involved

**adolescence**
a developmental transition from childhood to adulthood that begins at the onset of puberty, between 10 and 12 years of age, and ends at 19 or 20 years of age

**ageism**
discrimination based on age

**amusive leisure**
a situation in which members of the leisure class are entertained by members of a performer class

**androgyny**
state of being specifically neither female nor male in terms of attitudes and behavior

**anorexia nervosa**
a disorder characterized by a prolonged refusal to eat, resulting in emaciation, cessation of menstruation, emotional disturbance concerning body image, and an abnormal fear of becoming obese

**attitude**
the tendency to feel toward or react to a given object or subject in a certain way

**attribution theory**
holds that whether people perceive the causes of events as being internal or external to themselves determines whether they feel confident or inadequate in dealing with situations

**autotelic (activity)**
having a purpose in and not apart from itself

**Baby Boomers**
Americans born in the post–World War II years between 1946 and 1964; this generation numbers about 77 million people

**bulimia**
an insatiable craving for food, often resulting in episodes of continuous eating and often followed by purging, depression, and self-deprivation

**caste system**
a division of society into rigid groups based on heredity, in which members of a given caste are restricted to certain occupations and are forbidden to associate with members of other castes; originated with the Hindu sect of India

**customs**
the whole body of usages, practices, or conventions that regulate social life

**disengagement theory**
views aging as a process of mutual (and mutually satisfactory) withdrawal: the individual from society and society from the individual

**drive**
behavior motivated toward eliminating physiological deprivation or moving away from noxious conditions

**dyad**
a human social unit composed of a male and a female

**early childhood**
the period of childhood between 18 months and 5 years of age

**Eastern bloc**
countries of eastern Europe that were under Soviet communist domination from the end of World War II until the collapse of communism in 1989

**egocentric**
concerned or preoccupied with the self

**ethnicity**
the affiliation of a large group of people classed according to a common racial, national, tribal, religious, linguistic, or cultural background

**evolution**
a process of continuous change from a lower, simpler, or worse to a higher, more complex, or better state

**extended family**
a family that includes other relatives such as grandparents or cousins in addition to parents and their children

**family**
the basic social unit, traditionally consisting of two parents rearing their own or adopted offspring

**fine motor skills**
precise, coordinated movements in such activities as writing, buttoning, cutting, tracing, or visual tracking

**gender**
the behavioral, cultural, or psychological traits typically associated with one sex

**generalized other**
the totality of attitudes and values of one's group or social circle whose judgment is used as the standard of one's behavior

**Generation X**
Americans born between 1965 and 1976; this generation numbers about 41 million people

**gross motor activity**
activity that uses the large-muscle groups that coordinate body movements required for normal living, such as walking, running, jumping, throwing, and balance

*infancy*
the period of childhood between birth and 18 months

**information rate**
the rate at which the brain processes information during a given time

*instinct*
a largely inherited and unalterable tendency of an organism to respond to environmental stimuli without the use of reason

**instrumental value**
a value that is both observable and testable

**leisure**
permission to do as one pleases at one's own pace, to participate in an activity of one's own choice, and to abandon the activity at will

**lifestyle**
the way one lives based on one's age, gender, occupation, and residence

**menarche**
onset of menstruation

**menopause**
termination of menstruation and the end of childbearing capability

**middle adult years**
the period of adulthood between 40 and 60 years of age

**middle childhood**
the period of childhood between 5 and 12 years of age

**modern society**
a society that has adopted or is moving toward a unified code of behavior; e.g., Great Britain

**mores**
the fixed, morally binding customs of a group

**motive**
a conscious or unconscious reason for behavior

**nuclear family**
a family that consists only of mother, father, and children; named for the "nuclear age" that began after World War II

**parallel play**
side-by-side activity with another child

**play**
activities in which one engages freely and from which he or she derives personal satisfaction

**preschooler**
a child between 3 and 5 years of age

**primary economy**
an economy in which the majority of the labor force is engaged in farming or extractive work

**puberty**
the period of life at which the ability to reproduce begins

**quaternary economy**
a predicted post-industrial economy in which more time will be available for recreation and leisure

**race**
a division of humankind possessing traits that are transmittable by descent

**recreation**
voluntary participation in leisure activities that are meaningful and enjoyable to the person involved

**reflex**
a simple segment of behavior in which a direct and immediate response occurs to a particular stimulus

**role confusion**
experienced by adolescents who have not achieved a sense of identity and who tend to exhibit erratic and sometimes self-destructive behavior

**satisfaction**
the fulfillment of a want or need; contentment; a source or means of enjoyment

**secondary economy**
an economy based on manufacturing

**secondary sex characteristics**
physical characteristics that appear in only one sex and are not directly related to reproduction (e.g., breasts in females, thickened vocal cords in males)

**senior adulthood**
the period of adulthood that begins at 60 years of age

**sensorimotor stage of development**
the stage from birth to 2 years of age during which children learn to deal with objects, time, and space on a concrete basis

**sex**
the physical characteristics that distinguish males from females

**skill**
the learned ability to perform a task competently

**socialization**
the process through which a novice gains understanding of the society's customs, values, and expectations

**society**
an enduring and cooperating social group whose members have developed organized patterns of relationships through interactions with one another

**sociology**
the study of the development, structure, interaction, and collective behavior of organized groups of human beings

**special population**
a group of people who share characteristics and needs that distinguish them from the general population

**taboo**
social prohibition of a certain behavior

**terminal value**
a value that is conceptual and has meaning within itself

**tertiary economy**
a service-based economy

**Third World**
a group of developing nations with largely agrarian economies, located mainly in Asia and Africa, that generally are not aligned with the ideologies of either the East or the West

**toddlerhood**
the period of childhood between 18 months and 3 years of age

**value**
the quality of being worthwhile, important, and desirable

**Western bloc**
a political classification formerly used to describe noncommunist countries with free-market economies, including the United States, Canada, Great Britain, western Europe, Australia, and New Zealand

**young adulthood**
the period of adulthood between 20 and 40 years of age

**youth at risk**
adolescents who are in trouble at home or school, who may be involved in substance abuse, and who may or may not have been brought into the juvenile justice system

# Credits

## Chapter 1
**p. 3, Figure 1.2**, From Ibrahim, H: "Leisure, idleness, and Ibn Khaldun," *Leisure Studies*, vol. 7, #1, January, 1988, p. 54. Used with permission.

## Chapter 3
**p. 40, Figure 3.1**, Source: U.S. Bureau of the Census, 2000; **p. 45, Figure 3.4**, From Ibrahim, H: *Leisure: a psychological approach*, Los Alamitos, CA: Hwong Publ Co., 1979. © Hilmi Ibrahim; **p. 46, Action Guide**, Reprinted by permission from *Glamour*, September, 1992. © Conde Nast Publs, New York City.

## Chapter 4
**p. 58, Figure 4.1**, Source: U.S. Bureau of the Census, 1999; **p. 59, Table 4.1**, From Werner, P: *A movement approach to games for children*, St. Louis: CV Mosby, 1979; **p. 60, Table 4.2**, Adapted from Frankenburg, WK: *Denver Developmental Screening Test*, Denver: University of Colorado Medical Center, 1978. Reprinted with permission; **p. 68, Figure 4.2**, Source: National Electronic Injury Surveillance System (NEISS) Special Study, April-December, 1988, and the US Consumer Product Commission/EPHA; **p. 70, Table 4.3**, From Coakley, J: "Play group versus organized competitive team: a comparison," in Eitzen, S (ed.): *Sport in contemporary society: an anthology*, New York: St. Martin's Press, 1993. Reprinted with permission.

## Chapter 5
**pp. 80 and 81, Figures 5.1 and 5.2**, Source: U.S. Bureau of the Census, 1999; **p. 82, Figure 5.3**, Adapted from National Household Survey on Drug Abuse, 1996; **p. 86, Figure 5.4**, Adapted from Juster, FT, and Stafford, FB (eds): *Time, goods, and well-being*, Ann Arbor: University of Michigan Institute for Social Research. Design by Jane Lammers; **p. 87, Table 5.1**, Adapted from Cardin, RJ: "A youth perspective on outdoor recreation," *Parks and Recreation*, pp. 58–59; **p. 89, Table 5.2**, From Seefeldt, V, Ewing, M, and Walk, S: "Overview of youth sports programs in the United States," Unpublished manuscript prepared for the *Carnegie Council on Adolescent Development*, Washington, DC, 1992. Reprinted with permission.

## Chapter 6

**p. 99, Table 6.1**, Source: Stubbs, H: The social consequences of long life, Springfield, IL: Charles C. Thomas, 1982, p. 15; **p. 100, Table 6.2**, From National Endowment for The Arts, *Research Division Report 39*. Washington, D.C., 1998, p. 45; **p. 101, Table 6.3**, From U.S. Department of Commerce, Economics, and Statistics Administration, and Bureau of the Census: *Statistical Abstract of the United States*, 1997, Washington, DC: U.S. Department of Commerce, October 1997, p. 25. **p. 113, A Closer Look**, Source: Elderhostel International catalog, Spring, 1994 and August, 1993, Boston: Elderhostel, Inc.

## Chapter 7

**p. 121, Figure 7.1**, From Ibrahim, H, and Cordes, KA: *Outdoor recreation*, Madison, WI: Brown & Benchmark, 1993. Source: Bosserman, P: "The evolution of and trends in work and non-work time in the United States society (1920–1970)," *Society and Leisure* 7(1):94. Modified to 1983; **p. 129, A Closer Look**, Source: Gunnell, J: *100 years of American cars*, Iola, WI: Krause Publ, 1993, pp. 73–84.

## Chapter 8

**p. 156, A Closer Look**, Sources: *Collier's Encyclopedia*, vol. 6, New York: PF Collier, 1994, p. 187, and *Encyclopedia Americana, International Edition*, vol. 6, Danbury, CT: Grolier, 1994, p. 409, and *New Encyclopedia Brittanica*, ed. 15, vol. 3, Chicago: Encyclopedia Brittanica, 1994, p. 178.

## Chapter 9

**p. 171, Figure 9.1**, Source: Hopper, et al: "A family fitness program," *JOPERD*, vol. 63, no. 7. This article is reprinted with permission from the *Journal of Physical Education, Recreation & Dance*, September, 1992. *JOPERD* is a publication of the American Alliance for Health, Physical Education, Recreation and Dance, 1900 Association Drive, Reston, VA 22091; **p. 174, Table 9.1**, Source: "Sports participation in 1990: series I" (copyright), Mt. Prospect, IL: National Sporting Goods Association, and adapted from *Statistical Abstracts of the U.S.*, Lanham, MD: Bernan Press; **p. 180, A Closer Look**, Reprinted by permission from *Glamour*, March, 1995, p. 250. © Conde Nast Publ, New York City; **p. 185, Table 9.2**, Adapted from Tacha, K, Edwards, V, and Miller, S: "Sports fitness school for children," *JOPERD*, vol. 55, no. 7, Reston, VA: American Alliance for Health, Physical Education, Recreation and Dance, September, 1984, p. 61; **p. 188, Figure 9.2**, Source: Roper Starch; *Outdoor Recreation in America 1999*, Washington, D.C.: The Recreation Roundtable, 1999, p. 9.

## Chapter 10

**pp. 200–201, Figure 10.1**, Prepared by the U.S. Geological Survey from information provided by the agencies whose areas are shown on this map; **p. 202, Figure 10.2**, Source: Various government sources, 1999 and 2000; **p. 203, A Closer Look**, Source: *Collier's Encyclopedia*, vol. 11, New York: PF Collier, 1994, pp. 305–307; **p. 215**, Reprinted with permission, *The Sun*, December 26th, 1993, p. D3 by Fred Smith.

## Chapter 11

**p. 230, Table 11.1**, Source: Bialeschki, MD: "The state of parks and recreation, and leisure studies curricula," *Parks and Recreation*, vol. 27, no. 7, p. 76; **p. 243, A Closer Look**, Source: Kendrick, D: "Horse play," *Parenting*, San Francisco: © Time Inc. Ventures, June/July, 1993, pp. 179–181.

## Chapter 12

**p. 259, A Closer Look**, Source: *Recreation policy of the State of California*, Sacramento: California State Printing Office, 1962; **p. 261, Table 12.1**, Source: Buccner (1971): "The National Park and Recreation Association recommends that a minimum of 25 percent of new towns, planned unit developments, and large subdivisions be devoted to park and recreation lands and open space." From Knudson, D: *Outdoor recreation*, New York: Macmillan, 1984, p. 335. Reprinted with permission; **p. 261, Table 12.2**, From Kraus, RG, and Curtis, JE: *Creative management in recreation, parks, and leisure services*, ed. 3, St. Louis: CV Mosby, 1982; p. 117.

## Chapter 13

**p. 277, A Closer Look**, Condensed from "Going to extremes—to lure the hot dogs back," by Sandra Dallas with Gary McWilliams, *Business Week (Industrial/Technical Edition)*, March 13, 1995, p. 100.

## Chapter 14

**p. 297, A Closer Look**, Source: "The greening of the games," *U.S. News & World Report*, January 17, 1994, pp. 53–55; **p. 300, A Closer Look**, Source: Robinson, B: *Overdoing it*, Deerfield Beach, FL: Health Communications, 1992, pp. 137–138.

# Index